# Textbook of
# Social and Preventive Pharmacy

# Textbook of
# Social and Preventive Pharmacy

**Guru Prasad Mohanta**
**M. Pharm., Ph.D., FIC.**
Professor, C. L. Baid Metha College of Pharmacy,
Thoraipakkam, Chennai - 600 097
(Former Professor and Head, Department of Pharmacy, Annamalai University;
Former National Technical Officer, WHO Country Office for India)

**T. Purushoth Prabhu**
**M. Pharm., Ph.D., MBA.**
Professor and Head, Department of Pharmacognosy, Placement Officer,
C. L. Baid Metha College of Pharmacy,
Thoraipakkam, Chennai - 600 097

Pharma Med PRESS An Imprint of BSP Books Pvt. Ltd.
(TM) **PharmaMed Press**
*An imprint of BSP Books Pvt. Ltd.*
4-4-309/316, Giriraj Lane,
Sultan Bazar, Hyderabad - 500 095.

**Textbook of Social and Preventive Pharmacy**
***by* Guru Prasad Mohatna and T. Purushoth Prabhu**



***Published by:***

**PharmaMed Press**™

*An imprint of BSP Books Pvt. Ltd.*
4-4-309/316, Giriraj Lane, Sultan Bazar, Hyderabad - 500 095.
Phone: 040-23445688; Fax: 91+40-23445611
e-mail: info@pharmamedpress.com
www.pharmamedpress.com/pharmamedpress.net

**ISBN: 978-93-49562-51-6 (Hardback)**

***Dedicated to***

**Late Reena Mohanta**

You have been the inspiration to all my work and life.

**- Guru Prasad Mohanta**

**Manjiri Gharat, M. Pharm., FFIP.**

- *I/C Principal, Prin. K M.Kundnani Pharmacy Polytechnic, Ulhasnagar, Maharashtra, India*
- *Former Vice-President, International Pharma-ceutical Federation (FIP) 2020-2024*
- *Immediate Past Vice-President, Indian Pharma-ceutical Association (IPA), Chairperson, Community Pharmacy Division (2012-2024)*
- Secretary, Pharmacy Practice, SEARPharm Forum of FIP and WHO

# Foreword

Prevention is better than cure, an age-old adage sounds the most relevant guiding approach in today's world. Though the average life span is increasing, the years lived are not healthy. Health cannot be seen in isolation and considering a broader picture of HEALTH with its social determinants has become imperative. Advancing global health will only be possible if preventive strategies are used effectively. That's the reason the subject **Social and Preventive Pharmacy** found its place in the syllabus of pharmacy degree and diploma programmes. Textbook of Social and Preventive Pharmacy authored by Guru Prasad Mohanta and T Purushoth Prabhu not only covers the syllabus of Pharmacy Council of India for this subject but goes much beyond to give an overall holistic view of the importance of interdisciplinary approaches to health, combining medicine, sociology, and public health principles in healthcare. Both the authors are experienced and long-standing teachers.

Each chapter is covered in depth in an easy-to-understand manner and includes latest happenings. Practical aspects related to each topic are covered very well. Most importantly, the role of pharmacist in health and disease conditions is described well with actual success stories from the field, making it very relevant and inspiring.

Medicines, an important tool in saving lives, come with the baggage of high expenses and undesirable side effects. And more so when these are not used appropriately. Understanding this situation, authors have included a very useful chapter on Responsible Use of Medicines. Misinformation and its negative role is covered well in a chapter which becomes very relevant and useful in today's world of information explosion. Antimicrobial resistance (AMR), a global public health threat is also covered in depth sensitising the young minds about the importance of rational use of antimicrobials.

Community Pharmacists are the first point of contact for the people and pharmacies are the gateway to healthcare. Educating and orienting aspiring pharmacists for various health related initiatives of the Government is essential for knowledge and action. Therefore, chapters on various National health programmes and Ayushman Bharat are very important and useful.

The authors, through their expertise and experience, have come out with very useful resources for pharmacy students, academicians and healthcare professionals. I wholeheartedly commend the authors for their vision and commitment.

31 March 2025

**- Manjiri S Gharat**

# Preface

Education is learning what you didn't even know you didn't know.

Daniel J. Boorstin

The Social and Preventive Pharmacy is relatively new subject in pharmacy curriculum. Medicines being the main domain of pharmacists, social pharmacy is the subject matter that deals with improving access and promoting appropriate use of medicines in the society. It consists of all societal factors which influence medicine use: medicine related believes, regulations, policy, attributes, medicine information, ethics and behaviour.

Preventive pharmacy deals with the various strategies that can be explored for preventing illness and diseases. This part discusses the tools like vaccines and their access & use. Medicine use cannot be separated from health. The text attempts to corelate health and medicine use. In fact, now we are all concerned with health products not just medicines.

Corona has taught us many things. Perhaps most important is: "we are not safe, unless our neighbours are". Health education is a must for everyone. Educating school children is perhaps most sustainable. Many other practices we started adopting at least during pandemic period: social distancing, hand washing, avoiding infodemic and so on. The authors attempted to include these contemporary topics too along with the pharmacy curriculum.

The subject is meant to sensitize the students on health and pharmaceutical issues; encourage critical thinking on current health scenario; and evaluate the different strategies available or can be designed to redress these issues. This education aims at promoting health of the people of the country.

Social Pharmacy is about changing the society's behaviour towards their health and medicine use. This is the modest attempt by the authors to educate and sensitize students and teachers to promote health and well-being of all.

Indeed, we are grateful to Professor Manjiri Gharat who has penned foreword for this text. She is pioneer in implementing community pharmacists' participation in RNTCP.

We are thankful to Mr Anil Shah, Director, BSP Books Pvt Ltd, who agreed to publish.

We shall be glad to receive feedback for further improving the text.

31 March 2025

Guru Prasad Mohanta [gpmohanta@gmail.com]

T. Purushoth Prabhu [pharmprabhu@gmail.com]

## Abbreviations

**A. aegypti:** Aedes aegypti
**A. albopictus:** Aedes albopictus
**AB PM-JAY:** Ayushman Bharat Pradhan Mantri Jan Arogya Yojana
**AB-HWC:** Ayushman Bharat – Health & Wellness Centres
**AB-PMJAY:** Ayushman Bharat – Pradhan Mantri Jan Arogya Yojana
**ACE:** Angiotensin-Converting Enzyme
**ACS:** Advocacy, Communication, and Social Mobilization
**ACT**: Artemisinin-based Combination Therapy
**ACT-AL:** Artemether-Lumefantrine Combination Therapy
**ACT-SP:** Artemisinin-based Combination Therapy with Sulfadoxine Pyrimethamine
**ADR:** Adverse Drug Reaction
**AEFI:** Adverse Events Following Immunization
**AFP:** Acute Flaccid Paralysis
**AIC:** Airborne Infection Control
**AIDS:** Acquired Immune Deficiency Syndrome
**AMB:** Anaemia Mukt Bharat
**AMI:** Acute Myocardial Infarction
**AMR:** Antimicrobial Resistance
**ANC:** Antenatal Care
**ANM:** Auxiliary Nurse Midwife
**ART:** Antiretroviral Therapy
**ARV:** Antiretroviral
**ASHA:** Accredited Social Health Activist
**ATS:** Amphetamine-Type Stimulants
**AWW:** Anganwadi Worker
**AYUSH:** Ayurveda, Yoga and Naturopathy, Unani, Siddha, and Homoeopathy
**BCC:** Behaviour Change Communication
**BCG:** Bacillus Calmette-Guerin
**BMI:** Body Mass Index
**BOPV:** Bivalent Oral Polio Vaccine
**BP:** Blood Pressure
**BPL:** Below Poverty Line

**CA 19-9:** Carbohydrate Antigen
**CAD:** Coronary Artery Disease
**CBHI:** Central Bureau of Health Intelligence
**CBO:** Community-Based Organizations
**CBS:** Community-Based Screening
**CCB:** Calcium Channel Blockers
**CCS:** Country Cooperation Strategy
**CD4:** Cluster of Differentiation 4 (Immune cells targeted by HIV)
**CDC:** Center for Disease Control and Prevention, USA
**CEA:** Carcinoembryonic Antigen
**CGHS:** Central Government Health Scheme
**CHC:** Community Health Centre
**CHCs:** Community Health Centres
**CHIK:** Chikungunya
**CHIKV**: Chikungunya Virus
**CKD:** Chronic Kidney Disease
**COPD:** Chronic Obstructive Pulmonary Disease
**COTPA:** Cigarettes and Other Tobacco Products Act
**COVID-19:** Coronavirus Disease 2019
**Co-WIN:** COVID-19 Vaccine Intelligence Network
**CPHC:** Comprehensive Primary Health Care
**CQ:** Chloroquine
**CSF:** Cerebrospinal Fluid
**CSIR:** Council of Scientific and Industrial Research
**CT:** Computed Tomography
**CVD:** Cardiovascular Disease
**CVDs:** Cardiovascular Diseases
**DALY:** Disability Adjusted Life Years
**DAPCU:** District AIDS Prevention and Control Unit
**dB:** Decibel
**DBT:** Department of Biotechnology
**DBT:** Direct Benefit Transfer
**DEC:** Diethylcarbamazine Citrate
**DEET:** N,N-Diethyl-meta-toluamide
**DH:** District Hospital

**DHF:** Dengue Hemorrhagic Fever
**DIC:** Drop-In Centre
**DMC:** Designated Microscopy Centre
**DMHP:** District Mental Health Programme
**DOTS:** Directly Observed Treatment, Short-course
**DPT:** Diphtheria, Pertussis, Tetanus
**DR:** Drug-Resistant
**DRC:** Democratic Republic of Congo
**DRTB:** Drug-Resistant Tuberculosis
**DS:** Drug-Sensitive
**DST:** Department of Science and Technology
**DSTB:** Drug-Sensitive Tuberculosis
**DTCC:** District Tobacco Control Cell
**ELISA:** Enzyme-Linked Immunosorbent Assay
**ESI:** Employees' State Insurance
**ESIS:** Employees' State Insurance Scheme
**FBNC:** Facility-Based Newborn Care
**FEV1:** Forced Expiratory Volume in 1 second
**FICTC:** Facility Integrated Counselling and Testing Centres
**FIXED:** Fixed Dose Combinations
**FP:** Family Planning
**FRU:** First Referral Unit
**FSSAI:** Food Safety and Standards Authority of India
**FSW:** Female Sex Workers
**FVC:** Forced Vital Capacity
**G6PD:** Glucose-6-Phosphate Dehydrogenase
**GDP:** Gross Domestic Product
**GGE:** General Government Expenditure
**GOI:** Government of India
**GPELF:** Global Programme to Eliminate Lymphatic Filariasis
**GTFCC:** Global Task Force on Cholera Control
**H1N1:** Hemagglutinin type 1 and Neuraminidase type 1 (Influenza A subtype)
**H3N2:** Hemagglutinin type 3 and Neuraminidase type 2 (Influenza A subtype)
**HAI:** Healthcare-Associated Infections
**HALE:** Healthy Life Expectancy at Birth

**HbA1c:** Glycosylated Hemoglobin
**HBYC:** Home-Based Care for Young Child
**HCTS:** HIV Counselling and Testing Services
**HCW:** Health Care Worker
**HDU:** High Dependency Unit
**Hep B:** Hepatitis B
**HIV:** Human Immunodeficiency Virus
**HIV/AIDS:** Human Immunodeficiency Virus/Acquired Immunodeficiency Syndrome
**HPV:** Human Papillomavirus
**HRH:** Human Resources for Health
**HWWS:** Hand Washing with Soap
**ICD:** International Classification of Diseases
**ICDS:** Integrated Child Development Services
**ICMR:** Indian Council of Medical Research
**ICTC:** Integrated Counselling and Testing Centres
**ICU:** Intensive Care Unit
**IDA:** Ivermectin, Diethylcarbamazine, Albendazole
**IDSP:** Integrated Disease Surveillance Programme
**IDUs:** Injection Drug Users
**IEC:** Information, Education, and Communication
**IFA:** Iron and Folic Acid
**IFG:** Impaired Fasting Glucose
**IgM/IgG:** Immunoglobulin M/Immunoglobulin G
**IGT:** Impaired Glucose Tolerance
**IHD:** Ischemic Heart Disease
**IHIP:** Integrated Health Information Platform
**IMD:** India Meteorological Department
**IMR:** Infant Mortality Rate
**IP:** Inpatient
**IPC:** Infection Prevention and Control
**IPHS:** Indian Public Health Standards
**IPR:** Intellectual Property Rights
**IPV:** Inactivated Polio Vaccine
**IRS:** Indoor Residual Spray
**ITS:** Index Terms Section

**IUCD:** Intrauterine Contraceptive Device
**JAMA:** Journal of American Medical Association
**JSSK:** Janani Shishu Suraksha Karyakram
**JSY:** Janani Suraksha Yojana
**KAP:** Knowledge, Attitude, and Practices
**LAC:** Link ART Centres
**LCDC:** Leprosy Case Detection Campaign
**LF:** Lymphatic Filariasis
**LLINs:** Long-Lasting Insecticidal Nets
**LMICs:** Low- and Middle-Income Countries
**LOS:** Length of Stay
**LPS:** Lipopolysaccharide
**LSD:** Lysergic Acid Diethylamide
**LTBI:** Latent Tuberculosis Infection
**MAC-ELISA:** IgM-Capture Enzyme-Linked Immunosorbent Assay
**MB:** Multibacillary
**MCP:** Mother and Child Protection
**MCUP:** Measles, Combined with Other Vaccines Program
**MDA:** Mass Drug Administration
**MDGs:** Millennium Development Goals
**MDR/RR:** Multi-Drug Resistant / Rifampicin-Resistant
**MDR-TB:** Multidrug-Resistant Tuberculosis
**MDT:** Multidrug Therapy
**MiP:** Mycobacterium indicus Pranii
**MMR:** Maternal Mortality Rate
**MO:** Medical Officer
**MoDWS:** Ministry of Drinking Water & Sanitation
**MoHFW:** Ministry of Health and Family Welfare
**MoU:** Memorandum of Understanding
**MPA:** Medroxyprogesterone Acetate
**Mpox:** Monkeypox
**MR:** Measles-Rubella
**MRI:** Magnetic Resonance Imaging
**MSF:** Médecins Sans Frontières (Doctors Without Borders)
**NABH:** National Accreditation Board for Hospitals and Healthcare Providers

**NABL:** National Accreditation Board for Testing and Calibration Laboratories

**NACO:** National AIDS Control Organization

**NACP:** National Anaemia Control Programme

**NAFLD:** Non-Alcoholic Fatty Liver Disease

**NAPDDR:** National Action Plan on Drug Demand Reduction

**NCC:** National Cadet Corps

**NCD:** Non-Communicable Disease

**NCEAR-A:** National Centre for Excellence and Advanced Research on Anaemia Control

**NDP:** Net Domestic Product

**NE:** North Eastern

**NFHS:** National Family Health Survey

**NGO:** Non-Governmental Organization

**NHM:** National Health Mission

**NHP:** National Health Profile

**NHSRC:** National Health Systems Resource Centre

**NICPR:** National Institute of Cancer Prevention and Research

**NIDs:** National Immunization Days

**NIMHANS:** National Institute of Mental Health and Neurosciences

**NIPI:** National Iron Plus Initiative

**NLEM:** National List of Essential Medicines

**NLEP:** National Leprosy Eradication Programme

**NMBA:** Nasha Mukt Bharat Abhiyaan

**NMHP:** National Mental Health Programme

**NNRTI:** Non-nucleoside Reverse Transcriptase Inhibitors

**NPCCHH:** National Programme for Climate Change and Human Health

**NPCDCS:** National Programme for Prevention and Control of Cancer, Diabetes, Cardiovascular Diseases & Stroke

**NPCDCS:** National Programme for Prevention and Control of Cancer, Diabetes, Cardiovascular Diseases and Stroke

**NPHCE:** National Programme for Health Care of Elderly

**NP-NCD:** National Programme for Prevention & Control of Non-Communicable Diseases

**NPPCD:** National Programme for Prevention and Control of Deafness.

**NRHM:** National Rural Health Mission

**NRLS:** National Reference Laboratory System

**NS1:** Non-Structural Protein 1
**NSAIDs:** Non-Steroidal Anti-Inflammatory Drugs
**NSP:** National Strategic Plan
**NsRTI:** Nucleoside Reverse Transcriptase Inhibitors
**NSS:** National Sample Survey
**NSS:** National Service Scheme
**NTCC:** National Tobacco Control Cell
**NTCP:** National Tobacco Control Programme
**NTQLS:** National Tobacco Quit Line Service
**NtRTI:** Nucleotide Reverse Transcriptase Inhibitors
**NUHM:** National Urban Health Mission
**NVBDCP:** National Vector Borne Disease Control Programme
**NYK:** Nehru Yuva Kendra
**ODF:** Open Defecation Free
**OI:** Opportunistic Infections
**OOP:** Out of Pocket (expenditure)
**OOPE:** Out-of-Pocket Expenditure
**OPD:** Outpatient Department
**OPV:** Oral Polio Vaccine
**OR:** Odds Ratio
**ORS:** Oral Rehydration Solution
**OST:** Opioid Substitution Therapy
**OTC:** Over the Counter
**PB:** Paucibacillary
**PCI:** Pharmacy Council of India
**PCR:** Polymerase Chain Reaction
**PCV:** Pneumococcal Conjugate Vaccine
**PET:** Positron Emission Tomography
**PHC:** Primary Health Centre
**PHCs:** Primary Health Centres
**PHEIC:** Public Health Emergency of International Concern
**PI:** Protease Inhibitors
**PIP:** Programme Implementation Plan
**PIP:** Project Implementation Plan
**PLHIV:** People Living with HIV

**PM:** Prime Minister

**PM-JAY:** Ayushman Bharat Pradhan Mantri Jan Arogya Yojana

**PMSMA:** Pradhan Mantri Surakshit Matritva Abhiyan

**PMTCT:** Prevention of Mother-To-Child Transmission

**PMUY:** Pradhan Mantri Ujjwala Yojana (Government scheme for clean cooking)

**POSHAN:** Prime Minister's Overarching Scheme for Holistic Nutrition

**PPE:** Personal Protective Equipment

**PPG:** Post Prandial Plasma Glucose

**PPICTC:** Public-Private Partnership Integrated Counselling and Testing Centres

**PPTCT:** Prevention of Parent to Child Transmission

**PQ:** Primaquine

**PSA:** Prostate-Specific Antigen

**PTB:** Pulmonary Tuberculosis

**PVD:** Peripheral Vascular Disease

**PWMI:** Persons With Mental Illness

**RBSK:** Rashtriya Bal Swasthya Karyakram

**RCC:** Regional Certification Commission

**RCH:** Reproductive and Child Health Programme

**RDTs:** Rapid Diagnostic Tests

**RI:** Routine Immunization

**RMNCH+A:** Reproductive, Maternal, Newborn, Child, and Adolescent Health

**RMNCH+A:** Reproductive-Maternal-Neonatal-Child and Adolescent Health

**RNA:** Ribonucleic Acid

**RNTCP:** Revised National Tuberculosis Control Programme

**RR-TB:** Rifampicin-Resistant Tuberculosis

**RSBY:** Rashtriya Swasthya Bima Yojana

**RT-PCR:** Reverse-Transcriptase Polymerase Chain Reaction

**SAANS:** Social Awareness and Actions to Neutralize Pneumonia Successfully

**SACS:** State AIDS Control Societies

**SAICTC:** Standalone Integrated Counselling and Testing Centres

**SBM:** Swachh Bharat Mission

**SC:** Sub-Centre

**SCs:** Sub Centres

**SDG:** Sustainable Development Goal

**SDG 13:** Sustainable Development Goal 13

**SDGs:** Sustainable Development Goals

**SDH:** Single Dose Rifampicin

**SEARO:** South East Asia Regional Office

**SECC:** Socio-Economic Caste Census

**SI:** Strategic Information

**SIAs:** Supplementary Immunization Activities

**SLEP:** Sparsh Leprosy Elimination Campaign

**SLT:** Smokeless Tobacco

**SN:** Staff Nurse

**SNIDs:** Sub-National Immunization Days

**SOP:** Standard Operating Procedure

**SP:** Sulfadoxine-Pyrimethamine

**SPECT:** Single-Photon Emission Computed Tomography

**$SpO_2$:** Peripheral Capillary Oxygen Saturation

**SRS:** Sample Registration System

**STCC:** State Tobacco Control Cell

**STD:** Sexually Transmitted Disease

**STG:** Standard Treatment Guidelines

**STI:** Sexually Transmitted Infection

**SUMAN:** Surakshit Matritva Aashwasan

**SWAAS:** Step Wise Approach to Airway Diseases

**Swachh Bharat Scheme:** An Indian government initiative aimed at improving sanitation and hygiene

**TB:** Tuberculosis

**TFR:** Total Fertility Rate

**TFR:** Total Fertility Rate

**THE:** Total Health Expenditure

**TI:** Targeted Interventions

**TNMSCL:** Tamil Nadu Medical Service Corporation Limited

**TT:** Tetanus Toxoid

**U5MR:** Under-Five Mortality Rate

**UCHC:** Urban Community Health Centre

**UHC:** Universal Health Coverage

**UN:** United Nations
**UNICEF:** United Nations International Children's Emergency Fund
**UPHC:** Urban Primary Health Centre
**US$:** United States Dollar.
**USAID:** United States Agency for International Development
**UT:** Union Territory
**UTI:** Urinary Tract Infection
**UTs:** Union Territories
**VEN Analysis:** Vital, Essential, and Non-essential Analysis
**VHSND:** Village Health, Sanitation and Nutrition Day
**VL:** Viral Load
**VMMC:** Voluntary Medical Male Circumcision
**VPD:** Vaccine Preventable Diseases
**VVM:** Vaccine Vial Monitor
**WASH:** Water, Sanitation, and Hygiene
**WHO:** World Health Organization
**WIFS:** Weekly Iron Folic Acid Supplementation
**X-ray:** Radiography

# Contents

*Foreword* ........ (vii)
*Preface* ........ (ix)
*Abbreviations* ........ (xi)

**Chapter 1**

**Health, Diseases and Medicines**

Theories of Disease Causation ........ 1
Health Policy ........ 7
National Health Mission (NHM) ........ 13
Health Determinants ........ 18
Health Care Delivery System in India and Use of Medicines ........ 22
Public Health – Role of Practicing Pharmacists ........ 27
Access to Medicines ........ 34
National Health Profile ........ 39
International Agencies Contributing to India's Public Health ........ 44
Sustainable Development Goals ........ 51

**Chapter 2**

**Hygiene and Health**

Hand Washing ........ 59
Swachh Bharat (Cleaner India) Mission – A Public Health Programme ........ 69
Social Distancing ........ 73

**Chapter 3**

**Nutrition and Health**

Nutrition and Health ........ 77

**Chapter 4**

**Sociology and Health**

Sociology and Health ........ 84

## Chapter 5

### Communicable Diseases: Disease, Prevention and Control

Communicable Diseases .... 89
Chikungunya .... 90
Cholera .... 95
COVID – 19 .... 100
Denguc .... 107
Ebola .... 115
Human Immunodeficiency Virus (HIV) Infection / Acquired Immunodeficiency Syndrome (AIDS) .... 119
Influenza .... 127
Leprosy .... 132
Lymphatic Filariasis .... 140
Malaria .... 147
Mpox .... 153
Pneumonia .... 159
Tuberculosis .... 164

## Chapter 6

### Non-Communicable Diseases: Disease, Prevention and Control

Non-Communicable Diseases .... 170
Cancer .... 173
COPD and Asthma .... 182
Diabetes Mellitus .... 192
Hypertension .... 201

## Chapter 7

### National Health Programmes and Roles of Pharmacists

National Health Programmes .... 208
Anaemia .... 209
Blindness .... 217

Deafness ........ 222
Drug / Substance Abuse ........ 227
Family Welfare ........ 232
HIV and AIDS ........ 238
Immunization ........ 249
Leprosy ........ 267
Malaria ........ 274
Mental Health ........ 282
Mother and Child Health [Reproductive, Maternal, Newborn, Child, Adolescent Health and Nutrition) ........ 291
Tobacco Control ........ 298
Tuberculosis ........ 306
Worm Infestation ........ 324
Pulse Polio Immunization ........ 329

**Chapter 8**

**Community Service and Health Promotion**

Environment and Health (Climate and Health) ........ 335
Antimicrobial Resistance (AMR) ........ 343
School Education and Health Promotion ........ 350

**Chapter 9**

**Miscellaneous**

Ayushman Bharat Pradhan Mantri Jan Arogya Yojana (PMJAY) .. 353
Responsible Use of Medicines ........ 358
Infodemic ........ 363

*Glossary* ........ 369
*Index* ........ 391

# CHAPTER 1

# Health, Diseases and Medicines

## Theories of Disease Causation

"Disease is a lack of health. Health is not the lack of disease."

**After reading this chapter, you would be able to know / understand:**

- Concept of Health and Disease;
- Various theories on causation of diseases;
- Classification of diseases; and
- Diseases and Use of Medicines.

**Concept of Health and Disease:** Health has been defined by World Health Organization (WHO) as "Health is a state of complete physical, mental and social well-being and not merely absence of disease or infirmity". Health is multidimensional this definition at least covers three dimensions: physical, mental and social. Though health is much broader it has priority in addressing diseases especially in healthcare system.

- **Physical dimension of health:** It refers to the functioning of every cell and functioning of the body. These are signs of good physical health: good complexion, clean skin, bright eyes, lustrous hair with a body well clothed with firm flesh, not too fat, sweet breath, good appetite, sound sleep, regular activity of bowels and bladder and smooth, easy, and coordinated bodily movements.
- **Mental dimension of health:** It is a state of balance between the individual and the surrounding world, a state of harmony between oneself and others, a coexistence between the realities of the self and that of other people and that of the environment. Mental health is not as precise as physical health.

- **Social dimension of health:** It is the "quantity and quality of an individual's interpersonal ties and the extent of involvement with the community". The social dimension of health includes the levels of social skills one possesses, social functioning and the ability to see oneself as a member of a larger society. Social health takes into account that every individual is part of a family and of wider community and focuses on social and economic conditions and well-being.

  Disease is not precisely defined. Broadly disease is referred to any harmful deviation from the normal structural or functional state of an organism, generally associated with certain signs and symptoms and differing in nature from physical injury. Disease is any deviation from normal functioning or state of complete physical or mental well-being - since health and disease are mutually exclusive.

## Causation of Diseases

Many ancient literatures mentioned about diseases and causes of them. In earlier days, diseases were thought to be due to evil spirits and supernatural forces. The people practiced rituals, made sacrifices, and uttered prayers to satisfy the spirits, and get rid of diseases. This is beyond the scope of present text to discuss historical review of causes of diseases. The text discusses only the modern and scientific aspects of causation of diseases. The causation of diseases in modern times may be segregated into (though it may have ambiguity or incompleteness):

- Infection by microorganisms: It includes all types of infections –
  - Bacterial infections: TB, Typhoid, Urinary tract infection etc.
  - Viral infections: HIV, Measles, COVID -19 etc.
  - Fungal infection: Ringworm, Fungal nail infections etc.
  - Parasitic infection / infestation: Malaria, Filaria etc.
- Deficiency of nutrition (including vitamins and minerals): Vitamin $B_2$, Scurvy (Vitamin C deficiency), Anaemia etc.
- Hereditary disorder: Thalassaemia, Haemophilia etc.
- Physiological disorder: Diabetes, Asthma, Glaucoma etc.

**Classification of Diseases:** Understanding diseases in ways that enable prevention, treatment, and the allocation of resources requires measurement. To be useful, measurement must be reliable, allow valid comparisons to be made between places and over time, and enable coherent summarization of large volumes of data. A classification of diseases and related things is essential for such measurement.

International Classification of Disease (ICD) is published by the World Health Organisation. The ICD is used world-wide for morbidity and mortality statistics, reimbursement systems and automated decision support in medicine. This system is designed to promote international comparability in the collection, processing, classification and presentation of these statistics. It has been the main basis for comparable statistics on causes of death and non-fatal disease.

A disease is a set of dysfunctions in any body system defined by:

| Property | Description |
|---|---|
| Symptomatology or manifestations | Known pattern of signs, symptoms, and related findings |
| Aetiology | An underlying explanatory mechanism |
| Course and outcome | A distinct pattern of development over time |
| Treatment response | A known pattern of response to interventions |
| Linkage to genetic factors | E.g. genotypes, patterns of gene expression, etc. |
| Linkage to environmental factors | Factors of the environment that trigger presence of a disease |

The ICD is a core classification of the WHO Family of International Classifications (WHO-FIC). ICD assigns a unique category and a code to classify diseases and a wide variety of signs, symptoms, abnormal findings, complaints, social circumstances and external causes of injury or disease. The ICD is important because it provides a common language for recording, reporting and monitoring diseases. This allows the world to compare and share data in a consistent and standard way – between hospitals, regions and countries and over periods of time. It facilitates the collection and storage of data for analysis and evidence-based decision-making.

The physicians, nurses, other providers, researchers, health information managers and coders, health information technology workers, policy-makers, insurers and patient organizations find this useful.

For more than a century, the International Classification of Diseases (ICD) has been the basis for comparable statistics on causes of mortality and morbidity between places and over time.

Currently, ICD -11 is the official version of classification. It has the following categories for morbidity and mortality statistics: Certain infectious and parasitic disease; Neoplasms; Diseases of blood and blood forming organs; Diseases of immune system; Endocrine, nutritional or metabolic diseases; Mental, behavioural or neurodevelopmental disorders; Sleep-wake disorders; Diseases of the nervous system; Diseases of the visual system; Diseases of the ear or mastoid process; Diseases of the circulatory system;

Diseases of the respiratory system; Diseases of the digestive system; Diseases of the skin; Diseases of the musculoskeletal system or connective tissue; Diseases of the genitourinary system; Conditions related to sexual health; Pregnancy, childbirth or the puerperium; Certain conditions originating in the perinatal period; Developmental anomalies; Symptoms, signs or clinical findings, not elsewhere classified; Injury, poisoning or certain other consequences of external causes; External causes of morbidity or mortality; Factors influencing health status or contact with health services; Codes for special purposes; and Traditional Medicine Conditions.

**Diseases and Use of Medicines:** The diseases are to be treated with proper medicines. Depending on disease, medicine may be used as single dose or multiple doses for long periods. Some features of medicine use:

- Medicines to be used for full course of treatment in case of infectious diseases even if one feels better after few doses.
- Adherence to instruction with respect to user guideline: timing of medication like before or after food, only at bed time, duration etc.
- It is advisable to use medicines with doctor's advice.
- Patients should be educated by the pharmacists on medicine use.

**Pharmacists' Role**

- Community pharmacists and Hospital pharmacists:
    - They can educate and guide the common man on use of medicines: when to take / use, how to use etc.
    - Educate them on need of completion of course of antimicrobial medicines.
    - Adhere to the instructions on medicine use.
    - They should use medicines when advised not to believe they need medicines for every illness.
    - Guide them to disposing off the unused / expired medicine.

**Bottom Lines**

- "Health is a state of complete physical, mental and social well-being and not merely absence of disease or infirmity". Health is multidimensional this definition at least covers three dimensions: physical, mental and social.
- Physical dimension of health refers to the functioning of every cell and functioning of the body.

- Mental dimension of health is a state of balance between the individual and the surrounding world, a state of harmony between oneself and others, a coexistence between the realities of the self and that of other people and that of the environment.
- Social dimension of health is the "quantity and quality of an individual's interpersonal ties and the extent of involvement with the community".
- Disease is any deviation from normal functioning or state of complete physical or mental well-being - since health and disease are mutually exclusive.
- The causation of diseases in modern times may be segregated into (though it may have ambiguity or incompleteness):
    - Infection by microorganisms: It includes all types of infections –
        - Bacterial infections: TB, Typhoid, Urinary tract infection etc.
        - Viral infections: HIV, Measles, COVID -19 etc.
        - Fungal infection: Ringworm, Fungal nail infections etc.
        - Parasitic infection / infestation: Malaria, Filaria etc.
    - Deficiency of nutrition (including vitamins and minerals): Vitamin $B_2$, Scurvy (Vitamin C deficiency), Anaemia etc.
    - Hereditary disorder: Thalassaemia, Haemophilia etc.
    - Physiological disorder: Diabetes, Asthma, Glaucoma etc.
- International Classification of Disease (ICD) is published by the World Health Organisation. The ICD is used world-wide for morbidity and mortality statistics, reimbursement systems and automated decision support in medicine.
- This system is designed to promote international comparability in the collection, processing, classification and presentation of these statistics. Currently, ICD -11 is the official version of classification.
- **Pharmacists' Role:** The knowledge of causation of diseases helps to guide the common man including patients to prevent diseases and promote health. They would be able to guide the patients for medication adherence and responsible use of medicines.

## Bibliography

1. Alfred S. Evans, Causation and Disease, A Chronological Journey, Springer Science+Business Media New York, 1993.
2. Concept of Diseases and Health in Integrative Approaches for Health, Academic Press 2015.
3. International Classification of Diseases – 11th Revision, World Health Organization, 2024.
4. K. Park, Park's Textbook Preventive and Social Medicine, 23rd Edition, BHANOT, 2015.

## Health Policy

"You treat a disease, you win, you lose. You treat a person,
I guarantee you, you'll win — no matter what the outcome."

- Patch Adams

**After reading this chapter, you would be able to know / understand:**

- Genesis of India's Health Policy;
- Salient features current health policy; and
- Responsibilities of pharmacists.

National Health Policy (NHP) 2017, the current policy, is announced after 14 years of last NHP (2003). The new policy is in alignment with Sustainable Development Goals of United Nations. In health scenario, there have substantial changes over the years:

- Change in health priorities: health burden is shifting from communicable diseases to non-communicable diseases.
- Emergence of robust health care industry.
- Growing incidence of catastrophic health care expenditure – one of the major reasons of poverty.
- Rising economic growth – enhanced fiscal capacity.

All these factors necessitated a New National Health Policy and the government has announced NHP 2017. A policy is a commitment to a goal and guide for action. It is an official document of government, which acts as a formal record of aspirations, aims, decisions, and commitments for solving problems associated.

Mile Stone in the development of health policy:

- Till 1983, there was no official health policy. Health activities were planned as a part of five year plan.
- Alma Ata declaration of Health For All by 2000 AD (WHO, 1978).
- First National Health Policy was announced in 1983: "universal, comprehensive primary health care services which are relevant to the actual needs and priorities of the community at a cost which people can afford".
- National Population Policy announced in 2000.

- National Health Policy 2002 announced: "to achieve acceptable good standard of health, to decentralize public health system, to ensure more equitable access health care services, to enhance contribution of private sector, to emphasise on rational use of drugs, to increase access to tried system of traditional medicines, and to give primacy for prevention and first line curative initiatives".
- National Health Policy 2017 announced: "goal is the attainment of the highest possible level of health and well-being for all at all ages, through a preventive and promotive health care orientation in all developmental policies, and universal access to good quality health care services without anyone having to face financial hardship as a consequence".

Salient Features of NHP 2017

- **Aim:** to inform, clarify, strengthen and prioritize the role of the Government in shaping health systems in all its dimensions- investments in health, organization of healthcare services, prevention of diseases and promotion of good health through cross sectoral actions, access to technologies, developing human resources, encouraging medical pluralism, building knowledge base, developing better financial protection strategies, strengthening regulation and health assurance.
- **Objectives:** To improve health status and expand preventive, promotive, curative, palliative, and rehabilitative services through quality public heallth service.
  - (a) Assuring availability of free, comprehensive primary health care services, for all aspects of reproductive, maternal, child and adolescent health and for the most prevalent communicable, non-communicable and occupational diseases in the population.
  - (b) Ensuring improved access and affordability, of quality secondary and tertiary care services through a combination of public hospitals and well measured strategic purchasing of services in health care deficit areas, from private care providers, especially the not-for profit providers.
  - (c) Achieving a significant reduction in out of pocket expenditure due to health care costs and achieving reduction in proportion of households experiencing catastrophic health expenditures and consequent impoverishment.
  - (d) Strengthening the trust of the common man in public health system.
  - (e) Alligning the growth of private health care sectors with public health goals.

(f) Life Expectancy and healthy life

a. Increase Life Expectancy at birth from 67.5 to 70 by 2025.

b. Establish regular tracking of Disability Adjusted Life Years (DALY) Index as a measure of burden of disease and its trends by major categories by 2022.

c. Reduction of TFR to 2.1 at national and sub-national level by 2025.

(g) Mortality by Age and/ or cause

a. Reduce Under Five Mortality to 23 by 2025 and MMR from current levels to 100 by 2020.

b. Reduce infant mortality rate to 28 by 2019.

c. Reduce neo-natal mortality to 16 and still birth rate to "single digit" by 2025.

(h) Reduction of disease prevalence/ incidence

a. Achieve global target of 2020 which is also termed as target of 90:90:90, for HIV/AIDS. [90% of all people living with HIV know their HIV status, - 90% of all people diagnosed with HIV infection receive sustained antiretroviral therapy and 90% of all people receiving antiretroviral therapy will have viral suppression].

b. Achieve and maintain elimination status of Leprosy by 2018, Kala-Azar by 2017 and Lymphatic Filariasis in endemic pockets by 2017.

c. To achieve and maintain a cure rate of >85% in new sputum positive patients for TB and reduce incidence of new cases, to reach elimination status by 2025.

d. To reduce the prevalence of blindness to 0.25/ 1000 by 2025 and disease burden by one third from current levels.

e. To reduce premature mortality from cardiovascular diseases, cancer, diabetes or chronic respiratory diseases by 25% by 2025.

(i) Coverage of Health Services

a. Increase utilization of public health facilities by 50% from current levels by 2025.

b. Antenatal care coverage to be sustained above 90% and skilled attendance at birth above 90% by 2025.

c. More than 90% of the newborn are fully immunized by one year of age by 2025.

   d. Meet need of family planning above 90% at national and sub national level by 2025
   e. 80% of known hypertensive and diabetic individuals at household level maintain controlled disease status by 2025.

(j) Cross Sectoral goals related to health
   a. Relative reduction in prevalence of current tobacco use by 15% by 2020 and 30% by 2025.
   b. Reduction of 40% in prevalence of stunting of under-five children by 2025.
   c. Access to safe water and sanitation to all by 2020 (Swachh Bharat Mission).
   d. Reduction of occupational injury by half from current levels of 334 per lakh agricultural workers by 2020.
   e. National/ State level tracking of selected health behaviour.

(k) Health finance
   a. Increase health expenditure by Government as a percentage of GDP from the existing 1.15% to 2.5 % by 2025.
   b. Increase State sector health spending to > 8% of their budget by 2020.
   c. Decrease in proportion of households facing catastrophic health expenditure from the current levels by 25%, by 2025.

(l) Health Infrastructure and Human Resource
   a. Ensure availability of paramedics and doctors as per Indian Public Health Standard (IPHS) norm in high priority districts by 2020.
   b. Increase community health volunteers to population ratio as per IPHS norm, in high priority districts by 2025.
   c. Establish primary and secondary care facility as per norms in high priority districts (population as well as time to reach norms) by 2025.

(m) Health Management Information
   a. Ensure district-level electronic database of information on health system components by 2020.
   b. Strengthen the health surveillance system and establish registries for diseases of public health importance by 2020.
   c. Establish federated integrated health information architecture, Health Information Exchanges and National Health Information Network by 2025.

## Pharmacists in Health Policy

- This is the first time, pharmacists are part of National Health Policy 2017. Earlier NHP did not have even the word pharmacists.
- Strengthening Professional Educational Regulation: Expanding the membership of the council. As of writing the manuscript, the all professional councils like Medical Council of India, Dental Council of India are replaced by National Medical Commission and National Dental Commission. The formation of National Commission replacing Pharmacy Council of India is yet to become reality.
- Grouped with allied professionals: Planned expansion of allied technical skills- radiographers, laboratory technicians, physiotherapists, pharmacists, audiologists, optometrists, occupational therapists with local employment opportunities, is a key policy direction.
    - Mid – level Service Providers: A bridge course on Community Health can skill the pharmacists to provide services at the sub-centre and other peripheral levels.

Though now three National Health Policies have been announed since independence in 1947, the policies are silent about making health as fundamental right. Right to Health is not mentioned in the constitution. However, Supremecourt's interpretation "the right to health is an integral fact of a meaningful right to life" and that the Right to Health is a fundamental right. However, Rajasthan has adopted " the Rajasthan Right to Health Care Act 2022" in the Assembly, making it the first state to do so in India.

**Bottom Line**

- The current National Health Policy 2017 is announced 14 years after the last policy of 2003.
- The policy is in alignment with UN's Sustainable Development Goals.
- Some of the important features are:
    - o Increase health expenditure by Government as a percentage of GDP from the existing 1.15% to 2.5 % by 2025.
    - o Objective is to improve health status and expand preventive, promotive, curative, palliative, and rehabilitative services through quality public heallth service.
    - o Increase Life Expectancy at birth from 67.5 to 70 by 2025.
    - o Strengthening the trust of the common man in public health system.
    - o Reduce Under Five Mortality to 23 by 2025.

- To achieve and maintain a cure rate of >85% in new sputum positive patients for TB and reduce incidence of new cases, to reach elimination status by 2025.
- 80% of known hypertensive and diabetic individuals at household level maintain controlled disease status by 2025.
- More than 90% of the newborn are fully immunized by one year of age by 2025.

- Pharmacists are first time recognised as healthcare professionals in National Health Policy.
  - Plans for strengthening pharmacy council by expanding membership. There is possibility of constitution of National Pharmacy Commission as done for medical, dental and nursing profession.
  - Pharmacists may be considered as mid level service providers after a bridge course.

## Bibliography

1. National Health Policy 2017, Ministry of Health and Family Welfare, Government of India, 2017.
2. Prof. I. Ramabrahmam & Ramya Chitrapu, An Overview of Health Policies in India, 1 (1), 2019.
3. Ravi Duggal, Evolution of Health Policy in India, CEHAT, 2001.
4. Situation Analysis, Backdrop to National Health Policy 2017, Ministry of Health and Family Welfare, Government of India.

# National Health Mission (NHM)

"Of all the forms of inequality, injustice in health is most shocking and inhuman."

- Martin Luther King, Jr.

**After reading this chapter, you would be able to know / understand:**

- Genesis of NHM;
- Aim of NHM;
- Achievements of NHM; and
- Role of Pharmacists.

National Health Mission (NHM) is conceptualized and launched in 2013 with the two Sub Missions viz. the National Rural Health Mission (NRHM) and the National Urban Health Mission (NUHM). The National Rural Health Mission was launched in 2005 with the objective of building public health systems to provide accessible, affordable, and quality health care to the rural population, especially the vulnerable groups, up to the District Hospitals (DH) level. In 2012, the National Urban Health Mission (NUHM) was launched.

The aim of NHM is to ensure progress towards the goals and targets set out in the National Health Policy, 2017 for ensuring "universal access to equitable, affordable and quality health care services, accountable and responsive to people's needs". This would also enable the country to advance towards meeting Sustainable Development Goal 3, i.e. "Ensure healthy lives and promote well-being for all at all ages", including Universal Health Coverage.

The main programmatic components include Health System Strengthening in rural and urban areas, Reproductive-Maternal- Neonatal-Child and Adolescent Health (RMNCH+A), and Communicable and Non-Communicable Diseases. Various works/initiatives carried out under NHM in the country are as below:

- **Ayushman Bharat – Health & Wellness Centres (AB-HWCs):** 1,50,000 Sub- Health Centres (SHC), Primary Health Centres (PHC) and Urban Primary Health Centres (UPHC) are transformed into Ayushman Bharat- Health and Wellness Centres (AB-HWCs) up to December, 2022 to deliver twelve packages of Comprehensive Primary Health Care (CPHC) that includes preventive, promotive, curative, palliative and rehabilitative services which is universal, free, and close to the community. These AB-HWCs will provide Comprehensive Primary Health Care (CPHC), by expanding and strengthening the existing Reproductive & Child Health (RCH) services and Communicable Diseases services and by including services related to Non-Communicable Diseases (NCD), to begin with the common NCDs such as, Hypertension, Diabetes and 3 common cancers of Oral, Breast and Cervix. It is also envisaged to incrementally add primary healthcare services for Mental health, ENT, Ophthalmology, Oral health, Geriatric and Palliative health care and Trauma care as well as Health promotion and wellness activities like Yoga. Against the target of 1,50,000, a total of 1,54,070 AB-HWCs have been operationalized in the country by 31st December, 2022.

- **National Free Drugs Initiative:** States/UTs are supported to provide essential drugs based on the level of public health facilities free of cost to all who access these facilities.
- **Free Diagnostics Initiatives (FDI):** Under the initiative, support provided to States/UTs to provide a set of essential diagnostics in 33 States/UTs at various levels of care, free of cost.
- **National Ambulance Services (NAS):** Under the NHM, technical and financial support is provided for emergency medical services in States/UTs through a functional National Ambulance Service (NAS) network linked with a centralized toll-free number 108/102.
- **Mobile Medical Units (MMU)** are supported to facilitate access to public health care at the doorstep particularly to people living in remote, difficult, under-served and unreached areas to provide primary care services.
- Some major initiatives under NHM focusing on women and children, including ST category women and children, throughout the country, are as follows:
  - o Ayushman Bharat- Pradhan Mantri Jan Arogya Yojana (AB-PMJAY), provides health coverage of up to Rs 5 lakh per family per year to around 10.74 crore poor and vulnerable families in the country as per Socio Economic Caste Census (SECC).
  - o Surakshit Matritva Aashwasan (SUMAN) provides assured, dignified, respectful and quality healthcare at no cost and zero tolerance for denial of services for every woman and newborn visiting public health facilities to end all preventable maternal and newborn deaths.
  - o Janani Suraksha Yojana (JSY), a demand promotion and conditional cash transfer scheme for promoting institutional delivery.
  - o Under Janani Shishu Suraksha Karyakram (JSSK), every pregnant woman is entitled to free delivery, including caesarean section, in

public health institutions along with the provision of free transport, diagnostics, medicines, other consumables & diet.

- Pradhan Mantri Surakshit Matritva Abhiyan (PMSMA) provides pregnant women a fixed day, free of cost assured and quality antenatal check up by a Specialist/Medical Officer on the 9th day of every month.
- LaQshya improves the quality of care in labour room and maternity operation theatres to ensure that pregnant women receive respectful and quality care during delivery and immediate post-partum.
- Monthly Village Health, Sanitation and Nutrition Day (VHSND) is an outreach activity at Anganwadi centers for provision of maternal and child care including nutrition in convergence with the ICDS.
- Reproductive and child health (RCH) portal is a name-based web-enabled tracking system for pregnant women and new born so as to ensure seamless provision of regular and complete services to them including antenatal care, institutional delivery and post-natal care.
- MCP Card and Safe Motherhood Booklet are distributed to the pregnant women for educating them on diet, rest, danger signs of pregnancy, benefit schemes and institutional deliveries.
- Delivery Points- Over 25,000 'Delivery Points' across the country have been strengthened in terms of infrastructure, equipment, and trained manpower for provision of comprehensive RMNCAH+N services.
- Setting up of Maternal and Child Health (MCH) Wings at high caseload facilities to improve the quality of care provided to mothers and children.
- Functionalization of First Referral Units (FRUs) by ensuring manpower, blood storage units, referral linkages to improve the access to quality of care for pregnant women.
- Further, initiatives such as Mission Parivar Vikas, Adolescent Friendly Health Clinics (AFHCs), Weekly Iron Folic Acid Supplementation (WIFS), Menstrual Hygiene Scheme, Facility Based Newborn Care (FBNC), Home Based Newborn Care Program, Social Awareness and Actions to Neutralize Pneumonia Successfully (SAANS), Home Based Care for Young Child (HBYC), Rashtriya Bal Swasthya Karyakram (RBSK), Early Childhood Development (ECD), Comprehensive Abortion Care (CAC), Anaemia Mukt Bharat (AMB) strategy, Nutrition Rehabilitation Centre (NRC) program are supported to increase access to quality healthcare services. Support is also provided to strengthen Universal Immunization programme, introduction of new vaccines.

- o In tribal, hilly, and desert areas, the norm can be relaxed to one ASHA per habitation, depending on the workload, geographic dispersion, and difficult terrain. To attract quality Human Resources special provisions like "You quote, we pay" / Hard area allowances.

The NHM has had a significant impact on the health system, enhancing care quality, financial allocation, responsiveness, and accountability. This mission, geared towards increased public health spending, reduced inequity, decentralization, and community involvement, reflects the government's commitment to elevate healthcare.

**Pharmacists' Role**: Pharmacists working in the health system should be familiar with NHM's role and responsibilities. Though they have no direct responsibilities in the administrative set up, they function in the health system. Their understanding of NHM would help guide the patients.

**Bottom Line**

- National Health Mission (NHM) is conceptualized and launched in 2013 with the two Sub Missions viz. the National Rural Health Mission (NRHM) and the National Urban Health Mission (NUHM).
- The aim of NHM is to ensure progress towards the goals and targets set out in the National Health Policy, 2017 for ensuring "universal access to equitable, affordable and quality health care services, accountable and responsive to people's needs".
- NHM would enable the country to advance towards meeting Sustainable Development Goal 3, i.e. "Ensure healthy lives and promote well-being for all at all ages", including Universal Health Coverage.
- The main programmatic components include Health System Strengthening in rural and urban areas, Reproductive-Maternal-Neonatal-Child and Adolescent Health (RMNCH+A), and Communicable and Non-Communicable Diseases.
- Various works/initiatives carried out under NHM:
- Establishment Ayushman Bharat – Health & Wellness Centres (AB-HWCs);
- National Free Drugs Initiative;
- Free Diagnostics Initiatives (FDI);
- National Ambulance Services (NAS);
- Mobile Medical Units (MMU); and
- Improved focus on women and children, throughout the country.

- The NHM has had a significant impact on the health system, enhancing care quality, financial allocation, responsiveness, and accountability.
- Pharmacists in health system can guide the patients to avail the facilities.

## Bibliography

1. National Health Mission Website, https://nhm.gov.in/, accessed on 08.9.2024.

# Health Determinants

"It is social circumstances that determine health,
not health that determines social circumstances".

**After reading this chapter, you would be able to know / understand:**

- Meaning of health determinants;
- Various health determinants with special emphasis on social determinants; and
- Pharmacists' contribution promoting health through intervention on social health determinants.

Health is dependent on many factors and they combinedly influence health. Health determinants are the factors which contribute to health of the population. These may be grouped into: social and economic environment; physical environment; and the person's individual characteristics and behaviours. In India, health of the population is determined largely by lifestyle (50%) followed by biological and environmental factor (20% each), whereas health systems related factors contribute only 10%. Social determinants are most important factors which can be intervened successfully. Achievement of national health goals would require addressing all the social determinants (distal and proximal) in the context of rapid economic growth and changing life styles with a focus on the most vulnerable and marginalized.

Social and Economic Environment:

- **Income and Social Status**: Income determines access to various resources that support health, including nutritious food, safe housing, and healthcare services. Higher social status often means better job opportunities, education, and living conditions, which collectively contribute to better health. Conversely, socioeconomic disparities lead to significant health inequalities, with poorer individuals experiencing worse health outcomes.
- **Education**: Education enhances health literacy, enabling individuals to make informed health decisions. Higher educational attainment is associated with better job prospects, higher income, and reduced stress, all of which contribute to better health. Lower education levels are linked to poorer health, higher stress, and lower self-confidence.
- **Employment and Working Conditions**: Employment provides financial stability and access to health benefits. Job security and

positive working conditions, including control over work tasks and a supportive work environment, are linked to better health. Unemployment, job insecurity, and poor working conditions contribute to stress, mental health issues, and physical health problems.

- **Social Support Networks**: Social connections with family, friends, and communities provide emotional support, practical help, and a sense of belonging, which are crucial for mental and physical well-being. Strong social networks are associated with lower levels of stress, better mental health, and reduced risk of chronic diseases.
- **Culture**: Cultural norms, values, and traditions influence health behaviors and perceptions. Beliefs about diet, exercise, healthcare utilization, and illness management are shaped by cultural background, affecting health outcomes. Understanding cultural factors is essential for providing culturally competent healthcare.

## Physical Environment

- **Safe Water and Clean Air**: Access to clean water and air is fundamental for health. Contaminated water and polluted air can cause a range of health issues, including respiratory diseases, gastrointestinal infections, and chronic conditions like asthma.
- **Healthy Workplaces**: Safe and healthy working environments protect workers from occupational hazards and promote physical and mental well-being. This includes ergonomic workspaces, exposure to natural light, and measures to prevent workplace injuries and illnesses.
- **Safe Housing and Communities**: Housing quality and neighbourhood conditions impact health significantly. Safe, affordable housing and well-designed communities with green spaces, recreational facilities, and low crime rates promote physical activity, reduce stress, and enhance overall quality of life.
- **Infrastructure and Transportation**: Well-maintained roads, reliable public transportation, and accessible healthcare facilities ensure that individuals can reach necessary services and engage in social and economic activities that support health.

**Individual Characteristics and Behaviour**

- **Genetics**: Genetic factors influence susceptibility to certain diseases, lifespan, and overall health. While individuals cannot change their genetic makeup, understanding genetic risks can inform preventive measures and personalized healthcare.

- **Personal Behaviour and Coping Skills**: Lifestyle choices such as diet, physical activity, smoking, and alcohol consumption significantly affect health. Developing healthy habits, such as balanced eating, regular exercise, and effective stress management, is crucial for preventing chronic diseases and promoting well-being.
- **Health Services**: Access to and utilization of healthcare services, including preventive care, screenings, and treatments, influence health outcomes. Ensuring equitable access to quality healthcare is essential for addressing health disparities and improving public health.
- **Gender**: Gender differences affect health risks, disease prevalence, and health behaviours. For instance, men and women may experience different health issues at various life stages, requiring gender-specific health interventions and support.

Social Determinants can be more important than health care or lifestyle choices in influencing health outcomes:

- Income and social protection
- Education
- Unemployment and job insecurity
- Working life conditions
- Food insecurity
- Housing, basic amenities and the environment
- Early childhood development
- Social inclusion and non-discrimination
- Structural conflict
- Access to affordable health services of decent quality.

## Pharmacists' Role

- **Community pharmacists:** They can sensitively counsel the patients and providing an opportunity for affordable medicines.
- **Hospital pharmacists:** Though no specific role is specified, they can interact with the patients addressing individual patient needs, identifying social risk factors, and addressing upstream causes of health disparities. They can guide the patients on government insurance available.

**Bottom Lines**

- Health is dependent on many factors: social and economic environment; physical environment; and the person's individual characteristics and behaviours. In India, health of the population is determined largely by lifestyle (50%) followed by biological and environmental factor (20% each), whereas health systems related factors contribute only 10%.
- Social and Economic Environment: Income and Social Status; Education; Employment and Working Conditions; Social Support Networks; and Culture.
- Physical Environment: Safe Water and Clean Air; Healthy Workplaces; Safe Housing and Communities; and Infrastructure & Transportation.
- Individual Characteristics and Behaviour: Genetics; Personal Behaviour and Coping Skills; Health Services; and Gender.
- Pharmacists' Role: Though the roles are not defined, they can interact with the patients sympathetically and guide them.

## Bibliography

1. https://www.who.int/news-room/questions-and-answers/item/determinants-of-health, accessed on 06.10.2024.
2. K. Park, Park's Textbook of Preventive and Social Medicine, BHANOT, 23rd Edition, 2015.
3. Keya Sengupta's Determinants of Health Status in India, Springer India, 2016.
4. Situation Analyses Backdrop to the National Health Policy – 2017, Ministry of Health and Family Welfare, Government of India.

# Health Care Delivery System in India and Use of Medicines

"You treat a disease, you win, you lose. You treat a person,
I guarantee you, you'll win — no matter what the outcome."

- Patch Adams

**After reading this chapter, you would be able to know / understand:**

- India's health care delivery system;
- Use of medicines;
- Indian Public Health Standards; and
- Pharmacists' contribution in India's healthcare delivery system.

Under the constitution, health is a state subject, and implementation of health programmes is left to state governments. The national government plays an overall stewardship role, providing vision and funds to policies and programmes. State governments play a larger role combining the role of vision, leadership, funding, regulation and delivery of health care. Health-care services are delivered by a range of public and private providers.

Health services in India are delivered by a diverse set of public, for-profit and not-for-profit private providers. These services are provided by public sector facilities: at the primary level, a sub-centre (SCs) established to serve a population of 3000 – 5000, primary health centre (PHCs) for a population of 20 000 – 30 000, community health centre (CHCs) for a population of 80 000 – 120 000, and district hospitals. A CHC, sub-divisional or district hospital also serves as a first referral unit (FRU). Above the level of district hospitals, tertiary care is provided by medical colleges and/or state-level super-specialty hospitals.

The National Health Mission (NHM) is the guiding force for the government. It encompasses its two Sub-Missions, The National Rural Health Mission (NRHM) and The National Urban Health Mission (NUHM). The main programmatic components include Health System Strengthening, Reproductive-Maternal- Neonatal-Child and Adolescent Health (RMNCH+A), and Communicable and Non-Communicable Diseases. The NHM envisages achievement of universal access to equitable, affordable & quality health care services that are accountable and responsive to people's needs.

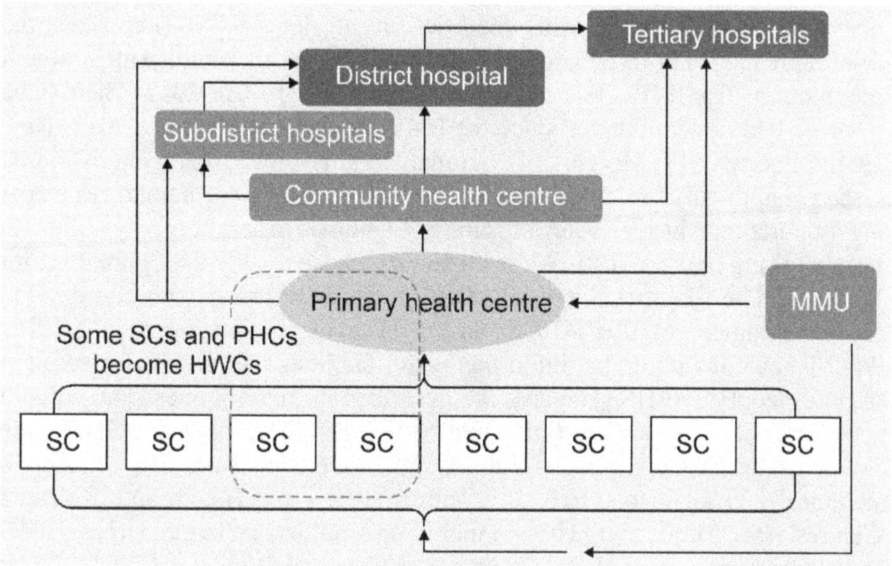


**Fig. 1.1** Service Delivery in Public Hospitals.
[Source: India health system review, Health system in transition, WHO Regional Office for SEA, 2022].

**Medicines Use in Public Hospitals**: Medicines are integral part of healthcare delivery system. Without medicines, sophisticated / high ended surgery is not feasible. But medicines are very expensive, they contribute the second most expense in public hospitals next to human resource expense.

Approximately only 10% of all medicines are prescribed and dispensed in government settings. In the government set-up, drugs are prescribed by medical doctors and specialists, and the dispensing function is undertaken by a dedicated dispensing unit in each health facility. Though patients are expected to receive medicines free in public health facilities, it is not feasible due to lack of funds and poor governance in procurement and distribution of medicines. In such situation, patient has to incur out of pocket (OOP) expenditure. The availability of essential medicines in public health facilities varies widely. Some study showed that in Bihar it is 43%, compared to 88% in Tamil Nadu public facilities. While the health facilities in Bihar registered average stockouts of about 41%, the proportion of stock-outs for Tamil Nadu was less than half, at around 16%.

## Indian Public Health Standards

The Government of India has released the Indian Public Health Standards (IPHS) 2022. IPHS are set of uniform standards to provide norms and benchmarks for quality of infrastructure, human resources, and services to be delivered from public health facilities at all levels. It prescribes the minimum standards to be adhered by the public health facilities at rural and urban areas. The IPHS 2022 is the revised version of IPHS 2012. There have been several new initiatives since the last revision of IPHS made 2012: New Health Policy 2017, Merging of National Rural Health Mission and National Urban Health Mission, and Ayushman Bharat. Norms for human resources are important. Always there is scarcity of human resources in health with long working hours and stress for those who chose to stay with public health facilities. The Member Secretary, Dr Himanshu Bhushan who coordinated the development of IPHS 2022, writes "The inspiration behind the IPHS 2022 is the conviction that build the health facilities that give rich treatment to poor people". IPHS standards are described in four volumes. The volume I is for District Hospitals (DH) and Sub – District Hospitals (SDH); the volume II is for Community Health Centres (CHC) – Rural and Urban; the volume III is for Primary Health Centres (PHC) and Health and Wellness Centres for Rural and Urban including multi speciality Urban PHC (polyclinic); and the volume IV is for Health and Wellness Centre – Sub Health Centre.

The details of standards are beyond the scope of this text. The relevant themes as applicable to pharmacists / pharmacy profession in District Level Hospitals are mentioned here:

- Responsibilities of pharmacists:
    - Dispense at least 120 prescriptions per day;
    - Maintain stock register;
    - Manage store; and
    - Manages inventory (a senior pharmacist may be assigned this job)
- No stock out of essential medicines. Pharmacists should be vigilant to ensure uninterrupted availability of essential medicines.
- Standard Operating Procedures (SOP) should be followed for indenting, stocking, logistics for stocking up and transportation.

The role of pharmacists has undergone big transformation worldwide. There has been paradigm shift from product-oriented approach to clinical and patient-oriented approach. Unfortunately, this is not reflected in IPHS.

## Pharmacists in Public Hospitals

- **Management of medicines:**
    - The pharmacist takes part in selection of medicines, essential medicine list.
    - Quantification and procurement: The pharmacist takes part in estimating medicine requirement and purchasing procedure.

  - o Receiving the supply either from the supplier or higher store / warehouse.
  - o Storing the supply appropriately: temperature controlled, restricted access for narcotics etc.
  - o Dispensing with counselling.
- **Members of various committees:**
  - o Member of Pharmacy and Therapeutic Committee (or, Drugs and Therapeutics Committee).
  - o Member of Antimicrobial Use Committee.
  - o Member of infection control committee.
  - o Member of prescription audit committee.
- **Other roles:**
  - o Providing information on medicines to healthcare professionals and general public.
  - o Taking part in pharmacovigilance activities: Adverse Drug Reaction Monitoring.

**Bottom Line**

- Health is a state subject, and implementation of health programmes is left to state governments.
- Health services in India are delivered by a diverse set of public, for-profit and not-for-profit private providers. The public sector health facilities include: sub-centre, primary health centre, community health centre, and district hospitals. Above the level of district hospitals, tertiary care is provided by medical colleges and/or state-level super-specialty hospitals.
- The National Health Mission is the guiding force for the government which aims to achieve universal access to equitable, affordable & quality health care services.
- Medicines are integral part of healthcare delivery system. Approximately only 10% of all medicines are prescribed and dispensed in government settings. The availability of essential medicines in public health facilities varies widely.
- Indian Public Health Standards (IPHS) 2022 fixes norms and benchmarks for quality of infrastructure, human resources, and services to be delivered from public health facilities at all levels. It prescribes the minimum standards to be adhered by the public health facilities at rural and urban areas.

- IPHS outlines the responsibilities of pharmacists:
  - Dispense at least 120 prescriptions per day;
  - Maintain stock register;
  - Manage store; and
  - Manages inventory (a senior pharmacist may be assigned this job)
- Pharmacists' contribution in public healthcare delivery system can be grouped into: Management of medicines, Members of various committees, Providing Medicine Information, Taking part in ADR monitoring.

## Bibliography

1. G. P. Mohanta and Raj Vaidya, Collaborative Health Care through Doctors and Pharmacist, The **Pharma Review,** April 2006.
2. Guru Prasad Mohanta and P. K. Manna, Empowering pharmacists for primary care, **Chronicle Pharmabiz**, 65$^{th}$ IPC 2013, 2013.
3. Guru Prasad Mohanta and P. Ravikrishnan, Pharmacists in IPHS – a missed opportunity! **Chronicle Pharmabiz, July 2022.**
4. Guru Prasad Mohanta and Prabal Kumar Manna, Continuing Commitment for Primary Healthcare, **Chronicle Pharmabiz, A Special Supplement, December 13, 2018.**
5. Guru Prasad Mohanta, Healthcare in need of intensive care, **OrissaPost, 11 June 2019.**
6. India health system review, Health system in transition, WHO Regional Office for SEA, 2022.
7. Lekshmi S, GP Mohanta, KG Revikumar, PK Manna, Development and Emerging Issues in Public and Private Health Care Systems of Kerala, **International Journal of Pharmacy and Pharmaceutical Sciences, 2014.**

## Public Health – Role of Practicing Pharmacists

"And I believe that the best buy in public health today must be a combination of regular physical exercise and a healthy diet."

- Julie Bishop

**After reading this chapter, you would be able to know / understand:**

- Public Health and Pharmaceutical Public Health;
- Essential Components of Public Health;
- Essential Components of Pharmaceutical Public Health; and
- Role of Practicing Pharmacists.

In simple sense, public health is the implementation of activities concerned with collective activities to improve health of the population. "Public health is the science and art of preventing diseases, prolonging life, and promoting health through the organised efforts and informed choices of society, organizations: public and private, communities and individuals". Public health focuses on the health of population rather than individuals. Clinical prevention and clinical treatment are of less significance. Healthcare services are important component of public health. The pharmacists have been part of the healthcare system participating in various public health activities. The focus on clinical treatment is on identifying the most appropriate medication(s) for the specific disease or illness. On the other hand, public health shifts its focus ensuring access to medicines, promoting safe and effective use of medicines. This aspect of pharmacy practice is termed as 'pharmaceutical public health'. Public health is more than providing treatment for an illness – a concern for the entire population. Public Health works on upstream rather than downstream [Proactive rather than Reactive]. Goal of Public Health is to ensure conditions in which people can be healthy [Funds can be used in programmes, policies and laws]

'Pharmaceutical public health', a comparatively new concept in pharmacy practice, is a service to the population in contrast to the 'clinical pharmacy' and 'pharmaceutical care', services at individual patient level. Pharmaceutical public health has been defined as "the application of pharmaceutical knowledge, skills and resources to the science and art of preventing disease, prolonging life, promoting and improving health for all through the organized efforts of society."

**Essential Components of Public Health**: The National Health Policy (2017) identified the following national priorities in public health:

- **Maternal, New Born and Child Health:** Maternal and child survival is a mirror that reflects the entire spectrum of social development.
- **Child and Adolescent Health:** The focus is on accelerated achieve-ment of neonatal mortality targets and „single digit" stillbirth rates through improved home based and facility based management of sick newborns.
- **Addressing Malnutrition and Micronutrient Deficiency:** Malnu-trition, especially micronutrient deficiencies, restricts survival, growth and development of children. micronutrient deficiencies are addressed through a well planned strategy on micronutrient interventions. Screening for multiple micronutrient deficiencies is advocated. During the critical period of pregnancy, lactation, early childhood, adolescence and old age, the consequences of deficiencies are particularly severe and many are irreversible. While dietary diversification remains the most desirable way forward, supplementation and fortification require to be considered as short and medium term solutions to fill nutrient gaps.
- **Universal Immunization:** Several initiatives like Mission Indra-dhanush are taken up to improve immunization coverage.
- **Communicable Diseases:** Control of Tuberculosis, Control of HIV / AIDS, Leprosy Elimination, and Vector Borne Disease Control are priority health programmes in India.
- **Noncommunicable Diseases:** Screening for oral, breast and cervical cancer and for Chronic Obstructive Pulmonary Disease (COPD) are focused in addition to hypertension and diabetes. There are initiatives for mainstreaming AYUSH as an integrated medical care.
- **Mental Health:** There has been proposal to create network of community members to provide psycho-social support to strengthen mental health services at primary level facilities and leveraging digital technology in a context where access to qualified psychiatrists is difficult.
- **Population Stabilization:** The attempt is to provide sterilization services on any day of the week or at least on a fixed day to improve quality and safety.

The World Health Organization has outlined 12 activities to operationalize public health:

- Public health surveillance and monitoring;
- Public health emergency management;
- Public health stewardship;
- Multisectoral planning, financing and management for public health;

- Health protection;
- Disease prevention and early detection;
- Health promotion;
- Community engagement and social participation;
- Public health workforce development;
- Health service quality and equity;
- Public health research, evaluation and knowledge; and
- Access to and utilization of health products, supplies, equipments and technology.

**Essential Components of Pharmaceutical Public Health:** The domain of pharmaceutical public health includes ensuring availability of local treatment guidelines, developing national medicine policies and essential medicine lists, pharmacovigilance, pharmacoepidemiology, Pharmacoeconomics, and medicine use evaluation. Predominantly in our country, the pharmacists have been participating in the preparation of essential medicine list, pharmacovigilance activities, Pharmacoeconomics, medicine use evaluation.

- Development of Local Treatment Guidelines: The treatment guideline is advocated to be prepared locally so that adherence to the guideline would be optimum. The Standard Treatment Guidelines (STGs) are the recommended treatment options for a disease or medical condition. This is evidence-based guideline which provide quality treatment.
- Indian Council of Medical Research (ICMR) developed STGs for many conditions. Of late, they are called Standard Treatment Workflows. Many state governments and civil societies involved in healthcare prepared the STG for their use.
- The process of developing STG is outlined in the website of National Health Systems Resource Centre: https://qps.nhsrcindia.org/standard-treatment-guidelines.

It is the basic source for developing essential medicine list.

- **Preparation of essential medicines list:** Essential Medicines are indispensable and necessary for the health needs of the population. They should be available at all times, in proper dosage forms, to all segments of the society. The use of the Essential Medicine List is practiced at hospital level to state level to country level. They are prepared based on standard treatment guidelines. The WHO advises the Countries to develop the essential medicines list for National level as well as for healthcare facility levels. Essential Medicines List is a continually changing tool which needs periodic revision based on change in disease epidemiology, new findings of old medicines and introduction of new medicines.

- **Pharmacovigilance activities:** Pharmacovigilance is the science of collecting, monitoring, researching, assessing and evaluating information from health care providers and patients on the adverse effects of medicines, biological products, herbals and traditional medicines with a view to identify the new information on hazards and preventing harm to patients. In simple terms, it is adverse event monitoring. Medicines are important components of many public health programmes. In our country, public health programmes like TB, HIV, Malaria uses medicines extensively. Immunization uses vaccines that too has potential to harm through adverse effects. All these programmes have inbuilt pharmacovigilance activities. India has full -fledged pharmacovigilance programme and India's programme coordination centre, Indian Pharmacopoeia Commission, is recognized as WHO Collaborating Centre for Pharmacovigilance in Public Health. India has several pharmacovigilance programmes: pharmacovigilance of medicines, pharmacovigilance of vaccines [adverse events following immunization (AEFI)], pharmacovigilance of medical devices (materiovigilance) and pharmacovigilance of blood and blood products (haemovigilance). All medical colleges have pharmacovigilance centre.

- **Pharmacoeconomics:** Pharmacoeconomics assesses the overall value of pharmaceutical health products, services and programmes. It helps making a choice. Once safety, efficacy and quality of medicines available in the market are established, it is the turn of cost of medicines that should be the determining factor for drug selection. A simple determination of price is inadequate for determining the actual cost of medicines for the health care system. The pharmacoeconomics provides a series of evaluating tools for assessing the medicines and their alternatives to select the most beneficial alternatives with minimum cost to the system.

  The pharmacoeconomic tools, like cost minimization and cost effectiveness analysis, are handy in assessing medicines for suitability of using them in public health care systems. The use of pharmacoeconomic tools together with ABC and VEN analysis helps in ensuring optimize utilization of resources available in medicine management in public health.

- **Medicine use evaluation:** This can be focussed under two heading:
  - o Medicine use in public health institutions: Irrational use of medicines is not uncommon. The following indicators are used to study medicine use in health facilities (WHO / INRUD):
    - ▪ Prescribing indicators:
      - Average number of medicines per prescription.
      - Percentage of antibiotics.
      - Percentage of injection.
      - Percentage of drugs in generic name.
      - Percentage of drugs from essential medicine list / formulary.
    - ▪ Patient care indicators:
      - Average consultation time.
      - Average dispensing time.
      - Percent medicines dispensed.
      - Percent medicines appropriately labelled.
      - Patient's knowledge on correct dosage.
    - ▪ Facility indicators:
      - Availability of essential medicine list / formulary.
      - Availability of key medicines.
  - o **Medicine use in the community:** It has been estimated that around 50 % of all medicines are prescribed, dispensed or sold inappropriately, while 50 % of patients fail to take their medicines appropriately. Promoting rational use / appropriate use of medicines helps in many ways –
    - ▪ It combats the antimicrobial resistance, one of the biggest public health challenges.
    - ▪ Scarce resources are optimally used – patients get the maximum benefits.

## Pharmacists' Role

- **Community pharmacists:**
  - o May organize / conduct outreach activities – organising health screening camps.
  - o May display posters for health awareness: responsible / rational use of medicines; tobacco use; drugs abuse etc.

- **Hospital pharmacists:**
  - Participate in public health activities organised by the hospital.
  - Participate in national health programmes like TB, HIV etc.
  - Ensure accessibility to required medicines through efficient medicine management system: developing the medicine list for procurement, procurement, and storing at appropriate condition etc.
  - Participate in ADR monitoring programme.
  - Participate in infection control programme; and antimicrobial stewardship programme.

**Bottom Line**

- Public health is the science and art of preventing diseases, prolonging life, and promoting health through the organised efforts and informed choices of society, organizations: public and private, communities and individuals.
- Pharmaceutical public health is the application of pharmaceutical knowledge, skills and resources to the science and art of preventing disease, prolonging life, promoting and improving health for all through the organized efforts of society.
- Essential Components of Public Health:
  - Maternal, New Born and Child Health;
  - Child and Adolescent Health;
  - Addressing Malnutrition and Micronutrient Deficiency;
  - Universal Immunization;
  - Communicable diseases;
  - Noncommunicable diseases;
  - Mental health; and
  - Population Stabilization.
- The World Health Organization has outlined 12 activities to operationalize public health of which 'Access to and utilization of health products, supplies, equipments and technology' is directly relevant to pharmacy.
- Essential Components of Pharmaceutical Public Health:
  - Development of Local Treatment Guidelines;
  - Preparation of essential medicines list;
  - Pharmacovigilance activities;
  - Pharmacoeconomics;

  - Medicine use evaluation.
  - Medicine use in the community.
- Practicing pharmacists at community pharmacy and hospital pharmacy level have ample opportunities to involve themselves in public health and pharmaceutical public health.

## Bibliography

1. Guru Prasad Mohanta, S. Parimalakrishnan and PK Manna, On Strengthening Pharmaceutical Public Health, Chronicle Pharmabiz, 17th December 2015.
2. National Health Policy, 2017, Ministry of Health and Family Welfare, Government of India.
3. Applications of the essential public health functions – an integrated and comprehensive approach, World Health Organization, Geneva, 2024.

## Access to Medicines

"Access to Medicines Transform Lives."

**After reading this chapter, you would be able to know / understand:**

- Meaning of access to medicine and its importance;
- The barriers to access to medicines;
- Available strategies to improve access to medicines; and
- Indian scenario on access to medicines.
- Pharmacists' contribution improving access of medicines.

Medicines are the most important component of healthcare after the human resources (health professionals). Modern healthcare is impossible without the availability of modern medicines. The medicines are not only essential components for curative care but also equally essential for preventive health care and for health promotion. Globally, access to essential medicines is well recognised as a part of rights to health. No medicines no health programmes. The increased longevity is mostly contributed by the availability of the medicines. The world leaders have committed to achieve Universal Health Coverage (UHC) by 2030 under Sustainable Development Goals (SDGs). Achieving UHC requires universal access to safe, effective, quality and affordable essential medicines and vaccines.

**Concept of Essential Medicines**: The WHO has defined as those medicines that satisfy the priority health care needs of the population. They are selected with due regard to disease prevalence, evidence on efficacy, safety and comparative cost effectiveness. They should be available all the time.

However, essential medicines alone are not the requirements but the requirements of health products: medicines, vaccines, diagnostics. The concept of essential medicines is basis of developing list of essential health products: equitable access to health products is a global priority.

Though access and availability of medicines are often used interchangeably, they are not same. The World Health Organization has defined access to medicine as "having medicines continuously available and affordable at public or private health facilities or medicine outlets that are an hour's walking distance from the home". The access to medicines has four dimensions: Accessibility (Geographical access to service point – health centre or private pharmacy); Availability (Availability of medicines either at service point or private pharmacy); Affordability (Economic Access – whether people are able to buy); and Acceptability (peoples' cultural belief and trust on service providers). Among the four factors, availability of medicines at service point and at private pharmacy; and affordability is crucial for India.

**Barriers to access to essential medicines**

1. Unreliable medicine management system at health delivery points. This often leads to stock outs in spite of having surplus fund.
2. Inadequate financing for procurement of medicines for the health facilities.
3. Medicines are often unaffordable.
4. The open market is often flooded with medicines which are not essential. Consumers and Health care professionals are often confused and market pressure promotes these unnecessary medicines.
5. The patent protection has an adverse effect on availability of new medicines.

Time Line on Implementation of Essential Medicine Concept in India:

1. First National Essential Drugs List (EDL) Developed – 1996
2. National List of Essential Medicines (NLEM) – 2003
3. Third National List of Essential Medicines – 2011
4. Fourth National List of Essential Medicines – 2015
5. Fifth National List of Essential Medicines – 2022

The healthcare is under the domain of state government. National list at present has two significances:

- Serve as guide for state governments to prepare their own essential medicines list.
- Serve as guide for price control under Drugs Price Control Order (DPCO).

Availability of medicines at service point is crucial for quality of service. No medicines no programmes. Several initiatives are taken to ensure uninterrupted availability of essential medicines at health facilities. These include establishing a system in every state to manage procurement and distribution of medicines and other health products. Tamil Nadu is the first state to introduce a system for centralised pooled procurement and distribution. This becomes the role model and is adopted by almost all state governments. Tamil Nadu Medical Service Corporation Limited (TNMSCL) is established as early as in 1994. Some of the innovative tools used are: estimating medicine requirements; pooled procurement (buying medicines for full state by one agency); establishing warehouses in different locations (for appropriate storage and easy distribution to health facilities). It uses the concept of essential medicines for procurement. These activities along with good governance have improved the availability of medicines in public health facilities.

Availability of medicines in private pharmacies is not an issue but still a concern in remote areas like where running a pharmacy is unsustainable. Affordability is an economic concern. India though known as pharmacy of the world supplying medicines to more than 200 countries, still affordability is an issue as sizeable population are at below poverty line. Improved availability at public health facilities is a solution.

**Strategies needed for improving access to essential medicines:**

- **Rational Selection of Medicines:** The Essential Medicines List is to be developed. These selective medicines must be made available all the time at health facilities.
- **Minimizing Medicine Cost:** The health facilities should use innovative methodologies to procure quality medicines at lowest possible cost. Centralized procurement and tendering process are examples.
- **Sustainable funding:** Adequate fund should be made available.
- **Ensuring best management practices:** Good Pharmaceutical Management Practices are to be followed for estimating medicine requirements, procurement, distribution and dispensing.
- **Balance between Patent and Access:** This is a policy decision at highest level of the government. At pharmacists' level, it is of little value.

## Indian Scenario

Availability of essential medicine is poor in India. The data is very fragmented. Some reports say average availability of medicines in public health facilities is only 35 %. Almost 68 % of the people in India have limited or no access to essential medicines. Poor availability of medicines in the public sector has pushed up household out-of-pocket (OOP) expenditure, making them the largest household expenditure item after food. Up to 90 % of the population in developing countries purchase medicines through OOP payments. Nearly 80 per cent of India's health care expenditure is borne by patients OOP, of which medicines constitute 70 %. The study has also reported that in Haryana, Punjab and Chandigarh medicines constituted 19-47 % of hospitalization expenditure and 59 to 86 per cent outpatient department (OPD) expenditure borne out of pocket by households in public sector.

The World Health Organization advocates that the enjoyment of the highest attainable standard of health is one of the fundamental rights of every human being without distinction of race, religion, political belief, economic or social condition. Everyone has the right to a standard of living adequate for the health of himself and of his family, including food, clothing, housing and medical care and necessary social services. Governments have an obligation to see the right to health progressively realized to ensure access to health facilities, goods and services which includes access to essential medicines.

## Pharmacists' Role

- **Community pharmacists:** They should ensure the availability of essential medicines. They should give priority on these products.
- **Hospital pharmacists:** They should use their pharmaceutical knowledge in appropriate management of medicines such as estimating the requirements, procurement (wherever feasible), distribution among the facilities and within, and storage to sustain the quality.

**Bottom Lines**

- Medicines are the most important component of healthcare after the human resources (health professionals). Achieving UHC requires universal access to safe, effective, quality and affordable essential medicines and vaccines.
- Essential medicines are those medicines that satisfy the priority health care needs of the population.
- Access to medicine is "having medicines continuously available and affordable at public or private health facilities or medicine outlets that are an hour's walking distance from the home.
- The access to medicines has four dimensions: Accessibility (Geographical access to service point – health centre or private pharmacy); Availability (Availability of medicines either at service point or private pharmacy); Affordability (Economic Access – whether people are able to buy); and Acceptability (peoples' cultural belief and trust on service providers).
- Unreliable medicine management system at health delivery points, inadequate financing for procurement of medicines, unaffordable, market is flooded with unnecessary medicines, and perverse patents are the major hurdles for access to medicines.
- Rational selection of medicines, minimizing medicine cost, sustainable funding, adopting best medicine management practices, and keeping a

balance between public interest and patent: are strategies for improving access.

- 35 % India's population has access to quality medicines.
- The pharmacists at community pharmacy and health facilities have ample opportunities to promote access to medicines.

## Bibliography


1. G. P. Mohanta and S. M. Baranidharan, National Essential Drugs list-an Overview, The Indian Journal of Hospital Pharmacy, November – December, 223-224, 1997.
2. G. P. Mohanta, Essential drugs and rational drug use, Pharma Pulse, 01st January 2004.
3. Guru Prasad Mohanta and PK Manna, Revising national essential medicine list, Pharmabiz, March 18, 2015.
4. Guru Prasad Mohanta, C. K. Dhanapal and P. K. Manna, Access to Essential Medicines -a fundamental human right, Pharmabiz, 5th February 2020.
5. Lekshmi S, Revikumar KG, Veena R, Mohanta GP, PK Manna, An Analytical Study of the Essential Medicine List of Kerala and Tamil Nadu, Hygeia Journal of Drugs and Medicines, 6(1), 40-47, April – September 2014.
6. Shankar Prinja, Pankaj Bahuguna, Jaya Prasad Tripathy and Rajesh Kumar, Availability of medicines in public sector health facilities of two North Indian States. BMC Pharmacology and Toxicology, 2015.
7. Sitanshu Kar, Himanshu Sekhar Pradhan, Guru Prasad Mohanta, Concept of Essential Medicines and Rational Use in Public Health, Indian Journal of Community Medicine, 35 (1), 10 - 13, January 2010.
8. World Health Organization, Road Map for Access to Medicines, Vaccines and Other Health Procucts,2019-2023, 2019.

# National Health Profile

"For he who has health has hope; and he who has hope, has everything."

- Owen Arthur

**After reading this chapter, you would be able to know / understand:**

- Need of health profile data base;
- Selected health profile of India; and
- Pharmacists' interest on health profile.

Reliable health data base is essential for decision making in public health. Central Bureau of Health Intelligence collects data from the health and other relevant sectors, ensuring their overall quality, relevance and timeliness, and converts data into information to support planning, management, and decision making. "National Health Profile" (NHP) has been methodically compiling data on demographic, socioeconomic, health status, health financing indicators, health infrastructure and human resources in health sector in India.

NHP provides extensive Health Information in the above-mentioned areas for specific year. All this information is required for efficient functioning of public health systems, so as to improve health outcomes.

Good Health confers on a person or groups freedom from illness - and enables to realize one's potential. Health is therefore regarded as the indispensable basis for defining a person's sense of well-being. Health care is not merely medical care, is aligned with cultural understanding of ill health and well-being, extent of socioeconomic disparities, reach of health services and quality and costs of care along with current bio-medical understanding about health and illness.

The salient features of National Health Profile 2022 are:

- **Demographic indicators**: It examines some of the key aspects that pertain to expected population increase from 121.1 crores to 151.8 crores during the period 2011-2036 - an increase of 25 percent in twenty- five years at the rate of 1.0 percent annually. Similarly, the sex ratio of the total population (females per 1000 males) is expected to increase from 943 in 2011 to 952 during 2036, and the sex ratio at birth is expected to increase from 906 in 2011 (SRS) to 909 in 2031. The proportion of population in the working age-group 15-59 years is expected to rise from 60.7 percent in 2011 to 65.1 percent in 2036. The average age of Indians is expected to be of 34.7 years in 2036 as compared to 24.9 years in 2011. Further, the SRS abridged tables 2013-17; which gives the Life Expectancy of Life at Birth show it has increased from 49.7 years in 1970-75 to 69.0 years in 2013-17. IMR for the country has come down to 28 in 2020 from 50 in 2009, a decline of 20 points over last 10 years and an annual average decline of about 1.6 points. The level of registration of births was 92.7% in 2019.

- **Socioeconomics data**: The gross enrolment ratio for both girls and boys in schools in India in primary grades in 2019-20 was 104.5 and 102.2, respectively. However, by the time students reach higher secondary grades, the enrolment ratio drops to 53.0 and 54.6, respectively. At the national level, the mean age at effective marriage of females remained almost constant at around 22 years from 2016 to 2019. Poverty levels are higher in rural India (26%) than urban (14%) as per Tendulkar Methodology, 2011-12. In 2019-20, among the populous states, per capita Net State Domestic Product at current price with base year 2013-14 was above INR 150,000 in Haryana, Karnataka, Tamil Nadu, and Telangana, while it was below INR of 50,000 in Bihar and Uttar Pradesh. In 2019-20, Delhi and Sikkim have the highest per capita NDP when Bihar and Uttar Pradesh have the lowest. From 2013 to 2020, the NDP growth rate was highest in Tripura.
- **Health status**: In 2020, total patients notified for TB was 18,12,151. Out of the total microbiologically confirmed cases (8,43,149 in 2020) of TB, 76% of the patients were successfully treated. With state-wise fluctuations, India has made significant progress in tackling HIV epidemic, from a prevalence of 0.80% in 2003 to 0.24% by 2018-19. In 2021, out of 5.91 crore people screened under National Programme for Prevention and Control of Cancer, Diabetes, Cardiovascular Diseases and Stroke (NPCDCS): 7.6% were diagnosed with hypertension, 5.93% with diabetes, 2.49% with Hypertension and Diabetes, 0.255% with CVDs, 0.11% with stroke and 0.19% with common cancers.
- **Health financing**: Appropriate Health Financing is a means to ensure adequate funds for health care provide equitable access to all population groups and reduce barriers to utilize health services. It provides (1) Public Expenditure on Health (2) Average Medical Expenditure and 3) Health Coverage and Insurance. Urban and rural health services constituted 70.11% of the public expenditure on medical and public health in 2018-19 the same has decreases to 69.54% in 2019-20. The per capita expenditure on CGHS during 2021-22 was Rs 10,835. As of 31st March 2021, around 13.16 crores

of beneficiaries were covered under ESIS. The per capita expenditure on medical benefit under ESIS is Rs. 716.82 for the year 2021

- **Health infrastructure**: This is an important indicator for understanding the health care delivery provisions and welfare mechanisms in a country. Medical education infrastructures have shown rapid growth over past few years with 648 medical colleges (396 Government, 252 Private), and 98013 MBBS seats till September, 2022. Currently there are 1962 Institutions for ANM with 59,085 seats for admission, and 9250 institutions with 3,50,679 Nursing seats in the country. As on 31st March 2021, there are total of 1,57,819 Sub Centres (SCs) (156101 rural + 1718 urban), 30,579 Primary Health Centres (PHCs) (25140 rural + 5439 urban), 5,951 Community Health Centres (CHCs) (5,481 rural + 470 urban), 1224 Sub-divisional Hospitals, 764 District Hospitals, and 307 Medical Colleges present across the country.
- **Human resources**: Data on human resources for health (HRH) is essential for planning, development, performance, management, retention, information, and research on human resources. With regard to the number of registered doctors, among the states, Maharashtra (1,88,540 doctors) has the highest number of registered doctors followed by Tamil Nadu (1,48,216 doctors), Karnataka (1,31,906), and Andhra Pradesh (1,05,795).

The Economic Survey, 2023-2024, says:

- 54 % disease burden in India is caused by unhealthy diets. High intake of ultra processed and restricted access nutritious foods is responsible for high obesity rate.
- 70 % of the urban population are either obese or over weight.
- India is the deemed capital of diabetes.

## Pharmacists' Interest on Health Profile

- **Community pharmacists:** Community pharmacists (retail pharmacists) are the first level health professionals for common man. The knowledge of health profile would help guiding the people.
- **Hospital pharmacists:** Though hospital pharmacists have no direct opportunity to provide healthcare, some states like Odisha empowered them to dispense / use medicines in absence of medical practitioners. The knowledge of health profile would help providing appropriate care.

Pharmacists are recognized in Indian Health Care System. It is evident from the list of important health days: 25th September (mentioned in National Health Profile 2022) is observed as world pharmacist day.

**Bottom Lines**

- Reliable health data base is essential for decision making in public health. Central Bureau of Health Intelligence compiles "National Health Profile" (NHP) giving data on demographic, socioeconomic, health status, health financing indicators, health infrastructure and human resources in health sector in India.
- The salient features of National Health Profile 2022 are:
    - **Demographic indicators**: The population is expected to increase from 121.1 crores to 151.8 crores during the period 2011-2036 - an increase of 25 percent in twenty- five years at the rate of 1.0 percent annually.
    - **Socioeconomics data**: The gross enrolment ratio for both girls and boys in schools in India in primary grades in 2019-20 was 104.5 and 102.2, respectively. However, by the time students reach higher secondary grades, the enrolment ratio drops to 53.0 and 54.6, respectively. At the national level, the mean age at effective marriage of females remained almost constant at around 22 years from 2016 to 2019.
    - **Health status**: In 2020, total patients notified for TB was 18,12,151. Out of the total microbiologically confirmed cases (8,43,149 in 2020) of TB, 76% of the patients were successfully treated. With state-wise fluctuations, India has made significant progress in tackling HIV epidemic, from a prevalence of 0.80% in 2003 to 0.24% by 2018-19.
    - **Health financing**: Urban and rural health services constituted 70.11% of the public expenditure on medical and public health in 2018-19 the same has decreases to 69.54% in 2019-20. The per capita expenditure on CGHS during 2021-22 was Rs 10,835.
    - **Health infrastructure**: There have been rapid growth over past few years with 648 medical colleges (396 Government, 252 Private), and 98013 MBBS seats till September, 2022. As on 31st March 2021, there are total of 1,57,819 Sub Centres (SCs) (156101 rural + 1718 urban), 30,579 Primary Health Centres (PHCs) (25140 rural + 5439 urban), 5,951 Community Health Centres (CHCs) (5,481 rural + 470 urban), 1224 Sub-divisional Hospitals, 764 District Hospitals, and 307 Medical Colleges present across the country.

- o **Human resources**: With regard to the number of registered doctors, among the states, Maharashtra (1,88,540 doctors) has the highest number of registered doctors followed by Tamil Nadu (1,48,216 doctors), Karnataka (1,31,906), and Andhra Pradesh (1,05,795).
- The knowledge of health profile helps the pharmacists to know the societal health issue.

## Bibliography

1. National Health Profile 2022, 17th Issue, Central Bureau of Health Intelligence, Government of India.

## International Agencies Contributing to India's Public Health

"Nothing on Earth is more International than Diseases"

- Paul Russel

**After reading this chapter, you should be able to understand and appreciate:**

- International Agencies actively participating / collaborating with India on health matters;
- Genesis of these organizations; and
- Their contribution to India's public health.

The International Organizations working to support countries can be divided into three groups: Multilateral Organizations; Bilateral Organizations and Non – Governmental Organizations (NGOs). Multilateral signifies funding from multiple governments and NGOs: WHO, UNICEF, World Bank. Bilateral Organizations: These are Government Agencies but provide aid to developing countries. United States Agency for International Development (USAID) is an example of bilateral organization. Most of the developed or industrialised countries have similar agencies. NGOs are private voluntary organizations: MSF falls in this category.

There are many organizations contributing for improving the health of the people of India. The text does not intent to cover all of them but just few. These organizations may be working in many other areas and the text just reflects their involvement in health sectors.

### World Health Organization (WHO)

World Health Organization, established in 1948, is an UN' specialised agency for Health works with mission to achieve "Attainment by all peoples of the highest possible levels of health" without discretion of race, religion, political belief, economic status or social condition. Being an inter-governmental organization, it works with the member states, usually with the Ministry of Health. The WHO was officially established in 1948 and is recognised as "Global Guardian of Health". It operates through its Head Quarter at Geneva, Six Regional Offices and the Country Office. The Country Office is headed by the WHO Representative. India comes under South East Asia Regional Office (SEARO) with office at New Delhi. WHO has 194 member states with more than 150 country offices.

WHO's birthday 7th April is celebrated as World Health Day to create awareness of a specific health theme to highlight a priority area of concern for the World Health Organization. WHO is a part of UN but not subordinate to it. It aims to build a better and healthier future for people all over the world. Currently, it is working (2019-2023) on three bold targets called triple billion targets:

- One billion more people to benefits from Universal Health Coverage;
- One billion more people better protected from health emergency; and
- One billion more people enjoying better health and well-being.

## WHO- India Country Cooperation

The WHO – India Country Cooperation Strategy (CCS) (2019-2023) is jointly prepared by Ministry of Health, Government of India and WHO Country Office for India. The CCS provides a strategic roadmap for WHO to work with the Government of India towards achieving its health sector goals, improving the health of its population and bringing in transformative changes in the health sector.

WHO's technical support to the Government of India falls under the following four strategic priorities to contribute India's health agenda:

**Strategic Priority 1:** Accelerate progress on UHC

- Implementing Ayushman Bharat: Health and Wellness Centres and hospital insurance scheme
- Monitoring and evaluation of health sector performance
- Improving access to priority health services such as immunizations, maternal and child health, tuberculosis, hepatitis
- Digital health ecosystem
- Eliminating neglected tropical diseases and control of vaccine-preventable and vector-borne diseases

**Strategic Priority 2:** Promote health and wellness by addressing determinants of health

- Non-communicable diseases (NCDs) action plan roll-out
- Environmental health, including air pollution
- Mental health promotion and suicide prevention
- Nutrition and food safety
- Road safety

- Tobacco control
- Integration of NCD and environmental risk factors in the digital health information platform

**Strategic Priority 3:** Better protect the population against health emergencies

- Disease surveillance and outbreak detection and response, including International Health Regulation
- Roll-out of integrated disease surveillance programme using the real-time integrated health information platform (IHIP)
- Preparedness for, and response to all, emergencies
- Containment of antimicrobial resistance

**Strategic Priority 4:** Enhance India's global leadership in health

- Improving access to medical products of assured quality made in India
- Development and information sharing of innovations in health practices and technologies including IHIP
- Strengthening India's leadership in digital health

The period of this CCS is expected to bring rapid and significant changes to India's health sector and to improve access to quality health care, especially to the vulnerable and underserved populations.

**Pharmaceutical Aspects**: Improving the access to quality medicinal products. The work areas on medicines include: policy (concept of essential medicines, STG, procurement, pricing), regulation (standards and strengthening the regulatory system), quality (safety and efficacy) and use (appropriate or rational use).

WHO has been instrumental making India polio free. India was certified polio free on 27$^{th}$ March 2014. In addition to routine immunization, it supports Intensified Mission Indradhanush, Measles – Rubella Campaign; Control of other vaccine preventable diseases including surveillance; Integrated disease surveillance programme; elimination of neglected tropical diseases: kala-azar, leprosy and lymphatic filariasis. It is also supporting India combating COVID – 19 pandemic.

## United Nation Children's Fund (UNICEF)

United Nations International Children's Emergency Fund (UNICEF) was initially established in 1946 as UN's temporary agency to deal with rehabilitation Second World War affected children. Later in 1953, the organization was renamed as "UN Children's Fund" but retained the acronym. UNICEF's Head Office is at New York, USA and South Central Asian Regional Office at New Delhi. It works in over 190 countries and territories to save children's life, to defend their rights, and to help them fulfil their potential from early childhood through adolescence.

UNICEF began its work in India in 1949. It provided equipment and technical assistance to India's first penicillin plant established in 1949 at Pimpri. Currently, being part of series of initiatives of GOI, it works on reducing child death including giving focus on pneumonia and diarrhoea. It aims in achieving single digit neonatal and still birth rate

It works across India to save children's lives, help them to fulfil their potential and defend their rights. Its health related work concentrates on improving maternal, new born, child and adolescent health through collaboration with communities, governments and partners. In short, UNICEF assists to improve services and quality care for children and women.

## World Bank

The World Bank was established as a specialised agency of UN with the purpose of helping the less developed countries to raise their living standards. The World Bank was founded in 1944 with head quarter at Washington DC.

It provides low interest loan, zero to low interest credits and grant to developing countries. Its priority areas: health, nutrition and population. It has been supporting health projects since early 1990s. The World Bank has recently sanctioned "$32 million Mizoram Health System Strengthening Project" to improve management capacity and quality of health services. The on-going projects in India are: Tamil Nadu Health System Strengthening Programme, Andhra Pradesh Health System Strengthening Project, Uttarakhand Health System Development Project, Programme towards Elimination of TB, National AIDS Control Support Project and Nagaland Health Project.

## US Agency for International Development (USAID)

USAID was created by US Government in 1961 to help lift lives, build communities and advance democracy. It works in over 100 countries to promote global health; support global stability; provide humanitarian assistance; catalyse innovation and partnership; and to empower women and girls.

USAID aims at generating sustainable solutions to improve health outcomes in India. The priority health areas include: Preventing child and

Maternal Deaths (focuses on urban poor, working to improve both reach and quality of health services, as well as reducing out of pocket medical cost); Championing a TB free India (training to health providers to expand access to TB services and to improve the quality and adherence to International TB standards for diagnosis, treatment and care); Controlling the HIV / AIDS epidemic (prevention and care for population most at risk of HIV); Combating infectious disease threat (strengthening India's capacity to prevent and reduce outbreaks, detect threat early to save lives, and respond with rapid and coordinated efforts).

## Doctors Without Borders/ Médecins Sans Frontières (MSF)

MSF is an international, independent medical organization, established in 1971 by a small group of French doctors. It provides medical assistance to people affected by conflict, epidemics, disasters, or exclusion from healthcare. Currently it is implementing several projects in India. In 1999, it was awarded Nobel Peace Prize for its worldwide campaign for affordable and effective medicines with key focus on the difficulties people face in getting hold of adequate and effective diagnostic tests, drugs and vaccines.

Its campaign focuses on safe guarding and strengthening policies that protect India's production and export of generic medicines. Because of this export, India is known as the pharmacy of the developing countries.

It has campaigned against the unwarranted patents and harmful provisions in trade agreements which would be obstacles to access. The current projects being implemented in India include: Mental health helpline for people affected by COVID – 9; Delivering specialist care for HIV, TB and Hepatitis in Manipur: Providing medical care for drug resistant TB in Mumbai; Meeting mental health needs in Jammu and Kashmir; Acting against Kala-Zar, HIV Co-infection, and Advanced HIV in Bihar; and Essential healthcare in remote areas of Andhra Pradesh, Chhattisgarh, and Telengana. Its publications like Clinical Guidelines and Essential Drugs are very valuable resources in public health.

## International Pharmaceutical Federation

The **International Pharmaceutical Federation (FIP)** was founded in **1912** as a global organization supporting pharmacy, pharmaceutical sciences, and education. Headquartered in the **Netherlands,** FIP collaborates with **158 national organizations** to advance pharmacy practice, scientific research, and workforce development. The Indian Pharmaceutical Association (IPA) is the partner of FIP in India. It plays a key role in transforming **molecules into medicines** by ensuring pharmacists optimize their responsible use for better health outcomes.

Recognized as a **global leader in pharmacy**, FIP influences policies, education, and innovation through partnerships with top health and science institutions. By strengthening the profession worldwide, FIP helps pharmacists meet global **healthcare challenges** efficiently. IPA in association with FIP has started empowering pharmacists to vaccinate the communities through training them as vaccinators.

**Bottom Line**

- Many multilateral, bilateral and NGOs have been contributing towards improving the health of people of India.
- WHO (multilateral organization), established in 1948, works with the mission "Attainment by all peoples of the highest possible levels of health". It supports India's activities in collaboration with Ministry of Health, GOI, with the strategic areas: Accelerate progress in UHC; Promote health and wellness by addressing determinants of health; Better protect the population against health emergencies; and Enhance India's global leadership in health.
- UN's Children Fund (multilateral organization), established in 1946, has been working across India to save children's lives, help them fulfil their full potential and defend their rights. Its activity concentrates on improving maternal, new born, child and adolescent health. It assists to improve services and quality care for children and women.
- World Bank (multilateral organization, established in 1944, with the purpose of helping the less developed countries to raise their living standard. Its projects in India mostly include capacity building: health system reform or development of state governments.
- USAID (bilateral organization), created in 1961, is working in over 100 countries to promote global health. Some of the areas of its work in India are: preventing child and maternal death; championing a TB free India; controlling HIV / AIDS epidemic; and combating infectious disease threat.
- MSF (NGO), established in 1971, is focussing on safe guarding and strengthening policies that protect India's production and export of generic medicines to the rest of the world especially to the developing nations.
- IPA in association with FIP started project empowering pharmacists as vaccinators.

## Bibliography


1. https://www.msfindia.in/projects-in-india/ ; accessed on 06th June 2021.
2. https://www.unicef.org/india/our-history; accessed on 06th June 2021.
3. https://www.usaid.gov/india/health; accessed on 06th June 2021.
4. https://www.who.int/about/what-we-do/thirteenth-general-programme-of-work-2019---2023; accessed on 06th June 2021.
5. https://www.who.int/india/country-cooperation-strategy-2019-2023; accessed on 06th June 2021.
6. https://www.worldbank.org/en/cpf/india/what-we-work/human-capital/health-care; accessed on 06th June 2021.

## Sustainable Development Goals

"I have always believed exercise is key not only to physical health but to peace of mind."

- Nelson Mandela

**After reading this chapter, you should be able to understand and appreciate:**

- Background of Sustainable Development Goals;
- Target date of achieving Sustainable Development Goals;
- Health and Sustainable Development Goals;
- India's position; and
- Pharmacists' contribution achieving Sustainable Development Goals.

The world leaders joined together at the United Nations (UN) Sustainable Development Summit at New York during 25-27 September 2015 to adopt new development agenda known as Sustainable Development Goals (SDGs). 193 world leaders committed to achieve sustainable development in three important dimensions: economic, social and environmental in a balanced and integrated manner. Commitment for ambitious 17 goals with 169 targets is an agenda for development for the next 15 years. The first line of the preamble of the sustainable development document 'Transforming our World: the 2030 Agenda for Sustainable Development' says "This agenda is a plan of action for people, planet and prosperity'. Though agenda are much diversified, the plan is to finish the unfinished agenda of millennium development goals SDGs are developed through a series of consultation among the member countries. MDGs focused on need of developing and poor countries, while SDGs are meant for everyone and have a holistic approach to achieve the goals to make the planet a better place to live.

| Goal | Theme |
|---|---|
| SDG – 1 | No Poverty – Aims to end poverty in all forms everywhere |
| SDG – 2 | Zero Hunger – Aims to end hunger and malnutrition by 2030 |
| SDG – 3 | Good Health and Well Being – Aims to ensure healthy lives and promoting well-being at all ages |
| SDG – 4 | Quality Education – Aims at ensuring inclusive and equitable quality education and promote lifelong learning opportunities for all |
| SDG – 5 | Gender Equality – Ensures to end all forms of discrimination against women and girls |
| SDG – 6 | Clean Water and Sanitation – Ensures availability and sustainable management of water and sanitation |

**Table *Contd...***

| Goal | Theme |
|---|---|
| SDG – 7 | Affordable and Clean Energy – Aims to improve energy, increase use of renewable resources and promotion of sustainable and modern energy |
| SDG – 8 | Decent Work and Economic Growth – Aims to promote sustained economic growth by achieving higher levels of productivity and through technological innovation |
| SDG – 9 | Industry, Innovation and Infrastructure – Aims to build resilient infrastructure, promote inclusive and sustainable industrialization and foster innovation |
| SDG – 10 | Reduced Inequalities – Focuses on reducing inequality within and among countries |
| SDG – 11 | Sustainable Cities and Communities – Focuses on cities as more than half of world's population lives in them |
| SDG – 12 | Responsible Consumption and Production – Aims at ensuring responsible consumption and production patterns |
| SDG – 13 | Climate Action – Calls for urgent action to combat climate change and its impacts |
| SDG - 14 | Life Below Water – Aims to conserve and sustainably use of oceans, seas and marine resources for sustainable development |
| SDG – 15 | Life on Land – Aims to protect, restore and promote sustainable use of terrestrial ecosystem, sustainably manage forests, combat desertification, and halt and reverse land degradation, halt biodiversity loss, which have already been at the centre of considerations while policy formulation relating to environment |
| SDG – 16 | Peace, Justice and Strong Institutions – Seeks to promote peaceful and inclusive societies for sustainable development, provide access to justice for all and build effective, accountable and inclusive institutions at all levels |
| SDG – 17 | Partnership for the Goals – Is critical to the achievement of all SDGs as goal seek to strengthen the means of implementation and revitalize the Global Partnership for sustainable development |

The SDG – 3 exclusively plans to achieve healthy lives and promote well being of all ages. This it-self is a paradigm shift from MDGs where focus was on specific groups: mother and children health; and on specific diseases: HIV/AIDS, Malaria, and TB. The SDGs covers all other aspects of health too like mental health, health for all age groups including elderly populations. The goal has 9 targets with four mechanisms of implementations.

These 9 targets are:

- reduce the global maternal mortality ratio to less than 70 per 100,000 live births;
- reduce neonatal mortality to at least as low as 12 per 1,000 live births and under-5 mortality to at least as low as 25 per 1,000 live births;
- end the epidemics of AIDS, tuberculosis, malaria and neglected tropical diseases and combat hepatitis, water-borne diseases and other communicable diseases;

- reduce by one third premature mortality from non-communicable diseases through prevention and treatment and promote mental health and well-being;
- strengthen the prevention and treatment of substance abuse, including narcotic drug abuse and harmful use of alcohol;
- ensure universal access to sexual and reproductive health-care services, including for family planning, information and education, and the integration of reproductive health into national strategies and programmes;
- achieve universal health coverage, including financial risk protection, access to quality essential health-care services and access to safe, effective, quality and affordable essential medicines and vaccines for all;
- substantially reduce the number of deaths and illnesses from hazardous chemicals and air, water and soil pollution and contamination by 2030;
- halve the number of global deaths and injuries from road traffic accidents by 2020.

The 4 mechanisms are: strengthening of implementation of WHO's frame work on Tobacco Control; supporting research and development of vaccines and medicines with improved access within the frame work of IPR; substantially increasing investment in health sector with increased trained health workforce; and strengthening the warning and management system of health risks. Among the four mechanisms, IPR provision associated with innovation often threatens access to new medicines and vaccines. Many anti-cancer drugs and drug treatment of hepatitis C are live examples of un-affordability. Even there are issues of monopolistic pricing of new drug in America. The new effective treatment for hepatitis C costing $1000 per pill for 12 week treatment is beyond the reach. While negotiating for stringent IPR protection, public health provision like compulsory licensing needs to be preserved.

Though apparently it looks that the health is not given due share as the health focus is reduced from '3 out of 8 goals in MDGs' to '1 out of 17 SDGs'. In reality, almost every one of the 17 SDGs has direct link with the health of the people or will contribute to health indirectly. The single health goal "Ensure healthy lives and promote well being for all at all ages" has link with other goals. World Health Organization has already formulated its task in the light of new developmental agenda and now it is the turn of member states to initiate the process of developing strategies and allocating resources to strengthen health system to achieve the much ambitious developmental goals by 2030!

India's progress (SDG 3: Ensure Healthy Lives and Promote Well Being for all at all ages):

| Target 3.1: By 2030, reduce the global maternal mortality ratio to less than 70 per 1,00,000 live births | |
|---|---|
| 3.1.1: Maternal Mortality Ratio, (per 1,00,000 live births | 103 (2017-2019) |
| 3.1.2: Percentage of births attended by skilled health personnel (Period 5 years), | 89.40 (2019-2021) |
| 3.1.3: Percentage of births attended by skilled health personnel (Period 1 year) | 90.90 (2019-2021) |
| 3.1.4: Percentage of women aged 15-49 years with a live birth, for last birth, who received antenatal care, four times or more (Period 5 years/1 year), | 58.50 (2019 – 2021) |
| Target 3.2: By 2030, end preventable deaths of newborns and children under 5 years of age, with all countries aiming to reduce neonatal mortality to at least as low as 12 per 1,000 live births and under-5 mortality to at least as low as 25 per 1,000 live births | |
| 3.2.1: Under-five mortality rate, (per 1,000 live births) | 35 (2019) |
| 3.2.2: Neonatal mortality rate (per 1,000 live births) | 22 (2019) |
| Target 3.3: By 2030, end the epidemics of AIDS, tuberculosis, malaria and neglected tropical diseases and combat hepatitis, water-borne diseases and other communicable diseases | |
| 3.3.1: Number of new HIV infections per 1,000 uninfected population | 0.05 (2021) |
| 3.3.2: Tuberculosis incidence per 1,00,000 population | 188 (2020) |
| 3.3.3: Malaria incidence per 1,000 population | 0.12 (2021) |
| 3.3.4: Prevalence of Hepatitis 'B' per 1,00,000 population | ------------ |
| 3.3.5: Dengue: Case Fatality Ratio | 0.16 (2021) |
| 3.3.6: Proportion of grade-2 cases amongst new cases of Leprosy, (Per million population) | 1.36 (2021-2022) |
| 3.3.7: Percentage of blocks reporting < 1 Kala Azar case per 10,000 population out of the total endemic blocks | 98.73 (2021) |
| 3.3.8: Percentage of districts reporting < 1% Microfilaria rate (MF) out of Targeted Endemic districts | 40.55 (2021) |
| Target 3.4: By 2030, reduce by one third premature mortality from non-communicable diseases through prevention and treatment and promote mental health and well-being | |
| 3.4.2: Suicide mortality rate, (per 1,00,000 population) | 11.3 (2020) |
| Target 3.5: Strengthen the prevention and treatment of substance abuse, including narcotic drug abuse and harmful use of alcohol | |
| 3.5.1: Number of persons treated in de-addiction centres | 2,85,559 (2021-2022) |

**Table *Contd...***

| | |
|---|---|
| 3.5.2: Percentage of population (men (15-49 years) & women (15 - 49 years)) who drink alcohol about once a week out of total population (men (15-49 years) & women (15 - 49 years)) who drink alcohol | Male – 43.4; Female – 36.6 (2019-2021) |
| 3.5.3: Percentage of population (15 years and above) who consume alcohol, by sex, | Male – 18.8; Female – 1.3 (2019-2021) |
| Target 3.6: By 2020, halve the number of global deaths and injuries from road traffic accidents | |
| 3.6.1: People killed/injured in road accidents (per 1,00,000 population) | 9.84 death rate; 24.76 injury rate (2020) |
| Target 3.7: By 2030, ensure universal access to sexual and reproductive health-care services, including for family planning, information and education, and the integration of reproductive health into national strategies and programmes | |
| 3.7.1: Percentage of currently married women aged 15-49 years who have their need for family planning satisfied with modern methods, | 74.10 (2019-2021) |
| 3.7.2: Adolescent birth rate (aged 15–19 years) per 1,000 women in that age group (Per 1,000 females) | 10.6 (2019) |
| 3.7.3: Percentage of Institutional Births (5 years/1 years) | 88.6 (5 years); 90.6 (1 Year); 2019-2021 |
| 3.7.4: Percentage of currently married women (15-49 years) who use any modern family planning methods | 56.5 (2019-2021) |
| 3.7.5: Percentage of women aged 15-19 years who were already mothers or pregnant | 6.80 (2019-2021) |
| Target 3.8: Achieve universal health coverage, including financial risk protection, access to quality essential health-care services and access to safe, effective, quality and affordable essential medicines and vaccines for all | |
| 3.8.1: Percentage of currently married women (15-49 years) who use any modern family planning methods | 56.50 (2019 - 2021) |
| 3.8.2: Proportion of population with large household expenditures on health as a share of total household expenditure or income | > 10 %, 4.48; > 25 %, 1.57 (2017-2018) |
| 3.8.3: Percentage of people living with HIV currently receiving ART among the detected number of adults and children living with HIV | 84 (2021-2022) |
| 3.8.4: Prevalence of hypertension among men and women age 15 years and above (in percentage) | Male 24.0, Female 21.3 (2019-2021) |
| 3.8.5: Percentage of population in age group 15-49 who reported sought treatment out of total population in that age group having diabetes, | Male 71.5, Female 80.7 (2019-2021) |
| 3.8.6: Percentage of women aged 30- 49 yeas who have ever undergone a screening test for cervical cancer | 1.80 (2019-2021) |

**Table *Contd...***

<table>
<tr><td>3.8.7: Percentage of TB cases successfully treated (cured plus treatment completed) among TB cases notified to the national health authorities during a specified period</td><td>83 (2021)</td></tr>
<tr><td colspan="2">Target 3.9: By 2030, substantially reduce the number of deaths and illnesses from hazardous chemicals and air, water and soil pollution and contamination</td></tr>
<tr><td>3.9.2: Proportion of men and women reporting Asthma in the age group 15-49 years,</td><td>Male – 1.20, Female – 1.60 (2019 -2021)</td></tr>
<tr><td>3.9.3: Mortality rate attributed to unintentional poisoning, (per 1,00,000 population)</td><td>1.64 (2020)</td></tr>
<tr><td colspan="2">Target 3.a: Strengthen the implementation of the World Health Organization Framework Convention on Tobacco Control in all countries, as appropriate</td></tr>
<tr><td>3.a.1: Percentage of adults 15 years and above with use of any kind of tobacco (smoking and smokeless),</td><td>28.6 (2016 – 2017)</td></tr>
<tr><td colspan="2">Target 3.b: Support the research and development of vaccines and medicines for the communicable and noncommunicable diseases that primarily affect developing countries, provide access to affordable essential medicines and vaccines, in accordance with the Doha Declaration on the agreement and public health, which affirms the right of developing countries to use to the full the provisions in the agreement on trade-Related aspects of Intellectual property Rights regarding flexibilities to protect public health, and, in particular, provide access to medicines for all</td></tr>
<tr><td>3.b.1: Percentage of children age 12-23 months fully vaccinated with BCG, measles and three doses each of polio and DPT or Penta vaccine (excluding polio vaccine given at birth),</td><td>76.6 (2019-2021)</td></tr>
<tr><td>3.b.2: Budgetary allocation for Department of Health Research, (in Rs. crore)</td><td>2663 (2021-2022)</td></tr>
<tr><td colspan="2">Target 3.c: Substantially increase health financing and the recruitment, development, training and retention of the health workforce in developing countries, especially in least developed countries and small island developing States</td></tr>
<tr><td>3.c.1: Health worker density</td><td>49.44 (2019)</td></tr>
<tr><td>3.c.2: Percentage of government spending (including current and capital expenditure) in health sector to GDP</td><td>1.59 (2020-2021)</td></tr>
<tr><td>3.d.1: International Health Regulations (IHR) capacity and health emergency preparedness</td><td>Legislation and Financing – 80,<br>IHR Coordination and National IHR Focal Point Functions – 90,<br>Zoonotic Events and the Human–animal Interface - 60,<br>Food Safety – 60,<br>Laboratory – 67,<br>Surveillance – 100,<br>Human Resources – 100,<br>National Health Emergency Framework – 80,<br>Health Service Provision – 33,<br>Risk Communication – 80,<br>Points of Entry – 80,<br>Chemical Events – 80.<br>Radiation Emergencies – 100.<br>[Data of 2019]</td></tr>
</table>

There have been many progresses in SDGs – 3, some notable achievements are:

| Parameter | Base line data | Achievements |
|---|---|---|
| Overall score has improved substantially from 52 in 2018 to 77 in 2023-24 | | |
| Maternal Mortality Ratio per 100,000 live births | 130 (2014-2016) | 97 |
| Under 5 mortality rate (per 1,000 live births) | 36 (2016-18) | 32 (2018-20) |
| Percentage of Women Aged 15-49 Years of live birth, for last birth, who received ante natal care four times or more | 51.20 (2015-2016) | 58.50 (2019-2020) |
| Institutional Birth | 82.6 (2015-2016) | 97.18 (2023-2024) |
| Percentage of children age 12-23 months fully vaccinated with BCG. Measles, and three doses each of polio and DPT or Penta vaccine (excluding polio vaccine at birth) | 62.0 (2015-2016) | 93.23 %(2023-2024) [Children 9-11 months] |
| 87.13% tuberculosis cases notified against target (2023-2024) | | |

## Pharmacists' Contribution Achieving Sustainable Development Goals

Pharmacists both in the community and hospital sector should sensitize common man to utilize the government schemes for healthcare including government insurance schemes. The services in the public health facilities and some charitable hospitals are free. Ayusman Bharat a central government scheme, health protection scheme, provides benefit of ₹ 5 lakh per poor and vulnerable family. The pharmacists can guide the beneficiary group to register under the scheme.

**Bottom Line**

- United Nations (UN) Sustainable Development Summit at New York during 25-27 September 2015 to adopt new development agenda known as Sustainable Development Goals (SDGs).
- The theme: 'Transforming our World: the 2030 Agenda for Sustainable Development'.
- SDGs have 17 goals with 169 targets. The SDG 3 concentrates on health: Good Health and Well Being – Aims to ensure healthy lives and promoting well-being at all ages.
- India has made many progresses over the period, notable achievements in the parameters are: Maternal Mortality Ratio per 100,000 live births; Percentage of Women Aged 15-49 Years of live birth, for last birth, who received ante natal care four times or more; Institutional Birth; and Percentage of children age 12-23 months fully vaccinated

with BCG, Measles, and three doses each of polio and DPT or Penta vaccine (excluding polio vaccine at birth).

- Pharmacists both in the community and hospital sector should sensitize common man to utilize the government schemes for healthcare including government insurance schemes.

## Bibliography

1. Guru Prasad Mohanta, Babita Sarangi and PK Manna, Health and Development Agenda, **Pharmabiz**, 14 January 2016.
2. Sustainable Development Goals, National Indicator Framework, Progress Report 2022, Government of India.
3. Release of SDG India Index 2023-2024, Posted by PIB, 12th July 2024.

# CHAPTER 2

# Hygiene and Health

## Hand Washing

**After reading this chapter, you should be able to understand and appreciate:**

- Definition of Hand Washing and Hand Hygiene;
- Importance of Hand Washing;
- Hand Washing Technique;
- Risk of Hand Shaking and
- Pharmacists' Role in Promoting Hand Washing.

The skin in our hands with natural secretions of oil form an ideal environment for microbes. Each square centimetre of human skin is home to about 40,000 bacteria. The number is much higher on hands because hands are in frequent contact with many everyday objects that may contain bacteria. The hands can easily carry bacteria or viruses from our gastro-intestinal tract after we cough, sneeze, rub our mouths or noses or use the rest room. Germs from contaminated food, water, and surfaces like dustbin bag, television remote, key board, kitchen mop, door knobs, mobile phones and floor mat too get entry through hands. People carry *Staphylococcus*, which can grow in foods to produce toxin. The uncooked food with bacteria can cause outbreaks of food borne illness. People frequently contaminate food during preparation because they fail to wash their hands.

A study reported in The Lancet, the prestigious medical journal, claim that a million deaths a year can be prevented if everyone starts routinely washing their hands. Poor hand hygiene is one of the major causes behind many infections like cold and flu, diarrhoea, respiratory tract infections, eye infections, and dangerous one like sepsis and hepatitis. 80% of the common infections are spread through hands. Hand hygiene is of utmost importance maintaining good health and prevent infectious diseases.

Hand washing has been a central component of personal hygiene for many years. But the link between hand washing and health is just about 200 years old.

Ignaz Semmelweis, a Hungarian doctor, working in Vienna General Hospital, first time introduced hand washing with chlorine for doctors which reduced the rate of maternity deaths in his maternity wards in 1840s. He is known as 'Father of Hand Hygiene'. Later, Florence Nightingale' introduced hand washing and other hygiene practices in the war hospital in Italy. Perhaps both them were ahead of their times and the concept of hand washing was not well received by then.

October 15 is observed as Global Hand Washing Day and May 5 is observed as World Hand Hygiene Day.

Clean hands are hands that carry no dirty matter or pathogens. Even though hands look clean and have no odour, still they can carry lot of germs. Simple washing with water alone does not remove all dirty matter and pathogens. Person to persons transmission of contagious diseases even occur through shaking hand and hugging. Hand washing with soap and water is recommended.

**When to Wash Hands?** [Center for Disease Control and Prevention, USA]

1. Before, during and after preparing food;
2. Before eating;
3. Before and after caring for someone at home who is sick with vomiting or diarrhoea;
4. Before and after treating a cut or wound;
5. After using a toilet;
6. After changing diapers or cleaning up a child who has used toilet;
7. After blowing nose;
8. After touching an animal, animal food or animal waste;
9. After handling pet food or pet treats; and
10. After touching garbage.

**Hand shake: an avoidable health hazard!**

While celebrating the 52$^{nd}$ Independence Day on October 9$^{th}$, President of Uganda, Museveni, advised his country's fellow citizens not to shake hands while greeting. He continues "this would reduce the highly infectious haemorrhagic fever Ebola". The country is on high alert for possible Ebola infection. This is not only appropriate for Uganda it is applicable for the whole world.

People shake hands with others to symbolize the greeting. This sort of greeting is deeply established in our custom or tradition. Handshaking is the common practice upon meeting, greeting, parting, congratulating, expressing gratitude, or completion of agreement. A good handshake wins the confidence of the person. Many believe that the handshaking is an indicator of individual's personality. Handshaking with few with an extra few shakes and holding on for few seconds communicate the positive thought. This lingering handshake is usually practiced among the people who know well each other. A handshake that isn't firm will signal a lack of authority. One that is too firm could make you seem overly aggressive and so on!

The numerous studies have demonstrated the risk of infection from handshaking. Recently in a simple experiment the British researchers have shown the transfer of germs through handshaking. A strong handshake is capable to spreading germs hand to hand in almost twice the quantities of a moderate handshake. After dipping a gloved hand into a dense culture of *Escherichia coli*, a bacterium commonly found in human intestines, an experimenter shook hands, bumped fists or high-fived with a person wearing a sterile glove. They repeated the tests several times and analysed the gloves for transmission of germs. The results showed about twice as many bacteria were transferred to the clean glove with a handshake as with a high-five, and the fist bump consistently produced the lowest transmission of all. This proves the fist bumping is healthier than handshaking.

The shaking hands with doctors or other health professionals while they are on duty in hospital or clinics may have two issues: you would be transferring germs to doctor who would get their way to patients or you are acquiring the germs from the hospital patients. The health professionals' hands are usually contaminated with pathogens from patients. The germs in the hospital are often resistant to common antibiotics putting you at high risk. If you get infected, it would be difficult to treat. Hand hygiene is a serious issue in hospitals and the Journal of American Medical Association (JAMA) in its editorial has called upon the banning of handshaking in health facilities. It advocates to making the health facilities as handshake free zone to protect your health and for those around you.

Of late, there has been increasing concern on hands as carrier of germs and infection irrespective of customs and types of handshaking. There are recommendations to follow good hand hygiene practices not only at health facilities but also at individual levels. This would go in a long way preventing spreading of infection from one to the other. The Indian

'Namaskar' or 'Namaste' does not involve touching with each other and perhaps the healthiest way of greeting people. You need to make your own effort to avoid shaking hands in different situation. This may look odd and people may look differently in the beginning but will understand your concern. They would appreciate too! Choice is yours. You need to protect yourself as you do not know how clean other person's hand is!

[Author's write up published in OrissaPost, 20th October 2014]

## Hand Washing with Soap (HWWS)

The study has shown that:

- The risk of diarrhoea can be reduced by 42 – 47% through hand washing intervention;
- Reduce the risk of acute respiratory infection by half in children under 5 years old; and
- Neonatal mortality was found to be significantly lower among the children of mothers who reported washing their hands.

**Steps for Effective Washing:**

1. Wet hands with clean running water, turn off the tap and apply soap – Running water is recommended because washing with stationary water in a bucket or basin may recontaminate the hands. Turning off the tap after wetting hands save water.
2. Using soap makes washing more effective as soap (surfactant) lift soil and microbes from skin. People tend to scrub hands more throughly when using soap which further removes the germs. In household washing, there is no added benefit of using antibacterial soap compared to plain bath soap. Use of antibacterial soap rather harmful as it adversely affect environment and encourage antibacterial resistance.
3. Lather your hands by rubbing them together with the soap. Lather the backs of your hands, between your fingers, and under your nails – lathering and scrubbing hands creates friction which helps lift dirt, grease, and microbes from skin. Microbes are present on all surfaces of the hand, often in particularly high concentration under the nails. The entire hand should be scrubbed.
4. Scrub your hands for at least 20 seconds – The optimal length of time for hand washing depends on many factors including the type and amount of soil on the hands and setting of the person washing hand. Healthcare workers require longer time than women preparing to go for making food. Washing for about 20 seconds followed 20 -30 seconds for drying is perhaps optimum.

5. Rinse your hands well under clean, running water – Hands could get re-contaminated if rinsed in standing water in a basin or bucket that has been contaminated through previous use. Clean running water is recommended.
6. Dry your hands using a clean towel or air dry them – Germs can be more easily transferred to and from wet hands. The hands need to be dried after washing using a clean towel or air drying hands are best methods.

The readers are advised to refer the figure of World Health Organization given in this chapter for looking at the steps of good hand washing practice.

If soap and water are not available, alcohol based hand sanitisers (containing at least 60% alcohol) may be used. While the sanitisers may quickly reduce the number of germs, it would not eliminate all types of germs and not remove harmful chemicals. They are not effective when hands are visibly dirty or greasy. Non-alcoholic sanitisers may be more irritating to skin. The steps for using hand sanitisers:

- Apply the product to thepalm of one hand;
- Rub your hands together; and
- Rub the product over all surfaces of your hands and fingers until your hands until your hands are dry.

Hand sanitisers are preferred in clinical settings like hospitals where hands come in contact with germs but generally are not heavily soiled or greasy.

**Namaskar – a Healthy Way of Greetings!**

Germs are everywhere. You can find them in air, foods, plants, pets, soil and almost on every other surface including your own body. Though many of them are harmless, but many are harmful. When these harmful microorganisms get transferred to the individuals, they may cause illness if the individual's capacity to fight (immunity) is less. Hand to hand transfers of the pathogenic microbes especially those responsible for cough and cold is very common. Shaking hands is a potent way to transfer germs from one individual to the other.

"If you drink or eat without washing your hands, or if you touch your nose, mouth, or eyes after shaking someone's hand, you can introduce the germs of others' palm to your own body risking an illness," Experts warned. Hand to hand contact is a potent way of passing germs. In present day culture, one needs to shake hands with several people at different points of the day whether it is office or social gathering or bus, train or airport terminals as part of greeting or welcoming. Handshake is perhaps the most common gesture of greetings in the modern times.

We have very poor hand hygiene practices. We do not wash our hands frequently. Keep eating even without washing our hands. Very poor toilet hygiene! Shaking hands not only brings germs to us but it spreads germs to others too. In short, it helps spreading infections. Washing hands is the single most important weapon we have to fight against diseases. Hand washing is considered to be one of the primary mechanisms to reduce the risk of transmission of infectious agents by both contact and fecal oral route. Hand surface especially under the finger nails are reservoir of microbes. Close environments, door knobs and other inanimate objects serve as resting ground for germs and the contaminated hands serve as vehicle of transmission. Study has shown that washing hands with soap and water drastically reduce bacterial count.

While shaking hands is the most common form of greetings, it is considered the unhealthiest way. Different way of Greetings is followed in different communities and different parts of the world. In western culture, we have seen people hugging, kissing and shaking hands as customary greetings. This is even practiced irrespective of gender, age or social status. On the other hand, Namskar (often as Namaste) is a customary salutation or greetings practiced in Odisha and other parts of our country when individuals meet and a salutation upon their parting.

Namaskar, with two hands (palms) pressed together, is a graceful and lovely way of greetings. It is the healthiest way too as there is no personal contact. No Gender Issue as well! It can be universally practiced when meeting a person of different gender, age or social status. Netas (political leaders) use Namaskar to greet thousands and thousands at a time in public meeting. Shaking hands is an impossible task in such situation. This also invites unnecessary security risk. Namaskar is believed to have spiritual benefit too.

Although one can't completely avoid germs in day to day life, developing good health hygiene culture at personal level can greatly reduce the chances of getting illness. Practice the following to keep yourself Healthy!

- Wash your hands after blowing your nose, coughing, sneezing, going to bathroom, taking out garbage, cleaning the house, shopping, caring sick, handling money, touching your ears, nose, mouth or ear.
- Say No to Handshake. If handshaking is a must, wash your hands thoroughly before touching your nose, mouth or eating food.
- Practice Namaskar, the Healthy and Indian Way of Greetings.

[Author's write up in OrissaPost, 17 December 2011]

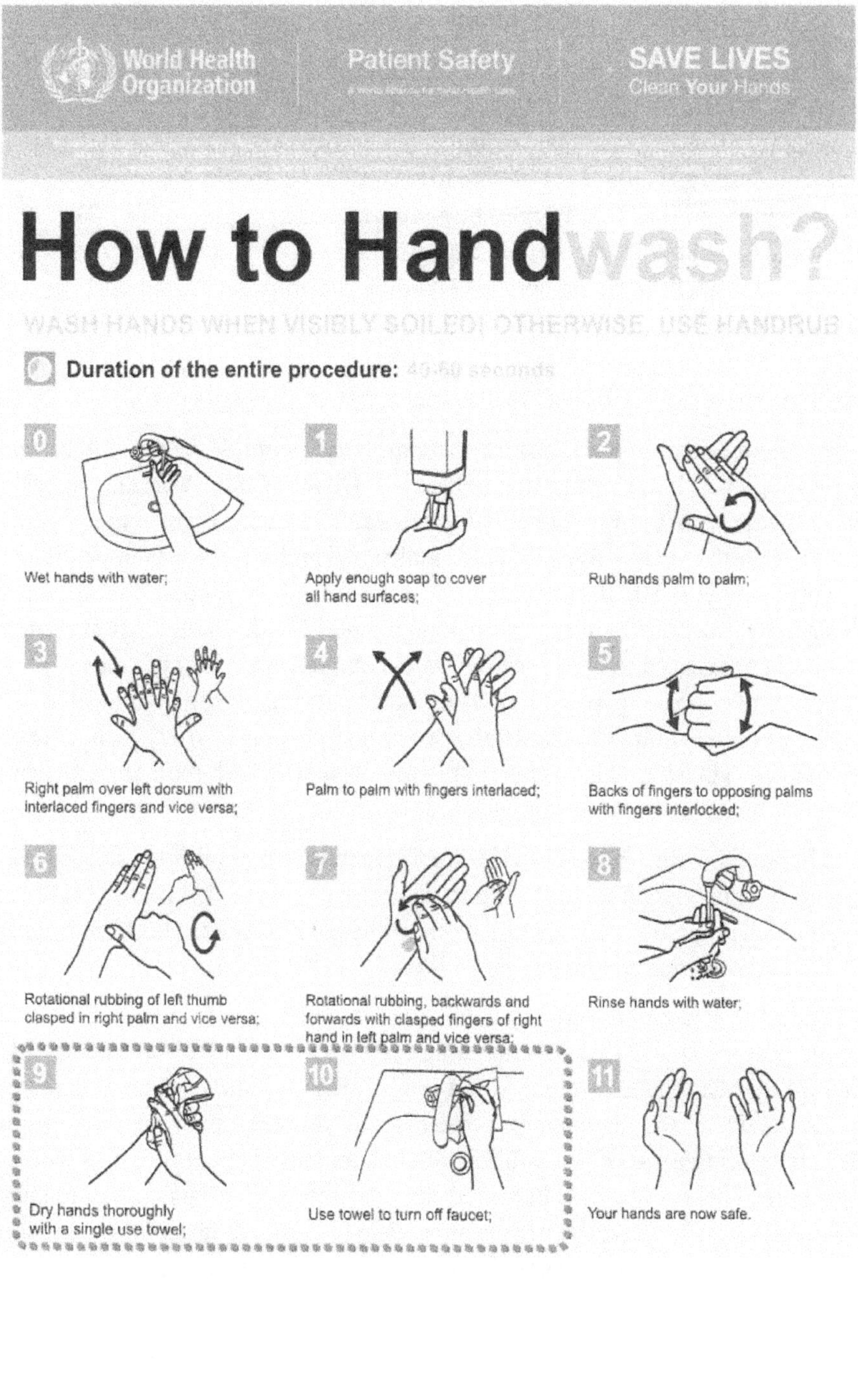
World Health Organization
Patient Safety
SAVE LIVES
Clean Your Hands
How to Handwash?
WASH HANDS WHEN VISIBLY SOILED! OTHERWISE, USE HANDRUB
Duration of the entire procedure: 40-60 seconds
0
Wet hands with water;
1
Apply enough soap to cover all hand surfaces;
2
Rub hands palm to palm;
3
Right palm over left dorsum with interlaced fingers and vice versa;
4
Palm to palm with fingers interlaced;
5
Backs of fingers to opposing palms with fingers interlocked;
6
Rotational rubbing of left thumb clasped in right palm and vice versa;
7
Rotational rubbing, backwards and forwards with clasped fingers of right hand in left palm and vice versa;
8
Rinse hands with water;
9
Dry hands thoroughly with a single use towel;
10
Use towel to turn off faucet;
11
Your hands are now safe.

**WASH Approach [Water, Sanitation and Hygiene Education]**

This aims to improve the health and learning performance of school aged children. The extension of this to their families causes the reduction of incidence of water and sanitation related diseases. The WASH strategy implementation would lead to positive influence the hygiene practices in their homes, among family members and in wider communities. The study shows that hand washing before eating in schools was far more frequent in districts with UNICEF supported WASH programme in schools than in control districts.

## Religious and Cultural Aspects of Hand Hygiene

The religious and cultural issues influence the peoples' behaviour towards hand hygiene. In general, the degree of Health Care Workers (HCWs') compliance with hand hygiene as fundamental infection control measure in a public health perspective is community oriented rather than individual oriented society. Hand cleaning as a measure of preventing the spread of disease is clearly in harmony with fundamental Hindu value of non – injury to other (Ahimsa) and care for their well-being (Daya). In the Hindu culture, hands are rubbed vigorously with ash or mud and rinsed with water. The believe behind their practice is that soap should not be used as it contains animal fat. The study has shown that hand cleansing with mud and ash are as efficient as with soap in terms of faecal coliform counts.

Human health related behaviour depends on multiple factors like environment, education and culture. The behavioural theory suggests that hand cleansing patterns are most likely to be established in the first 10 years of life and this influences the rest of life.

Judaism, Islam and Sikhism have precise rules for hand washing included in the holy texts and this practice punctuates several crucial moments of the day. In Sikhism, hand hygiene is not only a holy act, but an essential element of daily life. Sikhs always wash their hands properly with soap and water before dressing a cut or wound. Personal cleanliness is paramount to worship in Islam. The Prophet Mohammed always urged Muslims to wash hands frequently and especially after some clearly defined tasks like repeating ablutions at least three times with running water before prayers.

# How to wash and dry hands with soap and water

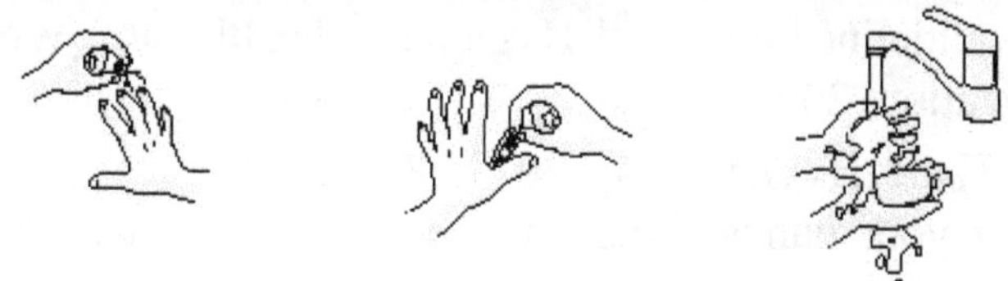

- Remove jewellery and cover abrasions
- Wet hands with warm water, then apply soap or liquid soap

- Lather for 15–20 seconds

- Rinse hands under running water
- Dry hands with clean towel

During the lather, pay particular attention to the backs of hands and fingers, fingernails, fingertips and the webbing between fingers.

Hand hygiene is crucial in reducing transmission of infections. It includes both handwashing with plain or antimicrobial soap and water, and use of alcohol-based products (gels, rinses, foams) containing an emollient that do not require the use of water.

If hands are visibly soiled or contaminated with respiratory secretions, wash hands with soap (either non-antimicrobial or antimicrobial) and water.

In the absence of visible soiling of hands, approved alcohol-based products for hand disinfection may be used. Ensure you have facilities for hand washing (i.e. sinks with warm and cold running water, plain or antimicrobial soap, and disposable paper towels) and hand disinfection (i.e. alcohol-based products) readily accessible.

Australian Government

Department of Health and Ageing

**Pharmacist's Role**

- Educating the common man on importance of hand washing.
- Educating the common man on effective hand washing technique,
- Educating people on healthy way of greeting.

## Bibliography


1. Guru Prasad Mohanta, Wash Your Hands of Hazard, **Orissa Post**, 06 May 2014.
2. WHO guidelines on Hand Hygiene in health care, World Health Organization, 2009.
3. World Hand Hygiene Day 2019: Prevent 6 infections simply by washing your hands, TheHealthSite.com [Accessed on 12th July 2019].
4. Water, Sanitation and Hygiene (WASH) in Schools, UNICEF, New York, July 2012.

# Swachh Bharat (Cleaner India) Mission – A Public Health Programme

**After reading this chapter, you should be able to understand and appreciate:**

- Swachh Bharat (Cleaner India) Mission and its health impact;
- Its correlation with SDG;
- Its aim and extended objectives;
- Achievements under Swachh Bharat Mission; and
- The Pharmacists' role in Swachh Bharat Mission.

Swachh Bharat Mission (SBM), flagship programme of the Government, aims to make India open defecation free by 2019. The programme was launched by the Prime Minister on 2nd October 2014, the birth anniversary of the Father of nation, Mahatma Gandhi. It functions under the administrative control of Department of Drinking Water & Sanitation, Ministry of Jal Shakti (Water Resource). It has two submissions: Swachh Bharat Mission (Gramin) and Swachh Bharat (Urban). The main objective is to bring about an improvement in general quality of life in the rural areas by promoting cleanliness, hygiene and eliminating open defecation. Swachh Bharat is not just a programme but a social movement! The goal of SBM is similar to that of United Nations Sustainable Goal (SDG). SDG 6 aims to achieve access to adequate and equitable sanitation and hygiene for all and end open defecation. Open defecation means disposal of faeces in open areas such as fields, forests, road side, beaches and open bodies of water.

There is a close link between diarrhoeal diseases and environment where we live. More defecation in open, there is more probability for faecal oral transmission and thus more chances of diarrhoeal diseases. Most diarrhoeal germs spread from the stools of one person to the mouth of another and are transmitted through contaminated water, food, or fomites. Contamination with stools happen if people practice open defecation near water sources, open spaces and fields.

**Achievements**: In 2014 (when the programme was initiated), 67 years after India's independence from British, around 10 crore rural and around 1 crore urban households were without a sanitary toilet. Half of the country's population still practice open defecation. At that time there were only 38.7% households with toilet and now it is 99.37% (as of 7th July 2019, http://swachhbharatmission.gov.in/sbmcms/index.htm). In total 30 States / Union Territories are declared open defecation free.

**Health Impact:** The World Health Organization in its preliminary estimation on the impact of SBM projected that:

- SBM (Gramin) will result in averting more than 3 lakh deaths (diarrhoea and protein energy malnutrition) between 2014 and October 2019;
- Unsafe sanitation caused an estimated 199 million cases of diarrhoea annually before the start of SBM in 2014. These have been gradually reducing and will almost be eliminated when universal use of safe sanitation facilities is achieved by October 2019; and
- More than 14 million disability adjusted life years (DALY) are estimated to be avoided (diarrhoea and protein energy malnutrition) between 2014 and October 2019.

The Economic Survey Report of 2018-19 confirmed the substantial improvement in the health scenario open defecation free region. Several villages have witnessed a reduction in deaths due to diarrhoea, malaria, especially under 5 mortality, still births, and new born with weight less than 2.5 kilogram. This shows the improvement in child health and nutrition.

| Indicator | Districts with low individual household latrine [Number of Cases] | | Districts with high individual household latrine [Number of Cases] | |
|---|---|---|---|---|
| | March 2015 | March 2019 | March 2015 | March 2019 |
| Diarrhoea | 6968 | 5683 | 5262 | 4550 |
| Malaria | 761 | 222 | 273 | 113 |
| Still Birth | 540 | 456 | 403 | 368 |
| Low Birth Weight | 3890 | 3686 | 3230 | 3198 |

The people of the districts with low individual household latrine coverage suffered from diarrhoea, malaria, still births and low birth weight compared to the people of high coverage districts. All these health indicators improved in the areas after implementation of SBM.

Subsequently, the Swachh Swasth Sarvatra scheme is launched. This is a joint initiative of Ministry of Health & Family Welfare and Ministry of Drinking Water & Sanitation to achieve high levels of sanitation and hygiene in and around Public Health Care facilities. It aims to ensure availability of separate male and female toilets facilities in all areas of the facility.

**Role of Pharmacists**

The community pharmacists have ample opportunities to educate the common men on ill effects of open defecation encouraging them to have toilets at their home.

This is part of their service role promoting health care through health education.

**Bottom Line**

- The flagship programme 'Swachh Bharat Mission (SBM)' aims to free of open defecation. The programme is managed by Department of Drinking Water & Sanitation, Ministry of Jal Shakti (Water Resource).
- The goal of SBM is similar to that of United Nations Sustainable Goal (SDG).
- As of $7^{th}$ July 2019, 99.37 % households have toilets.
- Open defecation has close link with diarrheal diseases.
- There has been substantial improvement in the health scenario open defecation free region. Several villages have witnessed a reduction in deaths due to diarrhoea, malaria, especially under 5 mortality, still births, and new born with weight less than 2.5 kilogram.
- The programme is extended to "Swachh Swasth Sarvatra".
- The community pharmacists have ample opportunity providing health education including discouraging open defecation.

## Bibliography

1. http://swachhbharatmission.gov.in/sbmcms/index.htm accessed on $7^{th}$ July 2019.
2. Dandabathula G, Bhardwaj P, Burra M, Rao PV, Rao SS. Impact assessment of India's Swachh Bharat Mission – Clean India Campaign on acute diarrheal disease outbreaks: Yes, there is a positive change. J Family Med Prim Care 8, 2019.

3. Summary of preliminary estimations of potential health impacts from increased sanitation coverage through Swachh Bharat Mission, WHO country office for India, August 2018.

# Social Distancing

Social Distancing: Increase social distance but decrease emotional or human distance.

- Narendra Modi

**After reading this chapter, you should be able to understand and appreciate:**

- Definition of Social Distancing;
- How does maintaining social distancing helps;
- Different guidelines of different countries;
- Healthiest way of Greeting People; and
- Pharmacists' Role in Promoting Social Distancing in hour of crisis.

'Social Distancing' perhaps new terminology that we came to know of and practiced as well during COVID – 19. Practicing social distancing is not easy in a populous country as India. It is also known as 'physical distancing'. This means keeping / maintaining a safe space / distance between one another to prevent or slow down transmission of infection in the community.

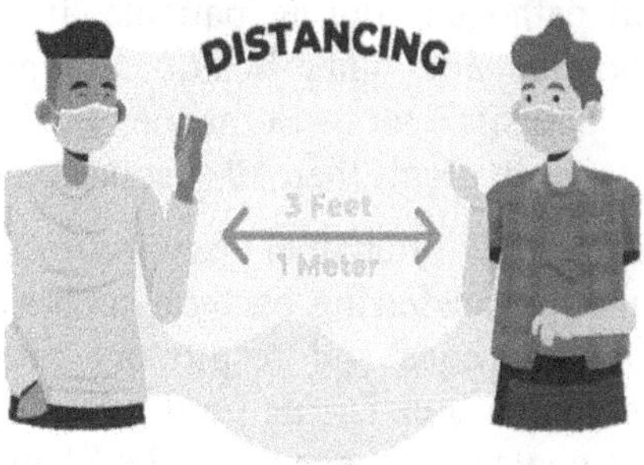


Social distancing is a non-pharmaceutical infection prevention and control intervention meant to avoid/decrease contact between those who are infected with a disease causing pathogen and those who are not, so as to stop or slow down the rate and extent of disease transmission in a community. This eventually leads to decrease in spread, morbidity and mortality due to the disease. Social distancing alone is not completely effective, the personal protective measures are also important. In addition to maintaining social distancing, it is advised to stay at home, avoid unnecessary social gathering, leave home for urgent work or medical need, and travel only if absolutely necessary. These were the guidelines to prevent transmission of COVID- 19. More intense and long term social distancing, it is better for preventing transmission of infective organism.

The diseases transmitted via respiratory droplet (sneezing, cough transmission, touching contaminated surfaces) are greatly influenced by social distancing. Social distancing with use of personal protecting equipments great helped preventing transmission of COVID – 19.

Below mentioned are country specific social distancing guideline:

| Country | Safe Distance |
|---|---|
| India | One meter distance between people. |
| UK | One meter distance between people. |
| USA | Maintain distance of at least 2 meters from others. |

In modern time, handshaking is used as a symbol of greeting people. Hands are exposed to millions of germs at schools, work place and home. In spite of using antibacterial agents for washing, hands continue to be dirty contaminated with germs including faecal matter. On an average, we carry 3200 bacteria from 150 species in our hands. Microbes survive on hands for different times. It has long been recognised that handshaking transfers germs from one hand to the other. The transfer of organisms is almost similar when the give hand is dry and when both hands are moist. The greatest transfer is found to the palms of the hands, in few instances to the fingers and least to finger tips. Contaminated hands could be vehicles for spread of bacteria and virus. Health care workers' hand is often colonised with commensal flora as well as with potential pathogens during patients. In health care facilities, shaking hand with doctors and other health care professionals we pass infection to other patients too. Someone has appropriately said "Handshaking transfers more germs than 10 seconds passionate kiss".

A strong handshake, what often feel very warmth, is almost twice as effective as a weak one in transferring bacteria such as *E. coli* which cause urinary tract infection, diarrhoea and respiratory problems. Handshaking seems to be more effective in transferring germs than use of common towel. The former is a direct contact between unwashed hands while the latter is indirect contact between washed hands. We could eliminate handshaking in our own interest. India has always shown the way out. We have shown "Namaste Trump" to the rest of the world as the way we greet our guests. It is time to 'Stop Handshake and Adopt Namaste (Namaskar) to protect us and protect others as well from common illness including new corona virus". 'Namaste' is our tradition and is the healthiest way of greeting!

**Pharmacist's Role**

- **Operation of retail pharmacy:**
  - Always wear face mask.
  - Advice customers to wear face mask or cover face using face covering.

- Maintain social distancing by signage / barriers / floor markers to keep at safe distance from the counter.
- Diverting the patients for delivery through window or promote home delivery.
- Offer sanitizers to all customers.

- **Operation of hospital pharmacy:**
  - Follow the infection control practices and other guidelines of the hospital.
  - Avoid overcrowding and make arrangement for keeping physical distance.
  - Always wear face mask.
  - Avoid crowding in store.
  - Encourage e-prescription services.
  - Use signage/barriers and floor markers to maintain social distance.
  - Schedule timing for dispensing.
- **Community education:**
  - Educate and sensitise the common man on importance of maintaining physical distance in community gathering. Encourage them to adhere the government guideline.
  - Avoid physical greetings such as handshaking or hugs. Do Namaste.
  - Stay at home and unnecessary movement can be avoided.
  - Visit hospital using face masks and not overcrowding.

Though maintaining social distancing in work place was extremely difficult in work places, government formulated SOP to be followed. Work from home is an alternative. Social distancing adversely affected the mental health and many even required counselling.

**Bottom Line**

- Social Distancing, also known as 'physical distancing', means keeping / maintaining a safe space / distance between one another to prevent or slow down transmission of infection in the community.
- Social distancing with use of personal protective equipments is very effective in preventing transmission of droplet infection.
- Keeping one metre distance between one person to another.
- Namaste is the healthiest way of greetings. It is preferable to hand shaking.

- Pharmacists should adhere maintaining social distancing in community and hospital pharmacy practice. They should also educate and sensitise common man on social distancing: essential for protecting individuals and others.

## Bibliography

1. Guru Prasad Mohanta, Namaskar: Healthy Way of Greeting! **Orissa Post**, 17 December, 2011.
2. Guru Prasad Mohanta, Namaste to Combat Corona Virus, **Orissa Post, 06 March 2020**
3. Centers for Disease Control (CDC). Implementation of Mitigation Strategies for Communities with Local COVID-19. Available at: https://www.who.int/emergencies/diseases/novel-coronavirus 2019.
4. COVID – 19, Response and Containment Measures, Training of ANM, ASHA, AWW, Ministry of Health & Welfare, Government of India.
5. Murphy C et al, Effectiveness of social distancing measures and lockdowns for reducing transmission of COVID – 19 in non-healthcare community-based settings, Phil. Trans. R.Soc. , 2023.

# CHAPTER 3

# Nutrition and Health

## Nutrition and Health

**After reading this chapter, you should be able to understand and appreciate:**

- Definition of Nutrition and its relation with Health;
- Indian Dietary Guideline;
- Diseases or illness associated with unhealthy diet; and
- Pharmacists' Role in Promoting Good Dietary Habits.

Our health and well-being predominantly depend on our eating habits and choice of food. Nutrition is the science of food and how the body uses it in health and disease. The nutrients present in the food profoundly influence our health. The body requires proteins, fats, carbohydrates, vitamins, minerals and water. The food not only provides energy but all essential nutrients to grow and function properly. The common nutritional problems of public health in our country are low birth weight, protein energy malnutrition in children, chronic energy deficiency in adults, micronutrient malnutrition and diet related communicable diseases. The coronary artery diseases (illness related to heart), high blood pressure, type 2 diabetes (non-insulin sensitive), certain cancers are related to diet and nutrition. Consumption of food rich with fibre and antioxidants are associated with decreased risk of certain cancers.

Nutrients may be divided into two groups: macronutrients comprising proteins, fats and carbohydrates and micronutrients consisting of vitamins and minerals. Macronutrients are required in large quantities and micro-nutrients are in small amounts.

**Proteins:** The proteins are the functional units of every living cell. They for the important parts of the body's main structural components: muscles and bones. They are also the important constituents of blood, enzymes, hormones etc. They constitute almost one-fifth of body's weight in adult. They are needed for body building. The requirements of proteins vary with age, physiological status and stress. Pregnant women and growing children require more proteins.

They are complex organic compounds composed of amino acids. Of the around 20 amino acids required for our body, 9 are called essential. These essential amino acids cannot be synthesized by the body and are to be supported by diet. These include histidine, isoleucine, leucine, lysine, methionine, phenylalanine, threonine, tryptophan and valine. Other amino acids are synthesized by the body.

Animal source proteins like meat, fish, egg, poultry, milk, cheese and soy provide all essential amino acids and thus are considered as complete proteins. The vegetable sources of proteins are pulses (legumes), cereals, beans, nuts, oil seed cakes etc. are also good sources of proteins, but lack in few essential amino acids. The combination of vegetable proteins allows each vegetable protein to make up for the amino acids missing in the other protein.

Consuming high level of protein, especially in the form of supplement, is not advisable.

**Carbohydrates:** Carbohydrates are the main source of energy and provide about 4 Kcal per gram. 70-80% of the total dietary calories are obtained from carbohydrate present in plant foods like cereals, millets, and pulses. The carbohydrates are divided into two types: simple carbohydrates and complex carbohydrates. The carbohydrates with type and sources are given in the table below:

<table>
<tr><td rowspan="2">Simple Carbohydrates</td><td>Examples</td><td>Glucose, Fructose</td><td>Sucrose</td><td colspan="2">Lactose</td></tr>
<tr><td>Sources</td><td>Fruits, Vegetables, Honey</td><td>Sugar</td><td colspan="2">Milk</td></tr>
<tr><td rowspan="2">Complex Carbohydrates</td><td>Examples</td><td>Starch</td><td>Glycogen</td><td>Cellulose</td><td>Gums and Pectin</td></tr>
<tr><td>Sources</td><td>Cereals, Millets, Pulses, Root Vegetables</td><td>Animal foods</td><td>Vegetables, Whole grains</td><td>Vegetables, Fruits and Cereals</td></tr>
</table>

Cellulose is indigestible (in human) but provides dietary fibre. They move through the digestive tract and out of the body. Insoluble fibres absorb water in digestive tract; give the stool bulk and decrease it takes the stool to move through the tract. Soluble fibres help reducing cholesterol level, keeping blood sugar level low and reducing the risk of colon cancer. The carbohydrate reserve (glycogen) of a human adult is about 500 g and this reserve gets rapidly exhausted when a person is on fasting.

**Fats (Lipids):** The fats are the most concentrated sources of energy providing around 9 calories per gram. They are the major fuels for the body during rest and light activity. They are stored in our body in the form of usable energy. The fat beneath the skin help insulting us against cold. The fats support and cushion our heart, kidney and intestine. Fats in the diet help in absorption of fat soluble vitamins.

Ghee, butter, milk, cheese, eggs, fats of meat and fish are the main source of animal fat while groundnut, mustard, sesame, coconut seeds provide the vegetable fats. Ghee, cooking oils (groundnut, soybean, sun flower, rice bran, safflower) are visible fats. Fats present in the diets but not visible to naked eye are non-visible fats. The sources for non-visible fats are cereals, pulses, nuts, milk, and eggs etc. The major contributory source of fat to our body is the invisible fats.

Dietary fats contain both saturated and unsaturated fatty acids. Food containing large amount of saturated fatty acids are usually solid at room temperature and they belong to animal fat. Foods containing large amounts of mono-unsaturated and poly-unsaturated fatty acids are usually from plant sources and liquid at room temperature. However, the process of unsaturated fatty acids (oils) converts the liquid oil to solid fat. The coconut and palm oil, though belong to vegetable source, have very high content of saturated fatty acids. Fish oils contain poly and mono-unsaturated fatty acids.

Saturated fatty acids are not considered as healthy food. The combination of cooking oils is suggested to ensure recommended in-take of fatty acids. Poly-unsaturated fatty acids are better as they reduce bad cholesterol. High intake of fats is associated with several health conditions like obesity, coronary heart diseases, cancer etc.

## Vitamins and Minerals

***Vitamins:*** The vitamins are required in small quantities but are not produced in the body. They are necessary for maintenance of structure of skin, bones, nerves, eye, brain, blood and mucous membrane. Vitamin A, D, E and K are fat soluble vitamins. Vitamin C and B Complex vitamins are water soluble. The B Complex vitamins are: Vitamin B1 (thiamine), Vitamin B2 (riboflavin), Niacin, Vitamin B6 (pyridoxine), Vitamin B9 (folic acid) and Vitamin B12 (cyanocobalamin). Fat soluble vitamins are stored if available in excess, often causing hypervitaminosis, and water soluble vitamins do not get stored (except vitamin B12 and folate) and easily get eliminated through urine. Vitamin B complex and Vitamin C are thermolabile and easily destroyed during cooking and food processing.

***Minerals:*** Sodium, Potassium, Calcium, Phosphorous, Magnesium and Sulphur are macro minerals. Iron, Zinc, Copper, Selenium, Molybdenum, Fluorine, Cobalt, Chromium and Iodine micro minerals. The minerals are necessary for maintenance and integrity of skin, hair, nails, blood and soft tissues.

The Food Safety and Standards (contaminants, toxins and residues) Regulation notified the acceptable limits of insecticides, antibiotics, other toxic materials and heavy metals.

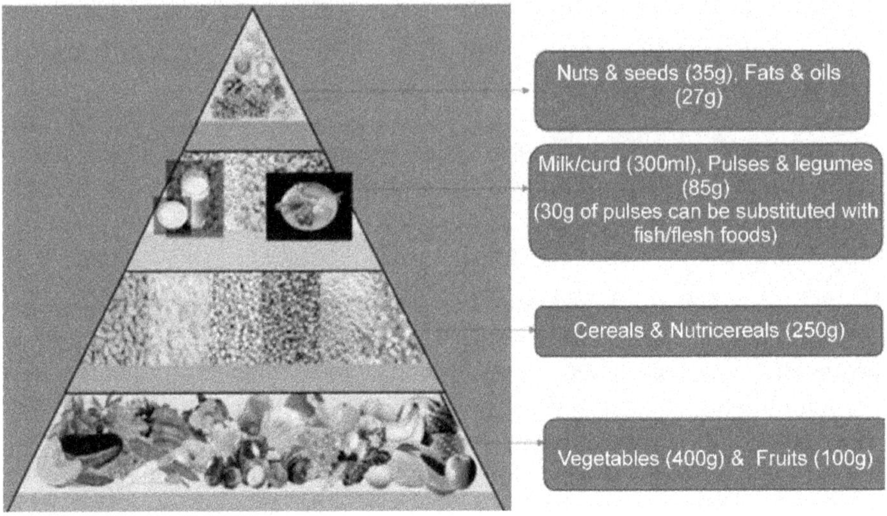


[Source: ICMR – NIN Expert Committee, Dietary Guidelines for Indians, 2024.]

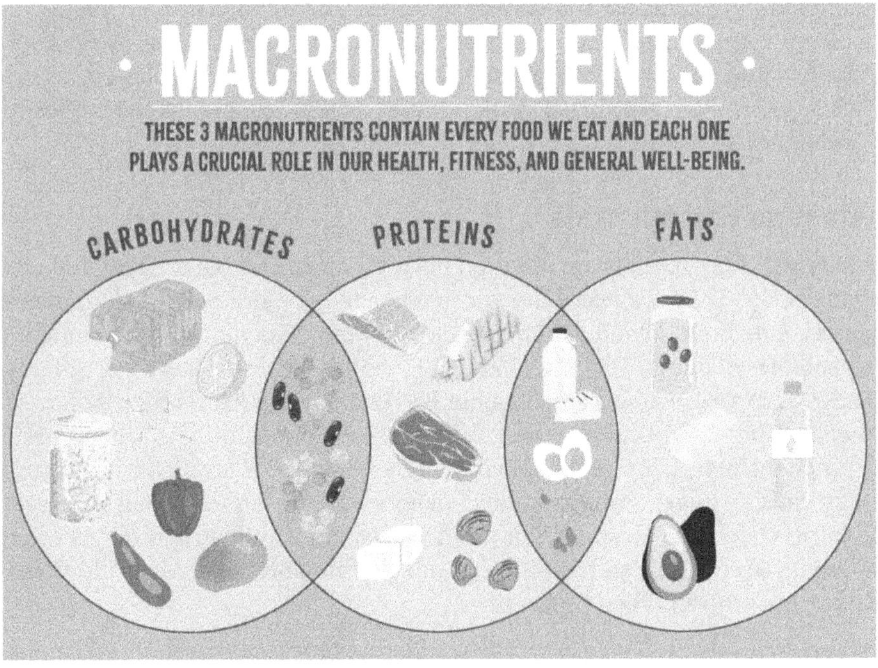


[Source: ICMR – NIN Expert Committee, Dietary Guidelines for Indians, 2024.]

**Health issues related with nutrition:** It is estimated that 56.4 % of total disease burden in our country is attributed to unhealthy diet. Health issues related to nutrition may be grouped under:

- **Under nutrition:** Severe form of under nutrition is almost disappeared because food security. This contributes increased morbidity and mortality. Eating too little food during infancy, childhood, adolescence, pregnancy and lactation may lead to under nutrition.
- **Micronutrient deficiency:** It includes deficiency of iron, Folate. If BMI is vitamin B 12, vitamin A, 25 hydroxy vitamin D and zinc.
- **Overweight:** Diet low in fats and calories prevents overweight. If BMI is 23.0 to 24.9, the person may be called overweight.
- **Obesity:** If the BMI is ≥ 25, the person may be called obese. Over eating along with decreased physical exercise are main reason for obesity. Abdominal obesity is prevalent in 53 % of urban and 19 % rural adults.
- **Diet Related Non-Communicable Diseases:** Coronary Heart Diseases, Hypertension and Type 2 Diabetes are predominant. Healthy diet can substantially reduce the risk factors.

The WHO advocates five keys to prevent food borne illnesses. These include:

1. Washing hands before handling foods and often during food preparation. One must wash hands before eating and after toileting. It is also recommended to clean eating, drinking and cooking utensils;
2. Separating raw and cooked food. Use of containers with lid is suggested for keeping foods in refrigerator to prevent cross contamination;
3. Thorough cooking at least at 70°C. Cooking at 70°C kills most of the disease producing bacteria within 30 seconds;
4. Keeping or storing foods at safe temperature. The microbes quickly multiply at room temperature. The cooked foods are to be kept in refrigerator within 2 hours of preparation. Keeping in refrigerator prevents bacterial growth in food; and
5. Using safe water and raw materials. Safe waters mean water free from pathogenic microbes and toxic chemicals. Untreated water from rivers or canals may contain parasites or bacteria which may cause diarrhoea. Boiling or chlorination may make water safe for use. Check the label of the packed foods to ensure they are fresh and within the usable period.

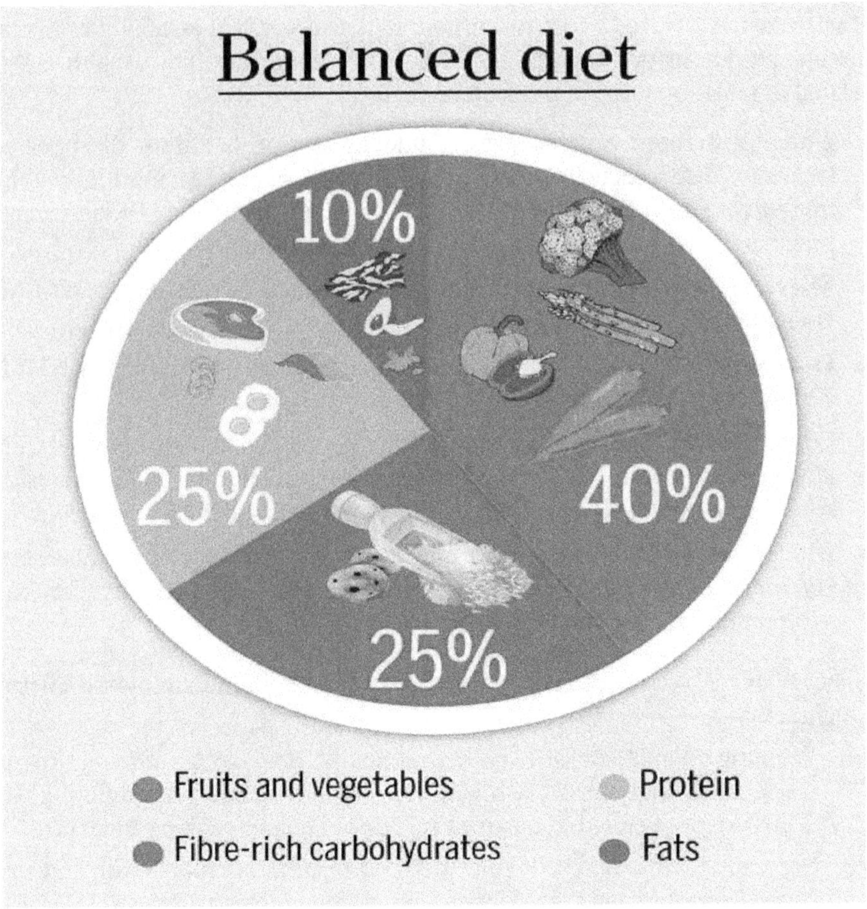


[Source: ICMR – NIN Expert Committee, Dietary Guidelines for Indians, 2024.]

## Pharmacists' Role

- The pharmacists can sensitize the people on need of balanced / healthy diets. They should encourage them to take natural food with minimal junk food.
- They should not promote food supplements.
- The food may interfere with functioning of some medicines. Some medicines like amoxicillin is preferred to taken in empty stomach. Medicine like non steroidal anti inflammatory agents are taken after food to avoid gastric irritation. "Before food means 30 minutes before taking food or two hours after taking food". Alcohol or alcoholic drinks are to be avoided while taking some medicines: paracetamol, metronidazole.

**Bottom Line**

- A balanced diet not only prevents nutritional deficiency but also promotes optimal growth and development.
- Balance diet provides all nutritional needs of the body. No single food can provide all essential nutrients.
- Balanced diet should be a combination of food items from variety of food groups. It provides required calories, proteins, vitamins, minerals and adequate fibres.
- Avoiding food and beverages with added sugar is necessary.
- Different age groups require different food groups.
- Physical activity is essential for appropriate utilization of all nutrients from balanced diet.
- Pharmacists can advice on healthy diets to common man and discourages on use food supplements. They can advice whether medicines can be taken before or after food.

## Bibliography

1. ICMR – NIN Expert Committee, Dietary Guidelines for Indians, 2024.
2. Guru Prasad Mohanta, *Balanced Diet – Need for Good Health and Well Being, **Science Horizon**, March 2013.*
3. Guru Prasad Mohanta, *Food Safety – a wake up call, **Orissa Post**, 23 June 2015.*
4. Guru Prasad Mohanta, *Five ways to ensure food safety, **Orissa Post**, 10 April 2015.*
5. G. P. Mohanta, *Does Food Affect Medicine? **The New Indian Express supplement- Health**, 28 February 2006.*
6. Guru Prasad Mohanta, *Food Poisoning – Prevention and Management, **Science Horizon, 5(7)**, July 2015.*

# CHAPTER 4

# Sociology and Health

## Sociology and Health

**After reading this chapter, you would be able to know / understand and:**

- The meaning of sociology;
- Socio-cultural factors influencing disease and health;
- Impact of urbanization on disease and health; and
- Relationship of economic status and health.

**Sociology:** Sociology is a subject of social science and is defined as study of individuals & society. Society is a group of individuals who have organised themselves and follow a given way of life. Sociology is concerned with the relationship between the human beings and human behaviour. Social environment immensely influences health outcomes.

Culture is the learned behaviour which has been socially acquired. A culture denotes total way of life. The cultural factors: customs, beliefs, values, and religious taboos create an environment that are deeply involved in all the affairs of man including health and sickness. They influence in matters of personal hygiene, nutritional and breast-feeding habits, weaning, and rearing practices, family planning, immunization and seeking early medical care.

The readers are encouraged to go through the chapter on determinants of health too for better understanding.

**Sociocultural factors in Disease and Health:** Family is primary unit of society. A family reflects the culture of wider society of which it forms a part and determines the behaviour and attitudes of its members. The behaviours of the individuals begin with family. The following are some of the factors which influence the disease and health in the community:

- **Family:** These are some of the functions which influence the health behaviour of individuals –
  - **Child rearing:** Pattern of child care such as feeding, nutrition, hygiene, sleep, clothing, discipline, habit training usually passes on from generation to the other.
  - **Socialization:** It is teaching of young ones the value of society.
  - **Development of personality:** Individual's capacity to withstand stress and strain is largely depend on his / her early experience in the family.
  - **Care of dependants:** Caring of the sick persons, caring of women during pregnancy & after child birth and caring of elderly influence the adult behaviour.
  - **Genetic susceptibility to diseases:** Some diseases like haemophilia, colour blindness, diabetes, some mental illnesses run through families.
- **Belief, Tradition & Education:** Education helps to understand what to believe or what not to believe. Even in this 21$^{st}$ century, people still believe the power of witch craft and ghosts. Some people believe in traditional method of treating snake bites. Education would help seeking rational health care.
- **Social Environment:** Social environment immensely influences the health of the community. Some of the measures required to promote healthy environment include:
  - **Ensuring availability of social security: Examples:** Free medical insurance, ESI.
  - Fair distribution of resources to ensure availability of basic necessities to every citizen: food and housing.
  - Facilities for exercise and leisure.
  - Facilities for education for all.
  - Propagation of healthy customs, freedom of expression
  - and thought.
  - Safe working place.
- **Socio economic status:** Socio-economic standard of people is conventionally expressed in terms of standard of living, status, and life style. Social class is determined by three parameters: education, occupation, and income. Education determines the knowledge, attitude, and value system of individuals and their socioeconomic growth potential.

**Urbanization and Health:** India is rapidly urbanizing and it estimated that around 40 % of the population will live in urban area by 2030. The term urban refers to towns (places with municipal corporation, municipal area committee, notified area committee or cantonment board). Urbanization is a complex and dynamic demographic phenomenon, which interacts with globalization, economic growth, income inequality, climate change, health, and sustainability. While urbanization has provided economic growth and socio-economic development opportunities, it has also brought adverse health issues, such as the rising burden of non-communicable diseases, road traffic injuries, emerging and re-emerging infectious diseases, antimicrobial resistance, and substance abuse. The health facilities such as hospital beds: 63 percentage are available in urban area compared to 27 percent on rural belt. The current lifestyle(s) of an average city dweller includes fast-paced life with sedentary jobs, a stressful environment, and unhealthy food habits predisposing them to noncommunicable diseases such as obesity, diabetes, and hypertension.

Rapid urbanisation has also led to increased influx of population and growth of slums. These habitations have poor access to basic facilities: safe water, drainage and sanitation, electricity, cooking fuel, pucca houses and public transport. These become a public health challenge. There has been an epidemiological transition from communicable to non-communicable disease owing to lifestyle and other factors. The National Health Policy in 2017 identified the need to focus on poor and vulnerable populations in cities, including the homeless, street children, rag-pickers, rickshaw pullers, construction workers, sex workers, and temporary migrants in urban settlements, listed and unlisted slums.

National Urban Health Mission (NUHM), a component of National Health Mission (NHM), aims to strengthening the existing health care service delivery system, targeting the people living in slums and converging with various schemes relating to wider determinants of health like drinking water, sanitation, school education, etc. implemented by the Ministries of Urban Development, Housing & Urban Poverty Alleviation, Human Resource Development and Women & Child Development. A total of 1162 cities are covered under the NUHM. The Urban Primary Health Centres (UPHCs) for 50,000 population near urban slums for primary health care services, and Urban Community Health Centres (UCHCs) for 2.5 lakh population in non-metros and 5 lakhs in metros, for secondary health care services are functional under NUHM. These are making a transformational change in urban poor.

In addition, the government has proposed development of healthy cities through appropriate planning and establishing the basic infrastructure.

**Economic status and Health:** Occupation determines the income generating capacity of individuals and their status. In India, there are two classifications in terms economic status: Below poverty line (BPL) and above poverty line. The' Poverty line' has been calculated for 2009-10 to be ₹ 672.8 per month per capita for rural India and ₹ 859.6 per month per capita for urban India. There is state sponsored health insurance scheme for BPL families. The central government has now extended Ayushman Bharat Pradhan Mantri Jan Arogya Yojana (AB PM-JAY) for senior citizens of 70 years and above irrespective income status. About 6 crore senior citizens are likely to benefited. This is a boon as longevity of Indian citizens has increased. India's elderly population projected to surge to 347 million by 2050. The major issue in Indian healthcare is that people is primarily pay out pocket; over 3/4$^{th}$ of hospitals and almost half of hospital beds are privately owned. The lower classes cannot pay private health insurance since it is mostly profit driven.

National Health Policy (2917) proposes an increase health expenditure by Government as a percentage of GDP from the existing 1.15% to 2.5 % by 2025. Though it is very ambitious, in terms of share in the General Government Expenditure (GGE), it has increased from 3.94% in 2014-15 to 6.12% in 2021-22. Increased investments in healthcare have contributed to better-equipped hospitals, expanded vaccination programs, and improved preventive care services. The share of out-of-pocket expenditure (OOPE) in the Total Health Expenditure (THE) declined from 62.6% to 39.4%. This reduction is a direct result of the government's efforts to increase public health spending, improve access to healthcare, and reduce financial hardship for individuals seeking medical care. About 7 % of the population (10 crore) are pushed into poverty every year due to the amount they spend on healthcare.

The socio-economic status can be measured using Kuppuswamy's scale. It is based on three variables - education, occupation, and income. A weightage is assigned to each variable according to seven-point predefined scale. The total of three weightages gives the socio-economic status: lower, upper lower, lower middle, upper middle and upper.

Higher income improves health seeking behaviour.

**Bottom Line**

- Sociology is a subject of social science and is defined as study of individuals & society. Social environment immensely influences health outcomes.
- Culture is socially acquired learned behaviour: customs, beliefs, values and religious taboos influence affairs of man including health and sickness.
- **Sociological Factors:** Family, Belief, Tradition & Education, Social Environment and socio – economic status.
- **Urbanization and Health:** India is rapidly urbanizing and it estimated that around 40 % of the population will live in urban area by 2030. While urbanization has provided economic growth and socio-economic development opportunities, it has also brought adverse health issues, such as the rising burden of non-communicable diseases, road traffic injuries, emerging and re-emerging infectious diseases, antimicrobial resistance, and substance abuse.
- Rapid urbanisation has also led to increased influx of population and growth of slums with no basic facilities: safe water, drainage and sanitation, electricity, cooking fuel, pucca houses and public transport.
- National Urban Health Mission is the agency strives to improve urban health. In addition, the government has proposed development of healthy cities through appropriate planning and establishing the basic infrastructure.
- AB PM-JAY provides health insurance to BPL and senior citizens of 70 years and above. The socio-economic status can be measured using Kuppuswamy's scale using parameters - education, occupation, and income.

## Bibliography


1. K. Park, Park's Textbook of Preventive and Social Medicine, 27th Edition, Banarasidas Bhanot, 2023.
2. Kumar S, Kumar S, Gupta B. Urban health: Needs urgent attention. Indian J Public Health 2018.
3. Rajvir Bhalwar (ed), Text Book of Public Health and Community Medicine, Department of Community Medicine, Armed Forces Medical College, 2009.

CHAPTER 5

# Communicable Diseases: Disease, Prevention and Control

## Communicable Diseases

Communicable diseases are the diseases that can spread from person to person. They are also called infectious diseases. Diseases that are spread from animals to people and from people to animals are called zoonotic diseases. Different communicable diseases spread in different ways. Common ways are through viruses or bacteria in food or water, blood or other body fluids, insect bites or air.

Communicable diseases like HIV/AIDS, tuberculosis (TB), malaria, viral hepatitis, sexually transmitted infections and neglected tropical diseases (NTDs) the leading causes of death and disability in low-income countries and marginalized populations. COVID – 19 is the new addition to infectious disease list.

In addition to the high proportion of deaths and suffering that they cause, communicable diseases hinder social and economic development. They can pose significant threats to international health security as seen during COVID-19 pandemic. In recognition of the high burden of communicable diseases, the SDGs include a specific target to end the epidemics of AIDS, TB, malaria and NTDs and to combat hepatitis and other communicable diseases.

The readers are encouraged to refer chapter on National Programmes too.

# Chikungunya

"No antiviral treatment for Chikungunya exists: however, timely dissemination of diagnosis and management is crucial."

- CDC

**After reading this chapter, you should be able to understand and appreciate:**

- Chikungunya as a public health problem of India;
- What causes Chikungunya and how it spreads;
- Symptoms of Chikungunya;
- Global and Indian Burden of Chikungunya;
- Diagnosis and Treatment available; and
- Prevention Control Strategies Practiced.

Chikungunya is a mosquito-borne viral disease that causes fever and severe joint pain. It is caused by a ribonucleic acid (RNA) virus. The name "chikungunya" derives from a word in the Kimakonde language of southern Tanzania, meaning "to become contorted" and describes the stooped appearance of sufferers with joint pain (arthralgia).

Once thought to have disappeared but has reemerged in 2006 in unprecedent magnitude with high morbidity rates and prolonged arthralgia causing substantial socio-economic impact. It is one of the public health problems. Almost all states are affected.

## Source of Infection and Mode of Transmission

Chikungunya virus (CHIKV) is transmitted to humans by the bites of infected female mosquitoes. Most commonly, the mosquitoes involved are *Aedes aegypti* and *Aedes albopictus*. These two species can also transmit other mosquito-borne viruses, including dengue and Zika viruses. They bite throughout daylight hours, although there may be peaks of activity in the early morning and late afternoon.

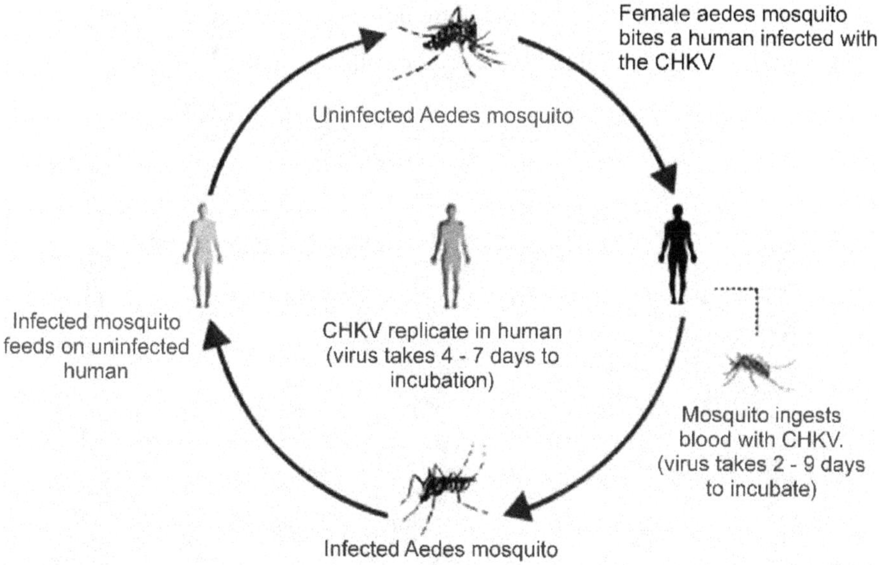


**Word of Mouth**

Symptoms: appear between 4 and 8 days after the patient has been bitten by the infected mosquito.

- Most symptoms are generally self-limiting and last for 2–3 days.
- Abrupt onset of fever frequently accompanied by joint pain.
- Other common signs and symptoms include muscle pain, headache, nausea, fatigue and rash. The joint pain is often debilitating and usually lasts for a few days to a few weeks.

**High Risks:**

- People with Hypertension / Diabetes / CAD/CVD / COPD / Hypothyroidism.
- Geriatric persons and pregnant women.
- People with Dengue / Malaria / Tuberculosis / Enteric fever / HIV.

CHIKV was first identified in the United Republic of Tanzania in 1952.

This virus was first isolated in Calcutta (Kolkata) in 1963.

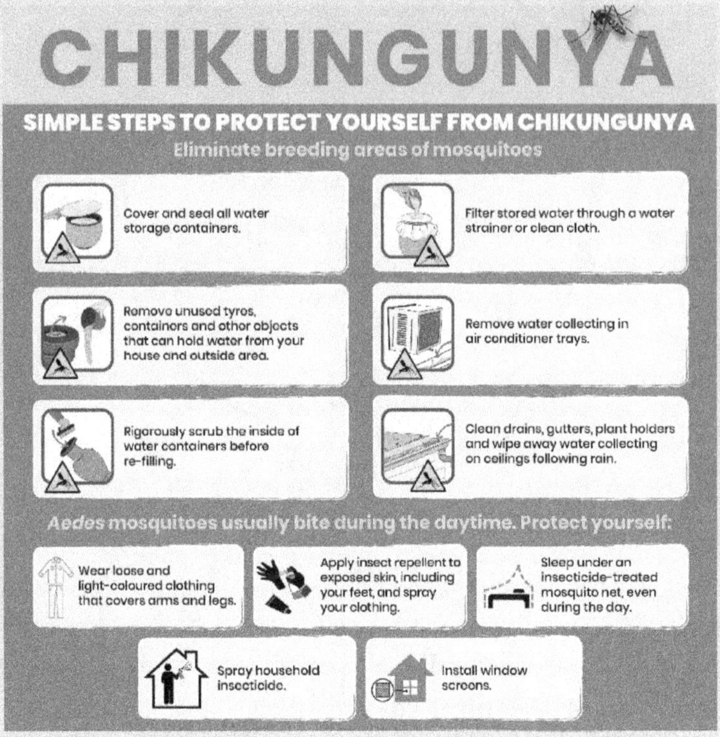


## Global Burden and Initiative

The disease has been reported in almost 40 countries from various WHO regions, including South-East Asia. The disease continues to cause epidemics in many countries in the region. The history of this disease epidemic has been known since 1952. A distinctive feature of the Chikungunya virus is that it causes explosive outbreaks before apparently disappearing for a period of several years to decades.

## India's Burden

During 2023 (Provisional), a total no. of 1,83,395 clinically suspected Chikungunya cases were reported from 32 States/UTs. Maximum cases were reported from Karnataka, followed by Maharashtra, Gujarat, Puducherry, Haryana and Madhya Pradesh.

This is covered under National Vector Borne Diseases Control Programme. National Guidelines on clinical management of Chikungunya fever is developed and release in 2023.

## Diagnosis and Treatment

***Diagnosis:*** The clinical manifestations of Chikungunya (CHIK) fever resemble those of Dengue. The laboratory diagnosis is essential to establish the cause of fever for individual case management and initiate specific public health response. The specimen is usually blood or serum, but in patients with neurological manifestations like meningoencephalitis, cerebrospinal fluid (CSF) may also be sent for analysis.

***Treatment:*** There is no specific antiviral drug treatment for chikungunya.

Treatment is directed primarily at relieving the symptoms, including joint pain. This is largely achieved by using anti-pyretic drugs to reduce fever, by optimizing the use of pain medication and by administering fluids. Aspirin and other non-steroidal anti-inflammatory drugs should not be administered until dengue can be ruled out to reduce the risk of bleeding.

## Prevention and Control

- Prevention and control rely heavily on reducing the number of water-filled habitats that allow mosquitoes to breed.
- During outbreaks, insecticides may be sprayed to kill flying mosquitoes; applied to surfaces in and around water-filled habitats where the mosquitoes land; and used to treat these habitats to kill the immature larvae.
- People with risk of exposure to infected mosquitoes are advised to wear clothing which minimizes skin exposure to day-biting mosquitoes. Repellents can be applied to exposed skin or to clothing in strict accordance with product label instructions.
- For those who sleep during the daytime, particularly young children or sick or older people, insecticide-treated mosquito nets afford good protection. Mosquito coils or other insecticide vaporizers may also reduce indoor biting.

**Role of Pharmacists:** There is no defined responsibilities as described under National TB programme. However, the pharmacists can:

- Participate in community education on awareness, prevention and control.

**Bottom Line**

- Chikungunya is a mosquito-borne viral disease that causes fever and severe joint pain.
- Once thought to have disappeared but has reemerged in 2006 in unprecedent magnitude with high morbidity rates and prolonged arthralgia causing substantial socio-economic impact.
- Chikungunya virus is transmitted to humans by the bites of infected female mosquitoes.
- The symptoms usually appear between 4 and 8 days after the patient has been bitten by the infected mosquito. Thcy are generally self-limiting and last for 2–3 days.
- People with Hypertension / Diabetes / CAD/CVD / COPD / Hypo-thyroidism; Geriatric persons and pregnant women and people with Dengue / Malaria / Tuberculosis / Enteric fever / HIV are at high risks.
- The disease has been reported in almost 40 countries. During 2023 maximum cases were reported from Karnataka, followed by Maharashtra, Gujarat, Puducherry, Haryana and Madhya Pradesh.
- This is covered under National Vector Borne Diseases Control Programme. National Guidelines on clinical management of Chikungunya fever is developed and release in 2023.
- The laboratory diagnosis is essential to establish the cause of fever as manifestations of Chikungunya fever resemble those of Dengue.
- There is no specific antiviral drug treatment for chikungunya it is primarily symptomatic. Anti-inflammatory drugs should not be administered until dengue is ruled out to reduce the risk of bleeding.
- Prevention and control rely heavily on reducing the number of water-filled habitats that allow mosquitoes to breed.
- The pharmacists can participate in community education on awareness, prevention and control.

## Bibliography


1. Annual Report 2023-2024, Department of Health & Family Welfare, Ministry of Health & Family Welfare, Government of India.
2. https://www.who.int/health-topics/chikungunya#tab=tab_1, accessed on 1st December 2024,
3. National Guidelines for Clinical Management of Chikungunya Fever, National Centre for Vector Borne Diseases Control, Government of India, 2023.

# Cholera

All that would be required to prevent cholera would be such a close attention to cleanliness in cooking and eating, to drainage and water supply, as is desirable at all times.

- John Snow

**After reading this chapter, you should be able to understand and appreciate:**

- Cholera as a public health problem of India;
- What causes cholera and how cholera;
- Symptoms of Cholera;
- Global and Indian Burden of Cholera;
- Diagnosis and Treatment available; and
- Prevention Control Strategies Practiced.

Cholera is an acute diarrhoeal infection caused by eating or drinking food or water that is contaminated with the bacterium *Vibrio cholerae*. Cholera remains a global threat to public health and is an indicator of inequity and lack of social development. It may spread like a wild fire in a community with overcrowding, poor sanitation and poor-hygiene.

Cholera is an extremely serious disease that can cause severe acute watery diarrhoea with severe dehydration. It takes between 12 hours and 5 days for a person to show symptoms after consuming contaminated food or water. Cholera affects both children and adults and can kill within hours if untreated.

## Source of Infection and Mode of Transmission

The main source of infection is human being who is a case or carrier. Infection occurs through consumption of contaminated water, food or drinks (usually faecal contamination). Direct personto-person contact, especially in overcrowded, low sanitation settings, also plays an important role.

**Word of Mouth**

**Symptoms:**

- Acute watery diarrhoea.
- Symptoms appear 12 hours to 5 days after infection.

  [Most people with the disease have mild or moderate symptoms. A minority of patients develop severe acute watery diarrhoea and life-threatening dehydration].

**Historical Perspective:**

History of cholera dates back to 18th Century when John Snow diagnosed a cholera outbreak in London city by pure epidemiological observation and analysis. He discovered that a handpump was responsible for the cholera outbreak and controlled the said outbreak by closure of that pump and water supply. This achievement of John Snow was commendable. He succeeded in the desired public health action long before the causative agent of cholera was discovered.

Cholera has been endemic in the Ganges Delta since time immemorial. There were annual epidemics in West Bengal and Bangladesh.

**Global Burden and Initiative:** WHO report released on 18$^{th}$ October 2024, from 1 January to 29 September 2024, a cumulative total of 439 724 cholera cases and 3432 deaths were reported globally. Although the number of cases in 2024 is 16% lower than last year, the 126% spike in deaths is deeply concerning. The increase in mortality may partly be attributed to the specific locations of these outbreaks, which include conflict-affected areas where access to healthcare is severely compromised, regions experiencing massive flooding that has damaged critical infrastructure, and areas with inadequate medical facilities. These challenges are particularly pronounced in rural and remote regions, where delays in accessing treatment are common due to poor infrastructure and limited healthcare resources.

Water, Sanitation and Hygiene (WASH) interventions help prevent many waterborne illnesses, including cholera, and contribute to the Sustainable Development Goals. During outbreaks, implementing WASH activities can reduce cholera transmission. These activities include improving WASH in healthcare facilities, conducting water quality monitoring, distributing WASH kits to communities and promoting protective hygiene practices.

The Global Task Force on Cholera Control (GTFCC) constituted in a partnership of governmental and nongovernmental organizations, UN agencies and academic institutions with a common mission to reduce the global cholera burden. It developed a road map to eliminate cholera by 2030.

**India's Burden and National Programme:** There are reports 29,400 cases from different states and Union Territories (UTs) during 2015–19. The study also advocated for piloting new intervention in states such as Karnataka, Madhya Pradesh, West Bengal, Orissa, and Maharashtra to prevent and control cholera. The data of 2021 shows the total cholera infection cases 264 of which 6 deaths. This shows situation has improved over the years due to improved living condition with quality of drinking water and initiatives like building toilets under Swachh Bharat scheme.

In the midst of all these initiatives, cholera cases continue to reported. Though there is no National Programme, India continues its surveillance and oral cholera vaccine campaign to end cholera.

## Diagnosis and Treatment

***Diagnosis:*** Signs and symptoms; and microscopic examination of stool.

***Treatment:*** Most people with cholera have mild or moderate diarrhoea and can be treated with oral rehydration solution (ORS). However, the disease can progress rapidly, so starting treatment quickly is vital to save lives. Patients with severe disease need intravenous fluids, ORS and antibiotics.

**ORS and its Preparation:**

Sodium chloride – 2.6 g

Glucose, anhydrous – 13. 5 g

Potassium chloride – 1.5 g

Trisodium citrate, dihydrate – 2.9 g

For dissolving in 1000 ml freshly boiled and drinking water. Few points:

- Quantity of water as mentioned in the sachet is to be maintained to ensure desired osmolarity. Avoid making concentrated solution.
- The left-over prepared solution is to be discarded after 24 h of the preparation.

## Prevention and Control

**For individual:**

- Drink water only from a safe source or water that has been disinfected (boiled or chlorinated).
- Cook food or reheat it thoroughly and eat it while it is still hot.
- Boil milk before drinking.
- Avoid ice creams from unreliable sources.
- Avoid uncooked food unless it can be peeled or shelled.
- Wash your hands after any contact with excreta and before preparing or eating food
- Dispose off human excreta promptly and safely.
- Avoid ice from unreliable sources.

**For Public:**

- Improve sanitation practice.
- Making provision for safe drinking water and food supply.
- Improving night soil / sewage disposal practice.

**Role of Pharmacists**

There are no defined responsibilities. The pharmacists can:

- Participate in community education on Cholera prevention and control.
- Guide the people on use of ORS.
- Community pharmacists should advice the customers and / or patients on personal hygiene and managing the ailment.

**Bottom Line**

- Cholera is an acute diarrhoeal infection caused by eating or drinking food or water that is contaminated with the bacterium *Vibrio cholerae.*
- Cholera is an extremely serious disease that can cause severe acute watery diarrhoea with severe dehydration.
- The main source of infection is human being who is a case or carrier.
- WHO report released on 18$^{th}$ October 2024, from 1 January to 29 September 2024, a cumulative total of 439 724 cholera cases and 3432 deaths were reported globally. Although the number of cases in 2024 is 16% lower than last year, the 126% spike in deaths is deeply concerning.
- Water, Sanitation and Hygiene (WASH) interventions help prevent many waterborne illnesses, including cholera.

- There are reports 29,400 cases from different states and Union Territories (UTs) during 2015–19. The data of 2021 shows the total cholera infection cases 264 of which 6 deaths.
- **Diagnosis:** Signs and symptoms; and microscopic examination of stool.
- **Treatment:** Most people with cholera have mild or moderate diarrhoea and can be treated with oral rehydration solution (ORS). Patients with severe disease need intravenous fluids, ORS and antibiotics.
- **Prevention strategies:** Drinking safe water; Cook food or reheat it thoroughly and eat it while it is still hot; Boil milk before drinking; Avoid ice creams from unreliable sources; Avoid uncooked food unless it can be peeled or shelled; Wash your hands after any contact with excreta and before preparing or eating food; and Avoid ice from unreliable sources.
- The pharmacists may participate in community education on Cholera prevention and control. They can advice on appropriate use of ORS.

## Bibliography

1. Cholera: A continuing challenge to Public Health, CDAlert, April-June 2008.
2. G. P. Mohanta, Fighting Cholera, The New Indian Express supplement-Health, 25 September 2007.
3. https://www.who.int/news-room/fact-sheets/detail/cholera?gad_source=1&gclid=Cj0KCQiAx9q6BhCDARIsACwUxu53LSY6wws7NWuTlQIY1UvOQFD3-s1Co0jtUv7RZyzv6c3ZstJdAWkaAmg0EALw_wcB accessed on 9th December 2024.
4. Multi- Country outbreak of cholera, WHO, 18th October 2024.

# COVID – 19

"To win over Covid, we have to give priority to expert and scientific advice."

- PM, Narendra Modi

**After reading this chapter, you should be able to understand and appreciate:**

- Covid – 19 was a public health problem of India;
- What causes Covid - 19 and how it spreads;
- Symptoms of Covid - 19;
- Global and India's Situation during Covid - 19;
- Diagnosis and Treatment available; and
- Prevention Control Strategies Advocated.

The world has seen the unprecedent human crisis in the name of covid – 19 (or, corona) with loss of uncounted number of lives during 2020 and 2021. Fortunately, the world has recovered from this through vaccination and other good infection prevention practices.

## Source of Infection and Mode of Transmission

The virus is transmitted through direct contact with respiratory droplets of an infected person (generated through coughing and sneezing), and touching surfaces contaminated with the virus. The COVID-19 virus may survive on surfaces for several hours, but simple disinfectants can kill it.

**Word of Mouth**

**Symptoms:**

- Fever, cough and shortness of breath.
- In more severe cases, infection can cause pneumonia or breathing difficulties.
- These symptoms are similar to the flu (influenza) or the common cold, which are a lot more common than COVID-19.

**High risk group:**

- Age > 60 years
- Cardiovascular disease and CAD
- Diabetes mellitus and other immunocompromised states (such as HIV)
- Active tuberculosis

- Chronic lung/kidney/liver disease
- Cerebrovascular disease
- Obesity
- Unvaccinated

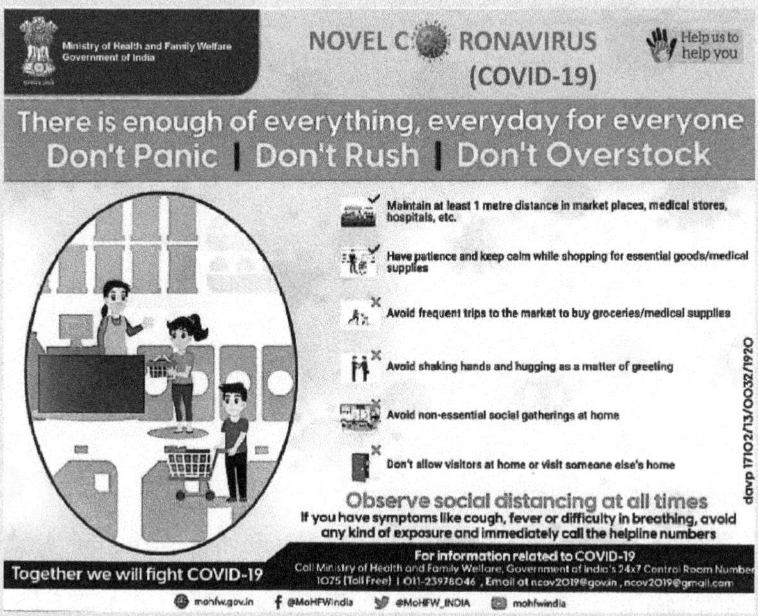


The novel coronavirus, the causative agent, was first identified in Wuhan, China. The disease has been named as corona-virus disease 2019 (COVID-19) – 'CO' stands for corona, 'VI' for virus, and 'D' for disease.

**Vaccination:**

- There has been lot of misinformation about Covid -19 vaccine causing vaccine hesitancy. In addition to the doubt on safety and efficacy of vaccines; wide spread rumours, false information and misinformed campaign further confuses the people.
- A survey conducted just before the launch of India's vaccination programme showed that about 59% of Indians were sceptical about COVID – 19 vaccines.
- More than 220 crore Covid-19 vaccine doses were made possible.
- Co-WIN, a comprehensive cloud-based IT solution is adopted for planning, implementing, monitoring, and evaluating Covid-19 vaccination in India, the Co-WIN system provided an end-to-end solution with utilities for the entire public health system.

- App based registration for vaccination was introduced: Co-WIN, Aarogya Setu, Umang.
- Covishield and Covaxin are two vaccines supplied under government scheme.
- The PM took the corona vaccine, Covaxin, on 01st March 2021 to build public confidence on India made vaccine.

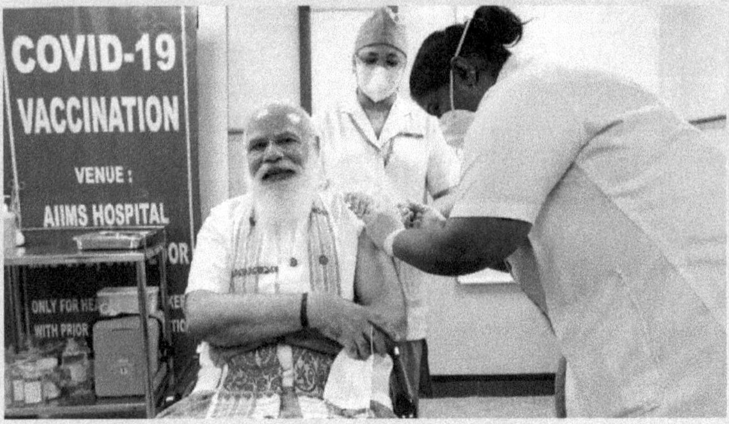


## Global Impact

The COVID-19 pandemic has led to a dramatic loss of human life worldwide and presents an unprecedented challenge to public health, food systems and the world of work. The economic and social disruption caused by the pandemic is devastating: tens of millions of people are at risk of falling into extreme poverty, while the number of undernourished people, currently estimated at nearly 690 million, could increase by up to 132 million by the end of the year (2020). About 3.4 million people died of COVID – 19.

COVID-19 pandemic reversed the trend of steady gain in life expectancy at birth and healthy life expectancy at birth (HALE). The pandemic wiped out nearly a decade of progress in improving life expectancy within just two years. Between 2019 and 2021, global life expectancy dropped by 1.8 years to 71.4 years (back to the level of 2012). Similarly, global healthy life expectancy dropped by 1.5 years to 61.9 years in 2021 (back to the level of 2012).

Millions of enterprises faced an existential threat. Nearly half of the world's 3.3 billion global workforce were at risk of losing their livelihoods. Informal economy workers were particularly vulnerable because the majority lack social protection and access to quality health care and had lost access to productive assets. Without the means to earn an income during lockdowns, many were unable to feed themselves and their families. For most, no income means no food, or, at best, less food and less nutritious food.

## India's Burden

India is one of the countries experiencing excess mortality caused by COVID-19 and has more than 10.3 million confirmed cases and 1.49 lakh deceased cases of COVID-19 pandemic disease in its first wave in the pandemic year 2020. This toll of deaths is almost one-third of that in the USA and half of that in Brazil. India ranks at the third position globally in terms of the toll of deaths attributable to COVID-19 disease in 2020. There are very limited number of active cases reported in 2024.

The outbreak of the COVID-19 pandemic in India led to a nation-wide lockdown starting from 25 March 2020. The pandemic and the lockdown involved restricted mobility of people as well as goods and services. This created severe challenges for vulnerable families due to the closure of shops, factories, and offices, and restricted access to public services. One of the biggest impacts of the lockdown was the loss of livelihoods, especially in urban locations, as a result of which millions of workers across India moved back to their villages. The post-lockdown challenges encompassed practically all sectors, including not only livelihoods, but also food availability, health and nutrition, education, and access to public facilities for people.

On 12 May 2020, Prime Minister had announced a special economic and comprehensive package of Rs.20 lakh crore - equivalent to 10% of India's GDP; to fight COVID-19 pandemic in India, Hon'ble Prime Minister gave a clarion call for Atmanirbhar Bharat or Self-Reliant India Movement.

45,041,748 cases of COVID-19 infection have been reported in India as of 19th August 2024. In Kerala, the first instance was documented on 30 January 2020. In March 2021, a second wave that was more damaging than the first broke out, leading to shortages of medical supplies such as oxygen cylinders, medical beds, and vaccines.

India's immunization program, which uses the AstraZeneca vaccine (Covishield) and the indigenous, Covaxin, was started on 16th January 2021. On 30th January 2022, India reported that over 720 million people had got all advised immunizations, totalling over 1.7 billion doses.

## Diagnosis and Treatment

***Diagnosis:*** Reverse-transcriptase polymerase-chain-reaction (RT-PCR) testing is regarded as most sensitive.

***Treatment:*** The treatment for adult is as follows –

- **Mild disease:** Upper respiratory tract symptoms and/or fever WITHOUT shortness of breath or hypoxia, Home Isolation & Care.
- **Moderate disease:** Anyone of –
  1. Respiratory rate $\geq 24$ / min, breathlessness.
  2. $SpO_2$: 90 %  $\leq 93$ % on room air. Admission to hospital.

- **Severe disease:** Anyone of –
    1. Respiratory rate > 30 / min, breathlessness.
    2. $SpO_2$< 90 % on room air. Admission to HDU / ICU.

## Prevention and Control

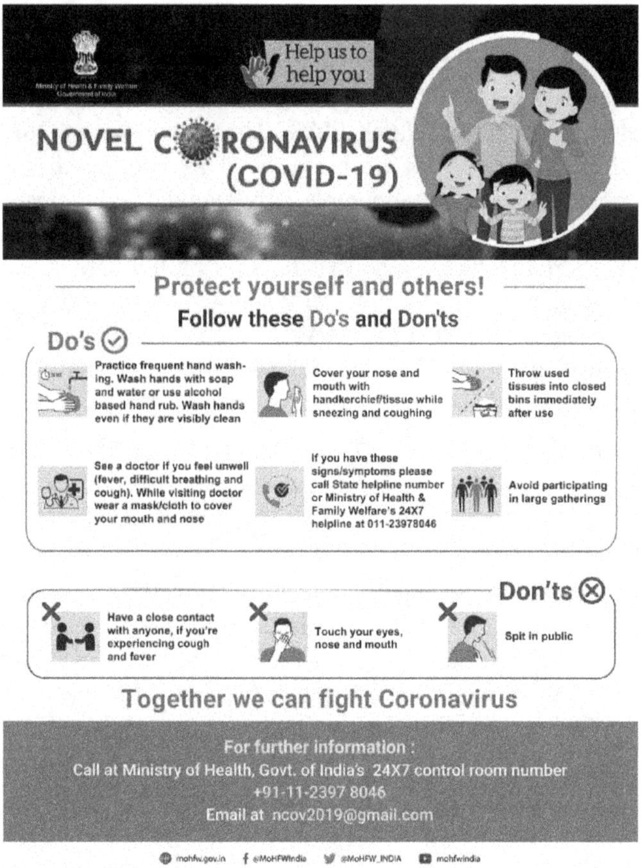


## Key Measures

- Frequent hand washing, and respiratory hygiene (cover your cough or sneeze with a flexed elbow or tissue, then throw away the tissue into a closed bin).
- Using mask.
- Avoiding close contact with anyone who has cold or flu-like symptoms.
- Keeping distance of at least one meter from others.

**Role of Pharmacists:** There is no defined responsibilities, the pharmacists can:

- Promote Good Hand Hygiene Practices.
- Help overcoming fake news about Covid-19 and try to build confidence among the public.
- Help overcoming the infodemic especially related to vaccine hesitancy.
- The pharmacists are first time trained to provide vaccination.
- Participate in community education on awareness, prevention and control.

**Bottom Line**

- The world has seen the unprecedent human crisis in the name of covid – 19 (or, corona) with loss of uncounted number of lives during 2020 and 2021.
- The virus is transmitted through direct contact with respiratory droplets of an infected person (generated through coughing and sneezing), and touching surfaces contaminated with the virus.
- Common symptoms are: Fever, cough and shortness of breath; In more severe cases, infection can cause pneumonia or breathing difficulties.
- People with age > 60 years, Cardiovascular disease and CAD, Diabetes mellitus and other immunocompromised states (such as HIV), Active tuberculosis, Chronic lung/kidney/liver disease, Cerebrovascular disease, Obesity and unvaccinated.
- The COVID-19 pandemic has led to a dramatic loss of human life worldwide and presents an unprecedented challenge to public health, food systems and the world of work. Globally, about 3.4 million people died of COVID – 19.
- India ranks at the third position globally in terms of the toll of deaths attributable to COVID-19 disease in 2020. There are very limited number of active cases reported in 2024.
- The outbreak of the COVID-19 pandemic in India led to a nation-wide lockdown starting from 25 March 2020.
- Reverse-transcriptase polymerase-chain-reaction (RT-PCR) testing is regarded as most sensitive diagnostic method.
- Treatment of mild cases is advocated for Home Isolation & Care. For Moderate disease, admission to hospital and severe disease, admission to ICU is adviced.

- Key measures for precaution: Frequent hand washing, and respiratory hygiene (cover your cough or sneeze with a flexed elbow or tissue, then throw away the tissue into a closed bin); Using mask; Avoiding close contact with anyone who has cold or flu-like symptoms and Keeping distance of at least one meter from others.
- Pharmacists' Role: Promote Good Hand Hygiene Practices; Help overcoming fake news about Covid-19 and try to build confidence among the public; Help overcoming the infodemic especially related to vaccine hesitancy; and Participate in community education on awareness, prevention and control.

## Bibliography

1. GP Mohanta, PK Manna, Fighting social stigma of coronavirus, Chronicle Pharmabiz, September 2, 2020.
2. https://www.unicef.org/india/coronavirus/covid-19 accessed on 3rd December 2024.
3. https://www.who.int/health-topics/coronavirus#tab=tab_1 accessed on 3rd December 2024

# Dengue

**After reading this chapter, you should be able to understand and appreciate:**

- Dengue as a public health issue;
- How does infection occur and spread;
- Symptoms of Dengue;
- Global and India's burden;
- Diagnosis and treatment options available; and
- Prevention and Control Strategies Practiced.

Dengue, a viral infection, is one of the most significant and prevalent arthropod borne communicable diseases, spread by the infective bite of a particular mosquito known as *Aedes aegypti*. Human being develops disease after 5 – 6 days of being bitten by an infective mosquito. It occurs in two forms: classical dengue fever (also called break bone fever) and dengue haemorrhagic fever (DHF). It is wide spread in tropical and subtropical regions. DHF is the serious form of dengue.

Dengue is known for long and the earliest record of dengue fever comes from Chinese Medical Encyclopedia back to 992 BC. It is believed that between 19$^{th}$ and 20$^{th}$ centuries, the virus spread through out the tropics and subtropics. The dengue virus was first isolated in India in 1945 and the first case was reported during 1956 from Vellore District of Tamil Nadu.

## Source of Infection and Mode of Transmission

Dengue virus is an RNA virus and the transmission of this virus occurs in a cycle. An infected human is bitten by a female mosquito (*Aedes aegypti)*. The infected mosquito then bites another human, and the cycle continues. It is 'man-mosquito-man' cycle. Human being develops disease after 5 – 6 days of being bitten by an infective mosquito. Female Aedes mosquito usually flies an average of 400 metres. But it may be transported accidently by humans from one place to another (e.g. in the back of the car, plants).

*Aedes aegypti* mosquitoes most commonly bite at dusk and dawn, indoors, in shady areas, or when the weather is cloudy. They can bite and spread infection at any time of day and all year long. Although the lifespan of an adult *A. aegypti* is two to four weeks depending on conditions, the eggs can be viable for over a year in dry state. This allows the mosquito to reappear after a cold winter or dry spell.

In addition to *Aedes aegypti,* there is one more species is involved in dengue transmission, *Aedes albopictus*. *Aedes* mosquitoes are small blackish mosquitoes with white strips on abdomen and legs. They are also known as 'tiger mosquitoes'. The dengue vector mosquitoes rest indoor houses mainly in corners under furniture, beds, shelves, almirah and dark clothing hanging inside. They bite during day time usually in morning (8-10 am) and afternoon (3-5 pm). Though they preferably bite legs, hands, face, neck and ears; they can bite any exposed body parts.

**Word of Mouth**

**Symptoms**

- Sudden onset of fever
- Headache (typically located behind the eyes)
- Muscle and joint pain
- Rash
- Chills (shivering)
- Facial flushing
- Loss of appetite
- Sore throat
- Abnormal bleeding such as nose bleeds, bleeding gums and / or blood in urine.

**Severe Dengue**

- Severe abdominal pain
- Persistent vomiting
- Bleeding gums
- Vomiting blood
- Rapid breathing
- Fatigue / Breathlessness

**Risk Groups**

- Pregnancy
- Infants
- Elderly
- Obesity
- Peptic ulcer diseases
- G6PD Deficiency
- Thalassemia

- Coronary artery disease
- Chronic diseases: diabetes, COPD, bronchial asthma, hypertension
- Patients on steroid, antiplatelet, anticoagulant medicines
- HIV infected persons / immune-compromised persons

## Global Burden and Initiative

Prior to 1970, the severe dengue epidemics was restricted to only 7 countries. Now the disease is endemic in more than 100 countries. The America, South East Asia and Western Pacific regions share 70 % of the global dengue burden. The largest number of dengue cases ever reported globally was in 2019. American region reported 3.1 million cases alone, Bangladesh reported 101,000, Malaysia reported 131,000, Philippines reported 420,000, and Vietnam 320,000 cases.

The estimated aggregate global cost of dengue illness was US$ 8.9 billion in 2013. Social, demographic, and environmental factors strongly influence transmission pattern of vector borne pathogens including that of dengue. Most of the vector borne diseases can be prevented by vector control. WHO's Global Vector Control Response aims to prevent vector diseases in all countries by 2030. WHO responds to dengue in the following ways [https://www.who.int/news-room/fact-sheets/detail/dengue-and-severe-dengue accessed on 01st April 2020]:

- supports countries in the confirmation of outbreaks through its collaborating network of laboratories;
- provides technical support and guidance to countries for the effective management of dengue outbreaks;
- supports countries to improve their reporting systems and capture the true burden of the disease;
- provides training on clinical management, diagnosis and vector control at the country and regional level with some of its collaborating centres;
- formulates evidence-based strategies and policies;
- support countries in the development of dengue prevention and control strategies and adopting the Global Vector Control Response (2017-2030)
- reviews the development of new tools, including insecticide products and application technologies;
- gathers official records of dengue and severe dengue from over 100 Member States; and
- publishes guidelines and handbooks for surveillance, case management, diagnosis, dengue prevention and control for Member States.

## India's Burden and National Programme

Dengue is endemic to 29 states and 6 union territories. Recurring outbreaks of Dengue have been reported from Andhra Pradesh, Assam, Delhi, Goa, Haryana, Gujarat, Karnataka, Kerala, Maharashtra, Odisha, Puducherry, Punjab, Rajasthan, Tamil Nadu, Telangana, Uttar Pradesh and West Bengal.

Every year during the period of July to November, there is an upsurge in the northern part of India. In Southern and Western parts, the disease becomes perennial. In 2018, a total of 101,192 cases and 172 deaths were reported from 29 states and 6 union territories. Maximum number of cases were reported from Punjab (14980) followed by Maharashtra (11011). The maximum deaths were reported from Maharashtra.

May 16 is observed as National Dengue Day to create awareness about dengue and to intensify preventive measures and preparedness for the control of disease.

The dengue prevention and control falls under the domain of National Vector Borne Disease Control Programme (NVBDCP). The state governments and the union territories are responsible for implementing the programme. The NVBDCP provides technical and financial assistance to the state governments.

Ministry of Health and Family Welfare of Government of India has made notification of dengue cases essential. Health institutions and private hospitals & clinics are required to inform the cases to the district health authority.

## Diagnosis and Treatment

Laboratory Diagnostics [Details are beyond the scope of the present text]:

- ELISA based NS1 antigen tests
- IgM – Capture enzyme – linked immunosorbent assay (MAC-ELISA)
- Isolation of dengue virus
- Polymerase chain reaction (PCR)
- IgG – ELISA
- Serological Tests
- RDTs

**Platelet Count and Dengue**: Platelet count is one of the laboratory parameter investigated during dengue season. Platelets less than or equal to 100,000 / $mm^3$ is erroneously viewed as an indicator of dengue. However, decrease in platelet count is always a cause of concern!

## Treatment

There is no anti-dengue medicine available at present. There is no vaccine too. However, tetravalent vaccine is available in some countries, but not included in India's dengue prevention programme.

Patients should be given rest and to drink plenty of fluids. Paracetamol can be used to bring down fever and reduce joint pains. However, **aspirin or ibuprofen should not be given since they can increase the risk of bleeding.**

## Prevention and Control

There is no vaccine available in India to prevent the dengue. Prevention and vector control interventions aim to reduce dengue transmission which would decrease the incidence of infection and prevent outbreaks of the disease. The best way to protect oneself from getting dengue is to avoid being bitten by mosquitoes.

**Prevention:** The following measures are advised:

- Using insect repellents and mosquito nets to avoid being bitten. Bodies could be protected from mosquito bite by applying insect repellent (containing DEET) on the clothes and exposed part of the body especially when you travel to Dengue Fever endemic areas;
- Wearing long-sleeved clothes and long trousers while going outdoors;
- Cleaning the places where the mosquito lays their eggs, primarily artificial containers that store water. Items that collect rainwater or are used to store water (for example, plastic containers, drums, buckets, or used automobile tires) should be cleaned or discarded. Pet watering containers and flower vases should be emptied and scrub dried at least once a week. This will eliminate the mosquito eggs, larvae and reduce the number of mosquitoes present in these areas;
- Screening the windows and doors with nets which would prevent the entry of mosquitoes;
- Staying under bed net or in a place with intact window/door screens to prevent Aedes mosquito bites during first week of illness. This will prevent further spread of dengue to other persons; and
- Covering water containers tightly so that mosquitoes can't get in to lay eggs.

**Vector Control:** The vector control should target source reduction. The vector control methods can be divided into the following categories:

- **Environmental Management:**
    - Detection and elimination of mosquito breeding sources;

  - Management of roof tops, porticos, and sunshades;
  - Proper covering of stored water;
  - Disposing of solid waste properly and removing artificial man made habitats that can hold water;
  - Reliable water supply; and
  - Observation of weekly dry day.
- **Biological Control:**
  - Use of larvivorous fishes in ornamental tanks, fountains; and
  - Use of biocides.
- **Chemical Control:**
  - Larval Control:
    - Temephos / abate in big breeding containers;
    - Diflubenzuron and Pyreproxifen as insect growth regulator.
  - Adult Control:
    - Pyrethrum aerosol space spray during day time.
    - Malathion fogging is used outdoor.
    - Cyphenothrin for outdoor and indoor fogging.
- **Community Participation:**
  - Educating community regarding the disease, vectors and risks involved; and
  - Sensitizing and involving the community for detection of breeding places and their elimination.

**Role of Pharmacists:** There is no defined responsibilities as described under National TB programme. However, the pharmacists can:

- Participate in community education on dengue awareness, prevention and control.
- Community pharmacists should not dispense aspirin /ibuprofen in dengue cases. They should strictly adhere not to dispense these medications without prescription during dengue season when the government directs.

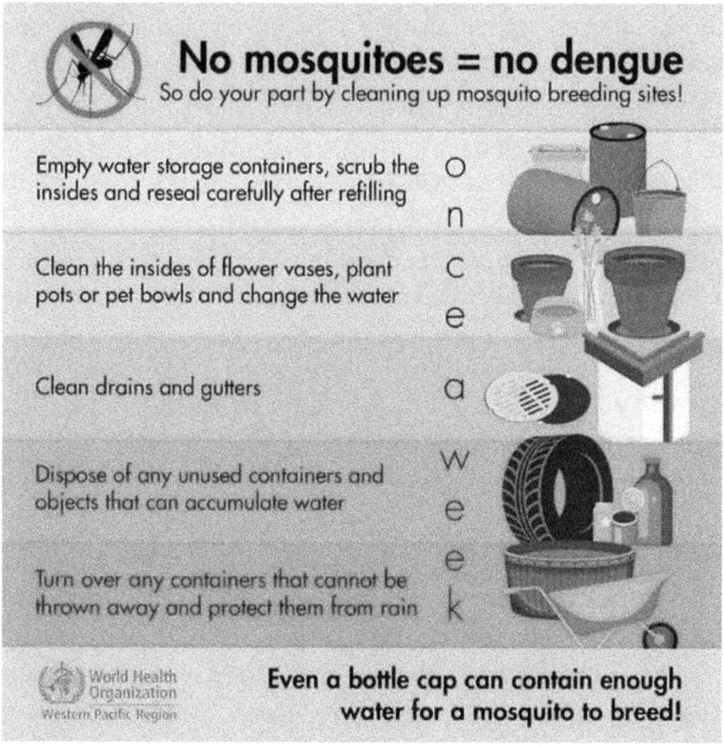


**Bottom Line**

- Dengue, a viral infection, is one of the public health issues, spread by the infective bite of *Aedes aegypti* mosquito. Human being develops disease after 5 – 6 days of being bitten by an infective mosquito. It occurs in two forms: classical dengue fever (also called break bone fever) and dengue haemorrhagic fever (DHF).
- The transmission is a 'man – mosquito – man' cycle.
- Common symptoms are: Sudden onset of fever, Headache (typically located behind the eyes), Muscle and joint pain, Rash, Chills (shivering), Facial flushing, Loss of appetite, Sore throat, and Abnormal bleeding such as nose bleeds, bleeding gums and / or blood in urine.
- Dengue is endemic in more than 100 countries. In India it is endemic to 29 states and 6 union territories. As of 2018, Punjab has the maximum number of cases.
- There are several diagnostic tests available: ELISA based NS1 antigen tests, IgM – Capture enzyme – linked immunosorbent assay (MAC-ELISA), Isolation of dengue virus, Polymerase chain reaction (PCR), IgG – ELISA, Serological Tests and RDTs

- National Vector Borne Disease Control Programme is the nodal agency for implementing the dengue prevention and control programme in the country.
- There is no vaccine and no treatment, patients should be given rest and plenty of fluids. Paracetamol can be given for fever, but aspirin and ibuprofen contraindicated.
- No mosquito – No Dengue is the mantra. All strategies for controlling dengue evolve around "prevent mosquito breeding and avoid mosquito bite".

## Bibliography

1. Annual Report 2018-2019, Ministry of Health and Welfare, Government of India.
2. Global Strategy for Dengue Prevention and Control: 2012-2020, World Health Organization, 2012.
3. Global Vector Control Response: 2017-2030, World Health Organization, 2017.
4. https://www.nhp.gov.in/disease/musculo-skeletal-bone-joints-/dengue-fever accessed on 1st April 2020.
5. https://www.who.int/health-topics/dengue-and-severe-dengue#tab=tab_1 accessed on 1st April 2020.
6. National Guidelines for Clinical Management of Dengue Fever, National Vector Borne Disease Control programme, Government of India, 2015.

# Ebola

"We must act now to prevent further spread of EBOLA VIRUS. If we do not act collectively, EBOLA VIRUS will wipe all whole populations and generations into their grave. The call to action is now."

- Lailah Gifty Akita

**After reading this chapter, you should be able to understand and appreciate:**

- Ebola as a public health problem;
- What causes Ebola infection and how Ebola spreads;
- Symptoms of Ebola infection;
- Global and Indian Burden of Ebola infection;
- Diagnosis and Treatment available; and
- Prevention Control Strategies Advocated.

Ebola (also known as Ebola virus disease) is a rare but severe illness in humans. It is often fatal. Earlier it was known as Ebola haemorrhagic fever. The average Ebola case fatality rate is around 50%. Case fatality rates have varied from 25% to 90% in past outbreaks.

Ebola first appeared in 1976 in 2 simultaneous outbreaks, one in what is now Nzara, South Sudan, and the other in Yambuku, Democratic Republic of the Congo. The latter occurred in a village near the Ebola River, from which the disease takes its name. There have been no indigenous reported cases from India. The first case was reported when a person landed at Delhi airport and undergone mandatory screening in November 2014.

## Source of Infection and Mode of Transmission

The four (Ebola, Sudan, Taï Forest, and Bundibugyo viruses) are known to cause disease in humans. Zaire ebolavirus is the most fatal Ebola virus.

Ebola is introduced into the human population through close contact with the blood, secretions, organs or other bodily fluids of infected animals, chimpanzee, gorilla, fruit bats, monkeys, forest antelopes and porcupines. The virus is likely maintained in the environment by spreading from host to host or through intermediate hosts or vectors. In Africa, fruit bats are considered natural hosts.

Human-to human transmission, with infection resulting from direct contact (through broken skin or mucous membranes e.g. the eyes, nose, or mouth, with the blood or secretions, organs or body fluids (urine, saliva, sweat, feces, vomit, breast milk, amniotic fluid, and semen) of an infected person or who died with it. Touching things that have the body fluids of an infected person like clothes or sheets.

*Ebola is not spread through the air or by water or, in general, by food.*

**Word of Mouth**

**Symptoms**

- Sudden fever, fatigue, muscle pain, headache and sore throat.
- Followed by vomiting, diarrhoea, rash, and internal and external bleeding.
- Onset of symptoms usually appears usually from 2 to 21 days after infection.
- After recovering from Ebola, some people may have symptoms for two years or longer.

**High risks group:**

- Healthcare workers
- Family and friends of patients with Ebola
- Handlers of body dead of an Ebola patient

**Global Burden and Initiative:** Most cases and outbreaks of Ebola Virus Disease have occurred in Africa. The cases were reported from Uganda, Guinea, and Democratic Republic of Congo.

**India's Burden and National Programme:** There have been no indigenous reported cases from India.

## Diagnosis and Treatment

**Diagnosis:**

- Antibody-capture enzyme-linked immunosorbent assay (ELISA)
- Antigen detection tests
- Serum neutralization test
- Reverse transcriptase polymerase chain reaction (RT-PCR) assay
- Electron microscopy
- Virus isolation by cell culture.

**Treatment:**

- Timely treatment of Ebola is important but challenging because the disease is difficult to diagnose clinically in the early stages of infection.

- **Isolation:** If a person has the early symptoms of Ebola VD and there is reason to believe that Ebola should be considered, the patient should be isolated and public health professionals notified.
- **Supportive therapy:** including intravenous fluids or oral rehydration with solutions including electrolytes and maintenance of oxygen status and blood pressure.
- Two monoclonal antibodies, REGN-EB3 (Inmazeb™) and mAb114 (Ebanga™) are available for the treatment of Ebola caused by Zaire ebolavirus.
- There are currently no licensed therapeutics for the treatment of EVD caused by Sudan ebolavirus.

## Prevention and Control

- Casual contact in public places with people that do not appear to be sick do not transmit Ebola. One cannot contract Ebola virus by handling money, groceries or swimming in a pool. Mosquitoes do not transmit the Ebola virus. Ebola virus is easily killed by soap, bleach, sunlight or drying. Ebola virus survives only a short time on surfaces that have dried in the sun.
- Raising awareness of the risk factors for Ebola infection and the protective measures individuals can take is the only way to reduce human infection and death.
- Reducing the consumption of their raw meat; Handling animals with gloves and other appropriate protective clothing.
- Avoiding close physical contact with Ebola patients; Wearing gloves and appropriate personal protective equipment; Regular hand washing; and cremation or burial under biosafety precaution.

**Bottom Line**

- Ebola (also known as Ebola virus disease) is a rare but severe illness in humans. It is often fatal. The average Ebola case fatality rate is around 50%.
- The four (Ebola, Sudan, Taï Forest, and Bundibugyo viruses) are known to cause disease in humans. Zaire ebolavirus is the most fatal Ebola virus.
- Human-to human transmission occurs from direct contact (through broken skin or mucous membranes e.g. the eyes, nose, or mouth, with the blood or secretions, organs or body fluids (urine, saliva, sweat, feces, vomit, breast milk, amniotic fluid, and semen) of an infected person or who died with it.

- The common symptoms: Sudden fever, fatigue, muscle pain, headache and sore throat; followed by vomiting, diarrhoea, rash, and internal and external bleeding.
- Onset of symptoms usually appears usually from 2 to 21 days after infection.
- High risk groups include: Healthcare workers, Family and friends of patients with Ebola, Handlers of body dead of an Ebola patient.
- Most cases and outbreaks of Ebola Virus Disease have occurred in Africa. There have been no indigenous reported cases from India.
- Important diagnostic tools include Antibody-capture enzyme-linked immunosorbent assay (ELISA) and RT-PCR assay.
- Isolation, Supportive therapylike intravenous fluids or oral rehydration with solutions including electrolytes and maintenance of oxygen status and blood pressure, Two monoclonal antibodies, REGN-EB3 (Inmazeb™) and mAb114 (Ebanga™) are available for the treatment.
- Casual contact in public places with people that do not appear to be sick do not transmit Ebola.
- Raising awareness of the risk factors for Ebola infection and the protective measures individuals can take is the only way to reduce human infection and death.

## Bibliography

1. CD Alert, National Centre for Disease Control, Government of India, December 2022.
2. https://www.who.int/health-topics/ebola#tab=tab_1 accessed on 11th December 2022.

## Human Immunodeficiency Virus (HIV) Infection / Acquired Immunodeficiency Syndrome (AIDS)

"A planet without AIDS is possible but to create that planet we must do away with the vestiges of the old planet where testing positive to the HIV effectively regulates an individual to the subclass of human society"

- Oche Otorkpa

**After reading this chapter, you should be able to understand and appreciate:**

- HIV Infection as a public health issue;
- How does HIV infection and AIDS differ;
- How does HIV spread;
- Symptoms of HIV Infection / AIDS;
- Global and India's burden; and
- The Pharmacists' participation in National AIDS Control programme.

The human immunodeficiency virus (HIV), a retrovirus, infects the cells of human immune system destroying or impairing their functions. The most advanced stage of HIV infection is Acquired Immunodeficiency Syndrome (AIDS). It takes about 10-15 years for an HIV infected person to develop AIDS.

In spite of all around efforts, the HIV infections continues to be a major global public health issue. Our country, India, has the third largest HIV epidemic in the world. There are two types of HIV: Type I and Type II. Type I is more common in India. There is no cure for HIV infection but there are many medicines to fight and control. The HIV infection in India was first detected in 1986among the female sex workers in Chennai (then it was Madras). Dr Selappan Nirmala, then a PG student at Madras Medical College working for her dissertation and her Professor Suniti Solomon were credited for the discovery of first HIV case in India.

**Difference between HIV and AIDS:** HIV infection's advanced stage is AIDS. HIV causes AIDS. The resultant effect is weakened immune system. As the effective anti-HIV therapy (Anti-Retroviral Therapy) is accessible to almost every one, most people infected with HIV do not progress to progress to AIDS. People will be living with HIV without being afraid of AIDS. HIV is the cause and AIDS is the effect.

Left untreated, HIV reduces the number of CD4 cells in the body, making it more difficult for the immune system to fight off infections and other diseases. With AIDS, the person becomes prone to opportunistic infections

(OI). Tuberculosis is the most common OI in India. Other common OIs are: oral candidiasis, diarrhoea, herpes zoster, respiratory and skin bacterial infections, cryptococcal meningitis and cytomegalovirus retinitis.

AIDS affects people primarily when they are most productive and leads to premature death there by severely affecting socio-economic structure of whole families, communities and countries.

**Source of Infection and Mode of Transmission:** HIV is found in the following body fluids of people with HIV infection: blood, semen, vaginal fluid, rectal fluid, and breast milk. HIV can be transmitted through:

- Unprotected vaginal or anal sex with a person living with HIV. In very rare case, transmission may occur through oral sex;
- Blood transfusion of contaminated blood;
- Sharing of needles, syringes, other injecting equippments, surgical equipment or other sharp instruments; and
- From HIV infected mother to infant during pregnancy, child birth or breast feeding.

Treatment with ART suppress the chances transmitting HIV.

As the HIV cannot reproduce outside human cell, it does not spread through air, water, insects, saliva, tears, sweat, shaking hands, sharing dishes or kissing.

**Word of Mouth (AIDS)**

**Symptoms:** The symptoms of HIV vary depending on the stage of infection.

***Acute Symptoms:*** *The majority of infected people develop influenza (flu) like illness within a month or two of entry of the virus.*

- Headache
- Fever
- Sore throat
- Muscle soreness
- Rash
- Mouth or Genital Ulcer
- Swollen lymph nodes mainly on the neck
- Joint pain
- Diarrhoea
- Night sweats

***Clinical Latency:*** Persistence swelling of lymph nodes.

***Severe Symptoms:***

- Headache
- Blurred and distorted vision
- Cough and shortness of breath
- Persistent white spots or unusual lesion on the tongue or mouth
- Soaking night sweats
- Shaking chills or fever higher than 100 °F / 38 °C for several weeks
- Chronic diarrhoea
- Persistent and unexplained fatigue
- Weight loss
- Skin rash

**Risk factors:** The following groups are at higher risk. Persons –

- Having unprotected anal or vaginal sex;
- Having another sexually transmitted infection such as syphilis, herpes, chlamydia, gonorrhoea, bacterial vaginosis;
- Sharing contaminated needles, syringes and other injecting equipments, and drug solutions when injecting drug;
- Receiving unsafe injection, blood transfusions and tissue transplantation and medical procedures that involve unsterile cutting or piercing; and
- Experiencing accidental needle stick injuries including among health workers.

**Global Burden of HIV and Initiatives**: HIV is one of the major global public health issue. As of 2018, there were approximately 39.9 million people living with HIV. The infection rate vary across the regions and countries. The highest HIV prevalence occurs in Sub – Sahara Africa accounting around 68% of HIV positive cases. The ART coverage is only 62%. Social stigma and discrimination continue to be a major challenge for people living with HIV.

Through concerted international efforts HIV service coverage has been steadily increasing, still service is not reaching to everyone who needs. As of 2018, 62% adults and 54% children with HIV have access to regular life-long ART in low and middle income countries. However, there are impressive achievements too. Between 2000 and 2018, the new HIV infections fell by 37% and HIV related death fell by 45%.

World Health Organization, Other International partners like USAID, Global Fund, Civil Societies etc. are working along with National HIV programme to achieve the global target of ending AIDS epidemic by 2030. This is one of the Sustainable Development Goal. By 2020, WHO targeted to achieve 90-90-90. WHO has raised a concern of missing 2020 target.

**India's HIV Burden and National Programmes:** HIV is epidemic in India. These are the salient features of HIV position in India as per the HIV estimation 2017 report:

- National adult (15-49 years) HIV prevalence was at 0.22%. There had been steady decline from an estimated peak of 0.38% in 2001-03 through 0.34% in 2007, 0.28% in 2012 and 0.26% in 2015 to 0.22% in 2017.
- Among the states and Union Territories, Mizoram has the highest adult prevalence of 2.04% followed by Manipur 1.43%, Nagaland 1.15%, Telangana 0.70% and Andhra Pradesh 0.63%. There are other states: Karnataka, Goa, Maharashtra, and Delhi too have more prevalence than the national average.
- The total number of people living with HIV in India was estimated at 21.40 lakh in 2017 and children below 15 years at 0.61 lakh and female adults accounted for 8.79 lakh.
- New HIV infection cases were around 87.58 thousand in 2017. This shows the decline rate by 85% since the peak of 1995 and 27% between 2010 and 2017. Annual new HIV infection are increasing in three states of north- eastern region: Assam, Mizoram and Meghalaya.
- India was estimated to have had 22.67thousand HIV positive women who gave birth in 2017. State wise Prevention to Mother to Child Transmission (PMTCT) number was highest in Maharashtra (2.41 thousand).

Shortly after the discovery of first case of HIV in Chennai in 1086, the Government of India launched National AIDS Control Programme (NACP). The programme is managed by National AIDS Control Organization (NACO). Currently NACP – IV (Extension) is under implementation for the period 2017-2020. India has drawn a strategic plan 2017-2024 to make AIDS free India. The strategic plan approved in June 2017 has proposed the following strategies:

- Accelerating HIV in key population and at risk group
- Expanding quality assured HIV testing with universal access to comprehensive HIV care
- Elimination of mother to child transmission of HIV and syphilis

- Addressing the critical enablers in HIV programming
- Restructuring the strategic information system to be efficient patient centric.

The NACO provides free ART to approximately 1.27 million people living with HIV.

**HIV Regulation:** The Parliament of India had unanimously adopted HIV and AIDS (Prevention and Control) Bill 2017 which provides the legal frame work for the government's commitment including in eliminating stigma and discrimination against people affected by HIV. This is the law to protect the rights of the people affected by HIV and promote 'Test and Treat Policy'. As per this test and treat policy, all people living with HIV (PLHIV) are to be treated with ART regardless of CD4 count, clinical stage, age or population.

## Diagnosis and Treatment

**Diagnosis:** The diagnosis and monitoring of HIV infection is performed on blood specimens. The test is based on the presence of antibodies. Commonly used screening tests are:

- Enzyme Linked Immunosorbent Assay (ELISA) – A positive test does not necessarily mean that the person has HIV. There are possibility of false positive result. A positive ELISA test is always followed by western blot test which confirms the HIV infection.
- Rapid Test – An immunoassay is used for screening.
    - Immunoconcentration / Dot blot assay
    - Agglutination assay
    - Immunochromatographic assay
    - Dipstick and comb assay based on enzyme immune assay

*No single test can provide a full HIV diagnosis; a confirmatory test is required.*

Patients in the window period and infants born to HIV positive mothers require Molecular and Other Assays.

**Treatment:** There is no definite cure for HIV/AIDS. However, medicines are available and their use can prolong the life of HIV positive persons. Even after treatment, people with HIV still will have virus in their bodies and they have the potential to spread HIV.

HIV can be suppressed by ART, a combination of three or more ARV drugs. There are six distinct classes of ARVs: Nucleoside Reverse

Transcriptase Inhibitors (NsRTIs); Non-nucleoside Reverse Transcriptase Inhibitors (NNRTIs); Protease Inhibitors (PIs); Nucleotide Reverse Transcriptase Inhibitor (NtRTI); Fusion Inhibitors and CRR 5 Co-receptors; and Integrase Inhibitors. NsRTI, NNRTI, PI, NtRTI and Integrase Inhibitors are available in NACO regimen.

*More details on Diagnosis and Treatment regimens are described in National AIDS Control Programme.*

**Prevention:** Limiting the exposure to risk factors is the primary strategy for HIV prevention. The key approaches are:

- Male and female condom use;
- Testing and Counselling for HIV and Sexually Transmitted Infections (STIs);
- Testing and Counselling – Linkage to TB care;
- Voluntary medical male circumcision (VMMC);
- Harm reduction for people who inject and use drugs; and
- Elimination of Mother to Child transmission of HIV.

**Pharmacists' Participation in HIV Care and Control in India:** The job responsibilities of pharmacists are clearly defined under National AIDS Control Programme. More details will be found in National Health Programme Chapter. The pharmacists' responsibilities can be summarised as: To

- Dispense ARV and OIs medicines
- Maintain medicines stock and medicines dispensing registers
- Ensure ART centre has stock of ARVs for at least 3 months
- Inform the ART Nodal Officer of the centre as and when the stock falls below the 3 month back up stock
- Ensure adequate stock of medicines required for treatment and prophylaxis of OIs
- Advise the patients and family about importance of adherence during each visit
- Advise the patient on possible medicines toxicities and reporting of the same if significant
- Maintain a monthly sheet for expiry of medicines stock.
- Do Pill count and report any adverse effects of ARVs or any OIs

**Bottom Line**

- HIV Infection is preventable. Treatment with ART reduces the chance of transmission. It is a public health problem not only for India but for entire globe.
- ART enables people living with HIV to lead a healthy productive life. It also prevents the progress of HIV to AIDS.
- HIV infection's advanced stage is AIDS. HIV is the cause and AIDS is the outcome. With AIDS, the person becomes more susceptible to opportunities infection like TB.
- The common symptoms are: headache, fever, sore throat, Muscle soreness, Rash, Mouth or Genital Ulcer, Swollen lymph nodes on the neck, Joint pain, Diarrhoea, Night sweats, Blurred and distorted vision, Cough and shortness of breath, Persistent white spots or unusual lesion on the tongue or mouth, Shaking chills or fever higher than 100 °F / 38 °C for several weeks, Persistent and unexplained fatigue, Weight loss.
- HIV is a major global public health problem and the highest prevalence was reported in Sub-Saharan Africa. The adult prevalence of HIV in India is reported at 0.22% in 2017. Mizoram has the highest prevalence at 2.04%.
- NACO is the nodal agency for implementing National AIDS Control Programme. India is a signatory to SDG on HIV elimination – Ending HIV epidemic by 2030. India has developed its strategic plan 2017-2024.
- Primarily ELISA and rapid tests are used for screening / diagnosing HIV. Molecular assay is required for testing patients in the window period and infants born to HIV positive mothers.
- While there is no cure, ART is successful in prolonging the life of HIV positive patients. NACO has well defined regimen – a combination of three or more ARV drugs.
- HIV can be transmitted through: Unprotected vaginal or anal sex with a person living with HIV; Blood transfusion of contaminated blood; Sharing of needles, syringes, other injecting equippments, surgical equipment or other sharp instruments; and From HIV infected mother to infant during pregnancy, chld birth or breast feeding.
- Limiting the exposure to risk factors is the primary strategy for HIV Infection.
- Pharmacists are part of National AIDS Control Programme and they have well defined responsibilities.

## Bibliography

1. https://www.nhp.gov.in/hiv-aids_pg accessed on 30th April 2020
2. https://www.who.int/health-topics/hiv-aids/#tab=tab_1 accessed on 30th April 2020
3. National Guidelines for HIV Testing, National AIDS Control Organization, GOI, 2015.
4. National Technical Guidelines on Anti-Retroviral Treatment, NACO, GOI, October 2018.
5. Training Manual on Intensified on TB/HIV Package for Pharmacists, Central TB Division and NACO, GOI, June 2008.

# Influenza

**After reading this chapter, you should be able to understand and appreciate:**

- Influenza as a public health problem of India;
- What causes Influenza and how Influenza spreads;
- Symptoms of Influenza;
- Global and Indian Burden of Influenza ;
- Diagnosis and Treatment available; and
- Prevention Control Strategies Practiced.

Seasonal influenza (the flu) is an acute respiratory infection caused by influenza viruses. It is common in all parts of the world. Most people recover without treatment.

## Source of Infection and Mode of Transmission

There are 4 types of influenza viruses, types A, B, C and D. Influenza A and B viruses circulate and cause seasonal epidemics of disease.

- Influenza A viruses are further classified into subtypes according to the combinations of the proteins on the surface of the virus. Currently circulating in humans are subtype A(H1N1) and A(H3N2) influenza viruses.
- Influenza B viruses are not classified into subtypes but can be broken down into lineages. Influenza type B viruses belong to either B/Yamagata or B/Victoria lineage.

Seasonal influenza spreads easily, with rapid transmission in crowded areas including schools and nursing homes. When an infected person coughs or sneezes, droplets containing viruses (infectious droplets) are dispersed into the air and can infect persons in close proximity. The virus can also be spread by hands contaminated with influenza viruses. To prevent transmission, people should cover their mouth and nose with a tissue when coughing and wash their hands regularly.

The time from infection to illness, known as the incubation period, is about 2 days, but ranges from 1–4 days.

**Word of Mouth**

**Symptoms:** [Symptoms begin 1–4 days after infection and usually last around a week.]

- Sudden onset of fever,
- Cough (usually dry) [The cough can be severe and can last two or more weeks].
- Headache,
- Muscle and joint pain,
- Severe malaise (feeling unwell), sore throat and a runny nose.
- Risk group:
- Age ≥ 65 years
- Pregnancy (including up to two weeks post-partum)
- Children aged less than 5 years especially less than 2 years
- Chronic respiratory disease
- Chronic heart, kidney, liver or neurological disease
- Diabetes mellitus
- Blood disorders (including haemoglobinopathies)
- Persons with immunosuppression (including HIV/ AIDS & use of long-term corticosteroids, Post- transplant patients)
- Extreme obesity (BMI ≥ 40 kg/m2)

**Global Burden and Initiative:** There are around a billion cases of seasonal influenza annually, including 3–5 million cases of severe illness. It causes 290 000 to 650 000 respiratory deaths annually. Ninety-nine percent of deaths in children under 5 years of age with influenza-related lower respiratory tract infections are in developing countries.

**India's Burden and National Programme:** Union Health Ministry is keeping a close watch on the Seasonal Influenza situation in various States/UTs through the Integrated Disease Surveillance Programme (IDSP) network on real-time basis. The Ministry is also tracking and keeping a close watch on morbidity and mortality due to the H3N2 subtype of the seasonal Influenza. Some deaths were reported from Karnataka and Haryana from H3N2 influenza.

India every year witnesses two peaks of seasonal influenza: one from Jan to March and other in post monsoon season. The cases arising from seasonal influenza are expected to decline from March end. State surveillance officers are fully geared to meet this public health challenge. During 2023, 8125 cases were reported with 129 deaths.

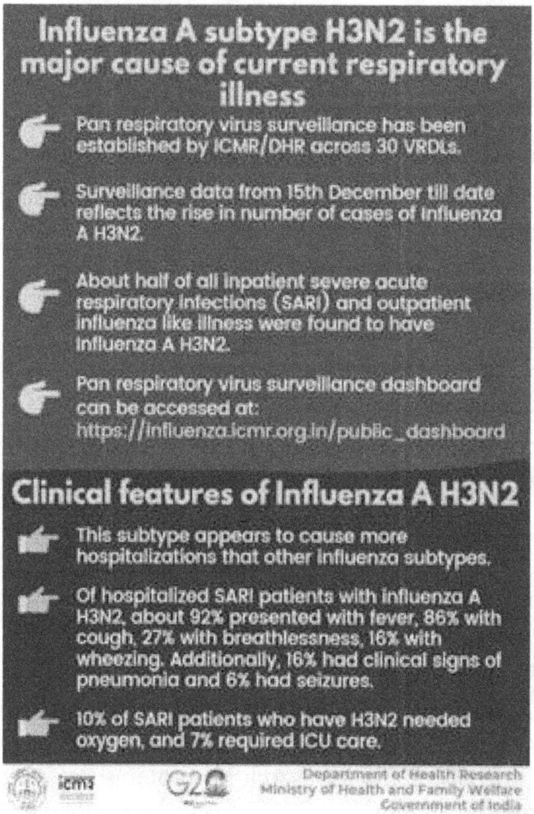


## Diagnosis and Treatment

**Diagnosis:** Clinical diagnosis and laboratory diagnostic tests are diagnostic tools.

**Treatment:** Most people recover from influenza on their own. People with severe symptoms or other medical conditions should seek medical care.

People with mild symptoms should:

- stay home to avoid infecting other people
- rest
- drink plenty of fluids
- treat other symptoms such as fever
- seek medical care if symptoms get worse.

People at high risk or with severe symptoms should be treated with antiviral medications as soon as possible.

## Prevention and Control

- Vaccination is the best way to prevent influenza.
- Isolation of the patients and avoiding direct contact.
- The patient and the care giver should use mask.
- Avoid hand shaking and frequent hand washing with soap and water are recommended.

**Role of Pharmacists:** There is no defined responsibilities. However, the pharmacists can:

- Participate in community education on Influenza awareness, prevention and control.
- Community pharmacists should advice the customers and / or patients on personal hygiene and managing influenza.

**Bottom Line**

- Seasonal influenza (the flu) is an acute respiratory infection caused by influenza viruses. It is common in all parts of the world. Most people recover without treatment.
- Influenza A and B viruses circulate and cause seasonal epidemics of disease. Influenza A viruses are further classified into subtypes according to the combinations of the proteins on the surface of the virus. Currently circulating in humans are subtype A(H1N1) and A(H3N2) influenza viruses.
- Seasonal influenza spreads easily, with rapid transmission in crowded areas including schools and nursing homes. When an infected person coughs or sneezes, droplets containing viruses (infectious droplets) are dispersed into the air and can infect persons in close proximity.
- The time from infection to illness is about 2 days, but ranges from 1–4 days.
- Common symptoms are: Sudden on set of fever, Cough (usually dry), Headache, Muscle and joint pain, Severe malaise (feeling unwell), sore throat and a runny nose.
- High risks group: Age $\geq$ 65 years, Pregnancy (including up to two weeks post-partum), Children aged less than 5 years, Chronic respiratory disease
- Chronic heart, kidney, liver or neurological disease, Diabetes mellitus, Blood disorders (including haemoglobinopathies), Persons with immunosuppression (including HIV/AIDS & use of long-term corticosteroids, Post- transplant patients) and Extreme obesity (BMI $\geq$ 40 $kg/m^2$)

- Globally there are around a billion cases of seasonal influenza annually, including 3–5 million cases of severe illness.
- Union Health Ministry is keeping a close watch on the Seasonal Influenza situation in various States/UTs through the Integrated Disease Surveillance Programme (IDSP) network on real-time basis.
- ***Diagnosis:*** Clinical diagnosis and laboratory diagnostic tests are diagnostic tools.
- ***Treatment:*** Most people recover from influenza on their own. People with severe symptoms or other medical conditions should seek medical care.
- People with mild symptoms should: stay home to avoid infecting other people, rest, drink plenty of fluids, treat other symptoms such as fever.
- People at high risk or with severe symptoms should be treated with antiviral medications as soon as possible.
- Vaccination is the best way to prevent influenza.
- Isolation of the patients and avoiding direct contact.
- The patient and the care giver should use mask.
- Avoid hand shaking and frequent hand washing with soap and water are recommended.
- Pharmacists may participate in community education on Influenza awareness, prevention and control.

## Bibliography

1. Flu Facts, WHO – India, January 2019.
2. https://www.who.int/health-topics/influenza-seasonal#tab=tab_3 accessed on 9th December 2024.
3. https://www.who.int/news-room/fact-sheets/detail/influenza-(seasonal) accessed on 9th December 2024.

# Leprosy

"Leprosy work is not merely medical relief, it is transforming frustration in life into the joy of dedication, personal ambition into selfless service"

- MK Gandhi

**After reading this chapter, you should be able to understand and appreciate:**

- Leprosy as a health issue;
- What causes Leprosy and how Leprosy spreads;
- Symptoms of Leprosy;
- Global and Indian Burden of Leprosy;
- Diagnosis and Treatment available; and
- Prevention Control Strategies Practiced.

Leprosy, also known as Hansen's disease, is a chronic mildly infectious disease caused by a slow growing bacillus, *Mycobacterium leprae.* It predominantly affects the skin and peripheral nerves resulting in neuropathy and long term consequences like deformities and disability. The disease is associated with stigma especially when deformities are present. The affected people are often abandoned by their families, isolated from society and deprived of their freedom. They face very harsh life.

The disease is very ancient to the mankind. In Sanskrit, leprosy is known as 'Kustha'. It finds reference in Atharva Veda (believed to be written 1400 BC). Caraka, the court physician to Emperor Kaniska, described the causes and symptoms of leprosy in his treatise 'Charaka – Samhita'. It is also written in Purana that Lord Krishna cursed his son 'Samba' to have Kustha. There are stories of lepers in Bible.

Though leprosy is no longer viewed as a public health problem, it is found in 159 countries including India. The current global prevalence rate is 0.2 per 10,000 population (2018). The leprosy is divided into two types based on number of skin lesions, presence of nerve involvement and identification of bacillus on slit – skin smear: Paucibacillary (PB) where there are few skin lesions (up to five); and Multibacillary (MB) where there are multiple lesions, nodules, plaques, thicken dermis or skin infiltration (more than five).

Dr Gerhard A. Hansen, a Norwegian Physician, discovered the cause of leprosy as bacterium, *Mycobacterium leprae in 1873.* Hence, the leprosy is named after him as Hansen's disease.

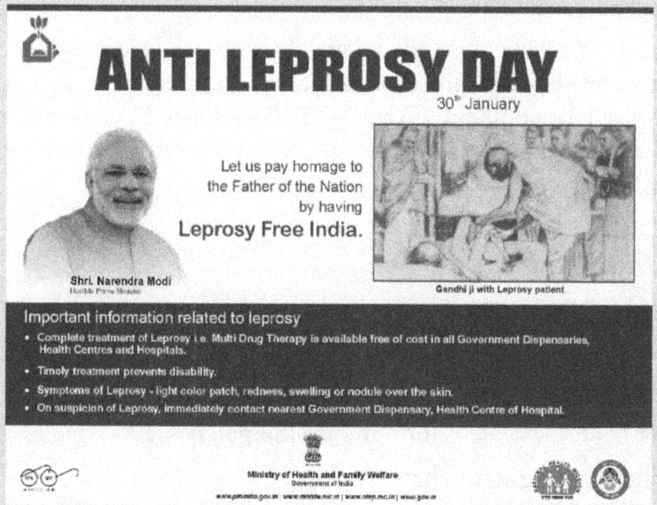


World Leprosy Day is celebrated on the last Sunday of every year to raise awareness of the disease. In India, it is celebrated 30th January each year to coincide with the death of Mahatma Gandhi as a tribute to Father of Nation who had compassion for the people affected with leprosy.

**Source of Infection and Mode of Transmission:** Untreated leprosy patient is the only source of bacteria and thus infection. The transmission occurs in this sequences:

- From respiratory tract of infected person into environment (droplets from nose / mouth)
- Organism enters the healthy body through respiratory system.

Organism migrates to nerves and skin (may cause permanent disability, if not treated). *M. leprae* multiplies slowly and the incubation period on an average is 5 years. The symptoms may appear within one year but may also take as long as twenty years or even longer.

**Regulations related to Leprosy:** Removing the discrimination against leprosy affected people -

1. In 2019, India made legislation to remove leprosy as a ground for divorce and made changes in five personal laws: Hindu Marriage Act; Dissolution of Muslim Marriage Act; Divorce Act (for Christians); Special Marriage Act; and Hindu Adoption & Maintenance Act.

2. In 2016, India repealed the Indian Lepers Act 1898. Under the Act, the affected persons were banished to colonies far from cities and towns to stop the spread as there no cure was available. This is a small but positive step towards eliminating discrimination against the leprosy affected persons.
3. Several states have amended laws to remove references to persons affected by leprosy in discriminatory provision: Example Tamil University (Amendment ) Act, 2022. This deleted the provision which was disqualifying persons from becoming the member of any of the authorities.

**Word of Mouth**

**Symptoms:**

- Light patches on the skin in the dark skinned person; Darker or reddish patches in the pale skinned person.
- Loss or decrease of sensation in the skin patches.
- Numbness or tingling in hand or feet.
- Weakness of hands, feet or eye lids.
- Painful nerves.
- Swelling or lumps in the face or ear lobes.
- Painless wounds or burns on hands or feet.

**Risk factors:**

Those living in endemic areas with poor conditions like:

- Inadequate bedding.
- Contaminated water.
- Insufficient diet
- Other diseases that compromise immune function.

**Global Burden and Initiative:** Though elimination of leprosy as public health problem [It is pragmatically defined as registered prevalence of less than one case of leprosy per 10,000 population] was achieved globally in 2000, around 2 lakh new cases appear every year. The prevalence rate at the end of 2018 was just 0.2 per 10,000 population.

The World Health Organization had launched global strategy 2016-20 titled "Acceleration towards leprosy free world". Leprosy related discrimination, stigma and prejudice are the most powerful barriers in ending leprosy. The global strategy is structured around three core pillars:

I. Strengthening government ownership, coordination and partnership;

II. Stopping leprosy and its complications; and
III. Stop discrimination and promote inclusion.

The strategy aims to achieve:

- Zero disabilities among new paediatric patients;
- Grade – 2 (Visible deformity in hands and feet; or severe visual impairments) disability rate of less than 1 case per 1 million people; and
- Zero countries with legislation allowing discrimination on the basis of leprosy.

Under the strategic plan WHO has developed tools like "Monitoring and Evaluation Guide"; "Guideline for the diagnosis, treatment and prevention of leprosy" in order help countries implementing the leprosy programmes.

Multi Drug Therapy (MDT), a combination of two or more of the following: Rifampicin, Clofazimine and Dapsone, is recommended for treatment. WHO supplies this free of cost. Besides WHO, International Federation of Anti-Leprosy Associations and Global Partnership for Zero Leprosy have been working to achieve the target "Zero transmission, Zero disability and Zero stigma".

## India's Burden and National Programme

In 2005, India was officially declared to have eliminated leprosy when the new cases fell to less than 1 in 10,000. Number of cases have steadily declined over the years, yet around 2 lakh fresh cases appear every year. State of Chhattisgarh and Dadra and Nagar Haveli (U.T.) have remained to achieve elimination. Other states namely Bihar, Jharkhand, Odisha and Lakshadweep (UT) have reported prevalence rate >1/10,000 population, as on 31stMarch 2018. This shows that Bihar, Chhattisgarh, Odisha, Jharkhand, Uttar Pradesh, West Bengal and Maharashtra continue to be the hotspots. During the period 10,287 child cases (8.15%) and 4552 Grade 2 disability cases (3.61%) were detected, making a concern for continued transmission and delayed case detection. India bears more than 50% of global burden of leprosy. High population density, poor sanitation and inadequate access to nutrition are the primary reasons continuing high incidence rate.

India started its National Leprosy Control Programme in 1954 and since then many initiatives are introduced. Currently the programme is called National Leprosy Eradication Programme (NLEP). Three pronged strategy was introduced in the NLEP since 2016-17:

I. Leprosy Case Detection Campaign (LCDC)
II. Focussed Leprosy Campaign
III. Special Plan to Hard to Reach Area

Since leprosy is no longer perceived as public health issue, the NLEP is absorbed into National Rural Health Mission. With this the state level programme is diluted.

Despite achievements, there have been large number of undetected cases in the community and transmission continues. Several innovative initiatives are introduced:

- Enhanced active and early case detection through three pronged strategy: (i) Leprosy Case Detection Campaign (LCDC) for endemic districts; (ii) Focussed leprosy campaign for hotspots; and (iii) Special plan for case detection in hard to reach areas.
- Enhanced early reporting of cases.
- Prevention of leprosy amongst contacts.
- Over all strengthening of programme with special emphasis on monitoring and feedback.

In addition various services are being provided under the programme for disability prevention and medical rehabilitation – reaction management, provision of MCR footwear, aids and appliances, referral services for management of cases and reconstructive surgery.

Sparsh Leprosy Elimination Campaign (SLEP) was launched on the 150$^{th}$ Birth Anniversary of Mahatma Gandhi focussing on conducting two rounds of leprosy case detection campaign: First round covered in September – October 2018 and Second round in February 2019 with significant success.

## Diagnosis and Treatment

**Diagnosis:** At least one of the following cardinal (unique and very important) signs must be present to diagnose leprosy:

- Hypo-pigmented or reddish skin lesion(s) with definite sensory deficit;
- Involvement of peripheral nerves, as demonstrated by definite thickening with loss of sensation and weakness / paralysis of the corresponding muscles of hands, feet or eyes; and
- Demonstration of *Mycobacterium leprae* in the lesion (examination of slit-skin smear).

**Treatment:** The multidrug therapy (MDT) is an effective and potential tool in curing leprosy. Adherence to treatment and completion of the full course are vital not only for obtaining complete cure but also for reducing the chance of antimicrobial resistance, another public health challenge.

| MDT Regimen (Adult)* | | | |
|---|---|---|---|
| Type of Leprosy | Drug, Dosage Form and Strength | Frequency of Administration | Duration of Treatment |
| MB Leprosy | Rifampicin Capsule -600 mg | Once a month | 12 months |
| | Dapsone Tablet – 100 mg | Daily | |
| | Clofazimine Capsule – 300 mg | Once a month | |
| | Clofazimine Capsule – 50 mg | Daily | |
| PB Leprosy | Rifampicin Capsule -600 mg | Once a month | 6 months |
| | Dapsone Tablet – 100 mg | Daily | |

*Appropriate dose adjustment on the basis of body weight needed for children.

| Side Effects of Anti-Leprosy MDT | | | |
|---|---|---|---|
| **Drug / Side Effect** | | **Sign and Symptoms** | **Management** |
| Dapsone | Anaemia | Pallor, Tiredness, edema of feet and breathlessness | Give anti-worm treatment and iron and folic acid tablets. Stop Dapsone if Hb< 8 g % |
| | Severe skin Rash (Exfoliative dermatitis) | Extensive scaling, itching, ulcers in the mouth and eyes, jaundice and reduced urine output | Stop Dapsone. Refer to hospital immediately. Never restart. |
| | Hepatitis Jaundice | Loss of appetite, vomiting | Stop Dapsone. Refer to treat Hepatitis. |
| | Nephritis | Edema of face and feet, reduced urine output | Stop Dapsone. Refer to treat Nephritis |
| Rifampicin | No significance | Reddish coloration of urine, saliva and sweat | Reassure the patient |
| | Hepatitis (liver damage) | Jaundice (yellow colour of skin, eyeballs and urine). Loss of appetite and vomiting | Stop Rifampicin. Refer to hospital. Restart after the jaundice subsides. |
| | Allergy | Urticaria, Skin rash | Stop Rifampicin |
| Clofazimine | Dark Colour | Brownish-red discoloration of skin, urine and body fluids | Reassure the patient that it Will fade after completion of treatment |
| | Ichthyosis | Dryness and scaling of the skin, itching | Apply oil to the skin. Reassure the patient. |
| | Eye | Conjunctiva- dryness | Moistening eye drops |
| | Abdominal symptoms | Abdominal pain, nausea and vomiting with high doses (used for Type II reaction) | Symptomatic treatment. Reassure the patient. Stop high doses |

**Key Points:**

- Leprosy is caused by a germ, *Mycobacterium leprae*. It is neither a curse nor hereditary.
- Casual touch like shaking hands or playing together or working in the same office will not transmit or spread leprosy.
- Leprosy usually starts as a patch without sensation:
    - No feeling of touch and pain
    - Can be anywhere on the body
- Can be cured with MDT within 6-12 months of treatment.

**Prevention and Control:** The NLEP recommends

- **Primary Prevention:** Chemoprophylaxis by single dose Rifampicin (SDR) / Immunoprophylaxis by *Mycobacterium indicus Pranii* (MiP). It provides around 60% protection.
- **Secondary Prevention:** Early diagnosis and complete treatment of leprosy cases prevents community transmission.
- **Teriary Prevention:** Disability prevention and medical rehabilitation is tool by which leprosy patient can lead a good quality life.

**Role of Pharmacists:** There are no defined responsibilities as described under National TB programme. However, the pharmacists can:

- Maintain and manage treatment register & drug stock register at health facilities level.
- Participate in community education on creating awareness on leprosy.
- Guide patients on medication adherence.
- Document the adverse drug reaction and submit the report to the pharmacovigilance programme national coordinating centre.

**Bottom Line**

- Leprosy, also known as Hansen's disease, is a curable infectious disease caused by *Mycobacterium leprae.*
- Common symptoms are: light patches on the skin of dark skinned person / darker or reddish patches in the pale skinned person; loss or decrease of sensation in the skin patches; numbness or tingling in hand or feet; weakness of hands, feet or eye lids; painful nerves; swelling or lumps in the face or ear lobes; and painless wounds or burns on hands or feet.
- Though leprosy is no longer perceived as a public health issue, globally around 2 lakh fresh cases appear every year of which India's share is more than 50%.

- The global goal is to achieve "zero transmission, zero disability and zero stigma". Discrimination and stigma are the major barriers to achieve the target.
- Through National Leprosy Eradication Programme, India introduced three pronged strategy:
- The MDT containing two or more combinations of the following: rifampicin, Dapsone and Clofazimine is an effective cure of leprosy. MDT is available free in health facilities. Adherence and completion of treatment is critical to achieve cure and prevent development of antimicrobial resistance, another public health threat.

## Bibliography

1. Annual Report 2018-2019, Ministry of Health and Welfare, Government of India.
2. Global Leprosy Strategy: 2016-2020, Accelerating towards a leprosy free world, World Health Organization, SEARO, 2016.
3. Guidelines for the Diagnosis, Treatment and Prevention of Leprosy, World Health Organization, 2018.
4. https://www.nhp.gov.in/disease/skin/leprosy accessed on 23.4.2020
5. Training Manual for Medical Officers, National Leprosy Eradication Programme, GOI, 2019.

# Lymphatic Filariasis

**After reading this chapter, you should be able to understand and appreciate:**

- Lymphatic Filariasis (LF) as a public health problem of India;
- What causes LF and how LF spreads;
- Symptoms of LF;
- Global and Indian Burden of LF;
- Diagnosis and Treatment available; and
- Prevention Control Strategies Practiced.

Lymphatic filariasis (LF), commonly known as 'Elephantiasis', is a public health problem in India. The disease has been known in India since ancient times. It is mentioned in our ancient 'Susruta Samhita', a treatise dates back to the sixth century BC. It is caused by infection with parasites classified as nematodes (roundworms) of the family Filarioidea. It is disfiguring, disabling disease usually occurred in childhood. In the early stages, there are no symptoms. Normal daily activities becomes difficult due to frequent infections. Though it is not fatal, it causes personal trauma, social stigma and economic burden to the affected person and family.

Yellapragada Subba Row, an Indian born Medical Scientist, discovered diethylcarbamazine, anti-filarial medicine, in 1947. He is known for many other discoveries like folic acid, methotrexate, tetracyclines.

## Source of Infection and Mode of Transmission

Filariasis is caused by several round, coiled and thread-like parasitic worms: *Wuchereria bancrofti* or *Brugia malayi* are main infecting agents in India. These parasites after getting deposited on skin penetrate on their own or through the opening created by mosquito bites to reach the lymphatic system. It is the man-mosquito contact that is critical of transmission.

Adult worms nest in the lymphatic vessels and disrupt the normal function of the lymphatic system. As these parasites live in lymphatic system are also called lymphatic parasites. The worms can live for approximately 6–

8 years and, during their life time, produce millions of microfilariae (immature larvae) that circulate in the blood.

Mosquitoes are infected with microfilariae by ingesting blood when biting an infected host. Microfilariae mature into infective larvae within the mosquito. When infected mosquitoes bite people, mature parasite larvae are deposited on the skin from where they can enter the body. The larvae then migrate to the lymphatic vessels where they develop into adult worms, thus continuing a cycle of transmission.

The microfilaria in mosquito develops into three stages and under optimum conditions of temperature and humidity; the duration of the cycle in the mosquito (extensive incubation period) is about 10-14 days. When the infective mosquito feeds on other human host, the infective larvae are deposited at the site of mosquito bite from where the infective larvae get into lymphatic system. In the human host, the infective larvae develop into adult male and female worms. The adult worms survive for about 5-8 years or sometimes as long as 15 years or more.

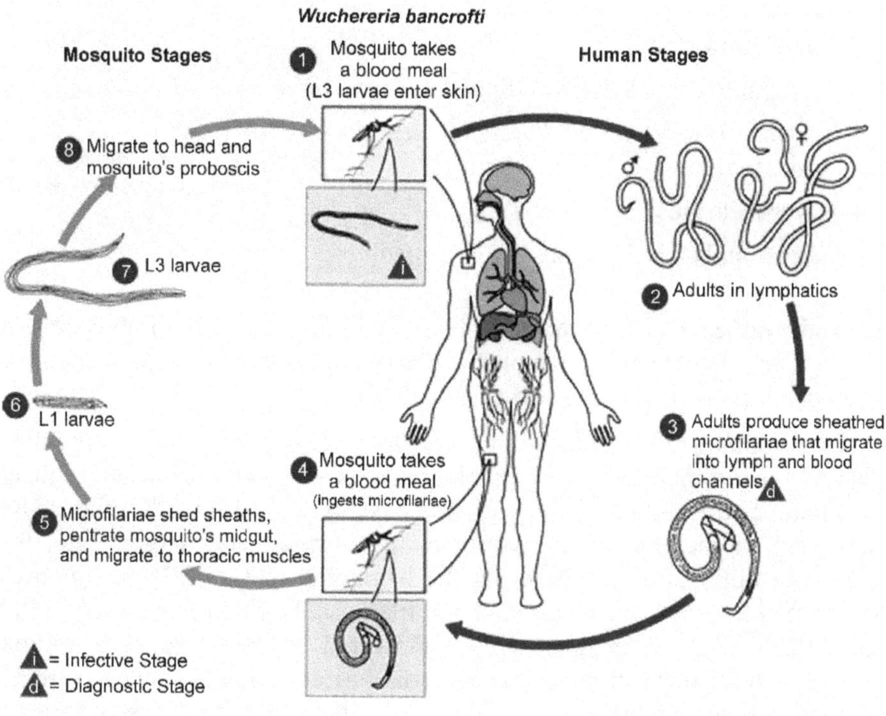


[Source: https://nvbdcp.gov.in/index4.php?lang=1&level=0&linkid=454&lid=3731]

Man is the definitive host i.e. where the mature adult male and female parasites mate and produce microfilariae whereas the mosquito is the intermediate host. The following mosquito species are involved: *Culex quinquefasciatus* and *Mansonia annulifera / M. uniformis*. The vector mosquitoes breed in polluted water, cess pits and in areas with inadequate drainage.

The clinical incubation period, time interval from the invasion of infective larvae to the appearance of clinical signs, is about 8-16 months.

**Word of Mouth**

**Symptoms:** Divided into - asymptomatic, acute, and chronic conditions.

**Asymptomatic condition:**

- No external signs of infection but continue transmission of parasites.

**Acute condition:**

- Local inflammation involving skin, lymph nodes and lymphatic vessels.

**Chronic condition:**

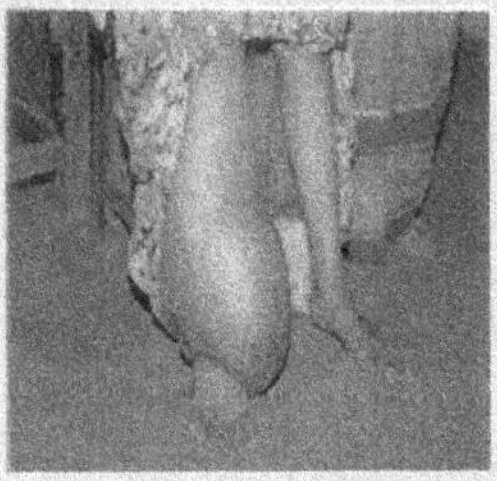

- Lymphoedema (tissue swelling)
- Elephantiasis (skin or tissue thickening of limbs)
- Hydrocele (scrotal swelling)
- Breast and Genital organs are also involved.

**Global Burden and Initiative:** Globally 893 million people of 49 countries are remain threatened by lymphatic filariasis and they require preventive chemotherapy to stop the spread of LF (2018).

In response to World Health Assembly resolution and to eliminate filariasis as a public health problem, in 2000 WHO launched Global Programme to Eliminate Lymphatic Filariasis (GPELF). In 2012, the WHO neglected tropical diseases roadmap reconfirmed the target date for achieving elimination by 2020. At the beginning of GPELF, 81 countries were considered endemic for lymphatic filariasis. During the period of 2000 to 2018, 7.7 billion treatments were delivered to more than 910 million people at least once in 68 countries. This has considerably reduced transmission in many places. The population requiring Mass Drug Administration has declined by 42% (597 million) where infection prevalence has been reduced below elimination thresholds. The overall economic benefit of the programme during 2000-2007 is conservatively estimated at US$ 24 billion. Treatments until 2015 are estimated to have averted at least US$ 100.5 billion of economic loss. The WHO's strategy to eliminate LF by 2020 is based on:

- stopping the spread of infection through large-scale annual treatment of all eligible people in an area or region where infection is present; and
- alleviating the suffering caused by lymphatic filariasis through provision of the recommended basic package of care.

Our neighbouring countries: Sri Lanka and Bangladesh are on the path of eliminating LF.

**India's Burden and National Programme:** The lymphatic filariasis is a public health problem in India. India shares about 40% of the global burden of LF. As of 2018, the country had more than 12.9 lakh cases of filariasis. The disease is endemic in 256 districts across 16 states and 5 union territories. Bihar has the maximum burden and accounts for about 25% of total lymphoedema cases.

Being a signatory to World Health Assembly's resolution on 1997 for Global Elimination of LF, the Government of India launched National Elimination of Lymphatic Filariasis Programme in 2004. Against the global target of eliminating filariasis by 2020, India planned to eliminate LF by 2015 and date was extended to 2017. Though the elimination target is not yet achieved, there has been significant improvement in the filariasis situation. At present, the LF programme falls under the umbrella of National Vector Borne Disease Control Programme (NVBDCP). The states are responsible for implementation of the programme while the Directorate of NVBDCP, located in Delhi, offers technical assistance, policies, and assistance to the states in the form of cash and commodity. Under the National Programme these two strategies are followed:

I. ***Transmission Control:*** Annual Mass Drug Administration with Diethyl-carbamazine Citrate (DEC) alone or DEC and Albendazole combination is practiced to prevent the occurrence of new infection and disease. Triple drug therapy is also now introduced in selected five districts [Arwal of Bihar, Simdega of Jharkhand, Varanasi of Uttar Pradesh, Nagpur of Maharastra and Yadgir of Karnataka]. Ivermectin is includes as third drug.

II. ***Disability Prevention and Morbidity Management*:** The states have been advised to provide hospital based and home based care to those infected patients for lymphoedema and hydrocele. The morbidity management kits are also provided. Health personnel including medical officers, paramedics, drug administrators, Lab technicians have been trained annually as a part of increasing capacity building. Under the morbidity management programme, 1.4 lakh hydrocele operations were done.

| **Milestones in Filariasis Control Programme** | | | |
|---|---|---|---|
| 1955 | National Filaria Control Programme launched | 2004 | National Elimination of Lymphatic Filariasis Programme launched |
| 1996-97 | Annual Mass Drug Administration introduced | 2006-07 | DEC + Albendazole combination introduced |
| 2002 | National Health Policy fixed the target to eliminate by 2015 | 2018-19 | Triple Drug Therapy (IDA) is launched in selected districts |
| 2003 | Convergence with other vector borne diseases | | |

**Mass Drug Administration**: DEC tablets have been administered to all eligible population in the affected areas on a single day, National Filaria Day. National Filaria Day is celebrated every year but not on fixed day like other health day. Albendazole was included later. In some districts, third drug, Ivermectin, is also included.

**Dosage of DEC Tablets (100 mg Strength)**

<table>
<tr><th>Age in Years</th><th>Number of DEC Tablets</th><td rowspan="5">Adverse Effects: Persons with high microfilariae density may experience adverse effects like headache, bodyache, nausea and vomiting which result from death of microfilariae. These effects are temporary and subsides within a day or two symptomatic treatment. Rarely localized reactions such as swelling and tenderness of lymph node occur.<br>Contraindications: Children below two years and pregnant or severely ill persons.</td></tr>
<tr><td>< 2</td><td>Not to use</td></tr>
<tr><td>2-5</td><td>One tablet</td></tr>
<tr><td>6-14</td><td>Two tablets</td></tr>
<tr><td>15 and above</td><td>Three tablets</td></tr>
</table>

## Diagnosis and Treatment

### Diagnosis

- Microscopic detection of microfilariae – The blood is collected at night as the microfilariae circulate in blood at night (nocturnal periodicity). A thick smear should be made and stained with giemsa or hematoxylin and eosin; and then examined under microscope. Presence of microfilariae is the confirmation.
- Serological test - Patients with active filarial infection typically have elevated levels of antifilarial IgG4 in the blood and these can be detected using routine assays.

### Treatment

- Drug treatment regimen - mass drug administration (MDA) in which a single dose of two medicines are given together - albendazole (400 mg) with either ivermectin (150-200 mcg/kg) in areas where onchocerciasis (river blindness) is also endemic or diethylcarbamazine citrate (DEC)

(6 mg/kg) in areas where onchocerciasis is not endemic. These medicines clear microfilariae from the bloodstream.

- Surgery for hydrocele.
- Maintenance of Good hygiene of the affected part prevents the worsening of the lymphoedema and secondary bacterial skin infections.
- The affected limb should be kept elevated and regular exercises should be done to improve the lymph flow.

## Prevention and Control

- Annual Mass Drug Administration (MDA) of single dose of DEC (Diethylcarbamazine citrate) and Albendazole for 5 years or more to the eligible population (except pregnant women, children below 2 years of age and seriously ill persons) to interrupt transmission of the disease.
- Avoiding mosquito bites is another type of prevention. The mosquitoes that bear the microscopic worms typically bite people during the night. If living in an area where Lymphatic Filariasis is prevalent, one should:
    - Apply insect repellent to uncovered skin.
    - Sleep under a mosquito net.
    - If possible, stay indoors between dusk and dawn.
    - Take an annual dose of medicine that kills the worms circulating in the blood.
    - When outdoors, wear long pants and long-sleeved shirts to protect against mosquito bites.

**Role of Pharmacists:** There is no defined responsibilities as described under National TB programme. However, the pharmacists can:

- Participate in community education on Filariasis awareness, prevention and control.
- They can participate in Mass Drug Administration Activity.
- Community pharmacists should advice the customers and / or patients on personal hygiene and managing the ailment.

**Bottom Line**

- Lymphatic Filariasis (LF), also called Elephantiasis, is a public health problem of India causing personal trauma, social stigma and economic burden to the affected person and family.
- LF is caused by nematodes parasites: *Wuchereria bancro-fti* or *Brugia malayi.* Man-mosquito contact is critical of transmission as it is spread by mosquito bite.

- Common symptoms are: Lymphoedema, Elephantiasis, and Hydrocele.
- It is a global problem: 893 million people of 49 countries are under threat of LF. India shares about 40% of global burden. As of 2018, LF if endemic in 256 districts of the country. Sri Lanka and Bangladesh are on the path of eliminating LF.
- Directorate of National Vector Borne Disease Control Programme is the nodal agency for implementation of LF elimination programme.
- Transmission through mass drug administration programme; and Disability Prevention & Morbidity Management are two pillars of prevention and control strategy.

## Bibliography

1. Annual Report 2018-2019, Ministry of Health and Welfare, Government of India.
2. https://nvbdcp.gov.in/index1.php?lang=1&level=1&sublinkid=5777&lid=3691 accessed on 21st April 2020.
3. https://www.nhp.gov.in/disease/blood-lymphatic/filariasis accessed on 21 April 2020
4. https://www.who.int/news-room/fact-sheets/detail/lymphatic-filariasis accessed on 21 April2020
5. Sabine Specht and colleagues, Elimination of lymphatic filariasis in South East Asia, Neglected Diseases and Innovation in South Asia, British Medical Journal, 22nd January 2019.

# Malaria

"Eradicating mosquitoes is a means to an end. An uninfected mosquito is harmless to humans – just a nuisance. An infected mosquito is a danger"

- T. K. Nalika

**After reading this chapter, you should be able to understand and appreciate:**

- Malaria as a public health issue;
- How does malaria occur and transmit;
- Symptoms of Malaria; and
- Global and India's burden.

Malaria is the most important parasitic disease of man and known for centuries. Malaria has been one of the public health problems of India. At one time it was considered to be a rural disease, but diversified under the pressure of developments into various ecotypes. These ecotypes have been identified as forest malaria, urban malaria, rural malaria, industrial malaria, border malaria and migration malaria. The name 'Malaria' is derived from Italian *mala* meaning 'bad' and *aria* meaning 'air'. The naming was done by the Italians in 18$^{th}$ Century. They believed that intermittent fevers were due to the 'bad odour' coming from the marshy areas and thus the name malaria. Even though the causative organism is known today, the name has stuck to this disease.

The reference to the persistence fever can be tracked back to earliest Hindu and Chinese Writings. The fifth century Greek Physician, 'Hippocrates' too described the clinical manifestation and some of the complications of malaria.

Sir Ronald Ross, Indian born British doctor, was awarded Nobel Prize in Physiology/Medicine in 1902 for his work on malaria. His discovery that the malaria parasites lodge in gastrointestinal tract of the female Anopheles mosquitoes and the transmission to humans through the biting of these mosquitoes laid the foundation for combating the disease. While examining each of the mosquitoes, on 20$^{th}$ August 1897 he noted different types of cells in the stomach of two mosquitoes which he assumed to be malaria parasites. He named this 20$^{th}$ August as Mosquito Day and even today the day has been celebrated as World Mosquito Day as a recognition of this remarkable discovery.

## Source of Infection and Mode of Transmission

The malaria is caused by the protozoa of genus *Plasmodium* and the four species of *Plasmodium* are known to cause malaria in humans: *Plasmodium malariae, Plasmodium vivax, Plasmodium falciparum, and Plasmodium ovale.* Malaria caused by *Plasmodium falciparum* and *Plasmodium vivax* is predominant in India. *Plasmodium vivax* is more prevalent in plain areas while *Plasmodium falciparum predominates* in forested and hilly areas. *Plasmodium falciparum* infections are known to cause severe form of malaria if not treated appropriately.

The malaria parasites are transmitted to humans by infective bite of female Anopheles mosquitoes. The transmission of vector borne diseases depends on prevalence of infective vectors and human-vector contact, which is further influenced by various factors such as climate, sleeping habits of people, density and biting of vectors etc. Man develops disease after 10 to 14 days of being bitten by an infective mosquito. The life cycle of malaria parasite in man and mosquito is given in the figure below:

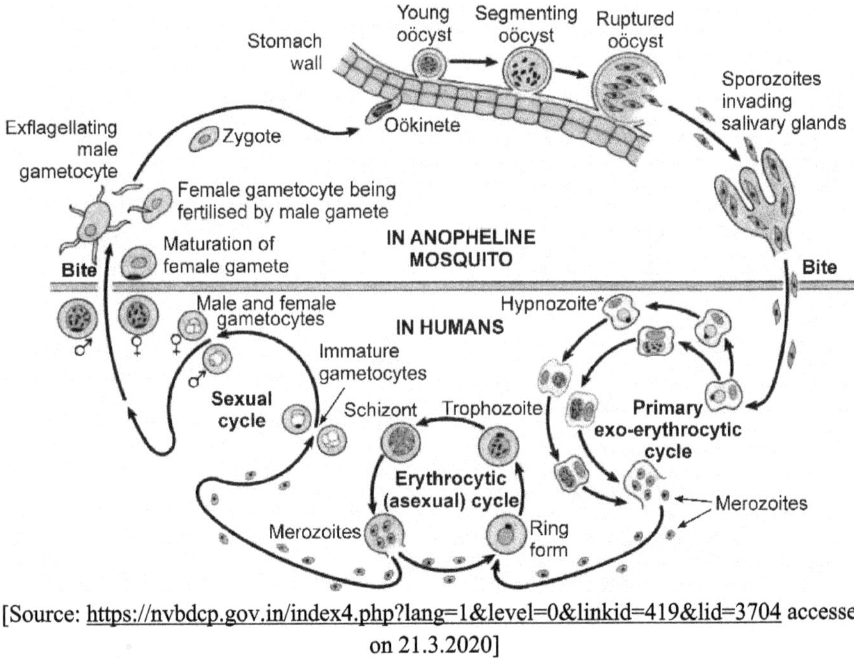


[Source: https://nvbdcp.gov.in/index4.php?lang=1&level=0&linkid=419&lid=3704 accessed on 21.3.2020]

**Word of Mouth**

**Symptoms**

- Fever, headache, vomiting and other flu-like symptoms
- Easy fatigue-ability due to anaemia, fits/convulsions and loss of consciousness

**Symptoms of Severe and Complicated Malaria:**

History of High Fever with at least one of the following:

- Prostration (inability to sit), altered consciousness lethargy or coma
- Breathing difficulties
- Severe anaemia
- Generalized convulsions/fits
- Inability to drink/vomiting
- Dark and/or limited production of urine

**Risk Factors:**

- Pregnancy poses a substantial risk to the mother, the foetus and the new born infant.

Malaria may be induced accidentally by hypodermic intra-muscular and intravenous injection of blood or plasma. Malaria parasites keep their infective activity for at least 14 days during storage at -4 °C.

**Global Burden and Initiatives:** An estimated 2.2 billion cases of malaria and 12.7 million deaths have been averted since 2000, but the disease remains a serious global health threat, particularly in the WHO African Region. According to WHO's latest *World malaria report (2024)*, there were an estimated 263 million cases and 597 000 malaria deaths worldwide in 2023. This represents about 11 million more cases in 2023 compared to 2022, and nearly the same number of deaths. Approximately 95% of the deaths occurred in the WHO African Region, where many at risk still lack access to the services they need to prevent, detect and treat the disease.

The burden of malaria and the challenges addressing it are most acute in Africa and its 11 countries bear about two-third of world's burden.

World Health Organization and Roll Back Malaria (RBM) Partnership to End Malaria launched the high burden to high impact (HBHI) country-led approach as a mechanism to prevent disease and save lives in the11 highest burden countries. The Global Fund is also offering partnership to fight against AIDS, TB and Malaria.

**India's Burden and National Programmes**: The malaria disease burden in India has declined by 80.53% (from 1.16 million to 0.23 million) and malaria deaths by 78.38% (from 384 to 83) in 2023 as compared to 2015. Malaria is more predominant in tribal districts of North-Eastern States, Odisha, Chhattisgarh and Jharkhand. Among 182 tribal and Left-Wing Extremist (LWE) districts, there has been 82.29% reduction in malaria morbidity and 77.01% reduction in malaria mortality in 2023 as compared to 2015. India has finally managed to control malaria, reduce mortality and has gotten out of the High-Burden-High-Impact (HBHI) group of endemic countries.

The National Vector Borne Disease Control Programme (NVBDCP) is initiated for prevention and control of malaria and other vector borne diseases. The States are responsible for the implementation of programme, while the Directorate of NVBDCP, Delhi, provides technical assistance, policies and assistance to the States in the form of cash & commodity. There have been consistently declining cases of malaria from 2.08 million in 2001 to 0.33 million in 2019 (provisional estimation). Similarly, *Plasmodium falciparum* cases have also declined from 1.0 million cases to 0.15 million during the same period. This indicates the declining of overall endemicity of malaria in the country. Annual Parasite Incidence (API), Annual Blood Smear Examination Rate (ABSER), Slide Positivity Rate (SPR), and Slide falciparum Rate (SfR) are the indicators used to measure malaria situation in the country.

Along with NHM, externally aided Global Fund project is being implemented in high endemic States. A total of 1.13 crores Long-Lasting Insecticidal Nets (LLINs) under GFTAM support are in the distribution process to the community residing in high malaria endemic areas of 7 North Eastern States, Chhattisgarh and Madhya Pradesh in 2023

Encouraged by the success achieved in malaria control in recent years, the vision of India's malaria control programme has now shifted to sustained malaria elimination to contribute more effectively to improved health and quality of life of the people. The National Framework for malaria elimination in India aims elimination of malaria by 2030.

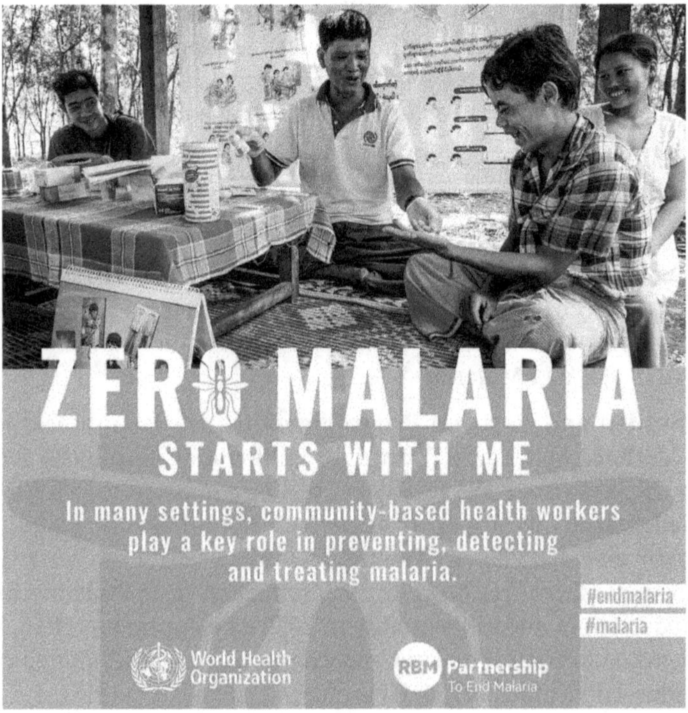

**Bottom Line**

- Malaria, a parasitic disease, is one of the major public health issues in India. It is caused by *Plasmodium malariae, Plasmodium vivax, Plasmodium falciparum, and Plasmodium ovale.* Malaria caused by *Plasmodium falciparum* and *Plasmodium vivax* is predominant in India.
- *Plasmodium falciparum* causes the serious form of malaria.
- The malaria parasites are transmitted to humans by infective bite of female Anopheles mosquitoes. The transmission of vector borne diseases depends on prevalence of infective vectors and human-vector contact
- The common symptoms are: Fever, headache, vomiting and other flu-like symptoms, Easy fatigue-ability due to anaemia, fits/convulsions and loss of consciousness.
- Symptoms of Severe and Complicated Malaria are: History of High Fever with at
- least one of the following: Prostration (inability to sit), altered consciousness lethargy or coma Breathing difficulties, Severe anaemia, Generalized convulsions/fits, Inability to drink/vomiting, Dark and/or limited production of urine.
- The burden of malaria and the challenges addressing it are most acute in Africa and its 11 countries bear about two-third of world's burden.
- India has finally managed to control malaria, reduce mortality and has gotten out of the High-Burden-High-Impact (HBHI) group of endemic countries.
- Malaria is more predominant in tribal districts of North-Eastern States, Odisha, Chhattisgarh and Jharkhand.
- Annual Parasite Incidence (API), Annual Blood Smear Examination Rate (ABSER), Slide Positivity Rate (SPR), and Slide falciparum Rate (SfR) are the indicators used to measure malaria situation in the country.
- India aims to eliminate malaria by 2030.

## Bibliography

1. Annual Report 2023-2024, Ministry of Health and Welfare, Government of India.
2. Guideline for Diagnosis and Treatment of Malaria in India, 2014, National Institute of Malaria Research and National Vector Borne Disease Control Programme, 2014.

3. Jai Prakash Narain & Lalit M Nath, Eliminating malaria in India by 2027: The Count Down begins! Indian Journal of Medical Research, 148, August 2018.
4. National Drug Policy on Malaria 2013, Directorate of National Vector Borne Disease Control Programme, Delhi.
5. National Framework for Malaria Elimination in India 2016-2030, Ministry of Health and Family Welfare, 2016.
6. National Health Profile 2019, 14th Issue, Central Bureau of Health Intelligence, Ministry of Health and Family Welfare, Government of India.
7. World Malaria Report 2024, World Health Organization, 2024.

# Mpox

"Mpox is not the new COVID"

- WHO

**After reading this chapter, you should be able to understand and appreciate:**

- Mpox as a public health issue;
- How does infection occur and spread;
- Symptoms of Mpox;
- Global and India's burden;
- Diagnosis and treatment options available; and
- Prevention Strategies advocated.

Mpox, earlier called as Monkeypox, is a viral disease of zoonotic origin with Smallpox like symptoms, but with less clinical severity. It is part of the same family of viruses as smallpox. WHO had declared it as a Public Health Emergency of International Concern (PHEIC) first in July 2022 and now again in August 2024. Mpox was first discovered in 1958 in colonies of monkeys kept for research, hence the name 'Mpox.' It was first identified in humans in 1970 in the Democratic Republic of the Congo (DRC) in a 9-year-old boy.

## Source of Infection and Mode of Transmission

Mpox can spread from animals to people, between people and from the environment to people. The virus can spread through:

- contact with lesions on the skin or infectious bodily fluids;
- contact with contaminated materials such as clothing, linen or sharps injuries in healthcare settings;
- contact with respiratory droplets, from an infected person's mouth or throat;
- contact with infected animals; and
- pregnant women can pass the virus on to their unborn baby.

**Word of Mouth**

**Symptoms:** Mpox is usually a self-limiting disease with symptoms lasting from 2-4 weeks.

- Fever
- Lymphadenopathy - Typically occurs with fever onset, Peri-auricular, axillary, cervical or inguinal, Unilateral or bilateral
- Headache, muscle aches, exhaustion
- Chills and/or sweats
- Sore throat and cough

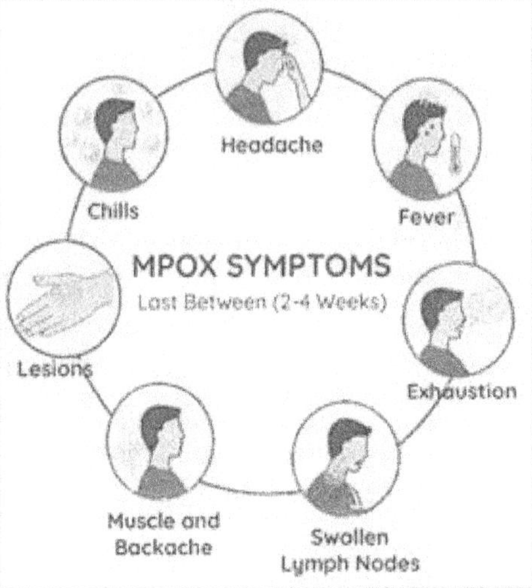


Skin rash occurs simultaneously and evolve together on any given part of the body. The evolution of lesions progresses through four stages — macular, papular, vesicular, to pustular —before scabbing over and desquamation. A person is contagious until after all scabs on the skin have fallen off and a fresh layer of intact skin has formed underneath.

**Risk Groups:**

- People in close contact. Close contact includes skin-to-skin (such as touching or sex) and mouth-to-mouth, or mouth-to-skin contact (such as kissing), and can also include being face-to-face with someone who has mpox (such as talking or breathing close to one another, which can generate infectious respiratory particles). People sharing clothing, bedding, towels, objects, electronics and other surfaces are also in risk.
- Children.
- Health workers caring patients.

## Global Burden and Initiative

Though Mpox was largely confined to Africa earlier, it is reported from Europe in 2022. Since 1st January 2022, Mpox cases have been reported to WHO from 121 Member States across all 6 WHO regions. As of 31st July 2024, a total of 1,02,997 laboratory confirmed cases and 186 probable cases, including 223 deaths, have been reported to WHO. As of July 2024, the number of monthly reported new cases has increased by 8.8%, compared to the previous month. The 10 most affected countries globally since 1 Jan 2022 are: USA, Brazil, Spain, DRC, France, Colombia, Mexico, UK, Peru, and Germany.

## India's Burden and National Programme

In India, the first case of Mpox was reported in Kollam, Kerala, on 14th July 2022. On 27th March 2024, the last case was also reported from Kerala. Total 30 laboratory confirmed cases were reported from Kerala (15 cases) and Delhi (15 cases).

India has been taking proactive measures against Mpox. The 35 laboratories across the country are equipped to test suspected cases of Mpox.

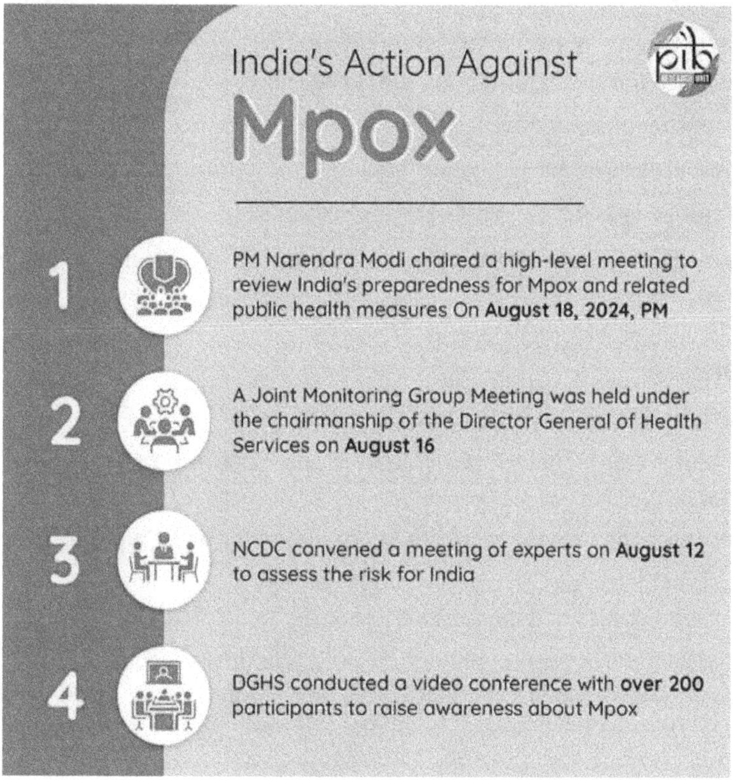

## Diagnosis and Treatment

Laboratory Diagnostics [Details are beyond the scope of the present text]:

Identifying is difficult because other infections and conditions look similar. It is important to distinguish mpox from chickenpox, measles, bacterial skin infections, scabies, herpes, syphilis, other sexually transmitted infections, and medication-associated allergies. Someone with Mpox may also have another sexually transmitted infection at the same time, such as syphilis or herpes.

Alternatively, a child with suspected Mpox may also have chickenpox. For these reasons, testing is key for people to get care as early as possible and prevent severe illness and further spread.

The preferred laboratory test for Mpox is detection of viral DNA by polymerase chain reaction (PCR). The best diagnostic specimens are taken directly from the rash – skin, fluid or crusts – collected by vigorous swabbing. In the absence of skin lesions, testing can be done using swabs of the throat or anus.

**Treatment:** Treatment of Mpox is primarily supportive. These include:

- Patient isolation
- Protection of compromised skin and mucous membranes
- Rehydration therapy and nutritional support
- Symptom alleviation
- Antibiotics to treat secondary bacterial infections if they develop
- Monitoring and treatment of complications

Drugs may be considered in special severe cases, strictly as per treating physician.

## Prevention

**Prevention:** The following measures are advised:

- Avoiding close contact with anyone who has mpox, including sexual contact.
- Cleaning hands frequently with soap and water or an alcohol-based hand rub.
- Isolating the infected persons and seeking medical advice.
- Avoiding unprotected contact with wild animals, especially those that are sick or dead (including their meat and blood). Any food containing animal parts or meat should be cooked thoroughly before eating.

**Role of Pharmacists:** There is no defined responsibilities as described under National TB programme. However, the pharmacists can:

- Participate in community education on Mpox awareness, prevention and control.

**Bottom Line**

- Mpox, earlier called as Monkeypox, is a viral disease with smallpox like symptoms but with less clinical severity.
- WHO had declared it as a Public Health Emergency of International Concern (PHEIC).
- Mpox can spread through: contact with lesions on the skin or infectious bodily fluids; contact with contaminated materials such as clothing, linen or sharps injuries in healthcare settings; contact with respiratory droplets, from an infected person's mouth or throat; contact with infected animals; and pregnant women to their unborn baby.
- Mpox is usually a self-limiting disease with symptoms lasting from 2-4 weeks: Fever; Lymphadenopathy; Headache, muscle aches, exhaustion; Chills and/or sweats; Sore throat and cough.
- High risk group: People in close contact; Children and Health workers caring patients.
- USA, Brazil, Spain, DRC, France, Colombia, Mexico, UK, Peru, and Germany are the most effected nations.
- In India, the first case of Mpox was reported in Kollam, Kerala. The 35 laboratories across the country are equipped to test suspected cases of Mpox.
- Identifying is difficult because other infections and conditions look similar. laboratory test for Mpox is detection of viral DNA by polymerase chain reaction (PCR).
- Treatment: Treatment of Mpox is primarily supportive: Patient isolation; Protection of compromised skin and mucous membranes; Rehydration therapy and nutritional support; Symptom alleviation; Antibiotics to treat secondary bacterial infections if they develop; Monitoring and treatment of complications.
- Preventive Measures: Avoiding close contact with anyone who has mpox, including sexual contact; Cleaning hands frequently with soap and water or an alcohol-based hand rub; Isolating the infected persons and seeking medical advice; Avoiding unprotected contact with wild animals, especially those that are sick or dead (including their meat and blood).
- Pharmacists may participate in community education on Mpox awareness, prevention and control.

## Bibliography

1. CD Alert, National Centre for Disease Control, Directorate General of Health Services. Government of India, https://ncdc.mohfw.gov.in/wp-content/uploads/2024/08/CD-Alert-Mpox-August-2024.pdf.
2. https://www.who.int/news-room/questions-and-answers/item/mpox, accessed on 27$^{th}$ November 2024.
3. https://www.who.int/news-room/fact-sheets/detail/mpox, accessed on 27$^{th}$ November 2024.

# Pneumonia

The most widespread and fatal of all acute infectious diseases, pneumonia, is now the "Captain of the Men of Death".

- William Osler

**After reading this chapter, you should be able to understand and appreciate:**

- Pneumonia as a public health problem of India;
- What causes pneumonia and how it spreads;
- Symptoms of pneumonia;
- Global and Indian Burden of pneumonia;
- Diagnosis and Treatment available; and
- Prevention Control Strategies Practiced.

Pneumonia is a form of acute respiratory infection. This is most commonly caused by viruses or bacteria. It can cause mild to life-threatening illness in people of all ages. It is the single largest infectious cause of death in children worldwide.

The lungs are made up of small sacs called alveoli, which fill with air when a healthy person breathes. When an individual has pneumonia, the alveoli are filled with pus and fluid, which makes breathing painful and limits oxygen intake.

## Source of Infection and Mode of Transmission

Pneumonia is caused by several infectious agents, including viruses, bacteria and fungi. The most common are the following.

- *Streptococcus pneumoniae* is the most common cause of bacterial pneumonia in children.
- *Haemophilus influenzae* type b (Hib) is the second most common cause of bacterial pneumonia.
- Respiratory syncytial virus is the most common viral cause of pneumonia.
- In infants infected with HIV, *Pneumocystis jiroveci* is one of the most common causes of pneumonia, responsible for at least one quarter of all pneumonia deaths in HIV-infected infants.

These infections are generally spread by direct contact with infected people.

**Word of Mouth**

**Symptoms:**

- Coughing,
- Trouble breathing
- Fever, sweating and shaking chills
- Fatigue
- Chest pain
- Nausea, vomiting or diarrhoea
- Confusion, especially in older adults
- Children with pneumonia usually experience fast breathing, or their lower chest may draw in or retract when they inhale (in a healthy person, the chest expands during inhalation).

**High Risks:**

- Children whose immune systems are compromised.
- A child's immune system may be weakened by malnutrition or undernourishment, especially in infants who are not exclusively breastfed.
- Pre-existing illnesses, such as symptomatic HIV infections and measles., also increase a child's risk of contracting pneumonia.
- Indoor air pollution caused by cooking and heating with biomass fuels (such as wood or dung), living in crowded homes and parental smoking.

**Global Burden and Initiative:** Pneumonia killed more than 808 000 children under the age of 5 in 2017, accounting for 15% of all deaths of children under 5 years. People at-risk for pneumonia also include adults over the age of 65 and people with preexisting health problems.

WHO and UNICEF developed Integrated Global Action Plan for Pneumonia and Diarrhoea (GAPPD) aims to accelerate pneumonia control with a combination of interventions to protect, prevent and treat pneumonia in children.

## India's Burden and National Programme

Childhood pneumonia continues to be the topmost infectious killer among under five children, contributing to 17.51 percent of under-five deaths in India (Cause of Death Statistics 2017-19). In order to achieve the National Health Policy goals, the Pneumonia mortality in children needs to reduce to less than 3 per 1000 live births.

The country had launched 'SAANS (Social Awareness & Action to Neutralize Pneumonia Successfully) campaign' on 12th November 2023 on the World Pneumonia Day to ensure health system strengthening and community awareness towards childhood pneumonia.

Pneumococcal Conjugate Vaccine (PCV) was introduced in a phased-manner by Government of India in May, 2017 under Universal Immunization Program (UIP) for reducing Under Five (U-5) mortality and morbidity caused by Pneumococcal Pneumonia.

## Diagnosis and Treatment

**Diagnosis:** Presence of symptoms and signs; Chest examination; X – ray of chest; and lab tests are diagnostic tools.

**Treatment:** Pneumonia may be treated with antibiotics, if it is bacterial. The antibiotic of choice is amoxicillin. Most cases of pneumonia require oral antibiotics, which are often prescribed at a health centre. These cases can also be diagnosed and treated with inexpensive oral antibiotics at the community level by trained community health workers. Hospitalization is recommended only for severe cases of pneumonia.

## Prevention and Control

- **Getting vaccinated:** Immunization against Hib, pneumococcus, measles, influenza and whooping cough (pertussis) is the most effective way to prevent pneumonia.
- **Washing hands:** Maintain good hygiene and washing your hands frequently, especially when caring for others who are sick or after blowing your nose, will keep germs from spreading.

- **Addressing environmental factors:** Reduce indoor air pollution by providing affordable clean indoor stoves and stop smoking.
- **Maintaining healthy lifestyle:** Eat a healthy diet, rest and get regular exercise to help you stay well.

**Role of Pharmacists:** There is no defined responsibilities.

- Pharmacists can participate in community education on Pneumonia awareness, prevention and control.
- Community pharmacists should advice the customers on need of completion of antibiotic course prescribed.
- They can advise the customers for vaccination and promote good hand hygiene practices.

**Bottom Line**

- Pneumonia is a form of acute respiratory infection commonly caused by viruses or bacteria.
- When an individual has pneumonia, the alveoli are filled with pus and fluid, which makes breathing painful and limits oxygen intake.
- These infections are generally spread by direct contact with infected people.
- Common symptoms include: Coughing, Trouble breathing, Fever, sweating and shaking chills, Fatigue, Chest pain, Nausea, vomiting or diarrhoea, Confusion, especially in older adults.
- Children with pneumonia usually experience fast breathing, or their lower chest may draw in or retract when they inhale (in a healthy person, the chest expands during inhalation).
- High risk persons include: Children with compromised immune system, malnutrition or undernourishment, exposed to indoor air pollution and parental smoking.
- Worldwide pneumonia killed more than 808 000 children under the age of 5 in 2017, accounting for 15% of all deaths of children under 5 years.
- In India, childhood pneumonia continues to be the topmost infectious killer among under five children, contributing to 17.51 percent of under-five deaths in India (Cause of Death Statistics 2017-19.
- The country had launched 'SAANS (Social Awareness & Action to Neutralize Pneumonia Successfully) campaign'.
- Pneumococcal Conjugate Vaccine (PCV) was introduced in a phased-manner by Government of India in May, 2017 under Universal Immunization Program (UIP).

- **Diagnosis:** Presence of symptoms and signs; Chest examination; X – ray of chest; and lab tests are diagnostic tools. *Treatment:* Pneumonia may be treated with antibiotics, if it is bacterial.
- Getting vaccinated and frequent handwashing are advocated for prevention and control.
- Pharmacists can participate in community education on Pneumonia awareness, prevention and control.

## Bibliography

1. Guidance Note, for Childhood Pneumonia Management, Social Awareness & Action Plan to Neutralize Pneumonia Successfully, Government of India.
2. https://www.who.int/health-topics/pneumonia#tab=tab_3 accessed on 8th December 2024.
3. https://www.who.int/news-room/fact-sheets/detail/pneumonia accessed on 8th December 2024.

# Tuberculosis

"The biggest disease today is not leprosy or TB, but rather the feeling of unwanted"

- Mother Teresa

**After reading this chapter, you should be able to understand and appreciate:**

- Tuberculosis as a public health issue;
- How does Tuberculosis occur and transmit;
- Symptoms of Tuberculosis;
- Global and India's burden; and
- The Pharmacists' participation in National TB programme.

Tuberculosis (TB) is an ancient disease reported to have originated in Europe and spread to Asia, Africa and America. The TB is ancient to India too. The literature reported that the Moon-god, the king of Brahmanas was the first to become the victim of TB and hence was known as Rajayakshma or King's disease (500 BCE). It is the leading infectious cause of death worldwide. TB is a dangerous epidemic disease, threat to life and is a public health problem with substantial morbidity and mortality in the country. Early diagnosis and complete treatment of the TB is the corner stone of TB control strategy. The global burden has slowly declined but increase in antibiotic resistance has made the TB control difficult. India has committed to make the country free of TB by 2025 much ahead of WHO's target and target of Sustainable Development Goals.

Robert Koch, German Physician and Microbiologist, had reported that he had isolated and grown the tubercle bacillus to the physiological society of Berlin on 24th March 1882. This day, 24th March, is celebrated as TB Day throughout the world.

TB is an infectious disease caused by *Mycobacterium tuberculosis*, a gram negative bacteria. The TB may be divided into two types depening on the organ affected by the TB bacteria: Pulmonary TB (TB of Lungs) and Extra-Pulmonary TB (TB of intestine, meninges, bones and joints,lymph glands, skin and other organs of the body). The disease primarily affects lungs and pulmonary TB (PTB) is most common. The text primarily concentrates on pulmonary TB.

## Source of Infection and Mode of Transmission

The most common source of infection is the TB patients. The bacteria spread through air. When the patient with PTB coughs or sneezes, the TB bacteria are spread in the air in the form of droplets. When these droplets are inhaled by healthy persons, the persons get infected. TB is contagious because infected persons are likely to transmit the bacteria to others. The particles must be fresh enough to carry a viable bacteria. The bacteria can stay alive for a few hours, especially in confined places with no fresh air. Fresh air scatters the bacteria and sunlight kills them.TB is not transmitted through use of dishes and other articles used by the patients.

Patients who have either received no treatment or have not been treated fully are the potential source of infection. One patient can infect on an average 10 – 15 persons in a year. The chances of getting infected depend on the amount of infectitous droplets exposed, the duration, the frequency of exposure, and the immune status of the individual. Patients, if do not get treated, would continue to be infective. Effective anti-bacetrial treatment reduces infectivity by 90% within 48 hours.

**Word of Mouth (TB)**

**Symptoms:**

**Pulmonary TB:**

- Cough lasting more than two weeks
- Weight loss
- Fever
- Episodes of night sweat
- Loss of appetite
- Coughing up blood
- Shortness of breath
- Tiredness

**Extra – Pulmonary TB:**

- Weight loss
- Fever
- Episodes of night sweat
- Loss of appetite
- Other symptom based on the organ involved

**Risk factors**

- HIV infection
- Diabetes
- Alcohol use
- Smoking
- Poverty and overcrowded housing
- Under Nutrition
- Indoor air pollution

## Global Burden of TB and Initiatives

TB is one of the top 10 causes of deaths and the leading cause from a single infectious agent. Millions of people continue to fall sick with TB each year. In 2017, TB is estimated to have killed 1.3 million persons among HIV negative persons. There were an additional 300 000 deaths from TB among HIV positive persons.

It is reported that 10 million people developed TB in 2017. Though disease occurs in all regions of globe, major TB burden countries are: India (27%), China (9%), Indonesia (8%), the Philippines (6%), Pakistan (5%), Nigeria (4%), Bangladesh (4%) and South Africa (3%). The incidence rate too vary. 2017 figure shows less than 10 new cases per 100 000 population in most high income countries and 150-400 new cases in most of the 30 high TB burden countries.

Globally, there were 558 000 new cases of rifampicin resistant TB (RR-TB) in 2017 of which around 50% were in three countries: India (24%), China (13%) and Russian Federation (10%). Among the RR-TB cases, 82% are estimated to be multi-drug resistant TB (MDR – TB).

The median cost of per patient treated in 2017 was $ 1224 for drug susceptible TB and $7141 for MDR- TB. There has been a gap between the requirement of fund and availability of the fund for achieving the target. It has been estimated that gap between the funding available in 2018 against the need of $2.5 billion is $0.5 billion. Study shows that the 27 – 81 percentage of TB patients and their house holds facing direct and indirect cost that exceeded 20% of their annual household income. About 10% of the world's population experience catastrophic expenditure on health. Access to TB care should not be looked in isolation but to be viewed as a part of Universal Health Coverage (UHC). UHC means everyone, irrespective of their living standards, receives the health services as needed and using health services does not cause financial hardship.

Many new TB cases are attributed to under nourishment, HIV infection, smoking, diabetes and alcohol use. Poverty is an important underlying driver of National TB epidemics. The elimination of extreme poverty and providing social protection can reduce TB incidences.

The TB incidence is falling globally at about 2% per year (new cases per 100 000). Globally, the number of deaths among HIV negative persons has fallen by 5% between 2015 and 2017. 2015 is the base year for the targets set in the 'End TB Strategy'. There has been a strong political commitment towards 'End TB'. On this effect, UN General Assembly had adopted the declaration of the high level meeting on 10th October 2018 to accelerate the progress on the fight against TB. WHO's End TB Strategy aims to end the Global TB epidemic with targets to reduce TB deaths by 95% and to cut new cases by 90% between 2015 and 2035; and to ensure that no family is burdened with catastrophic expenses due to TB. Under the Sustainable Development Goals (SDG), the world sets the specific target for 2030, to achieve a 90% reduction in absolute number of TB deaths and an 80% reduction in TB incidence compared to the levels. WHO's End TB target time 2035 while the target year for achieving SDGs is 2030.

## India's TB Burden and National Programmes

To ensure proper TB diagnosis and management in patients and their contacts; and to reduce TB transmission and to address the problems of emergence and spread of drug resistance TB, it is necessary to collect complete information of all TB patients. In order to achieve this, TB is made a notifiable disease. India aims to eliminate TB by 2025 well ahead of global time line.

**Pharmacists and TB Control: Regulations**

1. The anti-TB drugs are brought under the Schedule H1 of Drugs and Cosmetics Rules which require them to be sold in retail only on the prescription of registered medical practitioner. The details of the prescriber as well the patient are to be recorded in a register by the pharmacist.
2. The pharmacy / chemist and druggist dispensing anti-tubercular medicines needs to notify the details of TB patients in the prescribed proforma to the District Nodal Officer or any other officer as designated. Failure to adhere to the notification requirement is viewed as negligent act likely to spread infection of disease dangerous to life or malignant act likely to spread infection of disease dangerous to life. Negligent act invites punishment with imprisonment extending to six months or fine or both. Malignant act invites punishment with imprisonment extending up to two years or fine or both. [The notification is also required by the medical practitioners/clinics/ hospitals and medical laboratories]

**Success Stories of Community Pharmacists' Participation in TB Care and Control in India**

A TB Fact Card Project (2005-2006) was initiated by the Indian Pharmaceutical Association to involve community pharmacists in TB care and control in Mumbai. The project was supported by Commonwealth Pharmaceutical Association, the International Pharmaceutical Students' Federation, and Maharashtra State Chemists and Druggists Association resulted in TB awareness and treatment adherence in target population; increased social awareness among the students and their roles & opportunities.

Following the success of TB Card and other pilot projects, another collaborative scale up programme "DOTS TB Pharmacists Project" was launched in Mumbai. This was the first of its kind where private pharmacists were allowed to stock patient wise DOTS TB medicine boxes in the pharmacies.

Success breeds success. Similarly the successful outcomes of various initiatives on the role and responsibilities of community pharmacists in TB control led to the historic moment. On 27th April 2012, a MOU is signed between Central TB Division of Government of India, Indian Pharmaceutical Association, All India Organization of Chemists and Druggists, Pharmacy Council of India and SEARPharm forum to set out the policy of engaging retail pharmacists in RNTCP for TB care and Control in India. The programme was further strengthened by extending the validity of MOU and escalating to National Level beyond Maharashtra. Under the programme a training module for Community Pharmacists was developed by Central TB Division and Indian Pharmaceutical Association.

The Private Public Partnership model of Central TB Division and Community Pharmacists created history as this was the first successful collaboration which proved the potential of community pharmacists' participation in health programmes. Data of 2014 – 2017 showed the participation 64 community pharmacists as DOTS providers enrolling 128 plus patients in Maharashtra. During 2014-2016, 39 community pharmacists with 60 patients had participated as DOTS providers in the states of Goa, Haryana, Karnataka, Madhya Pradesh, Tamil Nadu and Uttarakhand.

[Source: Pharmacists at the Frontlines – A Novel Approach at Combating TB, Indian Pharmaceutical Association, 2017)

**Bottom Line**

- Tuberculosis (TB) is an ancient infectious disease with significant public health concern which causes substantial morbidity and mortality.
- TB is caused by a gram negative bacteria, *Mycobacterium tuberculosis.* There are two types of TB: Pulmonary TB and Extra-Pulmonary TB.
- Most common source of infection is the TB patients. Patients who have not received treatment or who have not been treated fully are the potential source of infection. On an average a patient can infect 10 -15 persons in a year.
- The common symptoms are: Pulmonary TB – cough lasting more than two weeks, weight loss, fever, episodes of night sweat, loss of appetite, coughing up blood, shortness of breath, and tiredness; Extra-Pulmonary TB – weight loss, fever, episodes of night sweat, loss of appetite, and other symptom based on organ involved.
- TB is one of the top 10 causes of death worldwide. India shares about 27% of the total global burden. WHO keeps the target of ending TB globally by 2035. India fixed an ambitious target of making country free of TB by 2025.
- In addition to TB, there are problems of multi-drug resistant TB.
- TB is a notified disease. Pharmacist needs to inform the health authority about the new patient. TB medicine falls under Schedule H1 of Drugs and Cosmetics Rules. These medicines are to be supplied only with prescription and maintaining some documenting procedure.

## Bibliography

1. Global Tuberculosis Report, 2018, World Health Organization, 2018.
2. India TB Report 2018, Revised National TB Control Programme, Annual Status Report, Central TB Division, Government of India, March 2018.
3. Pharmacists at the Frontlines – A Novel Approach at Combating TB, The DOTS TB Pharmacist Project, Indian Pharmaceutical Association, 2017.
4. Revised National Tuberculosis Programme – Training Module for Community Pharmacists, Central TB division and Indian Pharmaceutical Association, 2013.

# CHAPTER 6

# Non-Communicable Diseases: Disease, Prevention and Control

## Non-Communicable Diseases

Non-Communicable Diseases (NCDs) are chronic diseases that are not transmissible from one person to another. NCDs may thus include wide spectrum of medical disorders both acute and chronic like Cancers, Diabetes, Hypertension, Cardiovascular Diseases and Stroke, Chronic Kidney Diseases (CKDs), Chronic Obstructive Pulmonary Diseases (COPDs) and Asthma, Non-Alcoholic Fatty Liver Disease (NAFLD), and a gamut of other diseases.

World Health Organization estimates that the NCDs are collectively responsible for more than 74 percent of all deaths worldwide including heart disease, stroke, cancer, chronic respiratory diseases, and diabetes. These diseases have public health importance globally and in India. NCDs cause significant morbidity and mortality, both in urban and rural population and across all socio-economic strata, with considerable loss in potentially productive years of life. NCDs are also responsible for the maximum out-of-pocket expenditure on health. The economic output lost due to NCDs excluding mental conditions is estimated to be $ 3.55 trillion for India for the period of 2012-2030. Taking cognizance of these facts, Sustainable Development Goal 3 (Target 3.4) aims to reduce premature mortality from NCDs by one-third by 2030 in the world. SDG-3 also stresses on prevention and control of tobacco and alcohol use.

The National Health Policy, 2017 emphasises the need to halt and reverse the incidence of NCDs and seeks to focus on common NCDs. NCDs are emerging as a major public health challenge worldwide and people above the age of 30 years are most at risk of getting such diseases. India is also experiencing rapid demographic and epidemiological transitions with a steep rise in the burden of lifestyle related chronic NCDs. With rapid epidemiological transition with higher Disability-Adjusted Life Years (DALYs) and mortalities, prevention, and control measures for NCDs are required to be accelerated to reduce the burden of NCDs in India.

The global NCD burden remains unacceptably high. NCDs are responsible for 41 million of the world's annual deaths. Burden is greatest within low- and middle-income countries, where 77 percent of all NCD deaths and 80% of premature deaths occurred. Among NCDs, the four top killers are: cardiovascular diseases, cancers, chronic respiratory diseases, and diabetes.

WHO – NCD India profile – 2018 shows that NCDs account for 63% of all deaths in country of which the cardiovascular diseases lead with 27% overall mortality cause followed by chronic respiratory diseases (11%), cancers (9%), diabetes (3%) and others (13%). Incorporating other NCDs in the domain of the National Programme, National Programme for Prevention and Control of Cancer, Diabetes, Cardiovascular Diseases & Stroke (NPCDCS) is now renamed as National Programme for Prevention & Control of Non-Communicable Diseases (NP-NCD).

The text describes only Hypertension, Diabetes, COPD and Asthma, and Cancer.

Life style modification helps in controlling non-communicable diseases:

**Healthy Diets:**

- All meals to be taken at regular intervals.
- Wash food items properly before cooking. Boiling, steaming, roasting, cooking with minimal oil, as methods of cooking should be used rather than deep frying or using excess amount of oil.
- Consume a variety of fresh, seasonal, and locally available fruits and vegetables.
- Eat whole fruits and whole cereals and pulses (with outer covering 'chilka') as they are rich in fiber or roughage. Fiber/roughage helps in slowing down the absorption of sugar and fats into the blood.
- Restrict eating processed foods or foods available in packets with high amount of fat/oil, salt, and sugar.
- Reduce the consumption of sugar rich foods. Those with family history of diabetes should be careful of the amount and type of food consumed. Adding extra salt to cooked food and salads should be avoided. Those with family history of high blood pressure should especially reduce their daily salt consumption. Reduce the amount of salt- not more than 1 teaspoon (5 g) of salt for each individual in the whole day.
- Restrict intake of red meat like mutton, liver, brain, etc. and consume lean meats like chicken, fish, etc.

- Use vegetables oils like mustard oil, groundnut oil, soybean oil, etc. for cooking. In practice, it is best to use a mixture of oils. Ghee, butter, coconut oil are harmful and should be used in small quantities.
- Drink plenty of water, at least 8-10 glasses daily. Increase intake of fluids in diet.

**Physical activity:**

- To promote weight control and maintain a healthy weight, physical activity on a regular basis is important. Exercise regularly (moderate to vigorous) for 5-7 days per week; start slowly and work up gradually.
- At least 30 minutes (accumulated) of physical activities per day for cardiovascular disease protection. 45 minutes/day (accumulated) for fitness. 60 minutes/day (accumulated) for weight reduction.
- Sedentary activities like spending long hours in front of computers and TV should be discouraged and outdoor activities like gardening, cycling etc should be encouraged.
- Yoga & Meditation: They promote health by improving control of mind and body for the overall well-being of a person.

**Tobacco and Alcohol Use:**

- Tobacco any form like cigarettes, bidi, cigars, hukkah, chewing, sucking, inhaling, applying to teeth and gums etc is to be avoided.
- Alcohol in any form like alcohol made from locally grown grains, vegetables and fruits: arrack, mahwa, tari (toddy) etc; distilled alcohol/ foreign alcohol like whisky, rum, etc; beer and locally made illegal drinks is to be avoided.
- Tobacco and alcohol use is associated with diseases of the heart, stroke, lungs, kidney, cancers of lungs, oral cavity, respiratory problems, increased risk of tuberculosis, results in blindness, high blood pressure, diabetes, tooth decay/gum disease, bad breath, etc.
- Tobacco use in pregnancy leads to low-birth-weight babies and still birth. Tobacco use leads to impotence and low fertility among men.
- Consumption of alcohol during pregnancy leads to complications during delivery and defects in the child.
- If a person is on diabetes medication, alcohol consumption increases the risk of low blood sugar (hypoglycaemia).
- Harmful use of alcohol and tobacco should be avoided.
- All smokers should be strongly encouraged to quit smoking. All non-smokers should be discouraged from starting smoking.

The readers are encouraged to refer chapter on National Programmes.

## Cancer

"You can be a victim of cancer, or survivor of cancer. It's mindset."

- Dave Pelzer

**After reading this chapter, you should be able to understand and appreciate:**

- Cancer as a public health issue;
- Symptoms of Cancer;
- Global and India's burden;
- Diagnosis and treatment options available;
- Prevention and Control Strategies Practiced; and
- Pharmacists in cancer prevention and treatment.

Cancer is a disease in which some of the body's cells grow uncontrollably and spread to other parts of the body. Cancer can start almost anywhere in the human body, which is made up of trillions of cells. The spreading process is called metastasizing and is a major cause of death from cancer. A neoplasm and malignant tumour are other common names for cancer. Cancer is a increasing health challenge in India, impacting lives across diverse socio-economic and geographies of the country. The burden of cancer in the country is on the rise, with an increasing number of cases reported each year.

**Word of Mouth**

**Symptoms:**

- Headaches, vision or hearing changes, or seizures;
- Fatigue or extreme tiredness that is not relieved by sleep or rest;
- Pain that does not improve or that worsens;
- Fever or night sweats for no known reason;
- Cough or hoarseness that does not improve;
- Weight gain or weight loss of at least 4.5 kg (or 10 pounds) for no known reason;
- Changes in appetite, such as loss of appetite, dysphagia, abdominal pain, nausea or vomiting;
- Changes in bowel habits (diarrhoea or constipation), melena or haematochezia;

- Sores on the tongue or mouth or bleeding, pain or numbness in the lip or mouth;
- Bladder changes, such as dysuria or haematuria;
- Lumps or swelling in the body;
- Lumps or thickening in the breast, or nipple changes or discharge from the nipple;
- Changes to skin, such as lumps that bleed or that turn scaly, new moles or changes to existing moles, sores that do not heal or jaundice; and
- Unusual bleeding or bruising for no known reason.

**Risk**

| Life Style | Cancer Risk (%) | Life Style | Cancer Risk (%) |
|---|---|---|---|
| Cigarette smoking | 19.3 | Low dietary fibre | 0.9 |
| Excess body weight | 7.6 | *H. pylori* infection | 0.7 |
| Alcohol consumption | 5.4 | Red meat | 0.6 |
| UV radiation | 4.6 | Hepatitis C infection | 0.5 |
| Physical inactivity | 3.1 | HIV infection | 0.5 |
| HPV infection | 1.8 | Low dietary calcium | 0.3 |
| Low fruit / vegetable | 1.4 | Second hand smoke | 0.3 |
| Processed meat | 1.0 | Epstein Barr infection | 0.2 |
| | | Hepatitis B infection | 0.1 |

**Global Burden and Initiatives:** Cancer is the second leading cause of death globally, accounting for an estimated 9.6 million deaths, or 1 in 6 deaths, in 2018. Lung, prostate, colorectal, stomach and liver cancer are the most common types of cancer in men, while breast, colorectal, lung, cervical and thyroid cancer are the most common among women. The cancer burden continues to grow globally, exerting tremendous physical, emotional and financial strain on individuals, families, communities and health systems.

SDG proposes to reduce by one third premature mortality from non-communicable diseases through prevention and treatment and promote mental health and well-being by 2030. WHO advocates for early diagnosis for effective treatment.

**India's Burden and Initiatives:** Cancer is an increasing health challenge in India, impacting lives across diverse socio-economic and geographies of the country. In 2022, the projected incidence rate of 100.4 per 100,000 individuals. Approximately one in nine people in India is expected to face a cancer diagnosis during their lifetime. Notably, lung cancer ranked highest among males, while breast cancer held the top spot for females. Within childhood cancers (0-14 years), lymphoid leukaemia emerged as the predominant site, accounting for 29.2% in boys and 24.2% in girls. Looking ahead, an estimated 12.8% increase in cancer incidence by 2025 is expected as compared to 2020.

The highest burden is seen in the north and northeast regions of the country. Cancer contributes to 18.1 % deaths. The rise in disability-adjusted life years for cancer indicates a decline in premature mortality.

The various initiatives are introduced on sustaining and scaling up NCD screening, education, health promotion, and tobacco control using digital innovations at the population level.

India observes National Cancer Awareness Day on 7th November. World Cancer Day is on 4th February.

**Diagnosis and Treatment:** Two strategies used –

- Based on signs and symptoms.
- Screening:
    - Laboratory tests — of blood, urine or other bodily fluids, which may test for tumour markers that are produced at higher levels by cancer cells, such as alpha-fetoprotein, CA 19-9, carcinoembryonic antigen and prostate-specific antigen;
    - Imaging tests — such as computed tomography scans, magnetic resonance imaging, single-photon emission computed tomography scans, positron emission tomography scans, nuclear and bone scans, ultrasounds and X-ray; and
    - Biopsies — during which a physician removes a tissue sample through needle aspiration, endoscopy (such as during colonoscopies or bronchoscopies) or surgery. The tissue sample is then reviewed by a pathologist and graded

**Treatment options:** surgery, cancer medicines and/or radiotherapy, administered alone or in combination. A multidisciplinary team of cancer professionals recommends the best possible treatment plan based on tumour type, cancer stage, clinical and other factors.

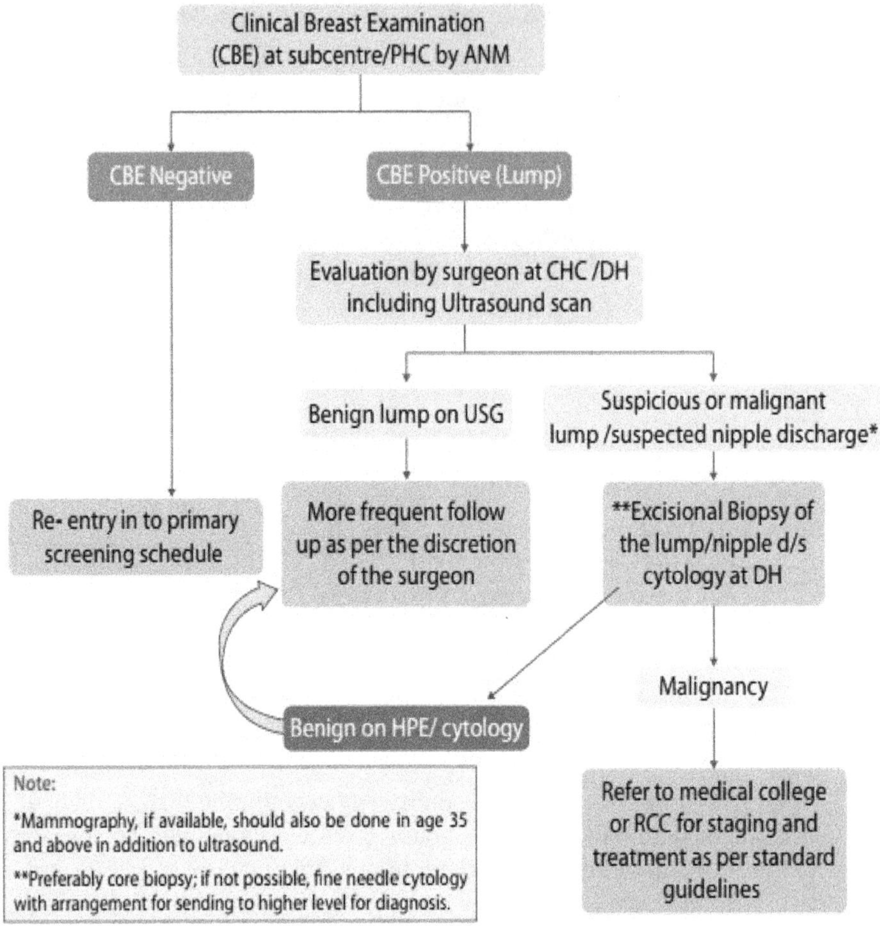


**Fig. 1.** Screening and Management Algorithm of Breast Cancer [Operational Frame Work: Management of Common Cancers].

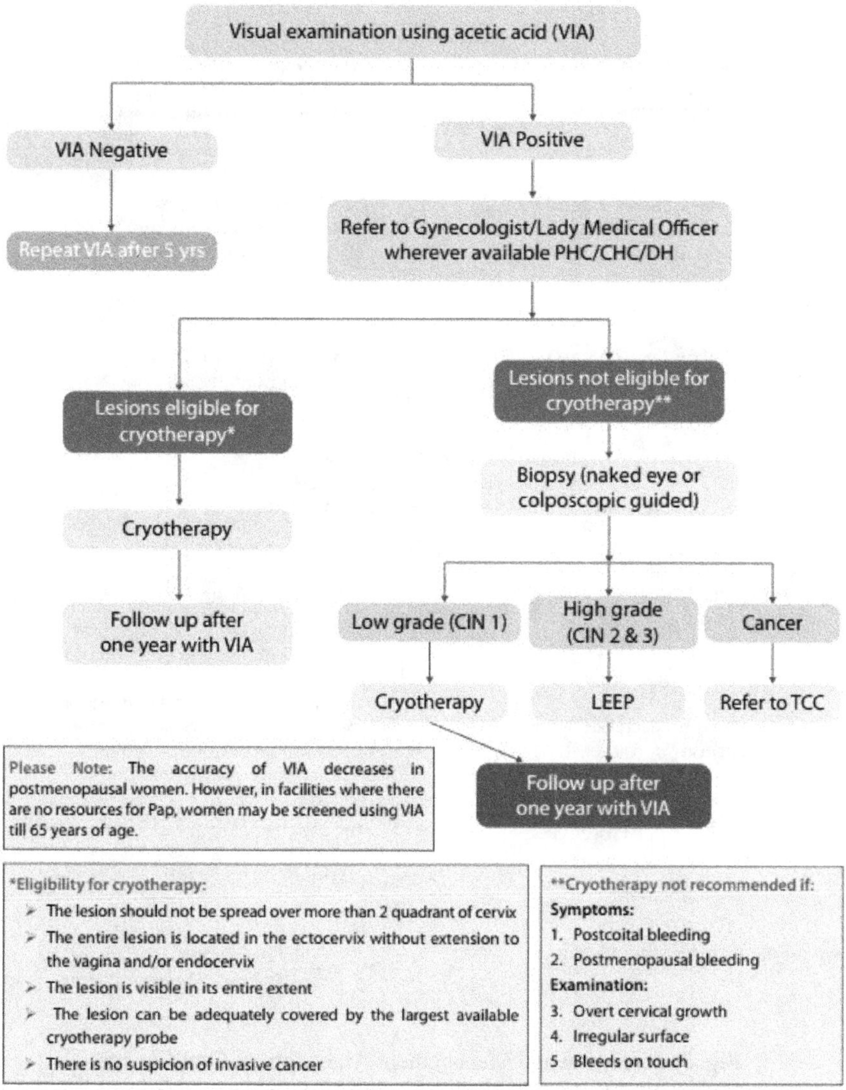


**Fig. 2.** Screening and Management Algorithm of Cervical Cancer [Operational Frame Work: Management of Common Cancers].

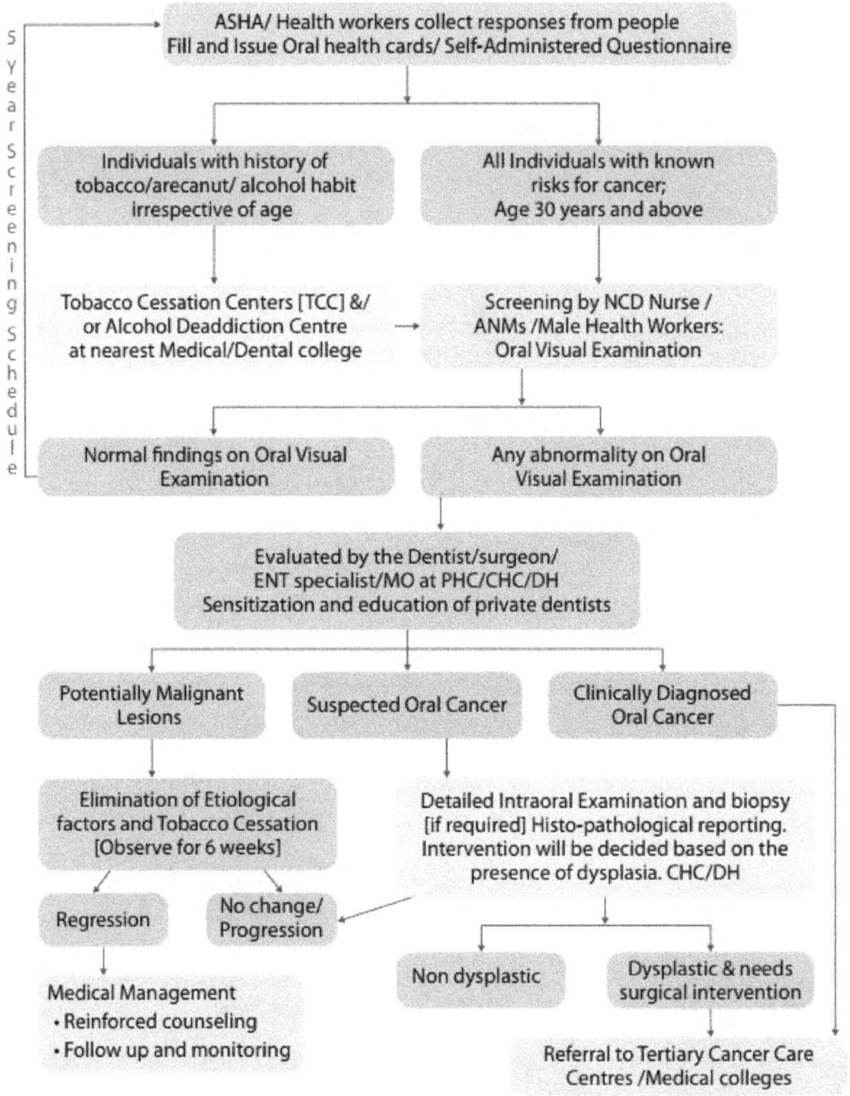


**Fig. 3.** Screening and Management Algorithm of Oral Cancer [Operational Frame Work: Management of Common Cancers].

**Prevention and Control:** The controlling risk factors helps in preventing cancer -

- Avoiding tobacco use, including cigarettes and smokeless tobacco;
- Maintaining a healthy weight;
- Eating healthy diet with plenty of fruit and vegetables;
- Exercising regularly;

- Limiting alcohol use;
- Practicing safe sex;
- Vaccinating against hepatitis B and human papillomavirus (HPV);
- Reducing exposure to ultraviolet radiation;
- Preventing unnecessary ionizing radiation exposure (e.g. minimize occupational exposure, ensure safe and appropriate medical use of radiation in diagnosis and treatment);
- Avoiding urban air pollution and indoor smoke from household use of solid fuels;
- Getting regular medical care; and
- Avoiding chronic infections.

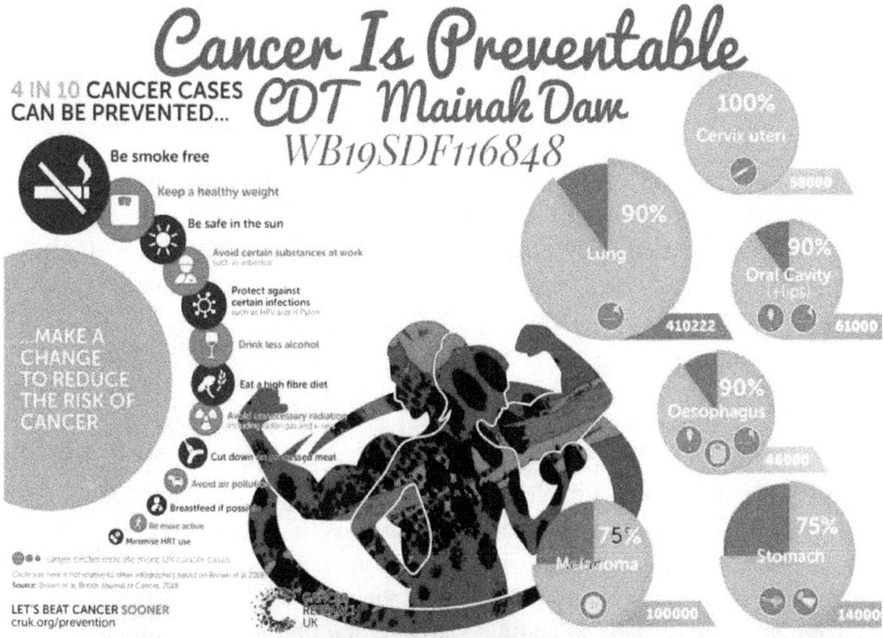


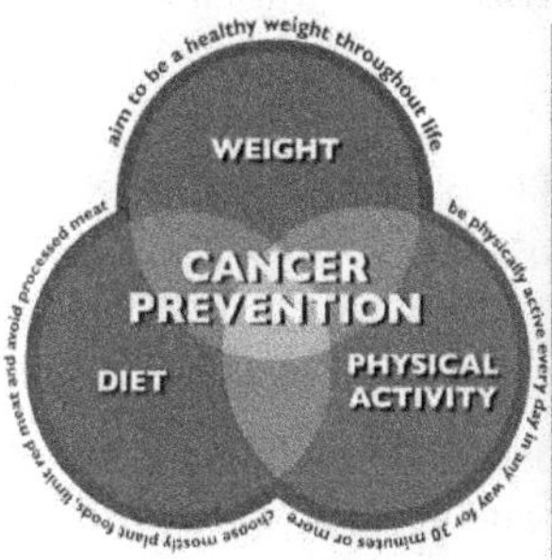

**Pharmacists' Role:** Though not specific involvement is specified the pharmacists can contribute in many ways for the well being of individuals in the society.

- **Community Pharmacists:**
    - Educating / Guiding the people on avoiding risk factors.
    - Guiding the general public on medication use and disposal of cancer treatment medicines. They are very toxic.
- **Hospital Pharmacists:**
    - Screening and cducating the people on need of avoiding risk factors.
    - Preparation of medications and adjustment of dose in consultation with physicians. Oncology pharmacists monitor the medication use including adverse events.
    - Responsible for disposal of unused / expired / spilled over cancer medicines.

**Bottom Line**

- Cancer is a disease in which some of the body's cells grow uncontrollably and spread to other parts of the body. The spreading process is called metastasizing and is a major cause of death from cancer. A neoplasm and malignant tumour are other common names for cancer.
- The common symptoms: Headaches, vision or hearing changes, or seizures; Fatigue or extreme tiredness that is not relieved by sleep or rest; Pain that does not improve or that worsens; Fever or night sweats for no known reason; Cough or hoarseness that does not improve; Weight gain or weight loss of at least 4.5 kg (or 10 pounds) for no known reason; Changes in appetite, such as loss of appetite, dysphagia, abdominal pain, nausea or vomiting; Changes in bowel habits (diarrhoea or constipation), melena or haematochezia; Sores on the tongue or mouth or bleeding, pain or numbness in the lip or mouth; Bladder changes, such as dysuria or haematuria; Lumps or swelling in the body; Lumps or thickening in the breast, or nipple changes or discharge from the nipple; Changes to skin, such as lumps that bleed or that turn scaly, new moles or changes to existing moles, sores that do not heal or jaundice; and Unusual bleeding or bruising for no known reason.
- Cancer is the second leading cause of death globally The cancer burden continues to grow globally, exerting tremendous physical, emotional and financial strain on individuals, families, communities and health systems.

- Cancer is an increasing health challenge in India. Approximately one in nine people in India is expected to face a cancer diagnosis during their lifetime.
- India observes National Cancer Awareness Day on $7^{th}$ November. World Cancer Day is on $4^{th}$ February.
- Diagnostic methods include: Laboratory tests, Imaging tests, and Biopsies.
- Treatment options: surgery, cancer medicines and/or radiotherapy, administered alone or in combination.
- The controlling risk factors helps in preventing cancer - Avoiding tobacco use, including cigarettes and smokeless tobacco; Maintaining a healthy weight; Eating healthy diet with plenty of fruit and vegetables; Exercising regularly; Limiting alcohol use; Practicing safe sex; Vaccinating against hepatitis B and human papillomavirus (HPV); Reducing exposure to ultraviolet radiation; Preventing unnecessary ionizing radiation exposure (e.g. minimize occupational exposure, ensure safe and appropriate medical use of radiation in diagnosis and treatment); Avoiding urban air pollution and indoor smoke from household use of solid fuels; Getting regular medical care; and Avoiding chronic infections.
- The pharmacists can educate the common man on risk factors and encourage them to avoid them.

## Bibliography

1. Cancer care, A handbook for pharmacists, International Pharmaceutical Federation, 2022.
2. https://www.who.int/health-topics/cancer#tab=tab_3, accessed on $08^{th}$ October 2024.
3. Operational Frame Work, Management of Common Cancers, National Health Mission, Ministry of Health and Family Welfare, Government of India.

# COPD and Asthma

When you can't breathe, nothing else matters.

- Canadian Lung Association

**After reading this chapter, you should be able to understand and appreciate:**

- COPD and Asthma as public health issues;
- Symptoms of COPD and Asthma;
- Global and India's burden;
- Diagnosis and treatment options available;
- Prevention and Control Strategies Practiced; and
- Pharmacists in COPD and Asthma prevention and treatment.

Chronic Obstructive Pulmonary Diseases (COPD) and Asthma are two most common chronic respiratory diseases. They are major public health problems world wide including India. COPD is a common, preventable and treatable disease characterized by persistent respiratory symptoms and airflow limitation that is due to airway and/or alveolar abnormalities usually caused by significant exposure to noxious particles or gases. Asthma is a heterogeneous disease, usually characterized by chronic inflammation and is defined by the history of respiratory symptoms such as wheeze, shortness of breath, chest tightness and cough that vary over time and in intensity, together with variable expiratory airflow limitation.

**Word of Mouth**

**Symptoms of COPD:**

- Difficulty breathing,
- Chronic cough (sometimes with phlegm), and
- Feeling tired.

COPD symptoms can get worse quickly.

***Symptoms of Asthma:***

- Persistent cough, especially at night,
- Wheezing when exhaling and sometimes when inhaling,
- Shortness of breath or difficulty breathing, sometimes even when resting, and
- Chest tightness, making it difficult to breathe deeply.

Some people will have worse symptoms when they have a cold or during changes in the weather.

**Global Burden:** Approximately half a billion people live with asthma and COPD and together these 2 conditions cause almost 4 million deaths every year. More than 1 million of these deaths occur "prematurely" – in people aged under 70 years. 90% of these premature deaths occur in low- and middle-income countries (LMICs). The SDGs:

- Target 3.4: By 2030, reduce by one third premature mortality from NCDs through prevention and treatment and promote mental health and well-being.
- Target 3.8: Achieve universal health coverage, including financial risk protection, access to quality essential health care services and access to safe, effective, quality and affordable essential medicines and vaccines for all.

## India's Burden and Initiatives

Global Burden of Disease Report (2019) says there are an estimated 37.8 million cases of COPD, contributing to 17.8% of the global burden in India. COPD is the second leading cause of death and DALYs in India. Although India contributes to 17.8% of the global burden of COPD, it contributes to a disproportionate 27.3% of the global deaths.

India contributes to 13% of the global asthma burden, and it contributes to a disproportionate 43% of the global asthma deaths. This has a significant long-term implication in terms of increasing burden to the patient, family, community, health care system, and economy.

The government proposes to provide the access to diagnostic tools at primary care level and developed guideline for control & treatment of COPD and Asthma. Kerala state has developed guideline "Step Wise Approach to Air Ways Diseases" in short called SWAAS.

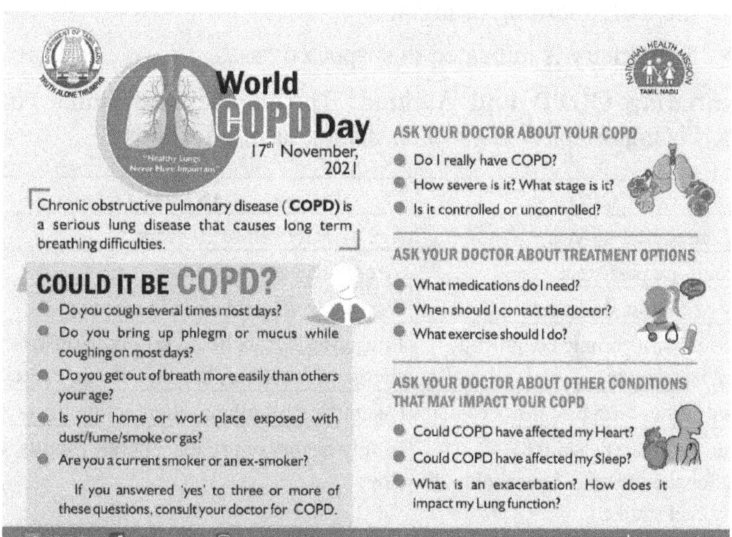

## Diagnosis and Treatment:

### I. Criteria for diagnosing COPD:

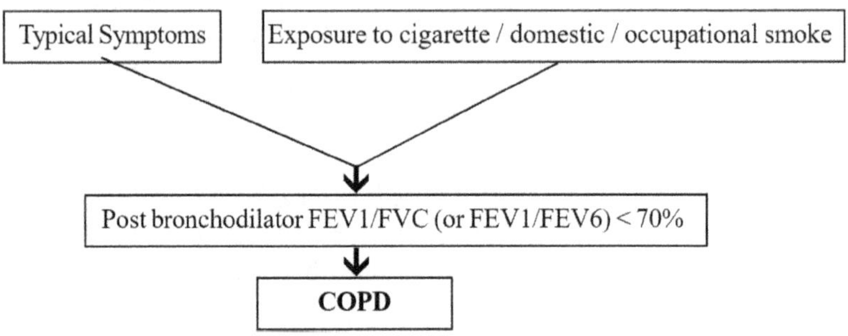


### II. Criteria for diagnosing Asthma:

- Presence of typical symptoms: wheeze, shortness of breath, cough and chest tightness. The symptoms are episodic and more severe in the early morning or night.
- Spirometry is indicated in suspected cases.

**Differentiating COPD and Asthma:** Though they are similar in many aspects, it is important to know their distinguishing features.

| COPD | ASTHMA |
|---|---|
| Age of onset after 40 years | Age of onset before 20 years |
| Symptoms are persistent | Symptoms vary over time |
| Mainly exertional dyspnoea | Worse during night or early morning |
| Associated with chronic cough and sputum, no triggers | Triggering factors like exposure to dust, allergens, emotions, laughter, drugs, exercise |
| No associations with past history | Past history of asthma, allergic rhinitis, or atopy |
| Exposure to cigarette smoke / occupational exposure / household biomass fuel smoke | Family history of asthma, allergic rhinitis, or atopy |

**Table *contd...***

| COPD | ASTHMA |
|---|---|
| Limited relief to treatment | Good response to treatment |
| Hyperinflammation or normal chest X-ray | Normal chest X – ray |
| Spirometry Post Bronchodilator No reversibility | Spirometry Post Bronchodilator reversibility [increase in FEV1 > 12 % maximal (mid-) expiratory flow > 200 ml] |

## Treatments:

- **COPD:**

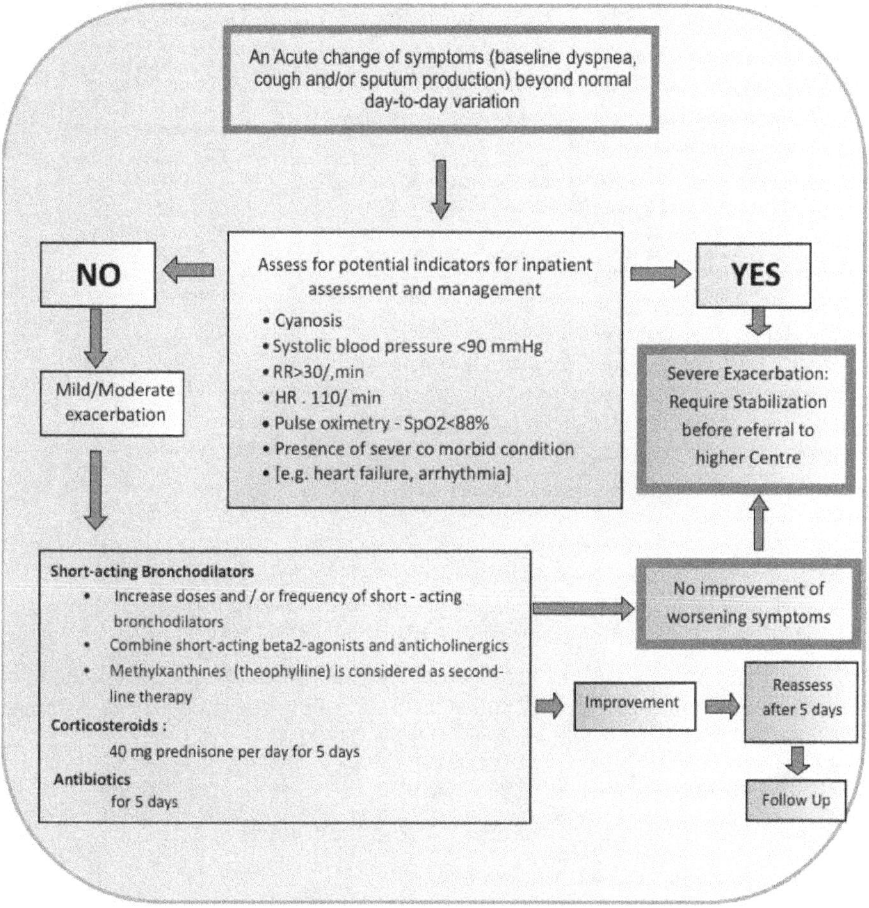


**Fig.** Algorithm: Management of Patient with Acute Exacerbation of COPD in Primary Care [Medical Officer's Manual for Prevention and Management of Chronic Obstructive Pulmonary Disease & Asthma, Government of India, 2021].

- **Asthma:**

OCS - Oral Corticosteroids; ICS - Inhaled Corticosteroids; SOS – as and when required; SABA – Short Acting Beta2 Agonists; LABA–Long Acting Beta2 Agonists; LAMA–Long-Acting Muscarinic Antagonists.

**Fig.** Algorithm: Management of Patient with Asthma [Medical Officer's Manual for Prevention and Management of Chronic Obstructive Pulmonary Disease & Asthma, Government of India, 2021].

### Using Spirometer:

Advising Patients prior to spirometry: Avoid the following activities -

- eating a large meal within 2 hours,
- vigorous exercise within 30 minutes,
- smoking within 1 hour and
- drinking alcohol within 4 hours

- for reversibility testing, patient should not take short acting bronchodilators
- within 6 hours, long acting bronchodilators within 24 hours

**Procedure:**

**Patient positioning:**

- Make the patient sit in upright position with feet flat on the
- ground and also to loosen the tight fitting clothes if any.
- Ask the patient to completely empty lungs and then to take in a quick full inspiration, followed by a full expiration into the hand held device through a disposable mouth piece. Enough encouragement should be given so that good results will be obtained

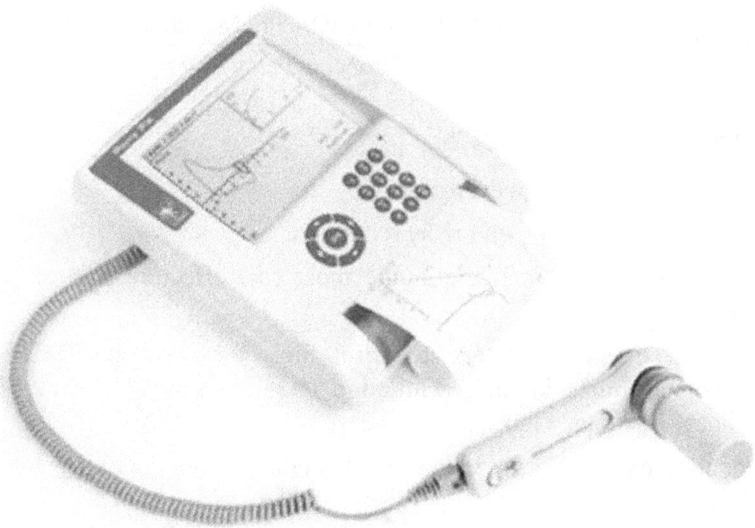

**An acceptable manoeuvre is:**

- An explosive start
- The manoeuvre is performed with a maximal inspiration and expiration.
- No glottis closure or cessation of airflow occurred during the manoeuvre (*e.g.* by hesitation or blocking the mouthpiece).
- No coughs (particularly during the first second), inspirations during the trace or evidence of leaks.

  The spirometry manoeuvre would be performed at least three times. The best two measurements must fulfil the reproducibility criteria.

- For FEV1 and FVC (FEV6), the best two values should be within 5% or 150 mL of each other, whichever is greater. The best FEV1 and FVC can be taken from different manoeuvres.

If this is not achieved, more manoeuvres are required. There is usually an upper limit of 5 manoeuvres.

When the FEV1/FEV6 is measured to be between 60 and 80 % is acceptable when measured by a mini-spirometer.

## Reversibility Testing

Spirometry is performed, after which a bronchodilator is given that can either be a short-acting -agonist or other agents, such as anticholinergics.

Spirometry is useful in differentiating between the two conditions. Presence of a post-bronchodilator FEV1 / FVC (or FEV1/FEV6) of less than 70% suggests a diagnosis of COPD whereas a post bronchodilator reversibility suggests a diagnosis of asthma.

$$\text{Reversibility (\%)} = \frac{\text{Post Bronchodilator FEV1} - \text{Pre Bronchodilator FEV1}}{\text{Pre Bronchodilator FEV1}} \times 100$$

## Prevention and Control

**For COPD – Exposure prevention**

- Life style modification and risks reduction.
- Smoking cessation: It is the single most cost effective way to manage COPD.
- Using clean energy instead of solid fuels for cooking (PMUY) and ensuring adequate kitchen ventilation (E.g., improve cross ventilation, chimney, or exhaust fan).
- Reducing exposure to second hand smoke if not smoking himself / herself.
- Adequate usage of respiratory protection in case occupational exposure is the cause.
- Avoid dusty and damp settings at home or outside.
- Avoid indoor air pollutants, (e.g., mosquito coils, fragrance sticks, dhoop-agarbatti,
- chemicals fumes used as mosquito repellents).
- Avoid going outside, doing exercise in heavy smoke outside, air pollution etc.

**Physical Activity**

- Aerobic exercise: Pursed lip breathing (breathing out slowly with the lips in a whistling position), diaphragmatic breathing (deep breathing focusing on the abdomen) and pranayama yoga breathing (timed breathing with a focus on exhalation) improve physical capacity. These exercises result in decrease in dynamic hyperinflation and exertional dyspnoea; improved exercise tolerance; and enhanced quality of life, with fewer disease exacerbations and reported sick days.

- Walking is also an important exercise with several benefits: at least 30 minutes of walking every day is extremely beneficial to COPD patients.
- Simple stretching and weight bearing exercises with filled water bottles can improve overall muscle mass.
- Resistance training: increase muscle mass and strength, augmenting patient' ability to perform tasks of daily living and improving health-related quality of life.

**For Asthma - Exposure prevention:**

- Avoid Asthma triggers mentioned in text box above.
- Avoid drugs like NSAIDs and selective beta blockers in those sensitive
- Use damp cloths to clean furniture, sprinkling the floor with water before sweeping, cleaning blades of fans regularly.
- Use mosquito nets rather than coils and avoid the use of incense sticks.
    - Do weight reduction (If obese or overweight)
    - Physical activity and regular exercises (including yoga)
    - Avoid smoking

**Patient and family education:**

- About the reversible nature of illness, that Asthma can be controlled but may need continuous therapy and regular follow up.
- Rationale for the inhaled drugs, different inhaler devices and inhalation techniques.
- Inhalers are not habit-forming. Inhalers are safe and better than tablets or Syrup.
- Emphasize the need for adherence with the prescribed controller drugs.
- Advice regarding dealing with triggers/ precipitants. Emphasize that diet has minimal role in causation of symptoms.

**Pharmacists' Role**

Community / Hospital Pharmacists:

- Educating the common man on preventive strategies [discussed above] emphasizing avoiding risk factors including smoking.
- Educating / Guiding patients on medication use especially metered dose inhalers and adherence.

**Bottom Line**

- Chronic Obstructive Pulmonary Diseases (COPD) and Asthma are two most common chronic respiratory diseases with significant public health issues.
- COPD is characterized by persistent respiratory symptoms and airflow limitation that is due to airway and/or alveolar abnormalities usually caused by significant exposure to noxious particles or gases.
- Asthma is a heterogeneous disease, usually characterized by chronic inflammation with symptoms of wheeze, shortness of breath, chest tightness and cough.
- Symptoms of COPD: Difficulty breathing, Chronic cough (sometimes with phlegm), and Feeling tired.
- Symptoms of Asthma: Persistent cough, especially at night, Wheezing when exhaling and sometimes when inhaling, Shortness of breath or difficulty breathing, sometimes even when resting, and Chest tightness, making it difficult to breathe deeply.
- Approximately half a billion people live with asthma and COPD and together these 2 conditions cause almost 4 million deaths every year worldwide.
- According to Global Burden of Disease Report (2019): COPD and asthma contribute 17.8 % and 13 % of the global burden in India.
- Differentiating COPD and Asthma: Asthma is reversible and COPD is not reversible in Post Bronchodilator spirometry.
- COPD – Exposure prevention: Smoking cessation, Using clean energy, Reducing exposure to second hand smoke, Adequate usage of respiratory protection, Avoid dusty and damp settings at home or outside, Avoid indoor air pollutants, Avoid going outside, doing exercise in heavy smoke outside, air pollution etc.
- Physical activities in COPD: Aerobic exercise, Walking, Simple stretching and weight bearing exercises.
- Asthma Exposure prevention:
    - Avoid Asthma triggers, Avoid drugs like NSAIDs and selective beta blockers, Using damp cloths to clean furniture, sprinkling the floor with water before sweeping, Using mosquito nets rather than coils and avoid the use of incense sticks.
    - Practice regular exercises (including yoga) and Avoid smoking.
- Community / Hospital Pharmacists' Contribution: Educating the common man on preventive strategies emphasizing avoiding risk factors including smoking. Educating / Guiding patients on medication use especially metered dose inhalers and adherence.

## Bibliography

1. SWAAS, Kerala State COPD Control Program, Module for Medical Officers, State NCD Division, Government of Kerala.
2. Medical Officer's Manual for Prevention and Management of Chronic Obstructive Pulmonary Disease & Asthma, National Programme for Prevention and Control of Cancer, Diabetes, Cardiovascular Diseases and Stroke, Government of India, 2021.
3. WHO Package of Essential Noncommunicable Disease Interventions for Primary Health Care, World Health Organization, 2020.

## Diabetes Mellitus

"If we want to get diabetes under control, we have to get our diets under control."

- Eric Adams

**After reading this chapter, you should be able to understand and appreciate:**

- Diabetes as a public health issue;
- Symptoms of Diabetes;
- Global and India's burden;
- Diagnosis and treatment options available;
- Prevention and Control Strategies Practiced; and
- Pharmacists in diabetes prevention and treatment.

Diabetes is a disease in which the body does not produce or properly use the hormone insulin. All food that we eat is broken down into a sugar called glucose. Glucose is carried by the blood to all the parts of the body to give energy. Insulin helps glucose move from the blood into the cells and keep the blood sugar levels normal. In diabetes, the glucose builds up in the blood, resulting in high blood glucose levels. Normally, a blood glucose level taken randomly (that is at any time of the day) of over 140 mg/dl should lead to a suspicion of diabetes.

Diabetes is classified into three types: Type 1 diabetes, Type 2 diabetes, and Gestational diabetes. Their features are:

**Type 1 diabetes:**

- Body does not produce insulin at all. People with this form of diabetes require daily injections of insulin in order to control the levels of glucose in their blood. This may be due to genetics, changes in environmental risk factors and/or viral infections.
- The disease can affect people of any age, but onset usually occurs in children, adolescents and younger people. The diagnosis of Type 1 Diabetes can be made throughout childhood but it is more likely below 15 yrs of age.
- The onset is usually acute and severe and insulin is required for survival.

**Type 2 diabetes:**

- This is the most common type of diabetes. The body produces some insulin, but not enough or the cells cannot use this insulin very well. People can be treated with oral medication, but may also require insulin injections.
- This type of diabetes used to be seen only in adults but it is now also occurring increasingly in children and adolescents. It is strongly associated with ageing populations, family history, excess body weight, unhealthy lifestyle- poor dietary habits, lack/low of physical activity, tobacco and alcohol consumption, etc.
- There is no insulin dependence till late in the course of illness.

**Gestational diabetes:**

- Diabetes which occurs among women during pregnancy.
- Women during pregnancy, and is associated with a risk of complications during pregnancy and delivery. The children of women with Gestational Diabetes are at an increased risk of type 2 diabetes in the future.

**Complications of untreated / uncontrolled diabetes:** If the blood glucose stays too high and is not treated on time, it can cause damage to the main organs such as:

- **Kidneys:** causing kidney failure with Heart and blood vessel disease- causing heart attack and stroke.
- **Nerves (Neuropathy):** Diabetes can damage blood vessels throughout the body. It causes numbness, tingling in hands and/or feet, making it hard to feel injuries. Diabetes also makes it harder for wounds to heal, easily leading to foot ulcers and infections. Fungus on the feet can also lead to infection. A foot infection can spread to the whole leg if not treated. The leg may become so infected that it needs to be removed (amputated). But good foot care and managing blood sugar levels can prevent amputation.
- **Eyes (Retinopathy):** Diabetes can damage blood vessels in the eyes, leading to gradual loss of vision or blindness. If an eye clinic is available, a person with diabetes should have their eyes tested once a year. If vision becomes blurry, keeping sugar levels down may help the eyes recover.
- **Oral cavity:** Diabetes worsens gum infections which, in turn, makes diabetes worse. People with diabetes should brush their teeth at least twice a day with a toothbrush or a chewstick (miswak, neem stick). A person with diabetes will benefit from seeing a dentist.

**Word of Mouth**

**Symptoms**

- Frequent urination;
- Increased hunger;
- Excessive thirst;
- Unexplained weight loss;
- Lack of energy, extreme tiredness;
- Lack of interest and concentration;
- Blurred vision;
- Repeated or severe infections such as vaginal infections;
- Slow healing of wounds, dry or itchy skin; and
- Impotence in men.

Persons at high risk:

- If he/she is overweight (BMI is more than 23 kg/m$^2$).
- If he/she is physically inactive, that is, he or she exercises less than 3 times a week.
- If he/she has high blood pressure.
- If he/she has impaired fasting glucose or impaired glucose tolerance.
- If his/her triglyceride and/or cholesterol levels are higher than normal.
- If his/her parents/siblings or grandparents have or had diabetes.
- If she delivered a baby whose birth weight was 4 kg or more.
- If she has had diabetes or even mild elevation of blood sugars during pregnancy.

**Global Burden:** About 422 million people worldwide have diabetes, the majority living in low-and middle-income countries, and 1.5 million deaths are directly attributed to diabetes each year. Both the number of cases and the prevalence of diabetes have been steadily increasing over the past few decades. In 2019, diabetes was the direct cause of 1.5 million deaths and 48% of all deaths due to diabetes occurred before the age of 70 years. Another 460 000 kidney disease deaths were caused by diabetes, and raised blood glucose causes around 20% of cardiovascular deaths.

## India's Burden and Initiatives

In 2019, diabetes was the direct cause of 1.5 million deaths and has prevalence of 9% among adults 18 years and above. 2018 data shows that 3 % of death is attributed to diabetes. More than 50% of people are unaware of their diabetic status which leads to health complications if not detected and treated early.

Adults with diabetes have a two- to three-fold increased risk of heart attacks and strokes. Combined with reduced blood flow, neuropathy (nerve damage) in the feet increases the chance of foot ulcers, infection, and the eventual need for limb amputation. Diabetic retinopathy is an important cause of blindness and occurs as a result of long-term accumulated damage to the small blood vessels in the retina. Diabetes is among the leading causes of kidney failure.

The government of India initiated and executed mDiabetes programme to reach a large number of people to improve their lifestyle and health-seeking behaviour

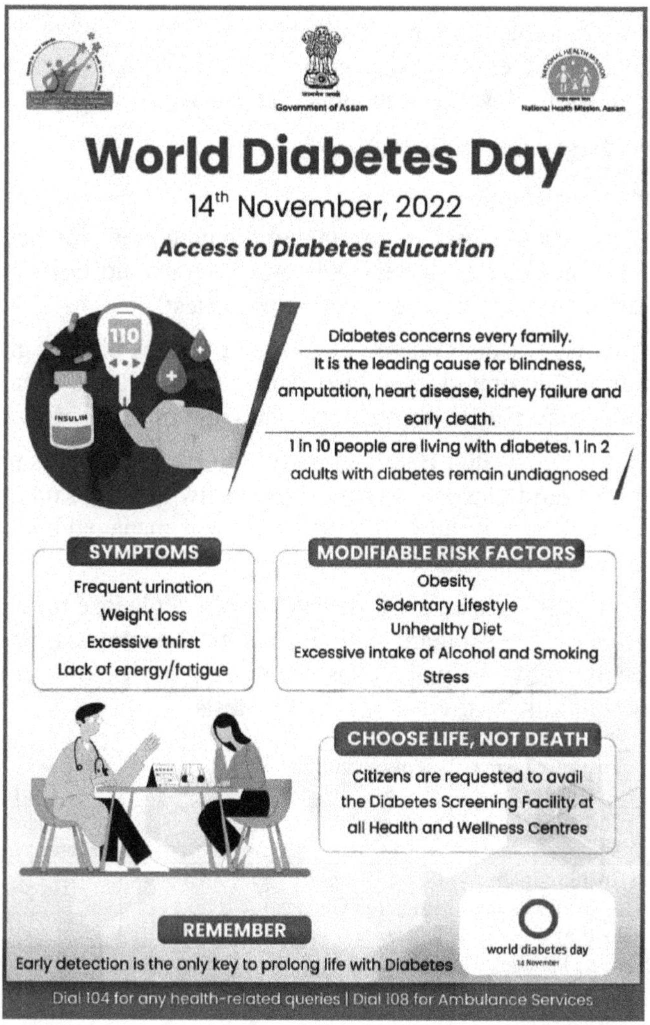

## Diagnosis and Treatment

**Screening by Strip Method:**

1. Take out the glucometer and place on a flat surface.
2. Remove a test strip from the container and place in the glucometer. One end will need to face the top of the glucometer; usually it has a darker colored line on it. This is where the blood will be placed for testing.
3. Turn on your glucometer.
4. Use a lancet to pierce the skin and obtain blood from the tip of a finger.
5. Place the blood sample on the test strip. The test strip package will have exact instructions, including blood sample size. Usually, this is accomplished by placing the blood drop against the edge or top of the strip.
6. Watch the glucometer screen. It should show a "waiting" or "processing" symbol, and will emit a beep when the sample has been tested. The results will be displayed as a number on the screen.

**Criteria for diagnosing diabetes**

**Testing for diagnosis**

- Fasting plasma glucose: Before taking the blood test, the person should have taken no food for at least 8 hours. They should fast overnight and must not have anything to eat until after the test.
- Post Prandial Plasma Glucose: Two- hour venous plasma glucose after ingestion of 75g oral glucose load. This is an indication of how well the body's cells are able to absorb a fixed amount of sugar or glucose.
- HBA1C (Glycosylated Haemoglobin): The HbA1c level is proportional to average blood glucose over the previous two to three months. It is an excellent indicator of how well the patient has managed his/her diabetes over the last four weeks to three months.
- Random Plasma Glucose: Sugar level or blood glucose measured at any time of day without regard to time since the last meal. It does not take into account what the patient has been eating or drinking. It is easier to perform but less sensitive than the other tests.

| Category | Fasting plasma glucose | Post Prandial Plasma Glucose | HBA1C | Random Plasma Glucose |
|---|---|---|---|---|
| Diabetes | ≥ 126 mg/dl | ≥ 200 mg/dl | ≥ 6.5 % | ≥ 200 mg/dl + diabetes symptoms |
| Prediabetes | 110 -125 mg/dl (Impaired Fasting Glucose) | 140 -199 mg/dl (Impaired Glucose Tolerance) | 5.7 – 6.4 % | |
| Criteria for suspected Diabetes case is reading of 140 mg/dl by glucostrip. The suspected case needs to undergo further tests to confirm the diabetes. | | | | |

**Treatment:** Glucose control is the key to diabetes management. Three strategies are effective:

- **Drug therapy:** The physician's prerogative to prescribing drugs.
- **Life style management:** Change in lifestyle behaviours is effective in preventing or delaying the occurrence of Type 2 diabetes. Eating a healthy diet, being physically active, avoiding the use of tobacco in any form/avoiding exposure to second-hand smoke, reducing the intake of alcohol amongst heavy drinkers, managing stress, reducing weight amongst overweight/obese individuals, etc. are the lifestyle changes.
- **Patient Education:**
  - Medication adherence.
  - Managing hypoglycaemia: Hypoglycaemia occurs when blood sugar (glucose) level falls below a level of 70 milligrams per decilitre (mg/dl) or less. If not treated, hypoglycaemia can be life-threatening. The only way to know if someone has hypoglycaemia is to check blood glucose.
  - Symptoms are tremours, nervousness or anxiety, sweating, irritability, confusion, rapid/fast heartbeat, dizziness, hunger, nausea, blurred/ impaired vision, headaches, weakness or fatigue, lack of coordination, falls, seizures, unconsciousness and can lead to accidents, injuries, coma and even death.

    The reasons are:

    - Missing or skipping a meal,
    - Long gap between two meals or delay in eating meals,
    - Taking more than recommended dosage of insulin or anti-diabetic drugs,
    - Side- effects of some anti-diabetic drugs, and
    - Increased physical activity If someone is having signs of hypoglycaemia, it's important to treat it right away.

Hypoglycaemia can be treated by consuming a small amount of sugar rich foods as soon as symptoms appear. For such an emergency, diabetic patients should be advised to always carry something to eat such as loose sugar, rock candy (misri) or toffee, etc.

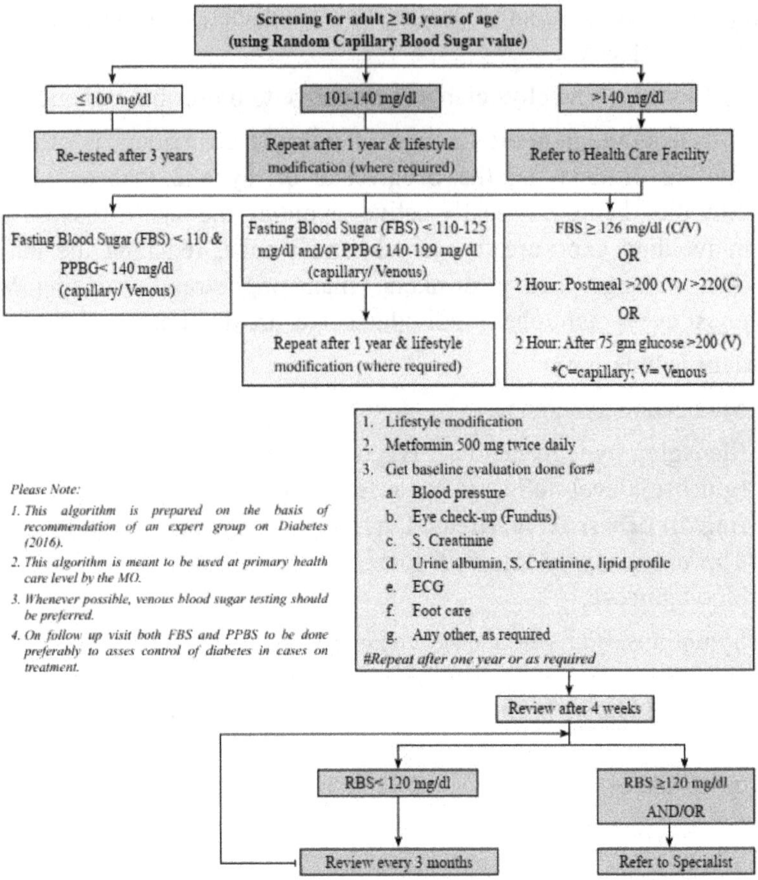


**Fig. 1.** Algorithm for Screening and Management of Diabetes [Source: Training Module for Medical Officers for Prevention, Control and Population Level Screening of Hypertension, Diabetes and Common Cancer (Oral, Breast & Cervical), National Centre for Disease Control, Government of India, 2017].

## Prevention and Control

People's education and sensitization are critical. Lifestyle changes are the best way to prevent or delay the onset of type 2 diabetes.

To help prevent type 2 diabetes and its complications, people should:

- reach and keep a healthy body weight
- stay physically active with at least 30 minutes of moderate exercise each day
- eat a healthy diet and avoid sugar and saturated fat
- not smoke tobacco.

**Pharmacists' Role**

- **Community Pharmacists:**
    - They can raise awareness of diabetes as a serious threat, support the screening and detection of diabetes, and counsel community members on healthy lifestyle.
    - They can guide the patients on medication adherence.
    - They should guide the patients on storing insulin at home: Using an airtight container to store their insulin inside household refrigerators to reduce temperature fluctuations.
    - If using cool bags with ice or ice packs to transport insulin, making sure the vials or pens are not in direct contact with the ice packs.
- **Hospital Pharmacists:**
    - They can ensure availability of medicines.
    - They should guide the patients on storing insulin at home: Using an airtight container to store their insulin inside household refrigerators to reduce temperature fluctuations.
    - If using cool bags with ice or ice packs to transport insulin, making sure the vials or pens are not in direct contact with the ice packs.
    - They can guide the patients on medication adherence.
    - They can be partner in field reach out activities promoting community health.

**Bottom Line**

- Diabetes is a disease in which the body does not produce or properly use the hormone insulin. In diabetes, the glucose builds up in the blood, resulting in high blood glucose levels.
- Diabetes is classified into three types: Type 1 diabetes - Body does not produce insulin at all. People with this form of diabetes require daily injections of insulin; Type 2 diabetes - This is the most common type of diabetes. The body produces some insulin, but not enough; and Gestational diabetes - Diabetes which occurs among women during pregnancy.
- If the blood glucose stays too high and is not treated on time, it can cause damage to the main organs such as Kidneys, Heart and blood vessels, Nerves, Eyes, and Oral cavity.
- Common Symptoms are: Frequent urination; Increased hunger; Excessive thirst; Unexplained weight loss; Lack of energy, extreme tiredness; Lack of interest and concentration; Blurred vision; Repeated or severe infections such as vaginal infections; Slow healing of wounds, dry or itchy skin; and Impotence in men.

- The following persons are at high risk: overweight, physically inactive, high blood pressure, impaired fasting glucose or impaired glucose tolerance, higher lipid levels, hereditary risk, baby's birth weight 4 kg or more, elevation of blood sugar level during pregnancy.
- About 422 million people worldwide have diabetes, the majority living in low-and middle-income countries, and 1.5 million deaths are directly attributed to diabetes each year.
- In India, diabetes was the direct cause of 1.5 million deaths with prevalence of 9% among adults 18 years and above in 2019.
- Diagnosis Criteria:

| Category | Fasting plasma glucose | Post Prandial Plasma Glucose | HBA1C | Random Plasma Glucose |
|---|---|---|---|---|
| Diabetes | ≥ 126 mg/dl | ≥ 200 mg/dl | ≥ 6.5 % | ≥ 200 mg/dl + diabetes symptoms |
| Prediabetes | 110 -125 mg/dl (Impaired Fasting Glucose) | 140 -199 mg/dl (Impaired Glucose Tolerance) | 5.7 – 6.4 % | |
| Criteria for suspected Diabetes case is reading of 140 mg/dl by glucostrip. The suspected case needs to undergo further tests to confirm the diabetes. | | | | |

- Glucose control is the key to diabetes management. Three strategies are Drug therapy, Life style management and patient education.
- Lifestyle changes are the best way to prevent or delay the onset of type 2 diabetes.
- Pharmacists can participate in community education on diabetes risk factors, preventing and adherence to medication are important.

## Bibliography

1. Diabetes prevention, screening and management, A handbook for pharmacists, FIP 2021.
2. https://www.who.int/health-topics/diabetes#tab=tab_1 accessed on 10th November 2024.
3. Module for Multi-Purpose Workers - Female / Male on Prevention, Screening and Control of Common Non-Communicable Diseases, National Health Mission, Government of India.

## Hypertension

If you don't know your blood pressure, it's like not knowing the value of your company.

- Mehmet Oz

**After reading this chapter, you should be able to understand and appreciate:**

- Hypertension as a public health issue;
- Symptoms of Hypertension;
- Global and India's burden;
- Diagnosis and treatment options available;
- Prevention and Control Strategies Practiced; and
- Pharmacists in hypertension prevention and treatment.

Hypertension, commonly known as high blood pressure, is defined as systolic blood pressure of 140 mm of Hg or greater and / or diastolic blood pressure of 90 mm of Hg. The systolic (first number) number represents the pressure in blood vessels when the heart contracts or beats. The diastolic (second) number represents the pressure in the vessels when the heart rests between beats.

Hypertension is recognized as one of the major risk factors for cardiovascular disease and premature deaths worldwide. This is 'Silent Killer' diseases today as it can exists without any signs or symptom, with every third person having suffered from it. International data suggest that fewer than half of those with hypertension are aware of their condition.

In high blood pressure, heart has to pump harder than normal for blood to get to all parts of the body. Hypertension is a serious medical condition that significantly increases the risk of heart, brain, kidney and other diseases. More people die each year from cardiovascular diseases than from any other cause.

**Word of Mouth**

**Symptoms:** Very high blood pressures can cause headaches, blurred vision, chest pain and other symptoms. Very high: 180/120 or higher have symptoms including:

- severe headaches
- chest pain
- dizziness

- difficulty breathing
- nausea
- vomiting
- blurred vision or other vision changes
- anxiety
- confusion
- buzzing in the ears
- nosebleeds
- abnormal heart rhythm

Maintaining Healthy Blood Pressure:

- Keeping Weight Healthy;
- Exercising Regularly (average of 30 minutes a day and Yoga);
- Eating plenty of fruit and/or vegetables every day;
- Cutting down on salt (less than 5 g daily) and reducing intake of fried food;
- Cutting down on fat and sugar;
- Stop smoking tobacco;
- Reducing caffeine intake;
- Avoiding drinking too much alcohol; and
- Relaxing: stress contributes to raising blood pressure.

**Global Burden:** An estimated 1.4 billion people worldwide have high blood pressure, but just 14% have it under control. An estimated 46% of adults with hypertension are unaware that they have the condition. Hypertension is a major cause of premature death worldwide.

The WHO African Region has the highest prevalence of hypertension (27%) while the WHO Region of the Americas has the lowest prevalence of hypertension (18%). One of the global targets for noncommunicable diseases is to reduce the prevalence of hypertension by 33% between 2010 and 2030.

**India's Burden and Initiatives:** Hypertension is one of the leading causes of premature deaths in India. Hypertension is attributable to 10.8% of all deaths in India. Hypertension is directly responsible for 29% of all stroke and 24% of heart attack. The adult Hypertension prevalence has shown a drastic increase in the past three decades in urban as well as rural areas. It is estimated that 16% of Ischaemic Heart Disease, 21% of Peripheral Vascular Disease, 24% of Acute Myocardial Infarctions and 29% of strokes are attributed to hypertension.

The various initiatives are introduced on sustaining and scaling up hypertension screening, education and health promotion using digital innovations at the population level.

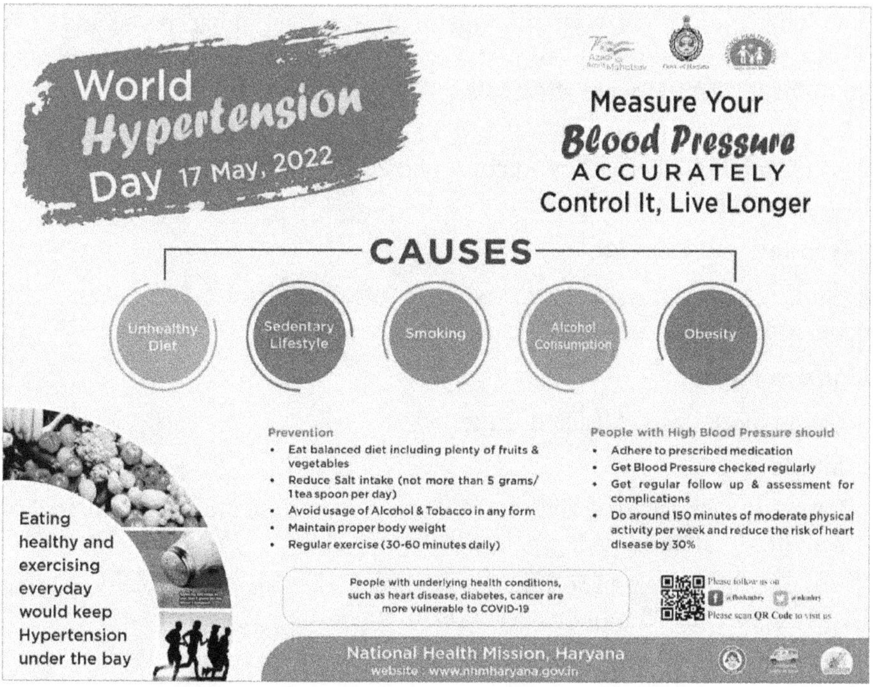


**Diagnosis and Treatment:** The blood pressure is of two types:

- Primary/essential: It has no known cause, however many of the above said lifestyle factors are associated with this condition.
- Secondary: Secondary hypertension is caused by some other medical conditions/problem or the use of certain medications. The causes of secondary hypertension include: kidney diseases: reno-vascular disease and chronic renal disease, endocrine disorders: hyperthyroidism, cushing's syndrome and pheocromocytoma, sleep disorders, coarctation of the aorta and non-specific aorto-arteritis.

**Criteria for diagnosing high blood pressure:**

| Category | Systolic (mm of Hg) | Diastolic (mm of Hg) |
|---|---|---|
| Normal | Less than 120 | Less than 80 |
| Pre-hypertension | 120-139 | 80-89 |
| High Blood Pressure | | |
| Stage 1 | 140-159 | 90-99 |
| Stage 2 | 160 or higher | 100 or higher |

The classification is based on consistent elevation during two or more properly measured BP readings in sitting position.

The treatment may be categorised into:

- **Therapeutic life style management:** Avoiding tobacco use and high salt, encouraging fruits and vegetables intake, encourage moderate physical activity are strategies.
- **Drug treatment:** Diuretics (Chlorthalidone/ Indapamide), Calcium channel blockers (Amlodipine) and ACE inhibitors (Ramipril/ Perindopril) are relatively cheap.

**Prevention and Control**

Lifestyle changes can help lower high blood pressure: The readers are encouraged to refer the materials given in textbox.

**Good practices:**

- Eating more vegetables and fruits.
- Sitting less.
- Improving physical activity: walking, running, swimming, dancing or activities that build strength, like lifting weights.
    - Getting at least 150 minutes per week of moderate-intensity aerobic activity or 75 minutes per week of vigorous aerobic activity.
    - Doing strength building exercises 2 or more days each week.
- Losing weight in case of overweight or obese.
- Adhering to prescribed medicines.
- Regularly checking BP.

**Avoiding unhealthy practices:**

- Eating too much salty food (try to stay under 2 grams per day)
- Eating foods of high in saturated or trans fats
- Smoking or using tobacco
- Drinking too much alcohol (1 drink daily max for women, 2 for men)

Reducing hypertension prevents heart attack, stroke and kidney damage, as well as other health problems.

**Reduce the risks of hypertension by:**

- reducing and managing stress
- regularly checking blood pressure
- treating high blood pressure
- managing other medical conditions
- reducing exposure to polluted air.

**WHO's Recommendation on Sodium Intake:**

- eat mostly fresh, minimally processed foods
- choose low-sodium products (less than 120mg/100g sodium)
- cook with little or no added sodium/salt
- use herbs and spices to flavour food, rather than salt
- limit the use of commercial sauces, dressings and instant products
- limit the consumption of processed foods
- remove the saltshaker/container from the table.

**Pharmacists' Role**: WHO suggests that pharmacological treatment of hypertension can be provided by nonphysician professionals such as pharmacists and nurses, as long as the following conditions are met: proper training, prescribing authority, specific management protocols and physician oversight.

**Community Pharmacists:**

- Educating the common man on importance of controlling blood pressure through life style changes.
- Educating / Guiding patients on medication adherence.

**Hospital Pharmacists:**

- Managing medicines ensuring uninterrupted availability.
- Educating / Guiding patients on medication adherence.
- Participating in screening activities as a part of outreach activities.
- Educating the common man on importance of controlling blood pressure through life style changes.

**Bottom Line**

- Hypertension, commonly known as high blood pressure, is defined as systolic blood pressure of 140 mm of Hg or greater and / or diastolic blood pressure of 90 mm of Hg. Hypertension is a serious medical condition that significantly increases the risk of heart, brain, kidney and other diseases.
- Very high blood pressures can cause headaches, blurred vision, chest pain and other symptoms.
- The healthy blood pressure can be maintained by Keeping Weight Healthy; Exercising Regularly (average of 30 minutes a day and Yoga); Eating plenty of fruit and/or vegetables every day; Cutting down on salt (less than 5 g daily) and reducing intake of fried food; Cutting down on fat and sugar; Stop smoking tobacco; Reducing caffeine

intake; Avoiding drinking too much alcohol; and Relaxing: stress contributes to raising blood pressure.

- An estimated 1.4 billion people worldwide have high blood pressure, but just 14% have it under control.
- Hypertension is one of the leading causes of premature deaths in India. Hypertension is attributable to 10.8% of all deaths in India.
- The blood pressure is of two types: Primary/essential and Secondary.

| Category | Systolic (mm of Hg) | Diastolic (mm of Hg) |
|---|---|---|
| Normal | Less than 120 | Less than 80 |
| Pre-hypertension | 120-139 | 80-89 |
| High Blood Pressure | | |
| Stage 1 | 140-159 | 90-99 |
| Stage 2 | 160 or higher | 100 or higher |

- The treatment may be categorised into: Therapeutic life style management and Drug treatment.
- Life tyle changes can help lower high blood pressure. Good practices include eating more vegetables and fruits; sitting less; improving physical activity: walking, running, swimming, dancing or activities that build strength, like lifting weights; losing weight in case of overweight or obese; adhering to prescribed medicines and regularly checking BP.
- Unhealthy practices include eating too much salty food; eating foods of high in saturated or trans fats; smoking or using tobacco; and drinking too much alcohol.
- Reduction of the risks of hypertension can be achieved by reducing and managing stress; regularly checking blood pressure; treating high blood pressure; managing other medical conditions; and reducing exposure to polluted air.
- Pharmacists' Role: Educating the common man on avoiding the risk factors and promoting medication adherence are important functions.

**Blood Pressure Awareness among Indians:** The awareness on diagnosis and treatment of the hypertension is significantly low. More than 50% of those with hypertension are unaware of their diagnosis, less than 1 in 7 (13%) take blood pressure lowering medication, less than 1 in 10 (10%) achieved any control over their condition. Awareness level was lowest in Chhattisgarh (22.1%) and highest in Puducherry over 80%.

In urban areas, 47.9% of hypertensive people were aware of their condition, whereas only 14.9% received treatment and 8.3% were controlled. The situation was worse in rural areas where 42.5% were aware, 12.3% got treatment and only 7.7% were controlled.

Improvement in access to hypertension diagnosis and treatment are important among men in rural areas and in populations with lower household wealth.

Women were found to have better control over their blood pressure than men. One study reported that while 10.9% of hypertensive women were taking medicine and had normal blood pressure. Only 5.3% of hypertensive men did so.

[The Times of India, Chennai, May 15, 2019]

## Bibliography

1. Guideline for pharmacological treatment of hypertension in adults, WHO, 2021.
2. https://www.who.int/news-room/fact-sheets/detail/hypertension/?gad_source=1&gclid=Cj0KCQiAire5BhCNARIsAM53K1gksASQryxl-Il55sXka_rFsGbnly7myFxls8yyqGLPnfXohieoTHAaAv2EEALw_wcB accessed on 09th November 2024.
3. Module for Multi-Purpose Workers - Female / Male on Prevention, Screening and Control of Common Non-Communicable Diseases, National Health Mission, Government of India.

# CHAPTER 7

# National Health Programmes and Roles of Pharmacists

## National Health Programmes

National Health Programmes are central government initiatives to improve public health and ensure access to health care to all citizens. They focus on education, prevention, treatment and building health infrastructure.

The National Health Policy listed the following National Health Programmes:

- RMNCH+A Services,
- Child and Adolescent Health,
- Interventions to Address Malnutrition and Micronutrient Deficiencies,
- Universal Immunization,
- Communicable Diseases,
- Control of Tuberculosis,
- Control of HIV/AIDS,
- Leprosy Elimination,
- Vector Borne Disease Control,
- Non-Communicable Diseases,
- Mental Health, and
- Population Stabilization.

# Anaemia

- Eat Iron. Kick anaemia.

**After reading this chapter, you should be able to understand and appreciate:**

- Anaemia as public health issue;
- Classification of anaemia on the basis of haemoglobin level;
- Initiatives to combat anaemia;
- Operation of the Anaemia Mukt Bharat Strategy; and
- Pharmacists' Role in Anaemia Control.

Anaemia is a condition in which the number and size of red blood cells, or the haemoglobin concentration, falls below an established cut-off value, consequently impairing the capacity of the blood to transport oxygen around the body. Oxygen requirement of the body varies by age, sex, altitude, smoking habits, and during pregnancy. Anaemia is an indicator of both poor nutrition and poor health. The manifestations of anaemia vary by its severity and range from fatigue, weakness, dizziness and drowsiness to impaired cognitive development of children and increased morbidity.

## Epidemiology

Though Anaemia is not a disease but just the manifestation, it is a public health issue in India. With huge interstate variations: 58% of the children aged 6-59 months in India are anaemic (<11.0 g/dl), while the anaemic level in children were highest in Dadra & Nagar Haveli (85 %) and lowest in Mizoram (18 %). 53 % of non-pregnant women aged 15-49 years were anaemic (<12.0 g/dl) and the anaemia levels among the non-pregnant women were highest in Dadra & Nagar Haveli (80 %) and lowest in Mizoram (22 %). Half of the pregnant women of 15-49 years were anaemic (<11.0 g/dl) and the anaemia level among the pregnant women are highest in Jharkhand (63 %) and lowest in Kerala (23 %). Among all women in India 53 % are anaemic and in the states / UTs this level is highest in Dadra & Nagar Haveli (80 %) and lowest in Mizoram (23 %). (Ref: National Family Health Survey, 2015-2016; National Health Profile 2019).

Globally too the anaemia is considered a serious public health problem that particularly affects young children and pregnant women. 42 % of children with less than 5 years of age and 40 % of the pregnant women worldwide are anaemic. It is estimated that one-third of all women of reproductive age are anaemic.

## Causes of Anaemia

The most common cause of anaemia worldwide is iron deficiency, resulting from prolonged negative iron balance, caused by inadequate dietary iron intake or absorption, increased needs for iron during pregnancy or growth periods, and increased iron losses as a result of menstruation and helminth (intestinal worms) infestation. An estimated 50% of anaemia in women worldwide is due to iron deficiency. Other causes are: infections, malaria and nutritional deficiency (especially folate and vitamins B12, A and C).

### Common Symptoms

The most common symptom of anaemia is fatigue or weakness. Other signs and symptoms of anaemia include: Shortness of breath; Dizziness; Headache; Coldness in the hands and feet; Pale skin; Chest pain. Iron deficiency anaemia rarely causes any serious or long-term complications. However, some of the complications are: tiredness; making a person more susceptible to illness and infection; heart and lung complications and increased risk of developing complications during pregnancy, particularly during and after the birth.

**Diagnosis** (Haemoglobin Levels in mg/dl)

| Population | Anaemia | | |
|---|---|---|---|
| | **Mild** | **Moderate** | **Severe** |
| Children 6–59 months of age | 10–10.9 | 7–9.9 | <7 |
| Children 5–11 years of age | 11–11.4 | 8–10.9 | <8 |
| Children 12–14 years of age | 11–11.9 | 8–10.9 | <8 |
| Non-pregnant women (15 years of age and above) | 11–11.9 | 8–10.9 | <8 |
| Pregnant women | 10–10.9 | 7–9.9 | <7 |
| Men (15 years of age and above) | 11–12.9 | 8–10.9 | <8 |
| *Source: WHO- Nutritional Anaemia: Tools for Effective Prevention and Control, 2017* | | | |

## Preventive Strategy and National Programme

India has a long history of anaemia control. But there have been no marked improvements in anaemia situation. The iron and folic acid supplementation had just 30 % compliance rate. Considering National and International commitment, the government of India launched the anaemia control under mission mode "Anaemia Mukt Bharat" in September 2018 for combating anaemia. The National Health Policy (2017) emphasised the need of intensified efforts to address all causes of anaemia. The government has also made a commitment to Global World Health Assembly Target of 50 % reduction of anaemia among women of reproductive age by 2025.

Anaemia Mukt Bharat Strategy is built up on POSHAN Abhiyaan (Holistic Nutrition), National Iron Plus Initiative (NIPI) and Weekly Iron and Folic Acid (WIFS) programmes. Anemia Mukt Bharat 6X6X6 strategy has defined 6 interventions:

1. Prophylactic Iron and Folic Acid Supplementation;
2. Deworming;
3. Intensified year-round Behaviour Change Communication Campaign (Solid Body, Smart Mind) including ensuring delayed cord clamping
4. Testing of anaemia using digital methods and point of care treatment
5. Mandatory provision of Iron Folic Acid fortified foods in public health programmes
6. Addressing non-nutritional causes of anaemia in endemic pockets, with special focus on malaria, haemoglobinopathies and fluorosis.

[the other 6 × 6 are 6 categories of beneficiaries (6 age groups) and participation of 6 ministries]

Prophylactic IFA Supplementation and Deworming are briefed below. Other four interventions are beyond the scope of this text.

| Time Line of Anaemia Control Programme in India | |
|---|---|
| 1970 | National Nutritional Anaemia Prophylaxis Programme |
| 1991 | National Anaemia Control Programme (NACP) |
| 1997 | NACP became the part of Reproductive and Child Health Programme (RCH) |
| 2005 | Included under NRHM (preventive and Treatment) |
| 2007 | 12 X 12 initiative to achieve haemoglobin of 12 g/dl for all adolescent by 2012 |
| 2013 | National Iron Plus Initiative (NIPI) |
| 2018 | Anaemia Mukt Bharat Strategy |

Anaemia Mukt Bharat Programme was launched to combat wide spread anaemia in the country in 2018. Iron deficiency is the major cause of anaemia. In order to raise awareness about the serious health consequences of iron deficiency, 'Iron Deficiency Day' is observed on 26th November every year.

## Target

The Anaemia Mukt Bharat strategy has been designed to reduce prevalence of anaemia by 3 percentage points per year among children, adolescents and women in the reproductive age group (15–49 years), between the year 2018 and 2022. The strategy is estimated to reach out to 450 million beneficiaries with specific anaemia prevalence targets for year 2022 to be achieved among various identified population groups.

Prophylactic Iron and Folic Acid (IFA) Supplementation

| **Prophylactic dose and regimen for Iron Folic Acid supplementation** | |
|---|---|
| **Age group** | **Dose and regime** |
| Children 6–59 months of age | Biweekly, 1 ml Iron and Folic Acid syrup<br>Each ml of Iron and Folic Acid syrup containing 20 mg elemental Iron + 100 mcg of Folic Acid<br>Bottle (50ml) to have an 'auto-dispenser' and information leaflet |
| Children 5–9 years of age | Weekly, 1 Iron and Folic Acid tablet<br>Each tablet containing 45 mg elemental Iron + 400 mcg Folic Acid, sugar-coated, pink colour |
| School-going adolescent girls and boys, 10–19 years of age Out-of-school adolescent girls, 10–19 years of age | Weekly, 1 Iron and Folic Acid tablet<br>Each tablet containing 60 mg elemental iron + 500 mcg Folic Acid, sugar-coated, blue colour |
| Women of reproductive age (non-pregnant, non-lactating) 20–49 years | Weekly, 1 Iron and Folic Acid tablet<br>Each tablet containing 60 mg elemental Iron + 500 mcg Folic Acid, sugar-coated, red colour |
| Pregnant women and lactating mothers (of 0–6 months child) | Daily, 1 Iron and Folic Acid tablet starting from the fourth month of pregnancy (that is from the second trimester), continued throughout pregnancy (minimum 180 days during pregnancy) and to be continued for 180 days, post-partum<br>Each tablet containing 60 mg elemental Iron + 500 mcg Folic Acid, sugar-coated, red colour |
| Prophylaxis with iron should be withheld in case of acute illness (fever, diarrhoea, pneumonia, etc.), and in a known case of thalassemia major/history of repeated blood transfusion.<br>All women in the reproductive age group in the pre-conception period and up to the first trimester of the pregnancy are advised to have 400 mcg of Folic Acid tablets, daily, to reduce the incidence of neural tube defects in the foetus. | |
| Guidance for appropriate use:<br>Advise to take drug with empty stomach for better action; and if patient have any symptoms like nausea, vomiting take the drug after food.<br>Warn patients, liquid preparations containing iron salts should take with plenty of water to prevent discoloration of the teeth.<br>Inform to patient medication may cause black stools, constipation or diarrhoea. | |

## Deworming

| Dose and regimen for deworming | |
|---|---|
| **Age group** | **Dose and regime** |
| Children 12–59 months of age | Biannual dose of 400 mg albendazole (Half tablet to children 12–24 months and 1 tablet to children 24–59 months) |
| Children 5–9 years of age | Biannual dose of 400 mg albendazole (1 tablet) |
| School-going adolescent girls and boys 10–19 years of age Out-of-school adolescent girls 10–19 years of age | Biannual dose of 400 mg albendazole (1 tablet) |
| Women of reproductive age (non-pregnant, non-lactating) 20–49 years | Biannual dose of 400 mg albendazole (1 tablet) |
| Pregnant women | One dose of 400 mg albendazole (1 tablet), after the first trimester, preferably during the second trimester |
| If the tablet is chewable, they should be chewed or crushed before swallowing. | |

## Roles of Stake Holders

All stake holders of the implementation have defined roles and responsibilities to implement the programme successfully.

| | |
|---|---|
| National Anemia Mukt Bharat Unit | Act as a nodal agency for policy and strategy formulation, resource allocation and monitoring expenditures, technical support for procurement and supply chain management, development of IEC/BCC materials and activity plan, establishing monitoring and digital reporting systems and reviewing progress.<br>• Provide support to states for roll-out of Anemia Mukt Bharat strategy.<br>• Coordinate external field assessments, validation of reported data, development of the digital dashboard cum knowledge repository and studies in consultation with National Centre for Excellence and Advanced Research on Anaemia Control (NCEAR-A) and other academic institutions |
| State Health Mission Unit | Establish the State Anemia Mukt Bharat Unit.<br>• Designate a nodal offi cer for overseeing the Anemia Mukt Bharat Unit.<br>• Support roll-out of the Anemia Mukt Bharat implementation strategy.<br>• Ensure quarterly review, reporting and supportive supervision as well as<br>• convergence with line departments and POSHAN Abhiyaan.<br>• Ensure uninterrupted supplies of micronutrients/commodities related to the Anaemia Mukt Bharat strategy. |
| AMB State Nodal Officer | Ensure budgeting for Anemia Mukt Bharat in Annual NHM-PIP under the respective FMR code for training, procurement, M&E, IEC/BCC activities, etc.<br>• Ensure convergence cum review meeting of state-level committee with<br>• participation from line departments.<br>• Ensure training of health functionaries and programme managers from the state level and below. |

**Table *contd...***

| | |
|---|---|
| | • Ensure timely procurement and supply of drugs, etc. till service delivery platforms.<br>• Ensure adequate IEC/BCC activities including printing and dissemination of materials.<br>• Ensure reporting, monitoring and supportive supervision of programme. |
| AMB District Nodal Officer | Ensure training/orientation of health functionaries and programme managers.<br>• Ensure district level review by the District Magistrate.<br>• Ensure timely supply of drugs as per adequate requirement, IEC materials, etc. till service delivery platforms.<br>• Ensure drug sampling as per protocol.<br>• Ensure adequate IEC/BCC activities at the district level.<br>• Ensure reporting, monitoring and supportive supervision of programme at the district level. |
| AMB Block Nodal Officer | Ensure training/orientation of ANM/ASHA/AWW, school teachers/SN/MO.<br>• Ensure availability of adequate supplies and maintain buffer stock at service delivery point.<br>• Ensure adequate IEC/BCC activities at the block level.<br>• Ensure reporting, monitoring and supportive supervision of programme. |

## Role of Pharmacists

The National Programme is being implemented involving ASHA workers and School Teachers. The pharmacists are not part of the National Programme implementation. However, the community pharmacists, being the first contact point for health needs of the people, have good opportunities to educate the members of the community. The members of the community visit pharmacy for various purposes including for buying medicines.

- Display of posters in the pharmacy: Posters educating common man on anaemia and advocating the need of iron and folic acid supplementation.
- Posters on nutrition related Anaemia Mukt Bharat.
- Guiding the customers when they buy iron and folic acid products. Providing patient counselling on appropriate use of these medicines: when to take – before or after food; discolouration of teeth; blackening of stool etc.
- Guiding the patients / customers on iron and folic acid rich foods: Iron rich foods – Leafy vegetables, Legumes, Dry fruits, Meat, Fish and Eggs. [Vitamin C containing fruits such as Amla, Guava and Citrus fruits are also encouraged for improving iron absorption]. Folate rich foods: Green Leafy Vegetables, Legumes, Nuts and Liver.

**Bottom Line**

- Anaemia is a major public health issue in India with high prevalence across the country irrespective of gender, age and geography.
- Almost 50 % of the pregnant women, 59 % of children under 5 years of age, 54 % of adolescent girls and 53 % of non-pregnant and non-lactating women of our country are anaemic.
- Based on haemoglobin level, anaemia is classified into mild, moderate and severe.
- Main contributing causes of anaemia are: Nutritional Deficiency of Iron, Vitamin $B_{12}$, Folate and Vitamin A. Infectious diseases: Malaria, Helminth Infections, Tuberculosis, Haemoglobinopathis too contribute.
- India has a long history of anaemia control initiatives. Current programme is Anaemia Mukt Bharat is being operationalized through well-defined mechanisms which are: National Anaemia Mukt Bharat Unit, State Health Mission Unit, AMB State Nodal Officer, AMB District Nodal Officer. It aims reduce prevalence of anaemia by 3 percentage points per year among children, adolescents and women in the reproductive age group (15–49 years), between the year 2018 and 2022.
- AMB Strategy has six defined interventions: Prophylactic Iron and Folic Acid Supplementation; Deworming; Intensified Year –Round Behaviour Changes Communication Campaign (Solid Body, Smart Mind) including ensuring delayed cord clamping; Testing of Anaemia using digital methods and point of care treatment; Mandatory provision of Iron Folic Acid fortified foods in public health programmes; and Addressing non-nutritional causes
- of anaemia in endemic pockets, with special focus on malaria, haemoglobinopathies and fluorosis.

- Though there is no specified role / responsibility specified in National Programme of Anaemia Control, the community pharmacists can engage themselves educating the community members on anaemia and its prevention. They can guide the common man: using the iron preparations; and nutritional resources of iron and folic acid.

## Bibliography:


1. https://www.who.int/health-topics/anaemia#tab=tab_1 accessed on 26th May 2021.
2. Anaemia Mukt Bharat, Intensified National Iron Plus Initiative, Operational Guidelines for Programme Managers, Government of India, April 2018.
3. National Health Profile, 2020, 15th Issue, Central Bureau of Health Intelligence, Government of India.
4. Annual Report 2020-21, Department of Health and Family Welfare, Ministry of Health and Family Welfare, Government of India.
5. Somarouthu Venkata Saibaba, Bandameedi Ramu. Role of Community Pharmacist in Management of Anaemia. *Open Science Journal of Clinical Medicine.* Vol. 6, No. 2, 2018, pp. 5-9.
6. WHA Global Nutrition Targets 2025, Anaemia Policy Brief, WHO/NMH/NHD/14.4, 2014

# Blindness

Eyes are useless when the mind is blind.

**After reading this chapter, you should be able to understand and appreciate:**

- Definition of Blindness;
- Prevalence and Burden of Blindness; and
- India's effort tackling Blindness.

Blindness means the person is not able to see. This is lack of vision. The blindness terminology is being replaced by visual impairment. "Total Blindness" was the term used in India in 1970 which referred to persons having no perception of light.

The current definition of blindness adopted under the National Programme for Controlling Blindness is presenting distance Visual Acuity less than 20/200 in the better eye.

## Epidemiology

**Global:** Globally, at least 2.2 billion people have a near or distance vision impairment. In at least 1 billion of these, vision impairment could have been prevented or is yet to be addressed. The leading causes of vision impairment and blindness at a global level are refractive errors and cataracts.

It is estimated that globally only 36% of people with a distance vision impairment due to refractive error and only 17% of people with vision impairment due to cataract have received access to an appropriate intervention.

**India:** Out of 93,108 enumerated individuals with aged > 50 years in 31 districts, 85,135 persons were examined with an overall response rate of 91.5%. The estimated prevalence of blindness was 1.99%, Severe visual impairment 1.96%, Moderate visual impairment 9.81%, Early visual impairment 12.92%, Moderate severe visual impairment 11.77% and Visual impairment 13.76%. Prevalence of functional low vision was 1.03% and that of blindness<3/60 (using pinhole) was 1.75%. The prevalence of blindness and visual impairment was lowest in Thrissur district (Kerala) and in Thoubal district (Manipur) respectively. Bijnor district (Uttar Pradesh) had the highest prevalence of both blindness and visual impairment.

## Disease and Economic Burden

Vision impairment and blindness impact the life of people everywhere. In low- and middle-income settings the burden of vision impairment can be even greater due to fewer opportunities to access the most essential eye care services.

Cataracts and uncorrected refractive errors are estimated to be the leading causes of vision impairment; however, other causes for vision impairment cannot be ignored. Age-related macular degeneration, glaucoma, long standing systemic conditions like diabetes causing diabetic retinopathy, infectious diseases of the eye and trauma to the eye are all equally important causes for vision impairment that need to be addressed.

Vision impairment can have profound effects on individuals at all stages of life:

- **Young Children:** Early onset severe vision impairment can delay motor, language, emotional, social, and cognitive development, leading to lifelong challenges.
- **School-age Children:** Vision impairment can result in lower educational achievement and limited future opportunities.
- **Adults:** Adults with vision impairment often face lower employment rates, higher instances of depression and anxiety, and reduced quality of life.
- **Older Adults:** Vision impairment in older adults can lead to social isolation, increased risk of falls and fractures, and a higher likelihood of early entry into nursing or care homes.

Vision impairment poses an enormous global financial burden with an estimate annual global productivity loss of about US$ 411 billion purchasing power parity. This figure far outweighs the estimated cost gap of addressing the unmet need of vision impairment (estimated at about US$ 25 billion).

**Blindness and Sustainable Development Goals**

Though there is no direct reflection of blindness and visual impairment in SDGs, it is part of SDG 3 and SDG 8.

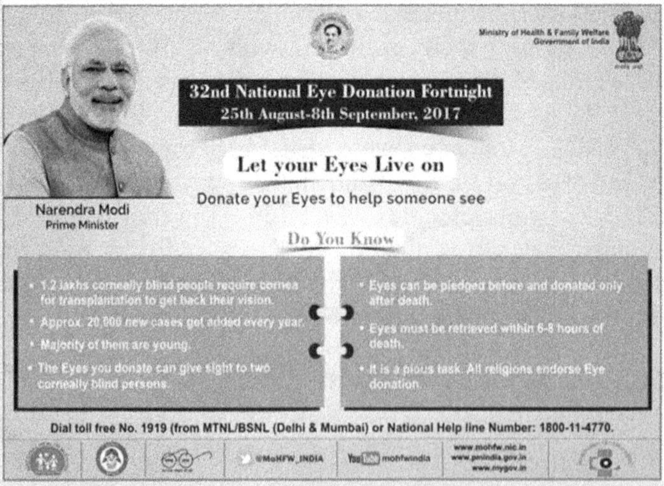

## Preventive Strategy and National Programme

National Programme for Control of Blindness & Visual Impairment (NPCBVI) was launched in the year 1976 as a 100% Centrally Sponsored scheme with the goal to reduce the prevalence of blindness from 1.4% to 0.3%. As per Survey in 2001-02, prevalence of blindness is estimated to be 1.1%. Rapid Survey on Avoidable Blindness conducted under NPCBVI during 2006-07 showed reduction in the prevalence of blindness from 1.1% (2001-02) to 1% (2006-07).

The programme continues to focus on development of comprehensive eye care services targeting common blinding disorders viz., Cataract, Refractive Errors, Glaucoma, Diabetic Retinopathy, Childhood Blindness, Corneal Blindness etc. to combat blindness and visual impairment in the country. The goal to reduce the prevalence of blindness to 0.25% by 2025.

**Goals & Objectives of NPCBVI in the XII Plan**

- To reduce the backlog of blindness through identification and treatment of blind at primary, secondary and tertiary levels. based on assessment of the overall burden of visual impairment in the country.
- Develop and strengthen the strategy of NPCBVI for "Eye Health" and prevention of visual impairment through provision of comprehensive Eye Care services and quality service delivery.
- Strengthening and upgradation of Regional Institute of Ophthalmology to become centre of excellence in various sub-specialities of ophthalmology.
- Strengthening the existing and developing additional human resources and infrastructure facilities for providing high quality comprehensive Eye Care in all Districts of the country.
- To enhance community awareness on eye care and lay stress on preventive measures.
- Increase and expand research for prevention of blindness and visual impairment.
- To secure participation of Voluntary Organizations/Private Practitioners in eye Care.

## Achievements

The following benchmark activities are being marked as key performance deliverable for regular monitoring and evaluation of the NPCBVI program:

Cataract Surgeries 1. Distribution of spectacles to school children

### Corneal Collection

In last three years: 2021-2022, 2022-2023 and 2023 – 2024, number of cataract operations performed exceeded the target.

However, the performance in No. of free spectacles provided to school children suffering from refractive errors and No. of donated eyes collected are much behind the target.

As a newer initiative Mission Mode Cataract Surgeries campaign (Netra JyotiAbhiyan) have been launched for the period: 2022-25 with an aim to finish off any prevailing cataract surgery backlogs and strengthened service delivery.

**Bottom Line**

- Blindness is distance Visual Acuity less than 20/200 in the better eye.
- Globally, at least 2.2 billion people have a near or distance vision impairment. The leading causes of vision impairment and blindness at a global level are refractive errors and cataracts.
- The estimated prevalence of blindness was 1.99%, Severe visual impairment 1.96%, Moderate visual impairment 9.81%, Early visual impairment 12.92%, Moderate severe visual impairment 11.77% and Visual impairment 13.76%. The prevalence of blindness and visual impairment was lowest in Thrissur district (Kerala) and in Thoubal district (Manipur) respectively. Bijnor district (Uttar Pradesh) had the highest prevalence of both blindness and visual impairment.
- Vision impairment and blindness impact the life of people everywhere. In low- and middle-income settings the burden of vision impairment can be even greater due to fewer opportunities to access the most essential eye care services.
- Vision impairment can have profound effects on individuals at all stages of life.
- National Programme for Control of Blindness & Visual Impairment (NPCBVI) was launched in the year 1976 as a 100% Centrally Sponsored scheme with the goal to reduce the prevalence of blindness from 1.4% to 0.3%. The goal to reduce the prevalence of blindness to 0.25% by 2025.
- In last three years: 2021-2022, 2022-2023 and 2023 – 2024, number of cataract operations performed exceeded the target.

## Bibliography

1. Annual Report 2023-24, Department of Health and Family Welfare, Ministry of Health and Family Welfare, Government of India.
2. https://www.who.int/news-room/fact-sheets/detail/blindness-and-visual-impairment accessed on 14th December 2024.
3. National Blindness & Visual Impairment Survey India 2015-2019, National Programme for Control of Blindness & Visual Impairment, Ministry of Health and Family Welfare, Government of India.

# Deafness

"Being deaf doesn't mean
I can't achieve things
that hearing people can do with ease"

**After reading this chapter, you should be able to understand and appreciate:**

- Definition of Deafness;
- Prevalence and Burden of Deafness;
- India's effort tackling deafness; and
- Pharmacists' Role in Deafness.

Deafness is defined as the inability to use hearing as a primary channel for receiving speech, even with amplification. Hearing loss is hearing impairment of various degrees. A person is said to have hearing loss if he/she is not able to hear as someone with normal hearing. Normal hearing is thresholds of 20 dB or better in both ears. It can be mild, moderate, moderately severe, severe or profound, and can affect one or both ears.

Hearing disability is defined as a difficulty in hearing day-to-day conversational speech but excluded unilateral hearing impairment.

## Prevalence

**Global:** Currently more than 1.5 billion people (nearly 20% of the global population) live with hearing loss; 430 million of them have disabling hearing loss. It is expected that by 2050, there could be over 700 million people with disabling hearing loss.

Globally, 34 million children have deafness or hearing loss, of which 60% of cases are due to preventable causes. At the other end of the lifespan, approximately 30% of people over 60 years of age have hearing loss.

**India:** More than 50 lakh people have hearing disability (2011 census). The 2002 National Sample Survey (NSS) found hearing loss was the second most common cause of disability and top cause of sensory deficit; 291 per 100 000 persons surveyed had hearing loss, which included mainly profound (32%) and severe (39%). National Sample Survey (NSS) (2017–2018) reported that hearing disability was estimated in 0.3% of the population. About 49.8% of them reported hearing only loud sounds or inability to hear at all.

Disabling hearing loss prevalence has been rapidly increasing due to three reasons: (i) an ageing population; (ii) better identification; and (iii) excessive exposure to noise.

**Disease and Economic Burden:** The disability due to hearing impairment is a major contributor to the loss of personal potential and a financial strain for the individual and the country. Low-income countries such as India are particularly susceptible due to patchy availability of screening programmes for the newborns, high prevalence of chronic ear infection in the young and the lack of resources for the elderly.

WHO estimates that unaddressed hearing loss costs the global economy US$ 980 billion annually due to health sector costs (excluding the cost of hearing devices), costs of educational support, loss of productivity and societal costs.

**Reasons for Hearing Loss**

- Ear Wax
- External auditory canal infections
- Otomycosis
- Acute Suppurative Otitis Media
- Chronic Suppurative Otitis Media
- Otitis Media with Effusion
- Excessive use of ototoxic drugs

Deafness and Sustainable Development Goals: Two SDG goals are directly relevant:

- SDG 3: Ensuring healthy lives and well being for all people.
- SDG 4: Ensuring quality education for all. Children with hearing loss who don't receive treatment may have difficulty accessing mainstream schooling and may have worse educational outcomes

World Hearing Day on 3rd March every year and World Deafness Week from 20th Sep-26th September every year is celebrated.

## Preventive Strategy and National Programme

WHO estimates that 50% of hearing loss can be prevented through public health measures. Some prevention strategies: reduction of exposure to loud sounds and music or wearing protective equipment such as earplugs. This can be assisted through implementing audio standards for personal audio systems and devices.

Further reductions in hearing loss can be gained through screening and early interventions in childhood, including application of assistive technologies or surgical options. Screenings can also prevent the use of damaging pharmaceuticals in high-risk cases.

Hearing loss and deafness can also occur as a complication of other diseases such as measles, meningitis, rubella and mumps. Work to prevent these diseases through vaccination and hygiene programs can have a beneficial impact on rates of hearing loss and deafness. Immunizing adolescent girls and women of reproductive age against rubella before pregnancy, and preventing cytomegalovirus infections in pregnant women, can reduce the risk of babies born with congenital hearing loss or deafness.

The National Programme for Prevention and Control of Deafness (NPPCD) was launched in 2008 with the following objectives:

- To prevent avoidable hearing loss on account of disease or injury.
- To have early identification, diagnosis and treatment of ear problems responsible for hearing loss and deafness.
- To medically rehabilitate persons of all age groups, suffering with deafness.
- To strengthen the existing inter-sectoral linkages for continuity of the rehabilitation programme, for persons with deafness.
- To develop institutional capacity for ear care services by providing support for
- equipment, material and training personnel.

**Achievements**

During 2023-2024 the following are achieved:

Total number of deafness cases examined: 239932;

Number of persons referred for rehabilitation: 35704; and

Number of hearing aids fitted: 6985

The programmes have been organised on World Hearing Day and during World Deafness Week to create public awareness.

**Pharmacists' Contribution in Hearing Loss and Deafness**

- Pharmacists are knowledgeable about medications that can potentially cause ototoxicity (damage to the ear) which leads to hearing loss. They should advice people while dispensing such medications.
- They can encourage the people to report of hearing loss to the health professionals.
- Providing information on the use and maintenance of hearing aids and other assistive listening devices.

**Bottom Line**

- Deafness is defined as the inability to use hearing as a primary channel for receiving speech, even with amplification. Hearing loss is hearing impairment of various degrees.
- Currently more than 1.5 billion people (nearly 20% of the global population) live with hearing loss; 430 million of them have disabling hearing loss. It is expected that by 2050, there could be over 700 million people with disabling hearing loss.
- In India. more than 50 lakh people have hearing disability (2011 census). Disabling hearing loss prevalence has been rapidly increasing due to three reasons: (i) an ageing population; (ii) better identification; and (iii) excessive exposure to noise.
- The disability due to hearing impairment is a major contributor to the loss of personal potential and a financial strain for the individual and the country. WHO estimates that unaddressed hearing loss costs the global economy US$ 980 billion annually due to health sector costs (excluding the cost of hearing devices), costs of educational support, loss of productivity and societal costs.
- Reasons for Hearing Loss: Ear Wax, External auditory canal infections, Otomycosis, Acute Suppurative Otitis Media, Chronic Suppurative Otitis Media, Otitis Media with Effusion and Excessive use of ototoxic drugs.
- SDG 3 and SCG 4 are linked to hearing impairment.
- Preventive Strategy: reduction of exposure to loud sounds and music or wearing protective equipment such as earplugs.
- Further reductions in hearing loss can be gained through screening and early interventions in childhood, including application of assistive technologies or surgical options. Screenings can also prevent the use of damaging pharmaceuticals in high-risk cases.
- National Programme for Prevention and Control of Deafness (NPPCD) was launched in 2008.

- Substantial benefits achieved in terms of creating public awareness, number of deafness cases examined, number of persons referred for rehabilitation, and number of persons provided with hearing aids.
- The pharmacists can advise the people on medicines which cause ototoxicity.

## Bibliography

1. Annual Report 2023-24, Department of Health and Family Welfare, Ministry of Health and Family Welfare, Government of India.
2. https://www.who.int/health-topics/hearing-loss#tab=tab_3 accessed on 28th December 2024.
3. National Programme for the Prevention & Control of Deafness (NPPCD), https://nhm.gov.in/index1.php?lang=1&level=2&sublinkid=1051&lid=606, accessed on 28th December 2024.

# Drug / Substance Abuse

Drugs take you to hell disguised as heaven.

**After reading this chapter, you should be able to understand and appreciate:**

- Definition of Drug Abuse;
- Prevalence and Burden of Drug Abuse;
- India's effort tackling Drug Abuse; and
- Pharmacists' Role in Drug Abuse.

Drug (substance) abuse is a patterned use of a drug (substance) in which the user consumes the substance in amounts or with methods which are harmful to them or others. It is excessive use of a drug (such as alcohol, narcotics, or cocaine) and/or use of a drug without any medical justification. Drug abuse has emerged as a serious concern, adversely affecting the physical and socio-economic well-being of the country. This issue is particularly alarming among the younger generation in India, exacerbated by the stresses of modern life. Addiction to substances like alcohol and drugs not only affects individuals but also has far-reaching implications for families and society at large.

"Drugs' and "Substances of abuse" are used inter changeably.

## Prevalence of Drug Abuse

**Global:** It is a global issue. World Health Organization (WHO) estimated that 2.6 million deaths per year were attributable to alcohol consumption, accounting for 4.7% of all deaths, and 0.6 million deaths to psychoactive drug use. Notably, 2 million of alcohol and 0.4 million of drug-attributable deaths were among men.

Cannabis remains the most widely used illicit substance globally. In the African Region, the highest prevalence and increase in use are reported in West and Central Africa, with rates between 5.2% and 13.5%. Amphetamine-type stimulants (ATS), such as "ecstasy" and methamphetamine, are now Africa's second most widely abused drug type. Other substances used by children and youth in Sierra Leone include benzodiazepines such as diazepam, chlorpromazine, and various inhalants, with 3.7% of the youth injecting drugs.

**India:** National Survey on Extent and Pattern of Substance Use in India released in February, 2019 has the following findings:

Alcohol is the most common psychoactive substance used by Indians followed by Cannabis and Opioids. About 16 Crore persons consume alcohol in the country, 3.1 Crore individuals use cannabis products and 2.26 Crore use opioids. More than 5.7 Crore individuals are affected by harmful or dependent alcohol use and need help for their alcohol use problems, about 25 lakh suffer from cannabis dependence and approximately 77 lakh individuals are estimated to need help for their opioid use problems. A sizeable number of individuals use sedatives and inhalants.

**Mode of Taking Drugs**

(a) **Orally:** One of the simplest ways of taking drugs is through the mouth and it allows the drugs to move to the stomach where they are absorbed by the stomach lining and then enter the bloodstream. The most common drugs to be taken in this way are alcohol, marijuana, opium, amphetamines, ecstasy, LSD and magic mushrooms.

(b) **Injecting:** It is a method of introducing a drug into the body with a hollow needle and a syringe which is pierced through the skin into the body (usually intravenous, but also intramuscular or subcutaneous). It often applies to substance dependence and recreational drug use.

(c) **Inhaling:** There are a broad range of intoxicative drugs whose volatile vapors or gases are taken in via the nose and trachea.

(d) **Snorting:** Inhaling the substance, usually as a powder or crushed pill, through the nose.

**Impact of Drug Abuse:** This causes drug addiction (also called substance dependence or chemical dependency). The followings are the impact (or, the addiction leads to):

- Accidents and injuries
- Absenteeism from the workplace, schools and colleges
- Poor educational performance
- Behavioural problems
- Low self-esteem
- Personality disorders
- Mental illness
- Depression
- Suicidal tendencies
- Health problems

## India's Effort Tackling Drug Abuse

Recognizing the severe implications of substance abuse, the Ministry of Social Justice and Empowerment has launched the National Action Plan on Drug Demand Reduction (NAPDDR). This comprehensive initiative focuses on:

- awareness generation,
- counselling, treatment, and
- rehabilitation of individuals affected by substance abuse.

The program adopts a community-based prevention approach, emphasizing educational programs and support for drug-dependent individuals and their caregivers.

India has initiated Nasha Mukt Bharat Abhiyaan (NMBA)aiming to reach out to the masses and spread awareness about substance abuse through various activities like

- Awareness generation programmes
- Focus on higher educational Institutions, university campuses and schools
- Reaching out to the Community and identifying dependent population
- Focus on counselling and treatment facilities in hospitals and rehabilitation centres that have been geo-tagged
- Capacity building programmes for service providers

**Nasha Mukt Bharat Abhiyaan** (an initiative of Ministry of Social Justice and Empowerment): This programme initiated in 2020 is extended to all districts.

**Achievements:**

- Creating toll free number:14446
- Community involvement is initiated.
- Till now, through the various activities undertaken on-ground, 10.80+ crore people have been sensitized on substance use including 3.40+ Crore Youth and 2.28+ Crore Women.
- **One Best Practice:** Organisation of interactive Cultural and Sports activities like Kabaddi tournaments, bike rallies, candle marches, marathon runs, musical nights and football matches to spread the message of NMBA among women, youth & children in Haryana, Punjab, Himachal Pradesh, Manipur and UT of Jammu & Kashmir.

**Drug Abuse and Initiatives:** Target 3.5 of UN Sustainable Development Goal 3 sets out a commitment by governments to strengthen the prevention and treatment of substance abuse.

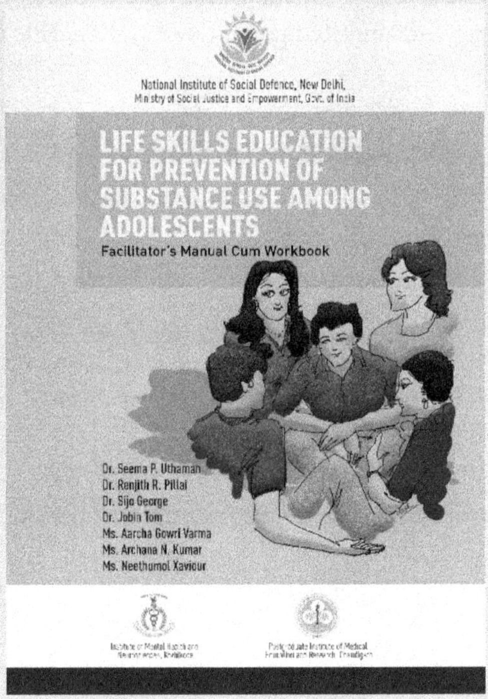


**Pharmacists' Contribution Tackling Drug Abuse**

- They can participate in community education on drug abuse.
- They should discourage people from use of the drugs: Not dispensing without prescription.
- They must keep these medicines under lock and key – no minimise the access.

**Bottom Line**

- Drug (substance) abuse is a patterned use of a drug (substance) in which the user consumes the substance in amounts or with methods which are harmful to them or others.
- It is a global issue. Cannabis remains the most widely used illicit substance globally.
- Alcohol is the most common psychoactive substance used by Indians followed by Cannabis and Opioids. A sizeable number of individuals use sedatives and inhalants.
- **Mode of Taking Drugs:** Oral, injections, inhalation, Snorting.

- **Impact of Drug Abuse:** Accidents and injuries, Absenteeism from the workplace, schools and colleges, Poor educational performance, Behavioural problems, Low self-esteem, Personality disorders, Mental illness, Depression, Suicidal tendencies, and Health problems
- **India's effort tackling Drug Abuse:** National Action Plan on Drug Demand Reduction and Nasha Mukt Bharat Abhiyaan.
- Pharmacists can participate in community education on drug abuse. They must not dispense addiction forming medicines without prescription.

## Bibliography

1. Annual Report 2023 -24, Ministry of Social Justice and Empowerment, Government of India.
2. https://www.nisd.gov.in/drug_abuse_prevention.html accessed on 24th December 2024.
3. https://www.who.int/health-topics/drugs-psychoactive#tab=tab_3 accessed on 24th December 2024.

# Family Welfare

"You cannot have maternal health without reproductive health. And reproductive health includes contraception and family planning and access to legal, safe abortion".

- Hillary Clinton

**After reading this chapter, you should be able to understand and appreciate:**

- Definition and Scope of Family Planning;
- India's population issue;
- National Family Planning Programme, History and Services Available;
- Achievements of Family Welfare Programme; and
- Pharmacists' Role in Family Welfare Programme.

Family Planning (FP) is the planning intended to determine the number and spacing of one's children through birth control. India has a long history of family planning initiative. India has launched world's first National Family Planning Programme in 1952 as a part of her first five year plan (1951-1956). The aim of the programme was to "reducing the birth rate to the extent necessary to stabilize the population at a level consistent with the requirements of the requirements of the national economy". The current focus of FP is not just restricted to birth control and population stabilization and is much beyond. It aims to promote reproductive health and reduce maternal, infant & child mortality and morbidity. It is the Planned Parenthood which means a conscious limitation or spacing of children within the economic limits of the family in order to create a happy home. For sometimes, FP was known as Family Welfare Programme. Family Welfare is much broader domain and Family Planning is the prime component.

India is the world's 7$^{th}$ largest country by area and the second most populous country harbouring more than 139 crore population accounting about 17.8 % of global population (2021). The 1971 census showed that the population was no longer a potential threat but a major problem that needed to be tackled on priority. The government gave this as one of the top priority programmes and substantial fund was allocated and many new initiatives were launched over the years.

## Demography (Population)

Across the world the concerns have been raised from time to time about the increasing population. The top five countries (2020) in terms of total population are: China (18.47 % global share), India (17.8 % global share), United States (4.25 % of global share), Indonesia (3.51 % of global share) and Pakistan (2.83 % global share). Population across the various Indian States too vary widely.

The population of India is expected to increase from 121.1 crores to 151.8 crores during the period 2011-2036 - an increase of 25 % in twenty-five years at the rate of 1.0 % annually. As a consequence, the density of population will increase from 368 to 462 persons per square kilometer. The top 5 populated states (based on 2021 projections) are Uttar Pradesh (23 crore), Maharashtra (12.44 crore), Bihar (12.30 crore), West Bengal (9.8 crore), and Madhya Pradesh (8.45 crore). Sikkim is the least populated state (6.77 lakh) followed by Mizoram (12.16 lakh) & Arunachal Pradesh (15.71 lakh).

**Factors influence Population Growth**

- Unmet need of family planning (12.9 % women do not have access) – 53.5 % married women use contraceptives.
- Age at marriage and first child birth – 26.8 % girls get married below the age of 18 years.
- Spacing between birth – Healthy spacing is three years to improve survival of infants and also to help reducing the impact of population momentum. 2017 figure shows spacing is less than recommended 3 years in 50.3 % births.

## National Family Planning Programme of India

India was the first country in the world to launch National Programme for Family Planning in 1952. Since then it has undergone many transformation in terms of policy and programme implementation. During Emergency (1975-1977) the FP was aggressively implemented with most aggressive and repressive sterilization. It was believed that only way to stop the disastrous rate of population growth and bring the birth rate down to an acceptable level was to force the people to act in their self-interest and submit to sterilization. As the people were fed up with excess done (forced sterilization because of target fixed for the officials), the new government in post emergency period changed the FP to Family Welfare.

Over the years, the programme has expanded to reach every nook and corner of the country. The FP of the country have been designed and modified in line with the goals and objectives of the policies: National Population Policies 2000; National Health Policy 2002 and National Health Policy 2017; India's International Commitments: International Conference on Population and Development; Sustainable Development Goals; and Family Planning 2020.

| Time Line of Family Welfare Initiatives in India (post-independence period) | |
|---|---|
| 1952 | National Programme on Family Planning Launched as a part of first five year plan [1951-1956]. |
| 1966 | Ministry of Health Created a separate Department: Department of Family Planning |
| 1976 | First National Population Policy Announced |
| 1977 | Population Control and Family Planning are made as Concurrent Subject.<br>National Family Planning Programme was renamed as National Family Welfare Programme |
| 1970s | Department of Family Welfare created at National /State/ District Level |
| 2000 | National Population Policy 2000 announced – to achieve population stabilization by 2045.<br>National Commission on Population constituted. |
| 2014 | Family Planning 2020 Vision Document Developed |

## Family Planning Methods / Services available under FP Programme

These methods are broadly divided into three categories: Spacing method; Limiting / Permanent Methods; and Emergency Contraceptive Pills. The programme is available up to Primary Health Centre (PHC) and Sub-Centres (SC) in rural areas; and as well as Urban Family Welfare Centres in urban areas. ASHA workers distribute contraceptives and pregnancy testing kits to direct beneficiaries at their doorsteps.

| Method | Advantages and Disadvantages | Examples | Service Delivery Points | Instruction / Counselling Points |
|---|---|---|---|---|
| Oral Contraceptive Pills | Reversible method and discontinued as per individual | Mala N (Combined Oral Contraceptive Pill); Centchroman (Chhaya) | All the spacing methods – all service are available in the public health facilities including sub-centre level. Oral Contraceptive pills, condoms, emergency contraceptive pills are available at village level through trained ASHAs. | Centchroman (Chhaya) is to be taken twice a week for the first 3 months followed by once a week thereafter |
| Condom | Use by men | Nirodh | | It protects against HIV / STD |
| Intrauterine Contraceptive Devices | Copper IUCDs | IUCD 380 A – Effective for 10 years; IUCD 375 – Effective for 5 years. | | AYUSH practitioners are also trained for IUCD Insertion in PHCs, and CHCs. |
| Contraceptive Injectable | Works for three months at a time | MPA – Antara | | Injected into a muscle (buttock or upper arm) to stop pregnancy by releasing progestogen in the body |

**Table *Contd...***

| Method | Advantages and Disadvantages | Examples | | Instruction / Counselling Points |
|---|---|---|---|---|
| Emergency Contraceptive Pill | Useful only if used within 72 hours of unprotected sex | E-Pills | | To be used within 72 hours of unprotected sex |
| Post Abortion Female Sterilization | With abortion procedure or within 7 days of abortion | | | |
| Post Abortion IUCD | Within 12 days of abortion (when no injury / infetion) | | | |
| Permanent Methods: Irreversible in Nature | Female Sterilisation includes Minilap and Laparoscopic; and Male Sterilisation includes conventional and non-scalpel vasectomy (no incision no stitches). | | | |

**Compensation Schemes**

1. The scheme indemnifies clients with a compensation amount in the unlikely event of deaths, complications, or failure following a sterilization process.
2. The providers / accredited institutes are identified against litigations in those eventualities.

**Achievements**

- Nationwide the small family norm is widely accepted and the general awareness of contraception is almost universal (98 % among women and 98.6 % among men NFHS – 3).

- India has witnessed a constant decline in Total Fertility Rate (TFR) from 3.2 in 2000 to 2.2 in 2018. The desired fertility rate is only 1.8

indicating that the couple on an average do not want more than two children. India is on the verge of achieving total fertility rate of 2.1 by 2025 as set out in the National Population Policy 2000 and through guidance of National Health Policy 2017.

- The 25 out of 36 states / UTs have already achieved the replacement level fertility of 2.1 or less. There are cause of concern too as some districts of Uttar Pradesh, Bihar, Rajasthan, Madhya Pradesh, Chhattisgarh, Jharkhand and Assam have shown TFR 3 and above. These seven states account for 44 % of the country's population.
- Improving the quality of contraceptives, augmenting the contraceptive demand through comprehensive IEC campaigns and focussed interventions in high fertility districts through Micro Paivar Vikas – strives to substantially reduce unmet need for contraception by 2030. Mission Parivar Vikas was launched in 2016 to substantially increasing acesss to contraceptive and family planning services in the states on Uttar Pradesh, Bihar, Rajasthan, Madhya Pradesh, Chhattisgarh, Jharkhand and Assam.

Uttar Pradesh's Population Policy 2021-2030 – unveiled on the occasion of world population day aims at bringing down the gross fertility rate among women to 2.1 by 2026 and to 1.9 by 2030. It aims at stabilizing the population in Uttar Pradesh and reducing maternal and infant deaths in a time bound manner.

In an affidavit filed in the Supreme Court, the Central Government said "The Family Welfare Programme in the country is voluntary in nature, which enables the couples to decide the size of their family and adopt family planning methods best suited to them, according to their choice and without compulsion".

**Pharmacists in Family Welfare Programmes:**

1. The pharmacies have trained pharmacists and they are often first line health care providers to many patients or customers. They have wide range of contraceptive commodities and information. They display the contraceptives at a prominent places in pharmacies with appropriate signage for helping the patients in choice of contraceptives; distributing the planning literatures freely; being counsellor next door spreading the message of small family and its advantages.

   They guide the customers on selecting the best possible family planning (welfare) method of their choice.
2. Large section of our society depends on public health facilities. The pharmacists, irrespective of their service point, guide the vulnerable population on facilities available in public health setup. The family planning facilities or services are available free.

**Bottom Line**

- Family planning is the planning intended to determine the number and spacing of one's children through birth control. India has begun its family planning programme as early as 1952.
- India has 17.8 % global share of population, second populous country.
- Unmet need of family planning; age at marriage and first child birth; and spacing between births are contributing factors for population growth.
- There are three categories of family planning methods: spacing methods; limiting / permanent methods; and emergency contraceptive pills. These services are available at all government health facilities including with ASHA workers.
- Nationwide small family norm is widely accepted and there have been constant decline in total fertility rate from 3.2 in 2000 to 2.2 in 2018.
- Uttar Pradesh, Bihar, Rajasthan, Madhya Pradesh, Chhattisgarh, Jharkhand and Assam have shown TFR 3 and above. These seven states account for 44 % of the country's population.
- Pharmacists by their education and training familiar with the various methods of contraception and guide the customers / seekers of family planning.

## Bibliography

1. A report on challenges and opportunities for pharmacists in health care in India, SEAR Pharm Forum, 2007.
2. Annual Report 2020-21, Department of Health and Family Welfare, Ministry of Health and Family Welfare, Government of India.
3. G. P. Mohanta and Uma Magesh, *Promotion of Family Welfare (Planning) programme: The role of Pharmacists;* ***The Eastern Pharmacist****; November 37-38, 1994.*
4. G. P. Mohanta, *Emergency Contraceptive Pills,* ***The New Indian Express supplement- Health****, 11th October 2005.*
5. G. P. Mohanta, P. K. Manna, and R. Manavalan, *Hormonal Contraceptive Delivery – A New Approach,* **Express Pharma Pulse,** *28th July, 2005.*
6. India's Vision FP 2020, Family Planning Division, Ministry of Health and Family Welfare, Government of India, November 2014.

# HIV and AIDS

"We can't fight AIDS unless we do much more to fight TB as well"
- Nelson Mandela

**After reading this chapter, you should be able to understand and appreciate:**

- The operation of National Programme on AIDS Control (NPAC);
- Milestones on NPAC;
- Strategic Plan of NPAC and its Monitoring;
- Treatment Protocol; and
- Pharmacists' Role in NPAC.

Shortly after the discovery of first case of HIV in India in 1986, Government of India (GOI) launched AIDS Control Programme in 1987. Subsequently the GOI established National AIDS Control Organization (NACO) and launched the National AIDS Control Programme (NACP) in 1992. NACP is a completely central sponsored scheme and is based on two pillars: Prevention; and Care, Support & Treatment. NACO is the nodal agency for implementation of NACP though state or union territories AIDS Control Societies (SACS). The programme is monitored through District AIDS Prevention and Control Unit (DAPCU).

Red Ribbon is an international symbol of AIDS awareness. People wear this on World AIDS Day (December 1 every year) to demonstrate care and concern about living with HIV/AIDS. The concept of World AIDS Day originated at the World Summit of Ministers of Health on programmes on AIDS prevention in 1988.

Currently NACP – Phase IV (Extension) is under operation for 2017-2020. The programme has the following components:

- **Prevention:** Targeted Interventions (TI) for high risk groups [female sex workers (FSW), Men who have sex with men (MSM), Injection Drug Users, Transgender] and bridge population (migrant and truckers) are planned. Prevention strategy aims to make these vulnerable groups HIV free through awareness generation, safe behaviour promotion, HIC testing etc. In addition, there are programmes for inmates of prison, people with Sexually Transmitted Infection (STI); safe blood transfusion (blood free of HIV, malaria, syphilis, hepatitis B and hepatitis C).

In addition to government agencies, more than 1400 civil societies are engaged for targeted intervention. TI projects provide a package of prevention, support and linkage services to high risk groups through drop in centres (DIC) and out-reached based service delivery model which includes screening for and treatment of STI, free condom and lubricants among core groups, behavioural change communications (BCC), creating an enabling environment with community involvement and participation linkage to integrated counselling and testing centre for HIV testing, linkage with care and support service for HIV positive high risk groups, community mobilization, ownership building and specially for injection drug users (IDUs), free distribution of sterile needles and syringes, abscess prevention and management, opioid substitution therapy (OST) and linkage with detoxification / rehabilitation services.

The programme is implemented in association with civil societies and state AIDS control societies.

- **Information, Education and Communication (IEC):** IEC is carried out through multi-media approach comprising of mass media, mid-media, and on ground mobilization and inter personal communication. IEC aims to generate awareness on the mode of transmission of HIV/AIDS, services available for testing and treatment.

  IEC is integrated with all programme components with the objectives of HIV prevention and increasing utilization of services. The various initiative introduces are: mass media campaigns, long format radio and TV programmes, outdoor activities, National Toll free AIDS help line, IEC van etc.

- **Testing:** The programme offers free HIV counselling and testing services (HCTS). Different types of HIV counselling and testing centres are established: Standalone integrated counselling and testing centres (SAICTC); mobile ICTC; Facility integrated counselling and testing centres (FICTC), public private partnership ICTC (PPICTC) and Community Based Screening (CBS). Counselling and Testing Service is integrated under general health services bringing the coverage below block level.

  Mother to child transmission is also included.

- **Treatment:** Free ART as well as comprehensive management of HIV people with respect to treatment and prevention of opportunistic infections. 'Test and Treat Policy' is adopted to offer ART treatment irrespective of CD4 count.

  Single window delivery of TB & HIV services across all ART Centres is proposed.

- **Laboratory Services:** Laboratory services not only for HIV testing but also for other laboratory services associated with prevention, care, support and treatment is covered under the programme. The external quality assurance was set up to ensure high reliability and validity to HIV and CD4 tests.
- **Main streaming & Partnership and Special Protection:** The multi-sectorial approach is adopted. The NACO has signed 17 MoUs with key ministries or departments of GOI: Ministry of Social Justice and Empowerment, Department of Higher Education of Ministry of Human Resource Development, Ministry of Development of North Eastern Region, Ministry of Labour and Employment etc.
- **Strategic Information (SI):** Strong SI is the first priority. It could generate evidence and successfully and effectively as well use such system to achieve the goal. SI and research are brought under one unit to ensure that rigorous and scientific evidence is available and becomes central to an effective response. India has one of the world's largest surveillance system for monitoring HIV epidemic. SI management system has real time data entry and analysis system. Twenty eight government institutions have collaborated with NACO and SACS for facilitating the data analysis and dissemination.

## National Strategic Plan (NSP): 2017-2024

Having already achieved Millennium Development Goals by 2015, (over 50% reduction in new annual HIV infections and AIDS related deaths), India committed now to "Ending the AIDS epidemic as public health threat by 2030" in line with Sustainable Development Goals.

India has also taken a bold step to attain 90-90-90 targets by 2020. At least 90% of the people living with HIV know their status, 90% of them are enrolled for treatment and 90% of those who are on treatment experience effective viral load suppression.

Despite the significant achievements made by the country through NACP, new HIV infections are still appearing across the country particularly among certain geographical areas and populations. Considering the epidemic trends and geographical variations, NSP 2017-24, is launched focussing on the attainable vision of "An AIDS Free India by 2030". The end of the strategic period, 2014, is in the middle of SDG period. The goal of this NSP is to achieve zero infection, zero related death and zero AIDS related stigma & discrimination. The NSP outlines the six objectives and the outcomes of them. This is given in the table below.

| NSP 2017-2024: towards fulfilling the vision of AIDS free India | |
|---|---|
| **Objectives** | **Outcomes** |
| 1. Reduce 80% of new infections by 2024 (base line 2010) | New infections reduced from >100,000 to <21,000 |
| 2. Ensure 95% of estimated PLHIV know their status by 2024 | 2.01 million PLHIV know their status |
| 3. Ensure 95% PLHIV have ART initiation and retention by 2024, for sustained viral suppression | 1.90 million PLHIV on ART are retained and have sustained virus suppression |
| 4. Eliminate mother to child transmission of HIV and syphilis by 2020 | Attain dual elimination by 2020 |
| 5. Eliminate HIV / AIDS related stigma and discrimination by 2020 | HIV/AIDS considered as chronic manageable disease |
| 6. Facilitate sustainable NACP service delivery by 2024 | 1. Integration of identified components of NACP with National Health Mission (NHM)<br>2. Domestic funding of NACP is 100% |

Three major strategies are proposed under the NSP to reach the milestones and goals fixed:

(i) **Fast Tracked Flexible Approach to HIV Programming:** HIV epidemic is not uniform in all states / UTs and so as within the state / UT. The critical elements identified for action are:

- Improving knowledge of level, trends and drivers of HIV epidemic and tailoring the response accordingly.
- Capacitating states / UTs and districts to fast track response.
- Active involvement of PLHIV / Non-Government Organizations (NGOs) / Community Based Organizations (CBOs) / Private as well as other sectors and departments.

(ii) **Leveraging Integration of the AIDS Programme with NHM:** With gradual decreasing of external support which have so far supporting NACP, there is need of increasing domestic funding. Besides, many components of NACP require support from general health systems and other programmes. Example: Prevention of Parent to Child Transmission (PPTCT) is heavily dependent of Reproductive, Maternal, Newborn, Child and Adolescent Health (RMNCH+A) programme to get pregnant mother under Antenatal care (ANC) and hence tested for HIV. NACP needs to integrate its principal activities in a phased manner with NHM for sustained and continuing service.

(iii) **Active Collaboration with Private Sectors:** The engagement of private sectors offers opportunity for expanding the coverage of services and achieve greater impact. Following initiatives are proposed:

- Developing an advocacy, communication and social mobilization approach

- Introducing policies and / or legislation on integration of private sector reporting with national programme management information systems
- Engaging public and private sector companies through their corporate social responsibility function and fund.

| Indicators for Monitoring the NSP Progress taking 2010 as base year | | |
|---|---|---|
| **Indicator** | **2020** | **2024** |
| 1. Number of people living with HIV/ AIDS (in million) | 2.13 | 2.25 |
| 2. Percentage of HIV response financed through domestic budget (sustainable service delivery) | 80% | 100% |
| 3. Percentage of condom use among key populations and sterile needles/ syringes among People Who Inject drugs (PWID) | 80% | 90% |
| 4. Number and percentage of PLHIVs who have been diagnosed with HIV (in million) | 1.75 (82%) | 2.14 (95%) |
| 5. Number and percentage of diagnosed PLHIVs currently on ART (in million) | 1.53 (87%) | 2.03 (95%) |
| 6. Percentage of PLHIVs retained and surviving on ART (12 months, 24 months and 60 months) | 78% - 12 months | 95% - 12 months |
| 7. Percentage of PLHIV undergone Viral Load (VL) test (in million) | 1.1 | 1.6 |
| 8. Number and percentage of PLHIV and on ART who are virologically suppressed (among all those currently on treatment who received a VL measurement regardless of when they started on ART) (in million) | 0.99 (90%) | 1.52 (95%) |
| 9. Number and percentage of pregnant women tested for HIV | 28.5 (90%) | 25.69 (95%) |
| 10. Number and percentage of HIV related deaths | TBD | TBD |
| 11. Number and percentage of new HIV infections (Incidence) | | < 21,000 (80%) |

**Treatment:** ART consists of the use of a combination of at least three anti-retroviral drugs from different classes to inhibit the replication of HIV and reduce viral load to an undetectable level. Continued suppression of viral replication leads to restoration of immune response.

ART should not be started in the presence of an opportunistic infections. In general, Opportunistic Infections should be treated or stabilized before commencing ART. The following regimens are recommended but the list is not complete:

| First-line ARV Regimen | |
|---|---|
| Regimen [First Line Regimen] | Recommended for |
| Tenofovir + Lamivudine + Efavirenz | First-line ART regimen for: All ARV naive PLHIV patients with HIV-1 infection, age > 10 years and body weight > 30 kg |

**Table *Contd...***

| First-line ARV Regimen | |
|---|---|
| Abacavir + Lamivudine +Efavirenz | First-line ART regimen for all patients with abnormal serum creatinine values - Refer to ART guidance for special situations.<br>All adults and adolescents with body weight less than 30 kg |
| Tenofovir + Lamivudine + Lopinavir/ritonavir | First-line ART regimen for: All women with single dose Nevirapine exposure in a past pregnancy;<br>All confirmed HIV-2 or HIV- 1 & HIV-2 co-infection |
| Zidovudine + Lamivudine + Nevirapine<br>Zidovudine + Lamivudine + Efavirenz | All patients who are on either of these first-line regimens initiated earlier in the programme need to be continued on the same regimen unless failing |
| **1. TENOFOVIR (TDF 300 mg) + LAMIVUDINE (3TC 300 mg) + EFAVIRENZ (EFV 600 mg) (TLE) as Fixed Dose Combination (FDC) in a single pill once a day.**<br>A single pill of TLE should be taken at bed time, 2- 3 hours after dinner; fatty food should be avoided as far as possible | |
| 2. In cases where the preferred first-line ARV regimen of TDF +3TC +EFV cannot be used, the alternative regimen of AZT +3TC +EFV, TDF +3TC +NVP, ABC +3TC +EFV or ABC +3TC +NVP can be used. | |
| **3. For patients with HIV-2 infection (HIV-2 alone or both HIV-1 and HIV-2 co-infections), the preferred first-line ART regimen shall be Tenofovir (300 mg) plus Lamivudine (300 mg) plus Lopinavir/Ritonavir (800/200 mg)** | |

## Commonly Used Drugs and Adverse Effects:

| Nucleoside/Nucleotide Reverse Transcriptase Inhibitors (NRTI) | | |
|---|---|---|
| Drug | Dose | Adverse Effects |
| Tenofovir (TDF) | 300 mg once daily | Renal toxicity, bone demineralization |
| Zidovudine (ZDV, AZT) | 300 mg twice daily | Anaemia, neutropenia, bone marrow suppression, gastrointestinal intolerance, headache, insomnia, myopathy, lactic acidosis, skin and nail hyperpigmentation |
| Lamivudine (3TC) | 150 mg twice daily or 300 mg once daily | Minimal toxicity, rash (though very rare) |
| Abacavir (ABC) | 300 mg twice daily or 600 mg once daily | Hypersensitivity reaction in 3 to 5% (can be fatal), fever, rash, fatigue, nausea, vomiting, anorexia, respiratory symptoms (sore throat, cough, shortness of breath); Re-challenging after reaction can be fatal. |
| **Non-Nucleoside Reverse Transcriptase Inhibitors (NNRTIs)** | | |
| Efavirenz (EFV) | 600 mg once daily (bed time administration is suggested to decrease CNS side-effects) [Avoid taking after high fat meals] | CNS symptoms (dizziness, somnolence, insomnia, confusion, hallucinations, agitation) and personality change. Rash occurs, but less common than NVP. |

Table *Contd...*

| Non-Nucleoside Reverse Transcriptase Inhibitors (NNRTIs) | | |
|---|---|---|
| Nevirapine (NVP) | 200 mg once daily for 14 days, followed by 200 mg twice daily | Hepatitis (usually within 12 weeks); sometime life-threatening hepatic toxicity. Skin rash occasionally progressing to severe conditions, including Stevens Johnson syndrome (SJS) and Toxic Epidermal Necrolysis (TEN). Patients who develop severe hepatic toxicity or grade 4 skin rashes should not be re-challenged. |
| **Integrase Inhibitors** | | |
| Raltegravir (RAL) | 400mg twice daily | Rhabdomyolysis, Myopathy, Myalgia, diarrhoea, fever, Rash, Stevens-Johnson syndrome, Toxic Epidermal Necrolysis, Hepatitis and Hepatic failure, |
| Dolutegravir (DTG) | 50mg once daily | Insomnia and headache. Dolutegravir can cause serious, life threatening side effects. These include hypersensitivity (allergic) reactions and liver problems. People with a history of Hepatitis B virus (HBV) or Hepatitis C virus (HCV) infection or who have elevated results on liver function tests may have an increased risk of developing new or worsening liver problems while taking dolutegravir. |
| **Protease Inhibitors (PIs)** | | |
| Atazanavir/ ritonavir (ATV/r) | 300 mg Atazanavir + 100 mg Ritonavir once daily | Unconjugated hyperbilirubinaemia, lipid abnormality, hyperglycaemia, fat maldistribution, nephrolithiasis, cholelithiasis, PR prolongation |
| Lopinavir / ritonavir (LPV/r) Heat stable tablets | 200 mg Lopinavir/50mg Ritonavir Fixed dose tablet 2 tablets twice daily | Diarrhoea, nausea, vomiting, abnormal lipid profiles, glucose intolerance. |
| Darunavir (DRV) | 600 mg twice a day (when used with Ritonavir 100 mg twice daily) | Hepatotoxicity, skin rash (10%), diarrhoea, nausea, headache, hyperlipidaemia, serum transaminase elevation, hyperglycaemia |
| Ritonavir (RTV) | 100 mg twice daily (used only to boost another PI) | Common-gastrointestinal (diarrhoea, nausea, vomiting, abdominal pain (upper and lower), rarely neurological disturbances (including paraesthesia) |

**Role of Pharmacists in National AIDS Control Programme:** The pharmacists' responsibilities in NACP are well defined. The responsibilities based on their place of work are divided into three categories:

(i) **Pharmacists in ART Services at ART Centres:** The pharmacists are entrusted with the following responsibilities:

- Dispensing ARV and Opportunistic Infection drugs with proper counselling;
- Advising the patients and family about the importance of adherence during each visit;
- Counselling the patients on possible drug toxicities and report the same if significant;
- Performing pill counting and reporting any adverse effects of drugs. Confirming the date of next visit to the patient;
- Preparing "Daily Due List" of patients who are scheduled for their appointment and provide the list of missed patients to the counsellor;
- Maintaining the drug store;
- Maintaining and updating drug stock & drug dispensing registers regularly every day. Informing the concerned medical officer for any discrepancy;
- Ensuring that the centre has enough ARV drugs for at least three months and informing the concerned authority about any near expiry or excess stocks well in time for relocation to other sites and ensuring First Expiry First Out protocol;
- Conducting physical verification of the drugs under the supervision of nodal officer;
- Facilitating transfer or availability of ARV drugs at LAC as per the number of patients linked to LAC; and
- Performing any other assigned duties.

(ii) **Pharmacists in Link ART Centres (LAC) / LAC Plus Centres:** LAC are drug dispensing units and are located in ICTC settings at district or lower level hospitals close to patients' home. LAC Plus Centres do the additional responsibility of Pre-ART functions. The responsibilities of the pharmacists of such centres are to:

- Dispense the ARV drugs as per first expiry first out principle;
- Maintain the drug stock register and drug dispensing register;
- Ensure that the centre has stock of ARV drugs for each patient which shall last till the next visit of the patient;

- Inform the LAC in charge if there is a problem with the drug stock (Examples: expiry, delay in release of drugs from nodal ART centre, improper package / damage) of the patients;
- Advise the patients and family about importance of adherence during each visit; and
- Advise the patients on possible drug toxicities and reporting of the same.

**(iii) Pharmacists at TB care Centre offering Prophylaxis Therapy to HIV Patients: The pharmacist of the centre is responsible for:**

- Checking the TB identity card for cotrimoxazole prophylaxis therapy prescription;
- Providing monthly pouch of cotrimoxazole prophylaxis therapy to HIV infected TB patients;
- Recording date of delivery on TB Card;
- Encouraging the HIV infected TB patients to meet Medical Officers for routine examination;
- Indenting cotrimoxazole prophylaxis therapy using monthly CPT report; and
- Maintaining the record of cotrimoxazole prophylaxis therapy in health facility's stock record.

**Challenges in HIV / AIDS Control Programme:** The National AIDS Control Programme has been a success story as it has achieved the MDG. Now on ahead to achieve SDG. In the midst of this there are many challenges and which need to be redressed appropriately. The key challenges identified are:

- Continuing stigma and discrimination which prevent the affected as well as high risk group from seeking vital health care services;
- Inadequate access to testing services for people from certain section of the society;

- Integrating the services of NACO with the health system (National Health Mission);
- Adequate funding from domestic sources as the external funding partners have reduced their support as public funding of healthcare has been consistently low in India;
- Reaching the unreached;
- Treatment adherence and development resistance; and
- Adequate medical, emotional, and social support for growing number of elderly persons with HIV. Now the people with HIV have been living longer and there are large numbers of elderly persons.

**Bottom Line**

- National AIDS Control Programme (NACP), centrally sponsored scheme, is managed by National AIDS Control Organization though State AIDS Control Societies.
- Currently NACP – Phase IV (Extension) is in operation for 2017 to 2020. The programme has the following components: prevention; information, education & communication; testing; treatment; laboratory services; mainstreaming & partnership and special protection; and strategic information.
- India has launched its National Strategic Plan (NSP) 2017-2024 focussing on attainable vision of "AIDS Free India by 2030" in consistence with Sustainable Goal. The goal of the NSP is to achieve "zero infection, zero HIV related deaths and zero AIDS related stigma & discrimination".
- Three major strategies proposed are: fast tracked flexible approaches to HIV programming; leveraging integration of AIDS control programme with National Health Mission; and active collaboration with private sectors. The NSP has in built monitoring indicators.
- ART is free and it consists of the use of a combination of at least three anti-retroviral drugs from different classes to inhibit the replication of HIV and reduce viral load to an undetectable level. Continued suppression of viral replication leads to restoration of immune response. There are fixed regimens recommended under the programme for different categories of patients.
- Pharmacists have well defined roles ranging from dispensing with counselling to managing the drug store.
- Stigma and discrimination still continues to be one of the big challenges of AIDS control programme.

## Bibliography

1. Annual Report 2018-2019, Ministry of Health and Welfare, Government of India.
2. National Health Profile 2019, 14th Issue, Central Bureau of Health Intelligence, Ministry of Health and Family Welfare, Government of India.
3. National Strategic Plan for HIV/AIDS and STI, 2017-2024, paving way for an AIDS free India, December 1, 2017, NACO, GOI.
4. National Technical Guidelines on Anti-Retroviral Treatment, National AIDS Control Programme, Care Support and Treatment Services, October 2018, NACO, GOI.
5. Operational Guidelines for ART Services, July 2012, NACO, GOI.
6. Operational Guidelines for Link ART & LAC Plus, January 2012, NACO, GOI.
7. Training Manual on Intensified TB/HIV Package for Pharmacists, Central TB Division and NACO, GOI, June 2008.

# Immunization

"Vaccines save lives; fear endangers them.
It's a simple message parents need to keep hearing."

- Jeffrey Kluger

**After reading this chapter, you should be able to understand and appreciate:**

- Definition of Immunization;
- India' Immunization Programme including Immunization Schedule; and
- Pharmacists' Role in Immunization

The World Health Organization (WHO) defines Immunization is the process whereby a person is made immune or resistant to an infectious disease, typically by the administration of a vaccine. Vaccines stimulate the body's own immune system to protect the person against the subsequent infection or disease. Though vaccination and immunization are often used interchangeably, one needs to know the difference. Vaccination is the process by which one gets immunised.

The word 'Vaccine' was derived from the Latin for cowpox 'Vaccinia'. Edward Jenner who successfully tested the folk belief that an attack of the relatively innocuous and localised disease, cowpox, provided immunity from the disfiguring and often fatal smallpox. This test resulted in the development of world's first vaccine in 1798 and Jenner was credited for it.

Today smallpox does not exist. The World Health Organization declared in World Health Assembly on 8th May 1980 "The world and all its people have won freedom from smallpox, which was the most devastating disease sweeping in epidemic from through many countries since earliest times, leaving death, blindness and disfigurement in its wake." The discovery changed the world.

Immunization is proven to be the most cost effective public health tool for controlling and eliminating life threatening infectious diseases. It is estimated to avert between 2 to 3 million death each year. Even then, there are about 20 million unvaccinated children in the world. In order to sensitise people and improve immunization coverage 'World Immunization Week' is celebrated in the last week of April (24-30 April) every year. The theme for the 2019 World Immunization Week was "Vaccines work: we are protected together". Fully immunized child is one of the sustainable development goal to be achieved by 2030. Two indicators are developed to test the progress of immunization: proportion of target population covered by all vaccines included in the National Programme; and Extent of Universal Health Coverage (Immunization is a tracer indicator).

The Government of India has launched the new initiative, Intensified Mission Indradhanush 2.0 from December 2019 to March 2020 to capture the information on the block wise target of children and pregnant women to be vaccinated during this period.

## Universal Immunization Programme

Though the first vaccination started in India with the imported smallpox vaccine lymph in 1802, it took almost 175 years to make India smallpox free in 1977. Following the success of smallpox vaccination India launched a regular separate National Immunization Programme named 'Expanded Programme of Immunization (EPI)' in 1978. BCG Vaccination was introduced in 1962 as a part of National TB programme. In the beginning, the EPI introduced BCG, OPV and typhoid-paratyphoid vaccines. The target of EPI was to have at least 80% coverage in infancy and the facilities offered though major hospitals largely restricting to urban areas. With major changes in the programme was brought and 'Universal Immunization Programme (UIP)' was rolled out in 1985. The UIP started in just 31 districts in 1985 and with time it covered the entire country. UIP is successful making the country polio free in 2014. Though the immunization programme started with the aim of reducing vaccine preventable diseases (VPDs), even after four decades we could not achieve 100% success. The significant proportion of VPDs still exists and largely due to sub-optimal coverage of immunization.

The UIP started (1985) with just six antigens: BCG, OPV, DPT and Measles. Later other vaccines are added to the immunization programme. National Vaccine Policy 2011 is the guiding force for functioning of immunization programme in India. In order to improve immunization coverage, the Government of India launched Mission Indradhanush (MI) in December 2014. MI was a targeted programme to immunize children who have either not received vaccine or partially vaccinated. MI led to just 6.7% increase in full immunization coverage. The intensified MI was launched targeting the population where immunization has been very low in spite of repeated phases of UIP and MI. Intensified MI aimed to rapidly build up full immunization coverage to more than 90%by December 2018.

| Milestones in India's Immunization Programme | |
|---|---|
| **Year** | **Event** |
| 1962 | BCG vaccination introduced as a part of TB programme |
| 1978 | Expanded Programme of immunization BCG, DPT, OPV, typhoid (urban areas) |
| 1983 | TT vaccine for pregnant women |
| 1985 | Universal Immunization Programme – measles added, typhoid removed, Focus on children less than 1yr of age |
| 1990 | Vitamin-A supplementation |
| 1992 | UIP is brought under Child Survival and Safe Motherhood Programme |
| 1995 | Polio National Immunization Days |

**Table *Contd...***

| Milestones in India's Immunization Programme | |
|---|---|
| **Year** | **Event** |
| 1997 | Brought under National Reproductive and Child Health Programme<br>VVM introduced on vaccines in UIP |
| 2002 | Hep B introduced as pilot in 33 districts & cities of 10 states |
| 2005 | Auto Disable (AD) Syringes introduced into UIP<br>Brought under NRHM |
| 2006 | JE vaccine introduced after campaigns in endemic districts |
| 2007-2008 | Hep B expanded to all districts in 10 states & schedule revised to 4 doses from 3 doses |
| 2010 | Measles 2nd dose introduced in RI and MCUP (14 states) |
| 2011 | • Hepatitis B universalized and *Haemophilus influenza* type b introduced as pentavalent in 2 states<br>• Open Vial Policy for vaccines in UIP<br>• Vaccine Policy Launched. |
| 2013 | • Pentavalent expanded to 9 states<br>• Second dose of JE vaccine |
| 2014 | • India is certified POLIO- FREE<br>• Mission Indradhanush launched |
| 2015 | • India validated for Maternal and Neonatal Tetanus elimination<br>• Pentavalent expanded to all states<br>• IPV Introduced |
| 2016 | • Rotavirus vaccine introduced in 4 states in Phase 1<br>• tOPV to bOPV Switch<br>• Switch to fractional IPV (Phased)<br>• Rotavirus vaccine introduced (Phased launch) |
| 2017 | • MR Vaccine introduced<br>• PCV (Phased launch)<br>• Use of adrenaline IM by ANM in AEFI |

The Government of India's polio immune strategy is aimed to make switch over from trivalent oral polio vaccine (OPV) to bivalent OPV in a phased manner to completely stop OPV and switch to inactivated polio vaccine (IPV) by2020. The trivalent OPV, containing three types of polio viruses (P1, P2 and P3), was used till April 2016. The bivalent OPV contains P1 and P3 virus. Type P2 component from OPV was removed as a part of Global Polio End Strategy.

**National Immunization Schedule (NIS) for Infants, Children and Pregnant Women**

| Vaccine | When to give | Dose | Route | Site |
|---|---|---|---|---|
| **For Pregnant Women** | | | | |
| TT-1 | Early in pregnancy | 0.5 ml | Intra-muscular | Upper Arm |
| TT-2 | 4 weeks after TT-1* | 0.5 ml | Intra-muscular | Upper Arm |
| TT- Booster | If received 2 TT doses in a pregnancy within the last 3 yrs* | 0.5 ml | Intra-muscular | Upper Arm |
| **For Infants** | | | | |
| BCG | At birth or as early as possible till one year of age | 0.1ml (0.05ml until 1 month age) | Intra-dermal | Left Upper Arm |
| Hepatitis B - Birth dose | At birth or as early as possible within 24 hours | 0.5 ml | Intra-muscular | Antero-lateral side of mid-thigh |
| OPV-0 | At birth or as early as possible within the first 15 days | 2 drops | Oral | Oral |
| OPV 1, 2 & 3 | At 6 weeks, 10 weeks & 14 weeks (OPV can be given till 5 years of age) | 2 drops | Oral | Oral |
| Pentavalent 1, 2 & 3 | At 6 weeks, 10 weeks & 14 weeks (can be given till one year of age) | 0.5 ml | Intra-muscular | Antero-lateral side of mid-thigh |
| Rotavirus# | At 6 weeks, 10 weeks & 14 weeks (can be given till one year of age) | 5 drops | Oral | Oral |
| IPV | Two fractional dose at 6 and 14 weeks of age | 0.1 ml | Intra dermal two fractional dose | Intra-dermal: Right upper arm |
| Measles /MR 1st Dose$ | 9 completed months-12 months. (can be given till 5 years of age) | 0.5 ml | Sub-cutaneous | Right upper Arm |
| JE - 1** | 9 completed months-12 months. | 0.5 ml | Sub-cutaneous | Left upper Arm |
| Vitamin A (1st dose) | At 9 completed months with measles-Rubella | 1 ml ( 1 lakh IU) | Oral | Oral |
| **For Children** | | | | |
| DPT booster-1 | 16-24 months | 0.5 ml | Intra-muscular | Antero-lateral side of mid-thigh |
| Measles/ MR 2nd dose $ | 16-24 months | 0.5 ml | Sub-cutaneous | Right upper Arm |
| OPV Booster | 16-24 months | 2 drops | Oral | Oral |
| JE-2 | 16-24 months | 0.5 ml | Sub-cutaneous | Left Upper Arm |
| Vitamin A*** (2nd to 9th dose) | 16-18 months. Then one dose every 6months up to the age of 5 years. | 2 ml (2 lakh IU) | Oral | Oral |
| DPT Booster-2 | 5-6 years | 0.5 ml. | Intra-muscular | Upper Arm |
| TT | 10 years & 16 years | 0.5 ml | Intra-muscular | Upper Arm |

- *Give TT-2 or Booster doses before 36 weeks of pregnancy. However, give these even if more than 36 weeks have passed. Give TT to a woman in labour, if she has not previously received TT.
- **JE Vaccine is introduced in select endemic districts after the campaign
- *** The 2nd to 9th doses of Vitamin A can be administered to children 1-5 years old during biannual rounds, in collaboration with ICDS.
- #Phased introduction, at present in Andhra Pradesh, Haryana, Himachal Pradesh and Orissa from 2016 & expanded in Madhya Pradesh, Assam, Rajasthan, and Tripura in February 2017 and planned in Tamil Nadu & Uttar Pradesh in 2017.
- $ Phased introduction, at present in five states namely Karnataka, Tamil Nadu, Goa, Lakshadweep and Puducherry. (As of Feb' 2017)
- **SOURCE: https://www.nhp.gov.in/universal-immunisation-programme_pg accessed on 22nd June 2019**

**National Immunization Schedule (Age-wise)**

| Age | Vaccines given |
|---|---|
| Birth | BCG, Oral Polio vaccine (OPV)-0 dose, Hepatitis B birth dose |
| 6 Weeks | OPV-1, Pentavalent-1 Rotavirus vaccine (RVV)-1^, fIPV-1, PCV-1# |
| 10 Weeks | OPV-2, Pentalalent-2, RVV-2^ |
| 14 Weeks | OPV-3, Pentalalent-3,fIPV-2, RVV-3^, PCV-2# |
| 9-12 months | Measles-1 or MR-1$, JE-1*, PCV-B# |
| 16-24 months | Measles-2 or MR-2$, JE-2*,DPT-Booster-1 OPV-Booster |
| 5-6 years | DPT-Booster-2 |
| 10 Years | TT |
| 16 Years | TT |
| Pregnant Mother | TT1, 2 or TT Booster** |

1. * In endemic districts only (at present in 216 out of 231 districts).
2. ** One dose if previously vaccinated within 3 years.
3. ^Rotavirus vaccine is provided in Andhra Pradesh, Haryana, Himachal Pradesh, Odisha, Assam, Madhya Pradesh, Rajastan, Tamil Nadu & Tripura.
4. $ MR vaccine has been introduced in 13 States namely Karnataka, Tamil Nadu, Goa, Lakshadweep & Puducherry, Andhra Pradesh, Chandigarh, Daman & Diu, Dadra & Nagar Haveli, Telangana, Himachal Pradesh & Uttarakhand. Planned to cover entire country.
5. #PCV in Himachal Pradesh and parts of UP & Bihar.
6. Adult JE vaccination as one time vaccination to adults aged 15-65 years in 31 endemic districts of Assam, West Bengal & UP.

*Being introduced/Scaled up.*

## Briefing of Vaccines (under UIP)

1. BCG Vaccine [Live Attenuated Bacterial Vaccine]: BCG stands for Bacillus Calmette Guerin and Calmette & Guerin are the Scientists who developed the vaccine.
   - (a) **Purpose:** To provide protection to infants against severe forms of childhood TB: TB meningitis and other severe forms.
   - (b) **When to give:** Should be given as soon as after birth and before 12 months of age.
   - (c) **When not to give:** in known HIV infection and other immune deficiency cases.
   - (d) **Availability and Storage:** Freeze dried form which should be reconstituted prior to vaccination reconstituted form is to be stored at 2 °C to 8 °C (Refrigerator but not to freeze).
   - (e) **AEFI:** Severe – Generalised disease or infection such as osteomyelitis (bone infection); abscess; lymph node inflammation. Mild – Injection site reaction in almost all children. A small raised lump

usually appears which disappear with time leaving a small scar. This small scar signifies that the child is immunised.

2. **Polio Vaccine:** There are two types: Oral Polio vaccine (OPV) [Live attenuated polio virus vaccine] and Inactivated Polio Vaccine (IPV) [Inactivated polio virus vaccine]. WHO recommends at least one dose of IPV along with OPV in immunisation schedule.
   - **(a) Purpose:** To protect the child against polio. Polio mainly affects children under 5 years of age.
   - **(b) When to give:** All children as per the schedule but begins with at birth.
   - **(c) When not to give:** Known hypersensitivity or anaphylaxis to a previous dose.
   - **(d)** Availability and Storage:
     - **(i)** OPV – multi-dose vial. Must be kept frozen during long term storage. Thawed product should be kept at 2 °C to 8 °C for a maximum of six months.
     - **(ii)** IPV – Single to multi-dose. Should be stored at 2 °C to 8 °C (not to be frozen).
   - **(e) AEFI:**
     - **(i) OPV – Serious:** Vaccine affected paralytic polio usually occurs in 2.7 million doses.
     - **(ii) IPV – Serious:** No serious reaction; Mild – Injection site redness, swelling and soreness.
3. **DPT Vaccine [Diphtheria toxoid, Cellular / whole-cell Pertussis and Tetanus toxoid]**
   - **(a) Purpose:** To provide protection of infants against three diseases: Diphtheria, Pertussis and Tetanus.
   - **(b) When to give:** As per the schedule given in UIP.
   - **(c) When not to give:** When the children are seriously ill or need hospitalization. Known hypersensitivity or anaphylactic reaction with previous dose.
   - **(d) Availability and Storage:** Multi-dose vial and to be stored at 2 °C to 8 °C [Not to freeze)
   - **(e) AEFI:**
     - **(i) Severe:** Neurological (Encephalitis/ Encephalopathy, prolonged convulsions, infantile spasm and Reye's syndrome). But they occur rarely.
     - **(ii) Mild:** Fever and mild local reactions are common.

4. **TT [Tetanus Toxoid]**
   (a) **Purpose:** To protect the individual. Pregnant women are given to protect neonates.
   (b) **When to give:** As required in UIP schedule.
   (c) **When not to give:**
   (d) **Availability and Storage:** Single dose ampoule and multi-dose vial. To be stored at 2 °C to 8 °C [Not to freeze)
   (e) **AEFI:**
      (i) **Severe:** Severe reactions are rare: anaphylactic reactions and neurological problems such as brachial neuritis (inflammation of arm nerves.
      (ii) **Mild:** Injection site pain, redness and /or swelling. Fever may develop in some cases.
5. **Pentavalent Vaccine [DPT + Hepatitis B (Hep B) and *Haemophilus influenzae typeB*(Hib) – It reduces the number of injection.**
   (a) **Purpose:** To provide protection against five diseases: Diphtheria, Pertussis, Tetanus, Hepatitis B and Influenza B.
   (b) **When to give:** As given in UIP schedule. It should be started for any child aged more than 6 weeks and can be started up to 1 year of age.
   (c) **When not to give:** Child of below 6 weeks; Child has already started receiving DPT; Severe allergic reactions / hypersensitivity; Children with moderate or severe acute illness.
   (d) **Availability and Storage:** Liquid and freeze dried form. UIP has only liquid form with multi-dose. To be stored at 2 °C to 8 °C [Not to freeze).
   (e) **AEFI:** Serious – No serious side effects; Minor – Redness, swelling and pain at the limb site. These symptoms usually appear the date after the injection and last from one to three days. Some children may develop fever for short time.
6. **Rota Virus Vaccine [Live attenuated virus vaccine]**
   (a) **Purpose:** To prevent severe rota virus disease (highly infectious diarrhoeal disease). It does not prevent all diarrhoeas.
   (b) **When to give:** As per the schedule specified in UIP.
   (c) **When not to give:** Not after 24 months of age; Severe allergic reaction to previous dose; severe immunodeficiency (but not HIV infection).

(d) **Availability and Storage:** Available as Freeze dried and liquid form. UIP has liquid form and is required to be stored at 2 °C to 8 °C [Not to freeze)

(e) **AEFI:** Severe – Intussusception (low risk); Mild – Irritability, runny nose, ear infection, vomiting and diarrhoea.

7. **Measles [Live attenuated virus] vaccine**

(a) **Purpose:** To protect the children against measles.

(b) **When to give:** First dose should be given at 9 or 12 month of age.

(c) **When not to give:** Known allergy to vaccine components (including neomycin and gelatine); pregnancy; severe congenital or acquired immune disorders including advanced HIV infection / AIDS.

(d) **Availability and Storage:** Freeze dried powders in vials. It is to be stored at 2 °C to 8 °C [Not to freeze) and protect from light.

(e) **AEFI:** Serious – events are rare: anaphylaxis, severe allergic reactions, thrombocytopenia (decreased platelet count); Mild – local injection site pain and tenderness, fever, rash. These may occur five to twelve days after vaccination.

8. **Measles – Rubella [Live attenuated viral vaccine]**

(a) **Purpose:** To protect the children from measles and rubella (replacing measles vaccine]

(b) **When to give:** The first dose: Children between 9 and12 months of age; Second dose: at 16 – 24 months.

(c) **When not to give:** High fever (> 102 °C / 38-39 °C); serious disease; pregnancy; hypersensitive reaction to neomycin, gelatin, or other components of MR vaccine; persons with severely immune compromised as a result of congenital disease, HIV (Full blown AIDS), advanced leukaemia, or lymphoma, serious malignant disease, or treatment with high dose steroid, alkylating agents or anti-metabolites or patients with immunosuppressive therapeutic radiation; taken immunoglobulin or other antibody containing blood products (Vaccine is to delayed for 3-11 months after blood products administration).

(d) **Availability and Storage:** Freeze dried multiple dose coloured vial; To be used within 4 hours of reconstitution; 2 – 8 °C (can be frozen without loss of potency), protect from light.

(e) **AEFI:** Serious – Anaphylaxis; arthralgia; joint pain in adolescent children or adults. Mild – Slight pain and tenderness at the site of injection (may occur within 24 hours) often with mild fever; fever 7 – 12 days after vaccination; transient rash; thrombocytopenic purpura.

9. **Japanese Encephalitis [Cell cultured live attenuated viral vaccine]**
   (a) **Purpose:** To protect the children against Japanese Encephalitis.
   (b) **When to give:** One dose to infants aged 9-12 months along with the first dose of measles vaccine and the second dose is scheduled along with DPT booster dose and measles vaccine's second dose.
   (c) **When not to give:** Anaphylaxis to the vaccine or any component of the vaccine, kanamycin or gentamycin; persons with fever, acute infectious disease, active untreated TB; cardiac, liver and kidney problems; pregnancy, allergy, and convulsion; and persons treated with any immunosuppressive therapy.
   (d) **Availability and Storage:** Powder for suspension and should be stored at 2 to 8 °C. It needs to be protected from light. Reconstituted vaccine should be used within6 hours.
   (e) **AEFI:** Serious – Rare, transient fever; Mild – local reactions at the site: tenderness, rash or irritability.

10. **Vitamin A [Not a vaccine, solution]**
   (a) **Purpose:** To strengthen resistance to infection and to increase child's chances of survival from infection, to promote growth and protect cornea.
   (b) **When to give:** As given in UIP.
   (c) **When not to give:** Usually no contraindication.
   (d) **Availability and Storage:** Bottle once opened, it should be used within 8 weeks. Protect from direct sunlight.
   (e) **Side Effects:** Usually no side effects. Rarely the child may experience headache, loss of appetite, or vomiting. The symptoms will disappear with time.

## Criteria for selection of vaccines for introduction to UIP

The selection of vaccines for possible introduction in National Immunization Schedule is a complex. Here are the basic criteria which are required to be considered while introducing new vaccine under UIP:

- Disease burden (incidence / prevalence, absolute number of morbidity / mortality, epidemic / pandemic potential);
- Safety and efficacy of vaccine under consideration;
- Affordability and financial sustainability of the vaccination programme; even if the initial introduction is supported by external funding agency;
- Programme capacity to introduce a new antigen including cold chain capacity;
- Availability of domestic or external vaccine production capacity; and

- Cost effectiveness of vaccination programme and also of the alternative other than vaccination.

**Achievements**

The GOI under the UIP is providing vaccinations free of cost against 12 vaccine preventable diseases. Eight vaccines: against diphtheria, pertussis, tetanus, polio, measles, severe form of childhood TB, hepatitis B and meningitis & pneumonia caused by *Haemophilus influenza* type B are provided across the country. The remaining four vaccines: against rotavirus diarrhoea, rubella, *Pneumococcal pneumonia*, and Japanese Encephalitis are provided in selected states and endemic districts.

The Health Management Information System data for 2016-2017 confirm full immunization coverage at 88.05%. A child is said to be fully immunized if he/she receives all due vaccines as per National Immunization Schedule within 1st year of the child. Mission Indradhanush has improved the coverage. The first two phases of MI have led to an increase of 6.7% in full immunization coverage in one year compared to 1% increase per year in the past.

The target date for achieving at least 90% coverage is advanced. MI initially aimed to increase the full immunization coverage to at least 90% by 2020 and is advanced to December 2018.

After several rounds of pulse polio immunization programme (pulse polio immunization programme launched in India in 1995), India could achieve the status of polio free country in March 2014. India has been maintaining the polio free status as the last polio case reported in 13th January 2011.

The below figure is adopted from Immunization Handbook for Medical Officers, Government of India, 2017 Reprint.

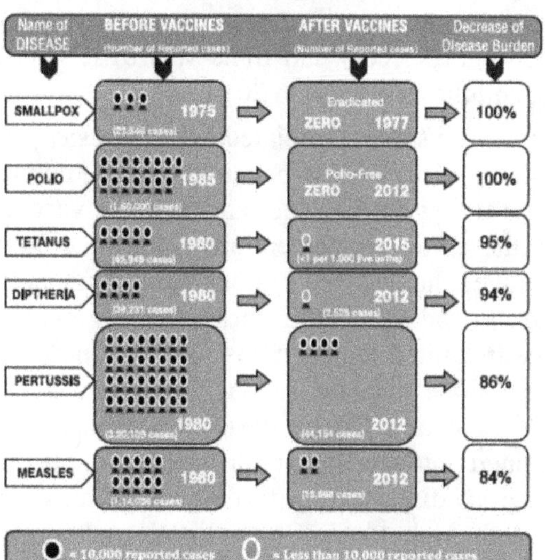

## Challenges

India's immunization programme has the following challenges:

- Weak VPDs surveillance system;
- Lack of data on disease burden in India and resulting perception that the disease is not important public health problem;
- Lack of diagnostic tools for certain vaccine preventable diseases that could be used without sophisticated instruments or specialized training;
- Lack of baseline surveillance data. It is a bottle neck in the monitoring of impact of vaccination;
- Limited economic evaluation to show cost effectiveness over other interventions to support decision making;
- Lack of financial sustainability plan for the introduction of new vaccines in UIP also affects decision making in the area; and
- Shortage of trained manpower at the central and state level, for innovation in vaccines, for disease surveillance and effective vaccine management.

**Stop Anti-Vaccine Movement**

It has been a very disturbing news for public health. 4th polio worker killed in a week in Pakistan. The gunmen on a motorcycle shot and killed the female polio worker. This is the latest surge of violence in Pakistan against efforts to make world free of polio. The hardliners against the vaccination say the polio vaccine is a foreign ploy to sterilize Muslims. Even false reports were broadcasted to the extent that the polio vaccine had madc children sick. India too faced spread of such misinformation. The myth that polio vaccine causes impotency was wide spread in some communities in India and the polio vaccination was viewed as a family planning strategy. The continuing persuasion, massive campaigns, involving religious leaders and celebrities, brought success and India was officially declared free of polio, a crippling childhood disease in 2014.

Several misperceptions are associated with measles vaccine too like: measles is a harmless disease; it is better to take immunity by getting the disease than by receiving the vaccine; and measles vaccination can cause autism. Though the three misperceptions contribute to the incomplete vaccination coverage, the vaccine's association with autism has caused maximum damage to the vaccination programme globally. In one of the worst health crisis in United States, it has recorded more than 600 cases of measles in this year alone since the disease was declared eliminated in 2000 in US. A New York county hit by measles outbreak declared a state of emergency ad banned non-vaccinated minors from public places in a bid to prevent the contagious disease from further spreading. The worst affected areas are those with high ultra – orthodox Jewish population. A local court's injunction requiring county officials to drop the ban against any child with a "religious exemption" complicated the immunization coverage further. The 'religious exemption' became central to the debate over the resurgence of measles and the rise of the anti-vaccine movement.

The myth of MMR vaccine (measles in combination with mumps and rubella) surfaced in 1998 when a scientist suggested a link between MMR vaccine and autism and gastrointestinal disease. This received high media attention. Even though the original article was retracted by the journal for falsified data, the fear caused by this flawed information continues preventing people from immunization against measles. Misinformed parents refuse to get the vaccine shot as required for the children. The Indian newspapers are not behind. In a recent incident in Hyderabad, two infants died because of a medicine goof up. Children were vaccinated but the health worker gave a wrong medicine to treat post vaccination fever which caused the death. One leading newspaper headlines "Two infants dead, 22 taken ill after vaccination". Such headlines causes damage to the vaccination programme creating distrust.

We have forgotten the success of vaccination. Small Pox is eradicated from the globe. No one remembers how many people used to become sick and die from this disease. Though all vaccines have potential side effects, they are usually mild. The spread of misinformation or fake news about vaccine safety despite of having good evidence to the contrary, strengthen the anti-vaccine movement. The people of all ages get heavily influenced by the negative messages spread through newspapers, internet and social media. A British Medical Journal article published in December 2018 quoted that there are 480 anti-vaccine websites and there has been big silence on the pro-vaccine side. World Health Organization promotes the use of vaccines to protect the people of all ages against the diseases. In WHO's words "Immunization saves millions of lives every year and is widely recognised as one of the world's most successful and cost effective health intervention, yet there are still nearly 20 million unvaccinated and under vaccinated children in the world".

Since the introduction of vaccination, a preventable strategy to fight against diseases, myths and misconceptions have been present. Studies showed that addressing these is not easy task. Mere reading a myth or even abut myth's refutation does not weaken its influence but strengthen it. Such is human's psychology. With high global mobility of the people from one corner to the other side of the globe, the infective organism too can travel widely creating health risk to the vulnerable population. It is necessary to stop the spread of rumours and misinformation against the vaccine use and their safety, the main reason for vaccine hesitancy. The vaccine hesitancy has been recognised as public health threat and requires global strategy to improve vaccination coverage.

[Author's article in OrisaPost: *06 May 2019.*

**Cost of Immunisation**

Understanding the cost of any programme is essential to plan, budget and sustain it. The UIP is not exception. The personnel cost takes away the major share (57%) of total immunisation cost at the facility level followed by vaccines and supplies and incentives for accredited social health activist (ASHA) workers. The unit cost (the cost per dose delivered / cost per fully immunised child) vary widely across the facilities, districts and states. The figure of 2013 – 2014 shows that the average cost per dose delivered at National level was USD 2.29. The cost of complete immunisation of DPT per child was USD 31.67 (Price of 2017). The cost per dose delivered varied from USD 1.38 in Bihar to USD 2.93 in Kerala. Similarly the cost per fully immunised child for DPT varied from USD 18.98 (Uttar Pradesh) to USD 35.50 (Kerala).

[Source: Chatterjee S. *et al,* Variation in cost and performance of routine immunization service delivery in India, BMJ Global Health, 3, 2018]

**Price in Private Sector**

The addition of sixth antigen (Hepatitis B) to a vaccine containing antigens against five diseases increases the cost from Rs. 2800/- to Rs. 3900/-. The market price of this sixth, Hepatitis B vaccine is just Rs. 60/-. Similarly another pentavalent vaccine costing just Rs 382/- has increased cost of Rs. 2392/- on addition of 6$^{th}$ vaccine (polio). This price aberration may discourage people from using the combo vaccine. Here is the example of combo vaccines' price:

| Vaccine | Price in Rupees | Combo Vaccines for Five Diseases | Price in Rupees |
|---|---|---|---|
| DPT | 13.50 | Easy Five (DPT + Bib + Hep B] | 382 |
| Hepatitis B | 60 - 100 | Pentaxim (DPT + Hib + Polio) | 2800 |
| Inactivated Polio | 350 - 440 | Combo Vaccines for Six Diseases | Price in Rupees |
| Pneumonia (Hib) | 250 - 350 | Easy Six | 2393 |
| Total cost of Six Vaccines | 674 - 904 | Infarix Hexa | 2599 |
| | | Hexaxim | 3900 |

[Source: Times of India, October 22, 2018]

**Innovative Strategy to improve Immunization Coverage [Vaccination Card Mandatory for Admission in Schools in Uttarakhand]**

The Uttarakhand Government has made the mandatory requirement of Vaccination Card of the child for admission to schools. The up to the age of vaccination card would help in identifying the children who are not completely covered under immunization. The ASHAs and ANMs of the respective areas are authorized to coordinate with the schools and collect the details of the children who are not immunized completely to the age. Then the steps would be taken to immunize them appropriately.

The strategy is to ensure that no child misses out vaccines intended.

**Uttar Pradesh's Success Story in MR Vaccination**: The state has achieved 98.8% vaccination of measles – rubella by February 14, 2019. There were some resistance over suspicion that the vaccine would cause impotency among children. The state has used innovative strategies: technology paired with social media to reach all children; GPS mapping of fixed MR session sites; use of electronic vaccine intelligence network, a system which digitises the vaccine stocks, monitoring temperature at cold chain points; and creating a sense of reassurance through district officials vaccinating their children in public. The state has redressed the resistance to vaccination due to alleged fake messages on social media about the adverse effects on children, awareness programmes over community radio stations, and peer to peer messages from parents helped debunking the rumours.

[Source: Times of India, Chennai, How UP used tech to reach the last child in vaccine drive, 23 February, 2019.]

**Social Issue on Polio Drops (India)**: The rumour spread over that polio vaccine (drops) cause impotency. Mass immunization with polio drops were believed to be part of Government's population control programme. Though it was not clear how the rumour spread, but costed heavily to the polio elimination programme. The impact of the rumour was largely felt in western Uttar Pradesh and Bihar. People had questioned "Why again and again these drops" to pulse polio. This resulted in the resurgence of polio and failure to eliminate the polio by the targeted date, end of 2002. The outbreak was more prominent among the Muslim community.

A two ways approach was used to counter the creeping rumours. In one approach, the social mobilization network was formed with UNICEF, CORE and Rotary. The network has appointed and trained the community level mobilisers. These mobilisers had systematically recorded and updated the list of under five year children in their locality, built local networks among religious leaders and local influential persons, and counselling mothers and mothers in law. The mobilisers were for counselling on the issue of impotency using examples from other countries that had already eradicated polio including Islamic countries.

The second approach was to focus on Muslim community due to their high rate of polio. This was known as underserved strategy introduced in

2004. Muslim academic institutions helped mobilizing Muslim intelligentsia and crafting messages with social mobilizations which was in resonate with Muslim community. Muslim clergy were involved to help in countering the negative fatwas. The universities complemented the work by issuing certificate assuring the safety of vaccine redressing the impotency rumour. A successful mass media campaigned was launched featuring Super star, Big B, Amitabh Bachchan since January 2003.

The combined effort was successful in sustaining the immunization coverage at 95% in polio outbreak year 2006-2007. The last polio case was detected in January 2011. India was removed from the list of polio endemic countries by WHO in February 2012.

**Pharmacists in Immunization Programme:** In India, the pharmacists are not directly involved in immunization programme administering vaccines to individuals. Most of the vaccines are given as injection and the pharmacists are legally not permitted to administer injection. However, they continue to perform the technical responsibilities like ensuring appropriate storage and dispensing vaccines.

The Indian Pharmaceutical Association with support from FIP has started Training Pharmacists for Vaccination.

Surveillance of Adverse Events Following Immunization (AEFI) is the part of National Immunization Programme. With collaboration of National Immunization Division and Indian Pharmacopeia Commission, National Coordinating Centre of Pharmacovigilance Programme, offers opportunities to report AEFI.

The Pharmacists of countries like Argentina, Australia, Philippines, South Africa, United Kingdom and United States of America have authorization for vaccination in pharmacies and/or by the pharmacists. Most of these cases, vaccination permission began with influenza vaccine and later expanded to include other vaccines from the immunization schedule. Vaccination authorization is linked to pharmacist training, management of vaccination records and specifications on premises, equipment and waste management.

In India, the ANM, ASHA workers are permitted to give vaccines, the Government should think of tapping the potential of pharmacists. In spite of all efforts, 100% immunization coverage is not yet reached. Involvement of pharmacists would certainly improve. The pharmacists have been identified as potential vaccinator for COVID – 19.

**Bottom Line**

- Immunization is the process whereby a person is made immune or resistant to an infectious disease, typically by the administration of a vaccine.
- Immunization is proven to be the most cost effective public health tool for controlling and eliminating life threatening infectious diseases.
- Mission Indradhanush is the scheme for complete and free immunization.
- BCG, Polio, DPT, TT, Pentavalent, Rota Virus, Measles, MR, and Japanese Encephalitis Vaccines are included in the National Programme. In addition, Vitamin A supplementation is initiated.
- The GOI under the UIP is providing vaccinations free of cost against 12 vaccine preventable diseases.
- The pharmacists are not directly involved in immunization programme administering vaccines to individuals. They continue to perform the technical responsibilities like ensuring appropriate storage and dispensing vaccines.
- India has been declared of free of Polio.
- *The Indian Pharmaceutical Association with support from FIP has started Training Pharmacists for Vaccination.*

## Bibliography


1. Annual Report 2017-18, Department of Health and Family Welfare, Ministry of Health and Family Welfare, Government of India,
2. G. P. Mohanta, P. K. Manna and R. Manavalan, Pharmacists and The Universal Immunization Programme, The Indian Journal of Hospital Pharmacy, p 94-96, May – June 1999.
3. Guru Prasad Mohanta, K. Chandrasekaran and P. K. Manna, Ensuring Vaccine Safety- a prime concern in immunization, **Chronicle Pharmabiz**, July 04, 2013.
4. Guru Prasad Mohanta, Stop anti-vaccine movement, **OrissaPost, Vol 9, Issue 35, Page 8, 06 May 2019.**
5. https://www.who.int/topics/immunization/en/ (accessed on 22$^{nd}$ June 2019).
6. Immunization Handbook for Medical Officers, Reprint 2017, Ministry of Health and Family Welfare, Government of India, 2016.
7. International Pharmaceutical Federation, An overview of current pharmacy impact on Immunization – A global Report, 2016. The Hague, FIP, 2016.

8. Juny Sebastian, Gurumurthy Parthasarathi, Mandyam Dhati Ravi, Is there a Role for Pharmacist in Safety Monitoring of Vaccines? Indian Journal of Pharmaceutical Education and Research, 52(2), 202-206, 2018.
9. National Vaccine Policy, Ministry of Health and Welfare, Government of India, 2011.

# Leprosy

"The biggest disease today is not leprosy or tuberculosis, but rather the feeling of being unwanted.

- Mother Teresa

**After reading this chapter, you should be able to understand and appreciate:**

- Definition of Leprosy;
- Prevalence and Burden of Leprosy;
- India's effort tackling Leprosy; and
- Pharmacists' Role in Leprosy.

Leprosy is an ancient disease with its earliest remains discovered at the Indus Valley Civilization. Leprosy (also known as Hansen's disease) is a chronic infectious disease caused by a bacillus, *Mycobacterium leprae*, which multiplies slowly and has a long incubation period, on an average, 5-7 years. Infection can lead to involvement of the nerves, respiratory tract, skin, and eyes. The nerve damage may result in a lack of ability to feel touch, pressure, pain, heat and cold, which may lead to the loss of parts of a person's extremities from repeated injuries or infection.

The disease leprosy is known as Hensen's disease named after Gerhard H. A. Hansen, the Norwegian physician, who discovered the causative agent of the disease. But he was also accused of unethical experiment: Human-to-Human Leprosy Transmission Experiment.

## Prevalence and Burden of Leprosy

**Global:** The registered prevalence has decreased substantially, from more than 5 million cases in the 1980s to 133 802 cases in 2021. New cases continued to occur, however, indicating continuing transmission of infection. Screening of contacts and chemoprophylaxis with single-dose rifampicin were recommended as a crucial step to break the chain of transmission. It is proposed to eliminate leprosy (interruption of transmission) by 2030.

**India:** India has achieved the elimination of leprosy as a public health problem i.e., defined as less than 1 case per 10,000 population, at the National level in December 2005. Thereafter, the trend is gradually declining. Prevalence Rate (PR) at National level was 0.84 per 10,000 population in 2005-06 which has been reduced to 0.66 per 10,000 population in 2015-16 which further reduced to 0.57 per 10,000 population in 2019-20. Due to COVID-19 pandemic, case detection was compromised, which led to sudden downward trend of Prevalence Rate (PR) to 0.40 and 0.45 per 10,000 population in 2020- 21 and 2021-22 respectively.

A total of 23 States/UTs have sustained the elimination status (Prevalence Rate < 1 per 10,000 population) at state level since 2009-10 until 2021-22. These States are Andhra Pradesh, Arunachal Pradesh, Assam, Gujarat, Haryana, Himachal Pradesh, Jammu& Kashmir, Karnataka, Kerala, Madhya Pradesh, Manipur, Meghalaya, Mizoram, Nagaland, Punjab, Rajasthan, Sikkim, Tamil Nadu, Tripura, Uttar Pradesh, Uttarakhand, A&N Islands and Puducherry. In addition to above, Telangana and Ladakh (UT) are sustaining the status of leprosy elimination since 2014-15 and 2019-20 respectively.

**Leprosy and Sustainable Development Goals:**

SDG target 3.3, which calls to "end the epidemics of AIDS, tuberculosis, malaria and neglected tropical diseases (NTDs) and combat hepatitis, water-borne diseases and other communicable diseases" by 2030. Leprosy is one of the NTDs.

**National Programme:** India being an endemic country for leprosy, is committed to its eradication. The National Leprosy Control Programme (NLCP) was launched in 1955. Multi Drug Therapy (MDT) for leprosy was introduced and the NLCP was renamed as National Leprosy Eradication Programme (NLEP) in 1983 and implemented as a Centrally Sponsored Scheme which significantly accelerated the elimination of leprosy as a public health problem.

The NLEP is a Centrally Sponsored Scheme under the umbrella of National Health Mission (NHM). NLEP programme has focussed its strategies towards the vision of "Leprosy Free India" since its inception. Current NLEP strategies include availability of quality diagnostic & treatment services, reduction of its transmission and the prevention of deformities and disabilities due to leprosy.

India achieved elimination status of leprosy at the National level in 2005 i.e., Prevalence Rate (PR) less than 1 case/10,000 population. Since then, India has introduced various programmatic strategies to reduce the transmission of leprosy. India continues to contribute to 60% of Global new leprosy cases. (Global Data by WHO 2023).

NLEP has released "National Strategic Plan & Roadmap for Leprosy 2023-27", which has enlisted strategies towards aim of "Interruption of transmission of leprosy in India by 2027" (3 years ahead of SDG 2030).

**Symbolizes beauty and purity in lotus:**

- Leprosy can be cured and a leprosy patient can be a useful member of the society in the form of a partially affected thumb; a normal fore-finger and the shape of house;
- the symbol of hope and optimism in a rising sun.

*World Leprosy Day, traditionally celebrated on the last Sunday of January globally, holds a special significance in India as it coincides with Mahatma Gandhi's Punyatithi on January 30 every year.*

The milestone of leprosy eradication programme is given below:

| Time | Activity |
|---|---|
| 1955 | National Leprosy Control Programme Launched |
| 1983 | National Leprosy Eradication Programme Launched |
| 1998-2004 | Modified Leprosy Elimination Campaign |
| 2002 | National Health Policy set the goal of Leprosy Elimination by 2005 |
| 2004 – 2005 | Block Leprosy Awareness Campaign |
| December 2005 | **India achieved elimination status of Leprosy (prevalence rate < 1/10000)** |
| 2016-17 | Three Pronged strategy Chemoprophylaxis |
| 2018 – 2019 | Sparsh Leprosy Elimination Campaign (SLEC) |
| 2019 | Convergence of leprosy screening under major programmes of National Health Mission |
| 2023 | National Strategic Plan & Roadmap for Leprosy 2023-27 launched - to achieve zero transmission by 2027. |

**Objectives:**

1. Strengthen leadership, commitment, and partnerships.
2. Acceleration of Case Detection
3. Provision of Quality Services
4. Enhanced measures for Prevention of Disease, Disabilities, Stigma, Discrimination and Violation of Human Rights
5. Digitalization of Surveillance Systems

Under the 4th objective the following are initiated:

- **Disease Prevention:**
    - o Expanding coverage of contacts with post exposure prophylaxis (PEP).
    - o Introduction of any newer and more efficacious PEP regimens, vaccines etc
- **Immuno-prophylaxis:**
    - o Promoting research on more effective immune-prophylaxis options
    - o Introduction of newly available effective and approved vaccines.
- **Prevention of Stigma, discrimination, and violation of Human Rights:**
    - o Community education by modern mass media methods.
    - o Taping resources for dissemination of messages around Anti-Leprosy Day.
    - o Sparsh Leprosy Awareness Campaign (SLAC).
    - o Sensitization of leaders, policy makers, faith-based leaders, gram panchayat leaders, Gram Pradhans (PRI reps), Ward members, Members of Legislative Assemblies, Members of Parliament, Resident Welfare Associations, Council members of Municipal corporations, Members of Social Welfare Organizations etc.

**Achievements**

- Convergence of leprosy screening under Comprehensive Primary Health Care (CPHC), Ayushman Bharat for population based screening of women and men of age 30 years and above.
- Urban Leprosy Screening under NUHM for Peri-Urban and Urban slums area/ colonies' migratory population.
- Sparsh Leprosy Awareness Campaigns (SLAC) at village level is started to stop discrimination.
- Contact tracing and Post Exposure chemoprophylaxis administration is initiated.
- Strengthening surveillance under NLEP by case based reporting of all the leprosy cases through Nikusth 2.0.
- Improving quality of services: National guidelines for AMR Surveillance in leprosy, ensuring the availability of Mental Health (MH) services to leprosy-affected individuals for better treatment outcome;
- Various other services are provided like free self-care kits and counselling/training for persons affected by leprosy for prevention of disability; free of cost specialized Micro-Cellular Rubber (MCR) footwear, Aids & Appliances for cases with disabilities & deformities

due to leprosy; Referral services for management of cases and Re-Constructive Surgery (RCS) at District Hospitals and Medical Colleges/Central Leprosy Institutions, including welfare allowance of ₹ 12,000/RCS as compensation for wage loss.

**Achievement during 2020:**

- Percentage of Grade II Disability (G2D)/visible deformity among new cases decreased from 3.05% in 2018-19 to 2.39% (2019-20).
- The G2D amongst new cases/ million population decreased from 2.65/million population as on 31st March, 2019 to 1.94/million population as on 31$^{st}$ March 2020.
- Child cases percentage has reduced from 7.67% as on 31st March 2019 to 6.86 % as on 31$^{st}$ March 2020.

**Treatment Regimen:**

**Duration:** Four weeks / 28 days

**Dosage:**

**Rifampicin:** 10mg/kg body weight, monthly once;

**Dapsone:** 2mg/kg body weight, daily.

**Clofazimine:** 1 mg/kg body weight daily & 6mg/kg body weight, monthly once.

**Pharmacists' Contribution to Leprosy Elimination**

Though no specific responsibilities are assigned to the pharmacists, they can:

- Ensure the availability of the medicines;
- Take part in pharmacovigilance activities;
- Take part in community education preventing stigma and discrimination; and
- Advocate the completion of the course of treatment.

**Bottom Line**

- Leprosy (also known as Hansen's disease) is a chronic infectious disease caused by a bacillus, *Mycobacterium leprae*, which multiplies slowly and has a long incubation period, on an average, 5-7 years.
- Infection can lead to involvement of the nerves, respiratory tract, skin, and eyes. The nerve damage may result in a lack of ability to feel touch, pressure, pain, heat and cold, which may lead to the loss of parts of a person's extremities from repeated injuries or infection.
- Globally, the registered prevalence has decreased substantially, from more than 5 million cases in the 1980s to 133 802 cases in 2021.

- India has achieved the elimination of leprosy as a public health problem at the National level in December 2005. Thereafter, the trend is gradually declining.
- A total of 23 States/UTs have sustained the elimination status (Prevalence Rate < 1 per 10,000 population) at state level since 2009-10 until 2021-22.
- Leprosy as a part neglected tropical diseases (NTDs) is included in SDG 3.3.
- The NLEP is a Centrally Sponsored Scheme under the umbrella of National Health Mission (NHM). NLEP programme has focussed its strategies towards the vision of "Leprosy Free India".
- NLEP has released "National Strategic Plan & Roadmap for Leprosy 2023-27", which has enlisted strategies towards aim of "Interruption of transmission of leprosy in India by 2027" (3 years ahead of SDG 2030).
- *World Leprosy Day, traditionally celebrated on the last Sunday of January globally, holds a special significance in India as it coincides with Mahatma Gandhi's Punyatithi on January 30 every year.*
- The milestone of leprosy eradication programme: National Leprosy Control Programme programme introduced in 1955 is renamed as National Leprosy Eradication Programme in 1983. **India achieved elimination status of Leprosy in December 2005.** National Strategic Plan & Roadmap for Leprosy 2023-27 launched in January 2023- to achieve zero transmission by 2027.
- The objectives of strategic plan: Strengthening leadership, commitment, and partnerships; Acceleration of Case Detection; Provision of Quality Services; Enhanced measures for Prevention of Disease, Disabilities, Stigma, Discrimination and Violation of Human Rights; and Digitalization of Surveillance Systems.
- **New Initiatives:** Convergence of leprosy screening under Comprehensive Primary Health Care (CPHC), Sparsh Leprosy Awareness Campaigns (SLAC) at village level is started to stop discrimination, Contact tracing and Post Exposure chemoprophylaxis administration is initiated etc.
- **Achievement during 2020:** Percentage of Grade II Disability (G2D)/ visible deformity among new cases decreased from 3.05% in 2018-19 to 2.39% (2019-20).
- **Treatment Regimen**: consists of Rifampicin, Dapsone and Clofazimine.
- **Pharmacists' Role:** Take part in pharmacovigilance activities, community education preventing stigma and discrimination.

## Bibliography

1. Annual Report 2023-24, Department of Health and Family Welfare, Ministry of Health and Family Welfare, Government of India.
2. National Strategic Plan and Roadmap for Leprosy, 2023 – 2027, Accelerating towards a Leprosy Free India, Central Leprosy Division, Government of India, January 2023.

# Malaria

**After reading this chapter, you should be able to understand and appreciate:**

- Malaria as public health issue;
- Strategy for prevention and control of malaria;
- India's efforts in managing malaria; and
- Pharmacists' role in malaria control programme.

Malaria has been the public health problem of India for centuries. Prior to 1940, there was no organized National Malaria Control Programme. The National Malaria Eradication Programme launched in 1958 was very successful but the impact could not be sustained. The malaria resurged during 1970s.Since then several initiatives are made but with limited success. The various initiatives of the malaria control over the years are given in the table (Milestones in Malaria Programmes in India).

| Year | Initiative | Year | Initiative |
|---|---|---|---|
| Prior to 1940 | No organized National Malaria Programme | 2005 | RDT (monovalent) introduced into the programme |
| 1953 | National Malaria Control Programmc [NMCP] launched | 2005 | Global Fund Assisted Intensified Malaria Control Project launched |
| 1958 | National Malaria Eradication Programme [NMEP] launched | 2006 | ACT introduced in areas showing Chloroquine resistance in falciparum malaria |
| 1971 | Urban Malaria Scheme launched | 2008 | Drug policy for malaria revised and ACT introduced in high *Plasmodium falciparum* predominant districts |
| 1977 | Modified Plan of Operation [MPO] implemented | 2008 | World Bank assisted National Vector Borne Disease Control Support Project initiated |
| 1995 | Modified Action Plan for Malaria Control implemented | 2009 | LLIN introduced, oral artemisinin monotherapy banned |
| 1997 | World Bank assisted Enhanced Malaria Control Project [EMCP] launched | 2010 | Malaria Drug Policy revised extending ACT for all cases. Global Fund (Round 9) assisted intensified Malaria Control Project [IMCP – II] launched. |
| 1999 | Programme renamed as National Anti-Malaria Programme [NAMP] | 2013 | RDT (bivalent) introduced; ACT introduced in Drug Policy for Malaria. |
| 2002 | Integration of Malaria Control Programme into National Vector Borne Disease Control Programme [NVBDCP] | 2014 | Newer insecticides and Larvicides introduced. |
| The National Frame Work for Malaria Elimination 2016-2030 launched in 2016 | | | |

In November 2015, the Prime Minister of India joined 17 Asia Pacific leaders in endorsing a plan and road map to eliminate malaria by 2030. India made its ambitious plan to eliminate malaria by 2027, three years ahead of Global Sustainable Development Goal. Over the last two decades, India has made impressive progress in Malaria control. The malaria has declined by over 80% (2.03 million cases in 2000 to 0.39 million in 2018) and malaria deaths by over 90% (932 deaths in 2000 to 85 in 2018). The National Vector Borne Disease Control Programme is responsible for Malaria programme in India. The GOI has developed National Framework for Malaria Elimination 2016-2030. Under the plan, the state governments are responsible for implementation and the apex agency (NVBDCP) offers assistance in the form of technical assistance, cash and commodity.

The states and the Union Territories are grouped into four categories for implementation: Category 0 (with no indigenous cases of malaria; at present no state or UT under this category), Category 1 (Low transmission areas), Category 2 (Moderate transmission areas), and Category 3 (High transmission areas). Efforts for malaria elimination are planned simultaneously: Elimination Phase for Category 1 areas, Pre-Elimination Phase in Category 2 areas and Intensified Control Phase in Category 3 areas.

The general strategy for prevention and control of malaria based on National Frame Work are:

I. Early Diagnosis and Radical Treatment;
II. Case based surveillance and rapid response;
III. Integrated Vector Management [IVM]:
   (a) Indoor residual spray [IRS];
   (b) Long Lasting Insecticidal Nets [LLINs] / Insecticide treated bed nets; and
   (c) Larval source management.
IV. Epidemic preparedness and early response;
V. Monitoring and Evaluation;
VI. Advocacy, Coordination and Partnership;
VII. Behavioural change commitment and community mobilization; and
VIII. Programme planning and management.

Of the above, the present text restricts its domain to 'diagnosis and treatment' & 'Integrated Vector Management'.

## Diagnosis and Treatment

### Diagnosis

**Suspected case (Criteria):** Patients with fever in an endemic area during transmission season who have recently visited an endemic area (But has no symptoms like cough and other signs of respiratory infection, running nose and other signs of cold, diarrhoea, pelvic inflammation indicated by severe low back ache with or without vaginal discharge and urinary symptoms, skin rash suggestive of eruptive illness, burning micturition, skin infections: boils, abscess, infected wounds, painful swelling of joints, and ear discharge).

**Confirmed cases:** Confirmed case is one in which the parasite has been detected by a diagnostic test: microscopy, rapid diagnostic test or molecular diagnostic test. Any trained volunteer, ASHA, health workers / professionals receiving a suspected malaria case must initiate or advise patient for a diagnostic test.

**Treatment:**

The treatment aims at: complete cure; prevention of progression of uncomplicated malaria to severe disease; prevention of death; interruption of transmission; and minimizing risk of selection and spread of drug resistant parasite.

The treatment protocol mentioned here is neither complete nor intends to encourage pharmacists to offer treatment. This intends to make pharmacists familiar with the national protocol to guide the patients.

## I. Treatment of Uncomplicated Malaria

*Plasmodium vivax* should be treated with Chloroquine (CQ) for 3 days and Primaquine (PQ) for 14 days. Primaquine is given to prevent relapse.

| Dosage [Number of Tablets] for Uncomplicated *P. vivax* malaria | | | | | | | |
|---|---|---|---|---|---|---|---|
| Age Group | Day 1 | | Day 2 | | Day 3 | | Day 4 -14 |
| | CQ (150 mg base) | PQ (2.5 mg) | CQ (150 mg base) | PQ (2.5 mg) | CQ (150 mg base) | PQ (2.5 mg) | PQ (2.5 mg) |
| Less than 1 year | ½ | 0 | ½ | 0 | ¼ | 0 | 0 |
| 1-4 years | 1 | 1 | 1 | 1 | ½ | 1 | 1 |
| 5-8 years | 2 | 2 | 2 | 2 | 1 | 2 | 2 |
| 9-14 years | 3 | 4 | 3 | 4 | 1½ | 4 | 4 |
| 15 years or more | 4 | 6 | 4 | 6 | 2 | 6 | 6 |
| CQ: Chloroquine (250 mg tablet contains 150 mg base); PQ: Primaquine | | | | | | | |
| Advice | Primaquine is contraindicated in infants, pregnant women and individuals with G6PD deficiency. Special care should be taken in patients with anaemia.<br>Symptoms of G6PD: dark coloured urine / yellow conjunctiva / bluish discoloration of lips / abdominal pain / nausea / vomiting / breathlessness | | | | | | |

## II. Treatment of Plasmodium falciparum malaria

Treatment of *P. falciparum* malaria should be started immediately on diagnosis to prevent progression of the disease and prevent deaths due to malaria.

| treatment of P. falciparum malaria in various age groups in all States and UTs except North Eastern States | | | | | | |
|---|---|---|---|---|---|---|
| Age group (in years) | Colour of blister pack | Day 1 | | Day 2 | | Day 3 |
| | | AS | SP | AS | PQ | AS |
| 0-1 | Pink | 1 Tablet (25 mg) | 1 tablet (250 mg + 12.5 mg) | 1 tablet (25 mg) | Nil | 1 tablet (25 mg) |
| 1-4 | Yellow | 1 tablet (50 mg) | 1 tablet (500 mg + 25 mg) | 1 tablet (50 mg) | 1 tablet (7.5 mg base) | 1 tablet (50 mg) |
| 5-8 | Green | 1 tablet (100 mg) | 1 tablet (750 mg + 37.5 mg) | 1 tablet (100 mg) | 2 tablets (7.5 mg base each) | 1 tablet (100 mg) |
| 9-14 | Red | 1 tablet (150 mg) | 2 tablets (500 mg +25 mg each) | 1 tablet (150 mg) | 4 tablets (7.5 mg base each) | 1 tablet (150 mg) |
| 15 & above | White | 1 tablet (200 mg) | 2 tablets (750 mg + 37.5 mg each) | 1 tablet (200 mg) | 6 tablets (7.5 mg base each) | 1 tablet (200 mg) |

- SP is not to be given to children below 5 months of age
- Primaquine and ACT-SP are not to given to pregnant women.

| Treatment of P. falciparum malaria in various age groups in NE States | | | | |
|---|---|---|---|---|
| ACT-AL | 5-14 Kg (5 months to < 3 years age) | 14-24 Kg (≥ 3 to 8 years) | 25-34 Kg (≥ 9 to 14 years) | More than 34 Kg (> 14 years |
| Dosage (in mg) | 20 mg/120 mg twice daily x 3 days | 40 mg/240 mg twice daily x 3 days | 60 mg/360 mg twice daily x 3 days | 80 mg/480 mg twice daily for 3 days |
| Dosage (in number of tablets) | 1 tablet twice daily x 3 days | 2 tablets twice daily x 3 days | 3 tablets twice daily x 3 days | 4 tablets twice daily x 3 days |
| Number of tablets in each pack | 6 | 12 | 18 | 24 |
| Colour of pack | Yellow | Green | Red | White |
| Artemether-lumefantrine (ACT-AL) | | | | |

- ACT-AL is not to be used in women in 1st trimester of pregnancy.
- Treat infants weighing < 5 kg with uncomplicated P. falciparum malaria with an ACT at the same mg/kg bw target dose as for children weighing 5 kg.

### Treatment of P. falciparum malaria in pregnancy:

The use of ACTs is safe in the second and third trimesters, and, in severe malaria it is considered that the benefits of artemisinin derivatives outweigh the possible side-effects. If the pregnancy test is negative, they should be treated with ACT. If the answer is yes, they should be referred to the sub-centre for treatment with quinine.

**Advice on Drug Use**: The first oral dose in malaria treatment should always be consumed in the presence of the health care provider. Children under 5 years of age and pregnant women should be asked to wait for 15 minutes after taking the dose. If there is no vomiting, the remaining part of the blister pack is given to the patient/caretaker to take home with the appropriate instructions.

If the patient vomits within the 15 minutes, he/she should be allowed to rest for 15 minutes and then the dose is repeated by opening a new blister pack and discarding what remains of the previous blister pack. If the patient vomits again, the case should be considered as a case of severe malaria and managed accordingly.

**III. Treatment of mixed infections with M. vivax and P. falciparum**

All mixed infections should be treated with a full course of ACT (ACT-AL in NE States and ACT-SP in other States) for 3 days and primaquine 0.25 mg/kg bw daily for 14 days.

**IV. Treatment of severe malaria**

The indications of severe malaria are: Impaired consciousness, Prostration, Multiple convulsions, Acidosis, Hypoglycaemia, Severe anaemia, Renal impairment, Jaundice, Pulmonary oedema, Significant bleeding, Shock and Hyperparasitaemia.

Parenteral artesunate is the treatment of choice for all severe malaria. It is essential that full doses of effective parenteral antimalarial treatment be given promptly in the initial 29 Diagnosis and Case Management 29 treatment of severe malaria, followed by a full dose of ACT orally. In case parenteral Artemisinin derivatives are not available readily, injection Quinine can be used.

Parenteral artesunate is the treatment of choice in all trimesters (pregnancy). If artesunate is not available, intramuscular artemether should be given, and if this is unavailable, then parenteral quinine should be started immediately until artesunate is obtained.

**V. Chemoprophylaxis**

Use of personal protection is encouraged. For short term chemoprophylaxis (up to 6 weeks) of malaria, doxycycline is used in a dose of 100 mg once daily for adults and 1.5 mg/kg once daily for children (contraindicated in pregnant women and children below 8 years age).

The drug should be started 2 days before travel and continued for 4 weeks after leaving the malarious area.

Chemoprophylaxis for stays more than 6 weeks is with mefloquine 250 mg weekly for adults and should be started two weeks before entering the high-risk area, continued during the stay and till four weeks after leaving the area. Mefloquine is contraindicated in individuals with history of convulsions, neuropsychiatric problems and cardiac conditions. Therefore, necessary precautions should be taken to ensure that individuals being administered mefloquine do not have these conditions.

**Integrated Vector Management**

I. **Indoor Residual Spray (IRS):** This is useful where mosquitoes enter house and rest on sprayed surface. The effectiveness of IRS depends on the adherence to the laid down criteria of the insecticide and spray procedure, public acceptance of spraying, use of well - maintained equipment, adequately trained personnel, good coverage and effective supervision.

   All interior walls and ceilings should be covered in the spray. All human dwellings including jhum huts where people sleep during plantation should be covered but not the cattle sheds.

   The insecticides used in IRS are: DDT, Malathion and a range of synthetic pyrethroids. Carbamate (Bendiocarb and Propoxur) formulations are recommended by WHO but not introduced in National Programme.

II. **LLINs:** The use of LLINs are very practical and cost effective intervention against malaria and are highly effective against vector mosquitoes which bite indoors at night. The nets not only provides a physical barrier against the mosquito bites but also either kill or shorten the life span.

   The LLINs are manufactured by incorporating synthetic pyrethroid insecticide into the net's fibre or coating impregnation of the insecticide on the fibre with a wash resistant binder system. They are more sustainable than conventional IINs.

III. **Larval Source Management:** This requires the management of aquatic habitats (water bodies) that are potential larval habitats for mosquitoes. This prevents the completion of development of immature stages. There are four types of LSM:

IV. **Habitat Modification:** It is the permanent alteration to the environment like landscaping, surface water drainage, filling and land reclamation, coverage of water storage containers with mosquito proof lids or permanent slabs and coverage of water surface with material impenetrable to mosquitoes.

(a) **Habitat Manipulation:** This is a recurrent activity including water level manipulation (stream flushing, keeping drains clear of vegetation so that water can flow too fast to support mosquitoes).

(b) **Larviciding:** Larviciding is the regular application of biological or chemical insecticides to water bodies.

(c) **Biological Control:** It is the introduction of natural predators into water bodies.

Larviciding measures should normally be used as a supplement to LLINs/ IRS but not as alternative to them.

V. **Personal Protective Measures:** Man – mosquito contact can be reduced by use of mosquito nets while sleeping or by use of mosquito coils or mats or liquids. Mosquito repellents applied to the skin give protection for 3-6 hours and are particularly useful for troops engaged in sentry duties and for those going outdoors from dusk to dawn for any other reason. Full sleeve loose shirts and trousers offer better protection from mosquito bites. Mosquito coils and mats are usually take about 30 minutes to reach their maximum effectiveness and they should be used accordingly before the mosquitoes become active in the evening.

**Pharmacists in Malaria Control Programme**

Unlike the National TB programme, Malaria Control Programme has not specified the fixed roles and responsibilities. Never the less, there are ample opportunities for the pharmacists to be part of the Malaria programme and serve the people.

I. Drug Management: National Programmes are vertical programmes and procurement of medicines are done centrally. The pharmacists can be part of it from quantifying the requirements to procurement and managing logistics. This would improve the access of medicines.

II. Pharmacists may advice the suspected patients for the need of diagnosis and treatment. They can help them taking medicines appropriately. They can also help the travellers on the need of prophylaxis.

III. ACT has potential for adverse effects. The National Programme needs pharmacovigilance of ACT. The pharmacists are in good position to act as pharmacovigilance expert and part of the programme.

IV. The Programme proposes to have partnership with various organizations including Pharmacists' Associations. The pharmacists' association can join hand at District and State level promoting implementation of National Programme on Malaria.

V. Community Participation: The pharmacists can participate in community education focussing on motivating behavioural change among the target audience in stead of just passing information.

Challenges in Malaria Control / Elimination Programme: The key challenges identified are:

I. Unrestricted population mobility across the states and union territories; and sharing of large international borders with malaria endemic countries (Myanmar and Bangladesh);

II. Shortage of skilled human resources; and

III. Insecticide resistance.

The 2012 estimate showed that the total economic malaria burden of the country was around US$ 1940 million with 75% from lost earnings and 25% from treatment costs borne by households. Estimates of 1990s showed that for every Rupee invested in malaria control, a direct return of Rupees 19.70 could be expected. This implies that implementing malaria elimination framework 2016-2030 would bring benefits at least 20 times greater than the total investment required for implementation of the programme.

## Bibliography

1. Annual Report 2018-2019, Ministry of Health and Welfare, Government of India.
2. Guideline for Diagnosis and Treatment of Malaria in India, 2014, National Institute of Malaria Research and National Vector Borne Disease Control Programme, 2014.
3. Jai Prakash Narain & Lalit M Nath, Eliminating malaria in India by 2027: The Count Down begins! Indian Journal of Medical Research, 148, August 2018.
4. National Drug Policy on Malaria 2013, Directorate of National Vector Borne Disease Control Programme, Delhi.
5. National Framework for Malaria Elimination in India 2016-2030, Ministry of Health and Family Welfare, 2016.
6. National Health Profile 2019, 14th Issue, Central Bureau of Health Intelligence, Ministry of Health and Family Welfare, Government of India.
7. Operational Manual for Malaria Elimination in India 2016 (version 1), Directorate of National Vector Borne Disease Control Programme, Ministry of Health & Family Welfare, Government of India.
8. World Malaria Report 2019, World Health Organization, 2019.

# Mental Health

"There is no health without Mental Health"

**After reading this chapter, you should be able to understand and appreciate:**

- Definition of Mental Health;
- Prevalence and Burden of Mental Health Disorder;
- India's effort tackling mental health issues; and
- Pharmacists' Role in Mental Health.

Mental Health is an integral and essential component of Health. World Health Organization definition of Health includes Physical, Social, Spiritual and Mental Health, not merely absence of disease or infirmity. Similar to the definition of health, mental health too is not just the absence of mental disorder. Mental health is defined as a state of well-being in which individuals realize their own abilities, can cope with normal stresses of life, can work productively, and are able to make positive contribution to their society. Mental health is also related to promotion of mental well-being, prevention of mental disorders, and treatment and rehabilitation of people affected by mental disorder.

## Epidemiology

**Global:** WHO estimates that at any given time 10 % of the global population suffers from some form of mental illness and one in four persons will be affected at least once in their life time. The mental disorder includes: depression, bipolar disorder, schizophrenia and other psychoses, dementia, and developmental disorders including autism. Depression is the most common mental disorder and an estimated 264 million people are affected by depression. The bipolar disorder affects about 45 million people worldwide. Schizophrenia is a severe mental disorder, affecting 20 million people worldwide. Worldwide, approximately 50 million people have dementia.

The burden of mental disorders globally is enormous, with an estimated 1·1 billion people affected by mental or substance use disorders worldwide. The surveys from China and India where more than 80 % of the world's population live with a mental or substance use disorder do not seek treatment.

**India:** One among every seven people in India was reported to have mental disorder ranging from mild to severe (2017). During 1990 to 2017, the proportional contribution of mental disorders to the total disease burden in India almost doubled. The National Mental Health Survey 2015-2016 showed:

- Prevalence of mental morbidity is more in urban metros. Fast paced life style, stress, complexities of living, break down of support systems, and challenges of economic instability are the major contributing factors;
- Common mental disorders including depression, anxiety disorders, and substance use disorder are huge burden affecting nearly 10 % of population;
- Prevalence of depression for both current and life time was 2.7 % and 5.2 %. The depression was reported to be higher in females and elderly groups;
- Nearly 1 % of the population reported high suicide risk. High suicide risk is an increasing concern. The prevalence of high suicidal risk was more in 40-49 years age group (1.19 %), among females (1.14 %) and those residing in urban metros (1.71 %);
- Nearly 1.9 % of the population were affected with severe mental disorders in the their life time and 0.8 % were identified as currently affected;
- The productive age groups (30 – 49 years)were affected most indicting that the mental disorders contribute to the greater morbidity in the productive population;
- The overall prevalence of mental morbidity was higher among males (13.9 %) than among females (7.5 %);
- Children and adolescents are too vulnerable to mental disorder;
- There are significant variations in overall morbidity among the surveyed states: 5.8 % in Assam to 14.1 % in Manipur; and
- Persons with mental disorders continue to be stigmatised and is a road block to seeking treatment. Nearly 80 % of the persons suffering had not received any treatment despite the presence of illness for more than 12 months.

## Disease and Economic Burden

Three out of four with a severe mental disorder experience significant disability in work, social and family life. Economic burden of mental disorder is very high as the treatment cost is out of pocket expenditure. Families had to spend nearly ₹ 1000 – 1500 per month for treatment and travel to access care. Poverty and disability with poor access to care significantly affect the quality of life with mental illness and their family.

COVID – 19 further increases mental health challenges. The uncertainties and fear associated with COVID – 19 outbreaks along with mass lock downs and economic recession has adversely affected the mental health of the people. There are reports of increase in psychological distress among the general population, persons with pre-existing mental disorder as well as health workers. The unprecedented threat to mental health is observed in both rich and poor nations. In post COVID time, mental ill-health is expected to be next epidemic.

**Mental Health and Sustainable Development Goals:** Mental health programmes usually have low priority. Treatment coverage is extremely low. In WHO's words "Mental Health has been neglected for far too long though it is crucial to the overall well -being of the individuals, societies and countries.

There are three basic principles of UN: No discrimination on the ground of mental illness; Every patient should have the rights to be treated and cared for in one's own community; and Every patient should have the right to be treated in the least restrictive environment with the least restrictive or intrusive treatment.

SDG Target 3.4: By 2030, there is one – third reduction of premature mortality from NCDs through provision of treatment and promotion of mental health and well-being.

SDG Target 3.5: To strengthen the prevention and treatment of substances of abuse including narcotic drug abuse and harmful use of alcohol.

## Preventive Strategy and National Programme

**Mental Health Policy**: The first ever National Mental Health Policy of India was formulated in 2014. The policy was formulated in consonance with the intent of World Health Assembly's resolution on global burden of mental disorders and the need for a comprehensive, coordinated response from the health and social sectors at the community levels. A need for a driving force to strengthen the National Programme was also felt as the programme was not universal and huge treatment gap. The National Policy was formulated with the following objectives in mind:

- To provide universal access to mental health care.
- To increase access to and utilization of comprehensive mental health services by persons with mental health problems.
- To increase to access to mental health services to vulnerable groups.

- To reduce prevalence and impact of risk factors associated with mental health problems.
- To reduce the risk and incidence of suicide and attempted suicide.
- To ensure respect for rights and protection of harms of persons with mental health problems.
- To enhance availability and equitable distribution of skilled human resources for mental health.
- To progressively enhance financial allocation and improve utilization of mental health promotion and care.
- To identify and address the social, biological and psychological determinants of mental health programmes and to provide appropriate interventions.

**National Programme on Mental Health:** In order to address the heavy burden of mental illness in the community and the absolute inadequacy of mental health care infrastructure in the country, the Government of India has launched the National Mental Health Programme (NMHP) in 1982. Programme was launched as a part of WHO initiative. India was the first major country to launch National Programme on Mental Health.

**Objectives:**

1. To ensure the availability and accessibility of minimum mental healthcare for all in the foreseeable future, particularly to the most vulnerable and underprivileged sections of the population;
2. To encourage the application of mental health knowledge in general healthcare and in social development; and
3. To promote community participation in the mental health service development and to stimulate efforts towards self-help in the community.

The Primary Health Centre (PHC) and Community Health Centres (CHC) were the service delivery points. The model faced many hurdles in terms of management and implementation. To overcome the limitations of National Programme, it was decided to make District as functional unit for management and programme implementation. In order to scale up the programme, under the National Programme for operation, the District Mental Health Programme was launched.

**District Mental Health Programme (DMHP):** Following the success of pilot project at the Bellary District of Karnataka by the National Institute of Mental Health and Neurosciences (NIMHANS), the DMHP was launched in 27 districts in 1996. The aim of the DMHP was to extend mental healthcare services through existing mechanism in the district. The model of DMHP had the following specific objectives:

- To develop and implement a decentralized training program in mental health for all categories of health personnel in a way that would be the least disruptive to on-going general healthcare activities
- To provide a range of essential drugs such as antipsychotics, antidepre-ssants, anticonvulsants, and minor tranquilizers for the management of PWMI
- To develop a system of simple recording and reporting of care by mental health personnel
- To monitor the effect of service of the mental health program in terms of treatment utilization and outcomes
- To reduce the stigma by bringing about a change of attitude through public health education
- Treatment and rehabilitation of patients within the community by adequate provision of medicines and strengthening the family support system

**Two authorities:** one at Centre and one at State Level were constituted under Mental Healthcare Act 2017. The Central Mental Health Authority is mandated with power of regulatory control over all central institutes / establishments providing mental health services. Besides, it maintains a national register of all mental health establishments of the country, maintains a national register of clinical psychologists, mental health nurses and psychiatric social workers. Similar the State Mental Health Authority is mandated to regulate, develop and coordinate mental health services offered by the respective state government.

| **Time Line of Mental Health Initiatives in India** | |
|---|---|
| 1982 | National Mental Health Programme (NMHP) launched |
| 1986 | District Mental Health Programme (DMHP) launched under NMHP (pilot study) |
| 1987 | Mental Health Act Enacted |
| 1990 | Central Mental Health Authority Rules 1990 |
| 1996 | DMHP launched on four districts. |
| 2003 | NMHP re-strategized: Modernization of Mental Hospitals; Manpower Development Scheme |
| 2007-2012 | In Xth Five Year Plan focus on Manpower Development |
| 2014 | National Mental Health Policy Announced |
| 2017 | Mental Healthcare Act 2017 (replaced Mental Healthcare Act 1987). Central Mental Health Authority and State Mental Health Authority were constituted. |

As a part of International Commitment on the Rights of Persons with Disabilities and its Optional Protocol and to provide mental healthcare and services for persons with mental illness and to protect, promote and fulfil the rights of such persons during delivery of mental health care and services, the GOI enacted 'The Mental Healthcare Act 2017'. Two Authorities are created: Central Mental Health Authority and State Mental Health Authority to ensure protection of Rights of Persons with mental illness.

World Mental Health Day is celebrated on $10^{th}$ October every year.

**National Programme**

Though the mental health is managed as a part of general healthcare for quite long time, it was in 1982 for the first time, a National Programme, called National Mental Health

**Mental Health and Medicines:** Access to medicines for mental disorders (Psychotropic Medicines) is always a challenge. Availability of essential medicines for mental health at all level of care is key to quality care. WHO emphasised the need to "procure and ensure the availability of basic medicines for mental disorders as included in WHO's list of essential medicines and to ensure their rational use".

The NLEM does not have adequate number of medicines for treatment of mental illness. The current list has just 13 psychotropic medicines. The NLEM should include all medicines as listed in WHO's list. The NLEM should be used for treatment not merely for price control.

Barriers for access to treatment (medicines) can be divided into two areas: Demand and Supply. The demand for psychotropic medicines depends on factors like: acceptability of mental health treatment; awareness of mental health problems in the community; reduced health seeking behaviours by individuals because of stigma, discrimination or other subcultural factors; poor recognition that the mental disorders are responsive to effective treatment; poor treatment adherence for various reasons; cost of services; and geographical distances from healthcare providers. Supply is affected cost, supply chain management and regulatory situation.

**Achievements:** The GOI has been supporting the DMHP under NMHP to address the burden of mental health. The programme has so far implemented 692 districts of the country for detection, management and treatment of mental disorders / illnesses with major components of counselling in schools and colleges, workplace stress managements, life skill training, suicide prevention of services IEC activities for generation of awareness and removal of stigma associated with mental illness.

**Some Concerns:**

- The implementation of NMHP is slow. Though first originated in 1982, the National Mental Health Policy was developed only in 2014;
- State Mental Health System Assessment showed wide diversity with respect to administrative and economic characteristics like number districts, talukas and villages covered under mental health programme. Gujarat, Kerala and Tamil Nadu have better system administration. Kerala has better coverage ensuring care for entire population;
- There is paucity of mental health specialists. Except Kerala, all other states fell short of requirements of at least one psychiatrist per one lakh population;
- Awareness on mental health is very poor;
- Susceptible to age old stigma, prejudices and fear; and
- Lack of funding: In 2021-22 budget centre has allocated ₹ 597 crore for mental healthcare. Out of this only 7 % is the real allocation for National Mental Health Programme which is grossly inadequate. The average budget remains as that of previous year.

**Pharmacists' Contribution to Mental Health**

- The pharmacists' participation in mental health programme varies widely in globe. FIP outlines the following areas for pharmacists' contribution: Triage; Health Promotion; Early Detection; Optimal Treatment Outcomes; Education; Helping to shape public policy; Inter-professional collaborative practices; and Research.
- In USA, the pharmacists are causing a huge impact on mental health outcome by educating patients about drugs to improve adherence; recognizing mental illness through observance and screening; providing resources and referrals for patients who need them; and evaluating medication list for drugs that may alter patient's mental status.

- In our NMHP, no specific role is specified. However, the community pharmacists can provide counselling while dispensing the medicines for mental health. As these medicines fall under restricted category, appropriate counselling not only improve rational use and improve adherence, there would be substantial health outcome as well.

**Bottom Line**

- Mental health is defined as a state of well-being in which individuals realize their own abilities, can cope with normal stresses of life, can work productively, and are able to make positive contribution to their society.
- At a given time, 10 %of the global population suffers from some form mental illness. The global burden of mental disorder is huge with an estimated 1.1 billion people affected by mental or substance use disorder.
- One among every seven persons in India is reported to have some form of mental disorder. Common mental disorders including depression, anxiety and substance use disorder affect around 10 % of the population. Prevalence of mental health morbidity is more in urban metros.
- Persons with mental disorders continue to be stigmatised and this factor discourages people from seeking medical help.
- Economic cost of treatment is high – A family spends around ₹ 1000 to ₹ 1500 per month for treatment and travel to care centre.
- India made several initiatives to tackle mental health issues in the country: importantly formulated mental health policy, initiated National Mental Health Programme and District Mental Health Programme.
- Though some progress has been made like programme implemented in 692 districts, the programme implementation still some concerns like inadequate funding.
- There is no specific role specified for pharmacists. The community pharmacists still have ample opportunities to contribute to mental health. They can counsel the patients or the care givers at the time of dispensing medicines which would improve adherence and therapeutic outcome.

## Bibliography

1. Annual Report 2020-21, Department of Health and Family Welfare, Ministry of Health and Family Welfare, Government of India.
2. International Pharmaceutical Federation (FIP) Focus on Mental Health, The Contribution of the Pharmacist, The Hague: International Pharmaceutical Federation, 2015.
3. Lalit Dandona *et al*, The burden of mental disorders across the states of India: the Global Burden of Disease Study 1990 – 2017, Lancet Psychiatry 2020; 7: 148–61.
4. National Health Profile, 2020, 15th Issue, Central Bureau of Health Intelligence, Government of India.
5. National Mental Health Survey of India, 2015-2016, Summary, National Institute of Mental Health and Neuro Sciences, Bengaluru, 2016.
6. New Pathways New Hope, National Mental Health Policy of India, Ministry of Health and Family Welfare, Government of India, October 2014.
7. The WHO Special Initiative for Mental Health (2019-2023): Universal Health Coverage for Mental Health, WHO, 2019.
8. World Health Report 2001, Mental Health: New Understanding, New Hope, WHO.

# Mother and Child Health

# [Reproductive, Maternal, Newborn, Child, Adolescent Health and Nutrition)

In order to improve maternal health, we have to focus on improving all women's health and access to care - not just during labor and delivery, but before and after pregnancy, and throughout our lives.

- Leana S. Wen

**After reading this chapter, you should be able to understand and appreciate:**

- Definition of Mother and Child Health;
- Prevalence and Burden of Illness of Mother and Child;
- India's effort tackling Mother and Child Health issues; and
- Pharmacists' Role in Mother and Child Health.

Maternal health (Mother Health) is defined as the health of women during pregnancy, childbirth, and the postnatal period. Each stage should be a positive experience that ensures women and their babies reach their full health and well-being potential. Improving quality of maternal healthcare services is key to reducing maternal mortality across developing nations, including India. Maternal health is one of the key priority areas for the country's health care system as the interventions strategized under this programme directly affect further reductions in maternal mortality and morbidity

Child health is a state of physical, mental, intellectual, social and emotional well-being and not merely the absence of disease or infirmity. Healthy children live in families, environments, and communities that provide them with the opportunity to reach their fullest developmental potential. Protecting and improving the health of children is of fundamental importance.

More mothers and children are surviving today than ever before.

The term maternal & child health refers to the promotive, preventive, curative & rehabilitative health care for mother & children which includes the sub areas of maternal health, child health, family planning and health aspects of care of children.

## Prevalence of Maternal and Child Health Issue

**Global:** About 287 000 women died during and following pregnancy and childbirth in 2020. This number is unacceptably high. The most common direct causes of maternal injury and death are excessive blood loss, infection, high blood pressure, unsafe abortion, and obstructed labour, as well as indirect causes such as anaemia, malaria, and heart disease.

Vast disparities exist around the world in a child's chances of survival, with low- and middle-income countries disproportionately affected. The leading causes of death among children include respiratory infections, diarrhoeal diseases, measles, malaria, malnutrition and newborn conditions. Many child deaths are preventable through vaccination, adequate home care, access to health care services, improved rates of breastfeeding and better nutrition. However, many of the life-saving interventions are beyond the reach of the world's poorest people.

Survival is just one of many issues relevant to children's health. Child health, growth and development are inseparable. In 2016, at least 250 million children were not able to reach their full physical or psychological development. This represents the staggering figure of 43%.

**India:** Maternal Mortality Ratio (MMR): A maternal death is the death of a woman while pregnant or within 42 days of termination of pregnancy, from any cause related to or aggravated by the pregnancy or its management, but not from accidental or incidental causes.

The MMR was 97 (2018-2020). This has declined over the years 97 (2010-2012).

Infant Mortality Rate (IMR): 35 (2021-2025) per 1000 live birth.

Under 5 Mortality Rate:47 (2021-2025) per 1000 live birth.

IMR for the country has declined to 28 in 2020 from 50 in 2009. Still, India continues to grapple with high maternal mortality.

**Mother and Child Health in Sustainable Development Goals:**

Maternal, Neonatal and Under 5 Mortality are linked to SDG 3.

## Preventive Strategy and National Programme

India programme on mother and child health are included in National Programme called 'Reproductive, Maternal, Newborn, Child, Adolescent Health and Nutrition (RMNCAH+N)'.

The various interventions under RMNCAH+N strategy are as below:

1. Promotion of Institutional deliveries through cash incentive under Janani Suraksha Yojana (JSY) and Janani Shishu Suraksha Karyakaram (JSSK) which entitles all pregnant women delivering in public health institutions to absolutely free delivery including Caesarean section, post-natal care and treatment of sick infants till one year of age. Pradhan Matritvya Vandana Yojana (PMMVY) is another maternity benefit programme under which cash incentive of Rs. 5000 is provided to pregnant women and lactating mothers.
2. Strengthening essential newborn care at all delivery points, establishment of Special Newborn Care Units (SNCU), Newborn Stabilization Units (NBSU) and Kangaroo Mother Care (KMC) units for care of sick and small babies. Home Based Newborn Care (HBNC) and Home Based Care of Young Children (HBYC) by ASHAs to improve child rearing practices and to identify sick newborn.
3. Early initiation and exclusive breastfeeding for first six months and appropriate Infant and Young Child Feeding (IYCF) practices are promoted under Mothers' Absolute Affection (MAA) in convergence with Ministry of Women and Child Development.
4. Village Health Sanitation and Nutrition Days (VHSNDs) are observed for provision of maternal and child health services and creating awareness on maternal and child care. Health and nutrition education through mass and social media is also promoted to improve healthy practices and to generate demand for service uptake.
5. Nutrition Rehabilitation Centres (NRCs) have been set up at public health facilities to treat and manage the children with Severe Acute Malnutrition (SAM) admitted with medical complications.
6. Universal Immunization Programme (UIP) is being supported to provide vaccination to children against life threatening diseases such as Tuberculosis, Diphtheria, Pertussis, Polio, Tetanus, Hepatitis B, Measles, Rubella, Pneumonia and Meningitis caused by Haemophilus Influenzae B. The Rotavirus vaccination has also been rolled out in the country for prevention of Rotaviral diarrhoea. "Mission Indradhanush is targeted to immunize children who are either unvaccinated or partially vaccinated i.e. those that have not been covered during the rounds of routine immunization for various reasons. Intensified Mission

Indradhanush (IMI) 2.0 is being planned as per road-map for achieving 90% full immunization coverage across the country.

7. All the children from 0 to 18 years of age are screened for 30 health conditions classified into 4Ds - Diseases, Deficiencies, Defects and Developmental delay under "Rastriya Bal Swasthya Karyakaram" (RBSK). District early intervention centre (DEIC) at district health facility level are established for confirmation and management of the 4D's.
8. National Deworming Day (NDD) is implemented biannually every year for deworming of children (one to nineteen year of age).
9. Name based tracking of mothers and children till two years of age is done through RCH portal to ensure complete antenatal, intranatal, postnatal care and immunization as per schedule.
10. Capacity building of health care providers is regularly done to build and upgrade the skills in basic and comprehensive obstetric care of mother during pregnancy, delivery and for essential new-born care.

Besides above programme and scheme, few newer initiatives started under RMNCAH+N are as follows:

(a) Pradhan Mantri Surakshit Matritva Abhiyan (PMSMA) has been launched to provide fixed-day assured, comprehensive and quality antenatal care universally to all pregnant women on the 9th of every month.

(b) "LaQshya" programme aims to improve the quality of care in Labour room and Maternity operation theatres.

(c) Surakshit Matritva Aashwasan (SUMAN) initiative is focussed on assured delivery of maternal and newborn health care services encompassing wider access to quality care services, at no cost, zero tolerance for denial of services, assured management of complications along with respect for women's autonomy and dignity.

(d) Defeat Diarrhoea (D2) initiative has been launched for promoting ORS and Zinc use and eliminating the diarrhoeal deaths by 2025.

(e) Social Awareness and Actions to Neutralize Pneumonia Successfully (SAANS) initiative for reduction of Childhood morbidity and mortality due to Pneumonia.

Anaemia Mukt Bharat (AMB) strategy as a part of Poshan Abhiyan aims to strengthen the existing mechanisms and foster newer strategies to tackle anaemia, which include testing & treatment of anaemia in school going adolescents & pregnant women, addressing non nutritional causes of anaemia and a comprehensive communication strategy.

**Achievements**

Maternal and Adolescent Health Care:

- In a significant achievement, Maternal Mortality Ratio (MMR) of India registered a decline by 33 points from 130 per 100,000 live births in SRS 2014-16 to 97 per 100,000 live births in Sample Registration System (SRS) 2018-20.
- India has achieved NHP's (National Health Policy) target for MMR of 100 per 1,00,000 live births by 2020.
- Institutional deliveries in India have nearly doubled, from 47% in 2007-08 (DLHS-3) to over 88.6% in 2019-21 (NFHS-5).
- Janani Suraksha Yojana (JSY): Safe motherhood intervention under NHM is being implemented with the objective of reducing maternal and neonatal mortality by promoting institutional delivery among pregnant women.
- Janani Shishu Suraksha Karyakram (JSSK): The scheme entitles all pregnant women delivering in public health institutions to absolutely free and no expense delivery including caesarean delivery. During the FY 2023-24 more than 1.37 crore beneficiaries availed the benefits under JSSK
- Pradhan Mantri Surakshit Matritva Abhiyan (PMSMA): Since inception (till 31st March 2024), more than 4.87 Crore antenatal check-ups have been conducted for comprehensive services under the programme and more than 62.40 Lakhs High Risk Pregnancies (HRP) have been identified.
- Surakshit Matritva Aashwashan (SUMAN): As on 31st March 2024, more than 40000 facilities have been notified under SUMAN.

**Child health and Immunization:**

- U5MR for the country has shown significant decline of 3 points (Annual Decline Rate: 8.6%) from 2019 SRS (32 per 1000 live births in 2020 against 35 per 1000 live births in 2019).
- IMR has also registered 2-point decline to 28 per 1000 live births in 2020 from 30 per 1000 live births in 2019 (Annual Decline Rate: 6.7%).
- NMR has also declined by 2 points from 22 per 1000 live births in 2019 to 20 per 1000 live births in 2020 (Annual Decline Rate: 9.1%).
- Six States/ UT have already attained SDG target of NMR (<=12 by 2030): Kerala (4), Delhi (9), Tamil Nadu (9), Maharashtra (11), Jammu and Kashmir (12) and Punjab (12).

**Pharmacists' Contribution to Maternal and Child Health**

- **Maternal Health:**
    - Encouraging pregnant women to have regular check up.
    - Encouraging pregnant women to go for Tetanus Toxoid, and Iron & Folic Acid treatment.
    - Advising them not to take any medications without consulting doctors / healthcare professionals.
    - Advising them on nutrition.
- **Child Health:**
    - Encouraging the parents to complete immunization of the child.
    - Advising the parents to take the sick child to health professionals.
    - Advising the parents not to give any medicine without advice from health care professionals.

**Bottom Line**

- Maternal health (Mother Health) is defined as the health of women during pregnancy, childbirth, and the postnatal period.
- Child health is a state of physical, mental, intellectual, social and emotional well-being and not merely the absence of disease or infirmity.
- Globally about 287 000 women died during and following pregnancy and childbirth in 2020. This number is unacceptably high.
- MMR, IMR Under 5 Mortality remain high in India.
- Maternal, Neonatal and Under 5 Mortality are linked to SDG 3.
- *India's programme on mother and child health are included in National Programme called* 'Reproductive, Maternal, Newborn, Child, Adolescent Health and Nutrition (RMNCAH+N)'. Many other relevant programmes are also available.
- In a significant achievement, Maternal Mortality Ratio (MMR) of India registered a decline by 33 points from 130 per 100,000 live births in SRS 2014-16 to 97 per 100,000 live births in Sample Registration System (SRS) 2018-20.
- U5MR for the country has shown significant decline of 3 points.
- IMR has Annual Decline Rate of 6.7%.
- NMR has also Annual Decline Rate: 9.1%.
- Kerala, Delhi, Tamil Nadu, Maharashtra, Jammu and Kashmir and Punjab have already achieved SDG target on NMR.
- Pharmacists can encourage the mothers go for regular check up, immunization for self and children, advicing not to any medications without health professionals' advice.

## Bibliography

1. A Strategic Approach to Reproductive, Maternal, New Born, Child and Adolescent Health ((RMNCH+A)) in India, for Healthy Mother and Child, Government of India, January 2013.
2. Annual Report 2023-24, Department of Health and Family Welfare, Ministry of Health and Family Welfare, Government of India.
3. https://www.who.int/health-topics/maternal-health#tab=tab_1 accessed on 29th December 2024.
4. https://www.who.int/teams/maternal-newborn-child-adolescent-health-and-ageing accessed on 29th December 2024.

# Tobacco Control

"A cigarette is a pinch of tobacco rolled in paper with fire at one end and a fool at the other"

- George Bernard Shaw

**After reading this chapter, you should be able to understand and appreciate:**

- The operation of National Tobacco Control Programme (NTCP);
- Milestones on Tobacco Control Programme in India;
- Various Forms of Tobacco Use in India;
- Ill effects of Tobacco Use and Benefits of Quitting Tobacco Use;
- Nicotine Replacement Therapy; and
- Pharmacists' Role in Tobacco Control.

Tobacco is the foremost preventable cause of death and disease in world today. It kills about the half of the people who use. Tobacco use is widespread in India. 26.7 crore people of 15 years and above use tobacco in one or other form with overall prevalence of tobacco use in India is at 28.6 % (males – 42.4 % and females – 14.2 %). The tobacco causing deaths are about 13 lakh per year in our country. The tobacco use is directly contributing to majority of CVDs, Cancers and Chronic Lung Diseases. Tobacco epidemic is a major public health challenge for India.

31 May is World No Tobacco Day. The theme of 2021 is "Commit to Quit". This yearly celebration informs the public on the dangers of using tobacco, the business practices of tobacco companies, what WHO is doing to fight the tobacco epidemic, and what people around the world can do to claim their right to health and healthy living and to protect future generations. WHO created this in 1987.

## Various Forms of Tobacco Use in India

There are two types of tobacco products available in India: Smoked and Smoke Less tobacco products. While for most countries cigarette smoking is the predominant form of tobacco use, In India the Smoke Less Tobacco (SLT) is more predominant.

**Smoked Form of Tobacco:** These are Beedi, Cigarette, Hukah, Chilum, Chutta. Beedi smoking is the most popular form followed by cigarette smoking. When a smoker inhales from a lit cigarette, the temperature at the tip rises to approximately 926 ° Celsius, as the oxygen is drawn through the tobacco, paper, and other additives. At this intense heat, more than four thousand separate compounds are oxidized and released through cigarette smoke. The smokers inhale these. Though all these chemicals are extremely harmful to the human health, the prominent among these include nicotine, tar and carbon monoxide.

**Smoke Less Form of Tobacco:** Smokeless Tobacco (SLT) is tobacco consumed in the unburnt form, either orally or nasally. SLT use is very common and they are available in different forms and used differently. In India, betel quid (pan) has been in use for centuries. It has been the socially accepted practice and a part of culture and religious customs. Soon after the arrival of tobacco (Portuguese traders brought tobacco to India in the early 1600s), it was added in the betel quid. This combination is now practiced. The various forms of SLT are given in the table below:

| Mode of Use | Products |
|---|---|
| *For chewing and sucking* | Betel Quid (Pan) with tobacco; Gutkha; Kharra; Mainpuri; Dohra; Mawa; Khaini; Zarda; Khiwam; Chewing Tobacco; Loose tobacco leaf. |
| *For application* | Mishri; Gul; Gudakhu; Tapkeer / Bajjar / Snuff; Tobacco Containing Toothpowder; Tobacco Containing Toothpaste. |
| *For gargling* | Tuibur. |

Global Adult Tobacco Survey, India, 2009 – 2010, showed different pattern of tobacco use in different states. The survey was conducted among the age group of 35 to 69 years and the highest prevalence tobacco smoking was found in Rajasthan (in men category) and Bihar (in women category). The smokeless tobacco use prevalence was highest in Bihar (in men category) and Odisha (in women category).

The Government of India launched the National Tobacco Control Programme (NTCP) in the year 2007-08, with the objectives to (i) create awareness about the harmful effects of tobacco consumption; (ii) reduce the production and supply of tobacco products; (iii) ensure effective implementation of the provisions made under "The Cigarettes and Other Tobacco Products (Prohibition of Advertisement and Regulation of Trade and Commerce, Production, Supply and Distribution) Act, 2003" (COTPA); (iv) help the people quit tobacco use through Tobacco Cessation Centres; and (v) facilitate implementation of strategies for prevention and control of tobacco advocated by WHO Framework Convention of Tobacco Control.

| Time Line on Tobacco Control in India | |
|---|---|
| 1975 | Cigarettes Act [Statutory Warning – Cigarette Smoking is Injurious to Health] |
| 1981 | Prevention and Control of Pollution Act [Smoking as Air Pollutant] |
| 1988 | Motor Vehicles Act [Smoking Illegal in Public Vehicle] |

**Table *Contd...***

| Time Line on Tobacco Control in India | |
|---|---|
| 1990 | Prevention of Food Adulteration Act, 1955 [Health Warning "Chewing of Tobacco is Injurious to Heath"] |
| 1992 | Drugs and Cosmetic Act, 1940 [Sale of Tobacco Containing Tooth Powders and Tooth Pastes Banned] |
| 2000 | Cable Television Networks Amendment Act [Prohibited the transmission of advertisements on Tobacco and Liquors] |
| 2003 | Comprehensive "Cigarettes and Other Tobacco Products Act" introduced. |
| 2008 | NTCP launched covering 42 Districts of 21 States / UTs. |
| 2012 | Operational Guidelines released |
| 2017 | National Programme for Tobacco Control and Drug Addiction Treatment [NPTCDAT] converged with NCDs and e-Health |
| 1st December, 2020. | Display of health warnings on all tobacco product packs |

NTCP is being implemented through a three-tier structure: (i) National Tobacco Control Cell (ii) State Tobacco Control Cell & (iii) District Tobacco Control Cell. The NTCP is being implemented in 677 districts across 36 States/UTs. The responsibilities of each tier:

- **National Tobacco Control Cell (NTCC):** The NTCC is responsible for overall policy formulation, planning, implementation, monitoring and evaluation of the different activities envisaged under the National Tobacco Control Programme (NTCP). The National Cell functions under the direct guidance and supervision of the programme in-charge from the MoHFW i.e. Joint Secretary.
- **State Tobacco Control Cell (STCC):** The STCC is responsible for over-all planning, implementation and monitoring of the different activities, and achievement of physical and financial targets planned under the programme in the State. The STCC is also responsible for documentation of activities, recruitment of staff at state/district level and sending timely activity as well as financial reports to the NTCC.

  The STCC is headed by a State Nodal Officer, who is a Senior Officer from State Department of Health preferably on a full time basis, to look after all the NCD programmes like [NPCDCS, NTCP, NMHP, and NPHCE]. This cell may operate under National Health Mission, within the State NCD Cell or as a part of the Health Department or Directorate General of Health Services, as the case may be, in the States/UTs.
- **District Tobacco Control Cell (DTCC):** The (DTCC) is established in a district under the umbrella of the District Health Society. The cell is the focal point for all the activities carried out under the National Tobacco Control Programme (NTCP) at the district and sub-district levels. It is responsible for overall planning, implementation, and monitoring of different activities and for achievement of physical and financial targets

under the programme. The role of the DTCC is extremely crucial as most of the activities under the NTCP are to be implemented at district and sub-district levels.

Key activities at the district-level include:

(a) Training of Key stakeholders: health and social workers, NGOs, school teachers, enforcement officers etc.

(b) Information, Education and Communication (IEC) activities.

(c) School Programmes.

(d) Monitoring tobacco control laws.

(e) Setting-up and strengthening of cessation facilities including provision of pharmacological treatment facilities at the district level.

(f) Co-ordination with Panchayati Raj Institutions for inculcating concept of tobacco control at the grassroots.

The DTCC is to be headed by a District Nodal Officer, preferably Chief Medical Officer/Civil Surgeon of the district on a full time basis. For achieving synergy, it is desirable that the District Nodal Officer under NTCP is also given the responsibility to look after the NCD programmes like Prevention and Control of Cancer, Diabetes, Cardiovascular Diseases & Stroke (NPCDCS), National Mental Health Programme (NMHP), National Oral Health Programme and National Programme for Health Care of Elderly (NPHCE). Other team members of this cell include a District Consultant, a Psychologist / Counsellor and a Social worker, appointed on a contractual basis under the NTCP. Every District should constitute an enforcement squad preferably under the Collector / District Magistrate (DM). The squad would be responsible for monitoring compliance with the tobacco control laws in the jurisdiction and for taking action against any violations in the district.

**Major Achievements:** Efforts made to discourage use of tobacco products in order to reduce prevalence of tobacco use amongst the population have achieved the following success:

1. Sale of cigarettes or any other tobacco products to and by persons below the age of 18 years and within 100 yards of educational institutions banned;
2. Promotion / advertisement of cigarettes or any other tobacco products banned;
3. Smoking in public places is banned;
4. Specified health warnings to be displayed on all tobacco product packs; and
5. Use of Electronic Cigarettes banned.

6. National Resource Centre for Tobacco Cessation and Oral Health is established at Maulana Azad Institute of Dental Sciences, New Delhi.
7. The National Tobacco Quit Line Service (NTQLS), a telephone based free of cost counselling service, is introduced to provide confidential and quality counselling services across the country. This can be accessed through toll free number: 1800-11-2356.
8. 'Global Knowledge Hub for Smokeless Tobacco (GKH for SLT)' is established at the National Institute of Cancer Prevention and Research (NICPR), Noida.
9. Several Training and Sensitization Programmes being organised throughout the countries.
10. The National Medical Commission has directed the medical colleges across the country to set up 'Tobacco Cessation Centre" to combat the adveorse effects of tobacco use and promote public health.

| Burden of Tobacco Use | Benefits of Quitting Tobacco Use |
|---|---|
| • Major risk factor for Cancer, Cardiovascular Diseases (CVD), Diabetes, Chronic Lung Disease, stroke, infertility, blindness, Tuberculosis (TB), Oral Cavity etc.<br>• 50% of cancers in males and 20% cancers in females<br>• 40% of TB and other related diseases<br>• The economic burden from tobacco constitutes more than 1% of India's GDP, and the direct health expenditures on treating tobacco-related diseases alone accounts for 5.3% of the total private and public health expenditures in India in a year. It shows that, for every INR 100 that is received as excise taxes from tobacco products, INR 816 of costs is imposed on society through its consumption.<br>• Economic costs attributable to tobacco use in 2011 for persons aged 35-69 is ₹ 1,04,500 crores.<br>• Loss to environment such as deforestation, pollution, litter, forest fires etc. | • In 8 hours: Oxygen levels return to normal.<br>• In 24 hours: Risk of heart attack begins to decrease.<br>• In 72 hours: Lung function improves.<br>• In 1-9 months: Coughing and shortness of breath decreases.<br>• In 12 months: Risk of heart disease is half as compared to tobacco user.<br>• In 5 years: Stroke risk is reduced.<br>• In 10 years: Risk of lung cancer is less than half as compared to tobacco user.<br>• In 15 years: Risk of heart disease is similar to a person who never smoked.<br>• Reduced risk of diseases attributable to tobacco use<br>• Reduced health care expenditure means more money for other essential expenditures<br>• You become a role model for your children as well as for your society |
| Source: https://ntcp.nhp.gov.in/ accessed on 20th May 2021. | |

| NRT Therapies and Counselling Points | | |
|---|---|---|
| **NRTs** | **Counselling Points** | **Contraindication / Side effects** |
| Nicotine gum | • Caution with dentures<br>• Caution with history of esophageal oral or pharyngeal inflammation<br>• Do not consume acidic beverages: soda, coffee, beer at least15 minutes before or after | Contraindication:<br>Pregnancy; Children; and Cardiovascular Diseases<br>Side Effects:<br>Nausea, vomiting, indigestion, and gastrointestinal disturbances;<br>Insomnia and sleep apnea;<br>Headaches; Oral ulcers;<br>Skin irritation;<br>Heart palpitations/chest pains;<br>Coughing; Throat soreness;<br>Dry mouth; Increase caries-risk profile;<br>Taste impairment; Difficulty in speech in denture wearers;<br>Hyperkeratosis;<br>Localized mucosal irritation |
| Nicotine patch | • place the patches over the clean and unbroken skin once in the morning, rather than using throughout the day.<br>• Do not use if patient has severe eczema or psoriasis | |
| Nicotine lozenge | • One lozenge at a time<br>• Limit 20 in 24 hours<br>• Do not eat or drink 15 minutes before or during use | |
| Nicotine inhaler | • Spray in the mouth (not inhaled nor swallowed for few seconds). Care should be taken that it does not touch the lips. | |
| Nicotine nasal spray | • Not to use during chronic nasal disorder<br>• Severe reactive airway disease | |

**Role of Pharmacists**

There is no specified role described under the National Control Programme. The pharmacists have been actively participating worldwide in tobacco use cessation programme. In India too, there are some initiates.

The community pharmacists are uniquely positioned in our society that people have easy access to them not only for their requirements of medicines but also for seeking guidance on variety of health related issues.

- In addition to other professional services, the pharmacists can also consider promoting smoking cessation activities in the community.
- Counselling patients on impact of smoking in their medication. Discuss with the patients on the benefits of quitting smoking and encourage & facilitate to stop using tobacco.
- The pharmacists have already been dealing with nicotine replacement therapy (NRT). They can guide the persons on appropriate use of NRT.
- Recommending behavioural intervention in response to key life events – New Year Resolution to Quit Smoking.
- Provide life style advice including withdrawal symptom management.

- Display of posters in the pharmacy: Posters related to harmful effects of smoking and "Pharmacy is Tobacco Free Zone". Keeping an advertisement board that smoking or tobacco cessation service available would add up the value to community pharmacy service. Remember the value added services add up the business too!

Pharmacists trained to provide behavioural support for smoking cessation are found to be effective in supporting smoking cessation.

**Bottom Line**

- Tobacco is the foremost preventable cause of death worldwide.
- Smokeless Tobacco Use is more common in India compared to smoked form. Examples of Smoked Form of Tobacco Use: Smoking of Cigarettes, Beedi. Examples of Smokeless Tobacco Use: Betel Quid (Pan) with tobacco, Gutkha, Gudakhu.
- Ill Effects of Tobacco Use: Major risk factor for Cancer, Cardiovascular Diseases (CVD), Diabetes, Chronic Lung Disease, stroke, infertility, blindness, Tuberculosis (TB), Oral Cavity.
- Quitting Tobacco use not only reduces the above risk factors but also gives many socioeconomic benefits.
- National Tobacco Control Programme was launched in 2008 with the objectives of creating awareness on the ill effects of tobacco use and discourages people from tobacco use.
- NTCP is being implemented through three tier system: National, State and District Cells.
- Nicotine Replacement Therapy available in various forms: Gum, Patch, Lozenge, Inhaler and Nasal Spray.
- Community Pharmacists can promote no tobacco use through keeping posters in the pharmacy and guiding the customers on quitting all forms of tobacco use. The pharmacists can guide the patients on appropriate use of Nicotine Replacement Therapy (Products).
- 31st May is the World No Tobacco Day.

## Bibliography


1. Annual Report 2017-18, Department of Health and Family Welfare, Ministry of Health and Family Welfare, Government of India.
2. Guru Prasad Mohanta, *Facilitating Quitting Tobacco Use! IPA CPD e Times, 3(3) May – June 2014.*
3. Guru Prasad Mohanta, *World No Tobacco Day: e- Cigarettes, Orissa Post, 31 May 2013.*

4. Guru Prasad Mohanta, *Quitting Tobacco Smoking, Science Horizon, November, 2012.*
5. Operational Guidelines, National Tobacco Control Programme, National Tobacco Control Cell, Ministry of Health and Family Welfare, Government of India, 2015.
6. Priya Mohan, Harry A Lando and Sigamani Panneer, Assessment of Tobacco Consumption and Control in India, Indian Journal of Clinical Medicine
7. Volume 9: 1–8, 2018.
8. Guru Prasad Mohanta, *Nicotine Replacement Medicines, The New Indian Express supplement- Health, 04 July 2006.*

## Tuberculosis

"Stopping TB requires a government programme that functions every day of the year and that is hard in certain parts of the world. And partly it is because of WHO tuberculosis affects: it tends to affect the poor and disenfranchised most"

- Tom Friedan

The Tuberculosis is a disease of public health importance since ages and it inflicts large quantum of socio-economic cost on the society. A single patient can infect 10 or more persons in a year. The incidence of TB in India was estimated to be 28, 00,000 accounting for about one-quarter of the World's TB cases. The country has been fighting TB under National Programme since 1962 and the current programme is known as National Tuberculosis Elimination Programme [The earlier name was Revised National Tuberculosis Programme (RNTCP) launched in 1997]. The RNTCP has achieved Millennium Development Goal in 2015 by halting and reversing the incidence of TB. Now, the programme intends to make India free of TB by 2025 ahead of WHO's and Sustainable Development Goal's target. The Health Ministry has signed the MoU with Ministry of AYUSH, Ministry of Defence and Ministry of Railways to strengthen the inter-ministerial coordination and efforts towards TB free India by 2025. The WHO in Global TB report 2024 acknowledges the India's achievement in tackling TB.

On line of commitment of the government to eliminate TB, The Government of India has renamed the RNTCP as TNEP.

**National Strategic Plan (NSP 2017-2025):** The bold and ambitious NSP for TB elimination is adopted as a frame work to provide guidance for the activities of stakeholders including National and State Governments, Development Partners, Civil Society Organizations, International Agencies, Research Institutions, Private Sector and many others whose work is relevant to TB elimination in our country, India. It is the guiding force to further strengthen the RNTCP. It aims to strengthen all activities which would bring significant changes in the incidence, prevalence and mortality of TB. NSP was developed in line with National Health Policy, WHO's End TB Strategy and Sustainable Goals of United Nations. NSP is led by the Central TB division of Government of India.

NSP is proposed to be implemented through National Project Implementation Plan (PIP), State PIPs, and District Action Plans (DHAP) under National Health Mission.

**Vision, Goal and Target of NSP:**

- **Vision:** TB free India with zero death, disease and poverty due to TB.
- **Goal:** To achieve a rapid decline in burden of TB, morbidity and mortality while working towards elimination of Tb in India by 2025.
- Impact and Outcome Indicators:

**New shorter and more efficacious treatment regimen for drug resistant TB**

BPaLM regimen consisting of four-drug combination – Bedaquiline, Pretomanid, Linezolid and Moxifloxacin, has been approved for a quicker treatment option than the previous MDR-TB treatment procedure. This move by the Union Government is expected to significantly boost the country's progress to achieve its national goal of Ending TB in India. While traditional MDRTB treatments can last up to 20 months with severe side effects, BPaLM regimen can cure the drug-resistant TB in just six months with high treatment success rate.

| Sl. No | | Base Line | Target | | |
|---|---|---|---|---|---|
| | **Impact Indicators** | **2015** | **2020** | **2023** | **2025** |
| 1 | To reduce estimated TB Incidence rate (per 100,000) | 217 (112-355) | 142 (76-255) | 77 (49-185) | 44 (36-158) |
| 2 | To reduce estimated TB prevalence rate (per 100,000) | 320 (280-380) | 170 (159-217) | 90 (81-125) | 65 (56-93) |
| 3 | To reduce estimated mortality due to TB (per 100,000) | 32 (29-35) | 15 (13-16) | 6 (5-7) | 3 (3-4) |
| 4 | To achieve zero catastrophic cost for affected families due to TB | 35% | 0% | 0% | 0% |
| | **Outcome Indicators** | | | | |
| 1 | Total TB patient notification | 1.74 mil | 3.6 mil | 2.7 mil | 2 mil |
| 2 | Total patient Private providers notification | 0.19 mil | 2 mil | 1.5 mil | 1.2 mil |
| 3 | MDR/RR TB patients notified | 28,096 | 92,000 | 69,000 | 55,000 |
| 4 | Proportion of notified patients initiated on treatment | 25% | 80% | 98% | 100% |
| 5 | Proportion of notified patients initiated on treatment | 90% | 95% | 95% | 95% |
| 6 | Treatment success rate among notified DSTB | 75% | 90% | 92% | 92% |
| 7 | Treatment success rate among notified DRTB | 46% | 65% | 73% | 75% |
| 8 | Proportion of identified targeted key affected population undergoing active case finding | 0% | 100% | 100% | 100% |
| 9 | Proportion of notified TB patients receiving financial support through DBT | 0% | 80% | 90% | 90% |
| 10 | Proportion of identified/eligible individuals for preventive therapy / LTBI s - initiated on treatment | 10% | 60% | 90% | 95% |

In order to achieve the target, it is necessary to ensure the decline of incidence of TB to more than 10-15% annually. The four strategic pillars: Detect – Treat – Prevent – Build (DTPB) are designed to achieve our goal.

**Detect:**

**Aim**: The NSP aims to find all Drug Sensitive TB (DSTB) and Drug Resistant TB (DRTB) cases with an emphasis on reaching TB patients seeking care from private practitioners and undiagnosed TB in high risk population.

**Process to achieve:**

- To use high efficiency diagnostic tools for early and accurate diagnosis linked treatment across the country:
    - Scaling up of rapid molecular tests;
    - Making provision for digital X – ray;
    - Universal DST to at least Rifampicin. DBT is to be used for the purchase of services in private sector;
    - Making diagnostics available for NTM detection and scaling of DST;
    - Introducing sentinel surveillance system with National TB Institute, Bangalore, as Nodal Centre;
    - Providing diagnostics to the private sector or provision of reimbursement;
    - To address the higher requirement of TB culture tests for follow up and outcomes;
    - Employing additional persons in laboratories;
    - Establishing 2 additional NRLS (West and North – East);
    - Introducing health insurance for health workers and laboratory personnel;
    - Empanelling the NABL accredited Laboratories for diagnostics; and
    - Implementing information management system and linking it to e-Nikshay.
- To strengthen surveillance systems including introduction and scale up of
- next generation sequencing platforms
- Purchasing services and ensuring notification through laboratories from the private sector and link to laboratory surveillance
- To promote and foster research for new diagnostic tools
- To build capacity for diagnosis of LTBI

Tamil Nadu's Initiative to Detect the TB Cases: Tamil Nadu developed a strategy document 'End TB in Tamil Nadu by 2025' which serves as a road map for achieving the target of eliminating TB by 2025. It has launched an active case finding campaign in all districts on 1st December 2019. It comprises door to door visit to check the persons with symptoms of TB and collection of sputum samples for testing. Based on a developed schedule it deploys mobile diagnostic vans that contain digital X-rays and Cartridge based Nucleic Acid Amplification Test (CB-NAAT) machines.

**Roles and Responsibilities of Community Pharmacists** [Source: Revised National Tuberculosis Control Programme, Training Module for Community Pharmacists, 2013, Developed by Central TB Division of Government of India (GOI) and Indian Pharmaceutical Association]: The GOI realised that the community pharmacists are often the first and repeated point of contact for the community seeking healthcare service. For the first time, the GOI has made the community pharmacists as partner in health care programme. Under the RNTCP, the GOI outlined the roles and responsibilities of the community pharmacists which are categorised into the following categories:

I. **Promoting Community Awareness through:**
   - Distribution of TB information leaflets to TB patients, suspects and others who are interested to know about TB.
   - Displaying posters / Boards / Stickers about DOTS programme in pharmacy.
   - Organizing and conducting TB and DOTS related activities in schools and community.

II. **Providing Patient Counselling:** The pharmacist needs to sensitize the patient about the disease and treatment. The TB is life threatening but curable if all the medicines prescribed taken as advised for the entire period of treatment. The pharmacist needs to explain the following points:
   - The TB and the way it spreads.
   - Symptoms of TB.
   - Treatment of TB in both Government and Private.
   - DOT (Directly Observed Treatment).
   - Importance of contact examination and chemoprophylaxis of children of less than six years.
   - Taking some drugs or irregularly taking the medicines may make the TB incurable.
   - Treatment requirements and expected duration of treatment.

The pharmacist should communicate the following information:

- Dose, dosage and duration of treatment.
- Possible side effects of the medicines and encourage them to report to doctor or pharmacist.
- Frequency and importance of sputum examination in sputum positive cases.
- Importance of evaluation of symptomatic contacts (family members with TB symptoms) of sputum positive patients.
- Possibility of transmission to children. The medical officer needs to be consulted regarding the preventive options.
- The patient should use handkerchief / tissue while coughing to prevent further transmission.
- The patient needs to be made aware that they may find orange or red colouration of body fluids especially urine if taking rifampicin. This is not adverse effect.
- If the patient is on oral contraceptive pill, she should be advised to use other method of contraception (birth control).
- Smokers need to be told about harmful health effects of smoking and possibility of poorer treatment outcomes. Encourage them to quit smoking.

III. **Promoting Case Detection and Referral of TB Suspects:** The pharmacist should help in case detection through referring to appropriate clinics. The following guidelines are helpful deciding which patients are to be referred to TB clinics (or any doctor for TB evaluation) and to identify chest symptomatic cases:

- Patients with cough of more than two weeks.
- Ascertain the duration of cough for patients seeking cough medicines.
- Ascertain other symptoms if the cough has persisted for long time.
- Ascertain whether the patient has specific TB patients: persistent cough, sputum or blood in cough, chest pain, fever, weight loss, loss of appetite etc.
- Ascertain whether the patient has already consulted doctor.
- Telling patients about the TB diagnosis and availability of effective treatment. TB treatment if government hospital is free and the patient can opt for free TB medicines in the pharmacy itself.
- Counsel and refer the suspect to the nearby Designated Microscopy Centre (DMC) with referral form for sputum examination. The pharmacist needs to fill up at least the person details in referral form

and keep a copy of the same in pharmacy. The filled form should be stamped with pharmacy seal and signed.

- Contact the DMC after referring the TB suspect for diagnosis to ascertain whether the person went to centre. Ascertain from the person whether he / she did go to the centre for testing. Try to convince the suspect to go for diagnosis. If the suspect does not go for diagnosis, inform the suspect details to TB health visitor for follow up.
- While handling private prescription for TB treatment, inform the prescribing physician about DOTS.
- Provide IEC materials like TB leaflets, pamphlets to suspects. Provide sputum cup and educate about sputum expectoration.

**Referral Form:**

Laboratory Form for Sputum Examination

Name of Referring Health Facility: Date:

Name of patient: Age: Sex: M/F

Complete Address: ..........................................................................................

..........................................................................................................................

Contact Phone number / Mobile ..................................................................

Type of suspect / disease: Pulmonary Extra-pulmonary Site:....................

Reason for examination: cough for more than 2 week, fever, loss of weight, haemoptysis

Diagnosis

Repeat Examination for Diagnosis

Follow-up examinations

For new and previously treated cases - Month of follow-up ................

For MDR-TB cases – Month of follow-up ..........................

Treatment Regimens (tick √ appropriate box):

New cases Previously treated MDR-TB

**(Name and signature of referring pharmacist with Pharmacy stamp)**

**Success Stories of Community Pharmacists' Participation in TB Control:** Community Pharmacies provide good opportunities to the patients to avail the services: long opening hours compared to short out-patient clinics in public health facilities; friendly environment as the patients have been visiting them for other benefits; and easier access to TB services thus reducing the cost of care. The community pharmacists can have multiple roles: DOTS provider, support case detection, and raising TB awareness.

A TB Fact Card Project (2005-2006) was initiated by the Indian Pharmaceutical Association to involve Community Pharmacists in TB care and control in Mumbai. The project was supported by Commonwealth Pharmaceutical Association (CPA), and the International Pharmaceutical Students' Federation (IPSF).

Following the TB Fact Card Project, Indian Pharmaceutical Association initiated a public-private partnership by involving retail pharmacists in DOTS service under RNTCP which was later scaled in Mumbai with support from FIP and SEARPharm Forum. This project was funded by Lilly MDR TB Partnership and supported by Maharashtra State Chemists and Druggists Association and TB Control Societies.

In 2007, SEARPharm Forum, in association with all stake holders including National Health Programme Managers and with support from WHO Country Office for India, explored possibilities of pharmacists' participation in National Health Programmes in a consultative meeting and prepared a road map. Professor Guru Prasad Mohanta, the then National Technical Officer on Essential Medicines at WHO Country Office, provided technical inputs in the deliberations and preparation of roadmap.

The success of the above projects and contributions of numerous pharmacists in TB control have finally resulted in MoU between the RNTCP; and the IPA, AIOCD, PCI and SEARPharm Forum on the role of pharmacists in TB control and care in India. Thus, officially the pharmacists became the part of National Health Programme. The MoU was signed on 27 April 2012.

The hard work and professional commitment of two personalities led to the success. They are Shri Prafull D Sheth, Former SEARPharm Forum Professional Secretary and Former Vice President FIP; Ms Manjiri S Gharat, Vice President of IPA and Executive Council Member of FIP Community Pharmacy Section (FIP CPS).

IV. **Tracing Contacts:** The pharmacist should help in tracing all child contacts and symptomatic adult contacts of smear positive cases. Irrespective of duration of symptoms, they should be traced, counselled and referred to identify, treat TB cases and to provide preventive treatment to children.

Acquiring infection and developing Tb is higher among contacts of TB patients.

V. **Providing DOTS Medicines:** The DOTS medicines can be provided in pharmacy for willing patients and pharmacist should supervise the administration of medicines. The health visitor brings the DOTS box (patient wise box with six months requirement) with treatment record card. The following are the procedures to be adhered by the pharmacist for providing DOTS service at pharmacy:

- Keep the patient wise DOTS medicine box and the treatment record card appropriately in the pharmacy.
- Fix the time for DOTS based on mutual convenience of the patient and the pharmacist.
- Patient will visit pharmacy on alternate day in intensive phase and once in a week in continuation phase for DOTS medicines.
- Offer a seat to the patient in the pharmacy, give the medicines from the kit and ensure that the patient swallows medicines in front of pharmacist with drinking water. Use disposable cup for water. The medicines may be given in a well- ventilated portion of the pharmacy (not in air conditioned part) ensuring the patient's comfort and privacy.
- Enquire about the well-being and record body weight of the patient if feasible.
- Make appropriate entry in the treatment record card and keep the card in secure place.
- **If the patient does not visit on scheduled day, immediately contact the patient through telephone or immediately inform the health visitor about the default.**
- Ensure collection of empty blister packs and preserve till the end of the treatment.
- Pursue the patient for follow up sputum test (if the patient is sputum positive) and give a copy of the referral form.
- If the patient experience side effects, advice the patient to go to medical officer if needed.

- Return the partially used patient wise boxes and treatment record card of the patients who have died / defaulted / failed treatment / transferred out to the health visitor.
- Permit the supervision of boxes and treatment cards any time to the RNTCP staff.
- Train the assistants working in pharmacy on DOTS administration and supervise the work. This would ensure continuity of administration even in absence of pharmacist.

VI. **Appropriately Documenting:** The pharmacist needs to make necessary entry in the treatment record card as the patient takes medicines.

VII. **Promoting Rational Use of Antibiotics and Anti-TB medicines:** Irrational Use of antibiotics is common by the doctors, pharmacists and the patients. Irrational Use has been recognised as one of the main reasons of antibiotic resistance. The antibiotic resistance has resulted in multi-drug TB, extra drug resistance TB and total drug resistance TB. The following guidelines are for the pharmacist to adhere to promote rational use of anti-Tb medicines:

- Do not sale first or second line TB medicines (MDR-TB medicines) without prescription. Discourage self-medication.
- Do not sell antibiotics like Fluoroquinolones (Ofloxacin, Ciprofloxacin etc.) without prescription. The patients need to be sensitised and made aware that the use of these medicines can masks the symptoms of active TB.
- Do not sell Schedule H1 medicines which include high ended antibiotics and anti-TB medicines.

VIII. **Patient Care in Special Situation:** The pharmacist should appropriately advise the patients in the following situations:

| Situation | Advise / Management |
|---|---|
| Treatment during pregnancy and post-natal period | • Streptomycin is contra-indicated during entire period of pregnancy. Advise to contact the physician.<br>• Breast feeding can be continued even when the mother is on TB treatment. The mother should continue to practice cough hygiene.<br>• Child should be given appropriate chemo-prophylaxis. |
| Treatment in patients with renal failure | • Rifampicin, Isoniazid, and Pyrazinamide can be safely given [they get excreted through entero-hepatic circulation].<br>• Dosage of Streptomycin and Ethambutol should be adjusted based on creatinine clearance. |
| Woman on contraceptive pills | • Rifampicin decreases the efficacy of oral contraceptive pills by increasing their metabolism. There is a need of increasing dose of oral contraceptives or advice the patient to use other form of contraception. |

The RNTCP provides Do and Don't guidelines for the pharmacist:

| Do | Don't |
|---|---|
| • Greet, Smile and Offer to seat inside.<br>• Provide opportunity to have interaction.<br>• Move your head to indicate that you are paying attention.<br>• Apologize for unexpected interruption.<br>• Ask open ended questions beginning with 'What', 'Why' and 'How'.<br>• Periodically summarize what the patient has said to ensure that you have under stood. Use their own words to repeat the ideas back to them.<br>• Convey that you understand their fears and apprehensions.<br>• Make them comfortable.<br>• Repeat important information in different ways each time you meet them.<br>• Emphasize them that your job is to help them.<br>• Emphasize that they will be cured.<br>• Use examples from your own experience.<br>• Tell them that the same recommendation is valid for your family members too.<br>• Compliment the other persons that they have done well.<br>• Recognise their progress.<br>• Emphasize that their welfare is your concern. | • Use technical terms..<br>• Ignore the efforts the other persons has made so far<br>• Overlook the patients' fear and anxiety..<br>• Ignore or minimise practical barriers |

## Treat

**Aim:** The programme plans to initiate and sustain all the patients on appropriate anti-TB treatment wherever they seek care with patient friendly system and social support.

**Process to achieve:**

- Ensuring treatment of patients in the private sector: to provide patient support for completion of the treatment.
- Ensuring patient friendly treatment of Drug Sensitive TB (DSTB): The daily dosing regimen is introduced as per patient's weight band.

| Types of TB case | Types of patient | Regimen |
|---|---|---|
| NEW | New Microbiologically Confirmed TB | 2* HRZE + 4* HRE |
| | New Clinically Diagnosed TB | |
| PREVIOUSLY TREATED | Recurrent TB | 2*HRZES + 1* HRZE + 5*HRE |
| | Treatment After Failure | |
| | Treatment after lost to follow up | |
| | Other Previously Treated | |

- ❖ H: Isoniazid, R: Rifampicin, z: Pyrazinamide, E: Ethambutol, S: Streptomycin
- ❖ **Prefix to the drugs stands for number of months**

DAILY DOSE SCHEDULE FOR ADULTS (as per weight bands) (RNTCP)

| Weight band | Number of tablets | | Inj. Streptomycin (Intensive phase only) |
|---|---|---|---|
| | **Intensive phase** | **Continuation phase** | |
| | **HRZE** | **HRE** | |
| | **75/150/400/275 mg** | **75/150/275 mg** | **gm** |
| 25-39 KG | 2 pills per day | 2 pills per day | 0.5 gm |
| 40-54 KG | 3 pills per day | 3 pills per day | 0.75gm |
| 55-69 KG | 4 pills per day | 4 pills per day | 1 gm |
| More than 70 KG | 5 pills per day | 5 pills per day | 1 gm |

DAILY DISPERSIBLE FDCs PAEDIATRIC ANTI-TB DRUGS (RNTCP)

| WEIGHT BAND | Number of tablets | | Ethambutol |
|---|---|---|---|
| | **Intensive phase** | **Continuation phase** | |
| | **RHZ 75/50/150 mg** | **RH 75/50 mg** | |
| 4-7 kg | 1 | 1 | 100 mg |
| 8-11 kg | 2 | 2 | 200 mg |
| 12-15 kg | 3 | 3 | 300 mg |
| 16-24 kg | 4 | 4 | 400 mg |
| 25 + kg | Adult dosage recommended | | |

- Ethambutol should be added in the intensive phase for children with extensive or living in settings where the prevalence of HIV or isoniazid resistance in high.
  - **Treating Drug Resistant TB (DRTB):**
    - o **Management of H mono poly resistance:** A specific 9-12 months treatment regimen to manage H monopoly resistance with available first line drugs substantiated with a fluoroquinolone and a second line injectable.
    - o **Shorter Multi Drug Resistant TB (MDR):** The shorter MDR – TB regimen is to be provided to all RR – TB patients by rapidly segregating patients susceptible to fluoroquinolone and second line injectable.
    - o **Introducing newer drug regimen:** Introduction of bedaquiline and delamanid in combination therapy to reduce the duration of DR TB regimen to 4-6 months.

- **DST guided DR-TB regimen:** Appropriate regimen is to be introduced based on DST results for RRTB. Introduction is proposed in phased manner.
- **NTM TB treatment:** Non Tubercular Mycobacteria are environmental opportunistic microorganisms that can cause human disease with signs and symptoms similar to MTB. Mix of diagnostic technologies are necessary: smear microscopy, rapid molecular tests, conventional culture and species identification. Treatment depends on the species.
- **Decentralization of DR TB treatment:** It is proposed to initiate decentralization of DR Tb centres. Standard H mono-poly or shorter MDR TB regimen would be available at every district level. This would promote initiation of treatment within 24-48 hours of diagnosis.
- **Palliative and rehabilitation:** Patients for whom no regimen is available and who need care beyond cure will be provided palliative care including pain relief, surgery, prosthesis, psychological support, respiratory, physiotherapy etc. the additional costs are to be met through insurance scheme.
- **Prevention of relapse and development of Drug Resistance:** Various strategies like pharmacokinetic and pharmacodynamic studies, nutritional support, exploration of targeted delivery, exploration of nano based aerosols etc.

- **Making care cascade monitoring a management priority:**
  - Incorporating local care cascade information into district plans.
  - Sensitization of state and district officers on the need of budget supplementary activities.
  - Regular monitoring through review meeting and on-site check list.
  - Training of programme staff, partners and volunteers on reporting formats.
  - Patient feedback through help line "call centre" and sharing this information with treatment providers through e-nikshay interface for remedial measure.
  - Direct beneficiary transfer to all health facilities and patients.
  - Logistic and coordination to be strengthened.
- **Empowering patients with information, support structures and honorarium to initiate and sustain treatment:**
  - Sensitization of communities through ACSM.
  - Each patient is to be enrolled for ICT enabled treatment adherence support and DBT.

- Patient support services to be linked with individual patient registry in the e-nikshay.
- Facility for ICT enabled benefit transfer through smart cards at district TB office.
- Provision for automated reminders on treatment initiation, integration and follow up to treatment providers and patients.
- Free an offline app would be made available for patient education.
- Nutritional support / enabler honorarium.
- Provision for a counsellor at each district.
- Replication of successful innovative models.

- **Expanding options for adherence monitoring – Different ICT based treatment support mechanism is to be introduced.**
  - Mobile based "pill –in hand" adherence monitoring tool – each time patient takes a dose of medication, a hidden number appears on the strip is to be sent to a particular contact number given.
  - Provision of Interactive Voice Response (IVR), SMS reminders to the patients through call centres.
  - Introduction of electronic pill boxes or strips with GSM connection and pressure sensor can be used to monitor the pill consumption.
  - Using patient compliance tool kit: The treatment provider can use the patient compliance toolkit, a mobile app for the patient to report patient compliance using video, audio or text message.
  - Use of automatic pill loading system: The medication dispenser will load the dosage as per pre-programmed setting.
  - Providing ICT enabled smart cards to treating doctors: The doctor will give these cards to the patients to enable them to register with customer care centre. The customer care centre (CCC) will send reminders to take medications, financial incentives, follow up calls etc.
  - Provision for short messaging services (SMS): The patient would be able to report day to day events like pill consumption, minor side effects or need of any help.
- Direct Benefit Transfer (DBT): The DBT is introduced to financially aid TB patients. This would cause improved adherence and treatment support.
- **Improved clinical support:**
  - Developing and implementing minimal clinical criteria for hospitalization / specialist consultation. Examples: in case of

hypoxic, high respiratory rate, BMI < 16 etc. the patients would be provided additional consultation facilities.

- o Developing criteria for identifying high risk patients for systematic referral to specialist / consultants. Examples: patients with extensive radiological disease, severe under-weight, comorbidities etc.
- o Provision of therapeutic nutrition in case of severe malnutrition (BMI less than 16). *Instead of providing food. Government has decided to introduce Energy Dense Nutritional Supplementation (EDNS), a sachet of sweetened peanut paste, milk powder and oil.*
- o Provision for systematic relapse surveillance: This is to find out whether the relapse has occurred and providing necessary treatment.

- Pharmacovigilance activities: The RNTCP linkage with Pharmacovigilance Programme of India is to be strengthened for monitoring, identification and detection of signals.

**Prevent**

**Aim:** The programme plans to prevent the emergence of TB in susceptible population.

**Process to achieve:** TB infection control is a combination of measures aims at minimizing the risk of TB transmission within the population.

- Scaling up of airborne infection control measures at healthcare facilities.

The infection control has many challenges and there are solutions too.

| **Challenges of achieving infection control** | |
|---|---|
| **Community Level** | **Health Facility Level** |
| Social Habits:<br>▪ Cough etiquette not being followed;<br>▪ Indiscriminating spitting;<br>▪ Sneezing without covering face;<br>▪ Delay in reaching health facility for specific diagnosis.<br>Special Groups:<br>▪ Migrant population, backward areas and tribal pockets;<br>▪ Old age homes, poor homes, children homes, jails and hard to reach areas;<br>▪ Delay in diagnosis in comorbid conditions like diabetes, HIV, cancer etc.<br>Environmental aspects:<br>▪ Environmental pollution | Out-patient facility:<br>▪ Patients with chest infection at outpatient settings;<br>Over-crowding: Mixing of patients in queues and waiting areas;<br>▪ Poor ventilation in the facilities.<br>Inpatient facility:<br>▪ Cough screening, separation, fast tracking mask and missing counselling provision;<br>▪ Infectious patients getting admitted at general wards;<br>▪ Cough etiquettes not followed in wards;<br>▪ Overcrowding in the wards – no restricted entries. |

Solutions at Health facility levels:

1. Certification of health facilities for AIC compliance;
2. Developing cough corners /counters – cough screening, separation, fast tracking, mask and counselling;
3. Posting of specific staff for fast tracking and providing masks;
4. Providing N 95 masks to the hospital staff in high risk settings;
5. ACSM at OPD and other settings like posters, clippings etc.;
6. Implementation of AIC in all settings;
7. In house AIC complaint facility for treating nomads, destitute, and homeless patients;
8. Separate IP facility for bacteriological positive DS / DR TB patients and other airborne infectious patients in major institutions;
9. Proper infection control measures in ART centres;
10. Proper follow up of daily reported cases;
11. Proper disposal sputum and infected materials;
12. Early diagnosis and initiation of treatment;
13. PPE for concerned staff;
14. Wet mopping and disinfection;
15. Periodic screening of staff;
16. Proper ventilation, innovation if necessary;
17. Facility risk assessment and reporting;
18. Periodic training of staff; and
19. On-going monitoring of dash board /check list for AIC practices at all levels.
    - Ensuring treatment for latent TB infection in contact of bacteriologically confirmed

      **Cases:**

      **Contact Tracing:**

      - All close contacts, especially household contacts, will be screened for TB using chest X – rays.
      - In case of paediatric TB patients, reverse
    - Addressing the social determinants of TB through inter-sectoral approach. During diagnosis and treatment, the system must ensure confidentiality and protect the dignity of the patient. The health system will ensure that the patient is treated successfully within the society to which the patient belongs to and enjoying the full support of the community. With this chain of infection is arrested at source

and the cured member enriches his/her material, social and cultural assets. Prevention, management and mitigation of stigma and discrimination is essential.

**Build**

**Aim:** The programme aims to build and strengthen enabling policies, empowered institutions, human resources with enhanced capacities and financial resources.

**Process to achieve:**

- Translating high level political commitment to action through supportive policy and institutional structure: High level political commitment is seen as the Prime Minister, Sri Narendra Modi, himself announced the commitment of the country to eliminate TB by 2025. To keep TB control high on health and development agenda; increasing budgetary provision; declaring TB as public health emergency are some of the initiatives proposed.

  It is also proposed to strengthen procurement and supply chain management system to ensure uninterrupted availability of anti-TB drugs and dignostics.

- Developing TB policy and regulation: It is proposed to bring a comprehensive TB Bill covering all aspects of TB prevention and care to protect; promote; and fulfil the rights of the persons with TB during delivery of TB care and services. The following regulations are proposed:
  - Mandatory notification of all TB patients – This has already been notified;
  - Assured access to quality diagnosis and treatment as a standard of care through all service providers;
  - Regulating the use of diagnostic tests;
  - Regulating the sale of anti-TB drugs in open market – Schedule H1 is introduced to restrict the sale anti-TB and high ended antibiotics;
  - Non stigmatization of TB patients and families;
  - Right to access to public healthcare;
  - Compensations;
  - Occupational screening, work place intervention;
  - Enforcements (immigration / admission to educational institutions);
  - Establishing linkage with existing health insurance schemes.

The programme aspires to convert RNTCP into 100% central programme.

- Restructuring RNTCP management structure & implementation arrangement:

National TB Elimination Board, the apex body, is proposed to be established at National level. The Board will facilitate policy development, coordinate multi-sectoral involvement, and over view the implementation of strategy towards TB elimination. The proposed composition of the Board are: Prime Minister as Patron; Union Minister of Health and Welfare as Chair Person; Secretary, Department of Health as Secretary; and other members. The other members include: Secretaries from other Departments; Representatives from affected communities; Representatives of Technical and Donor partners; and Representative of Non-Government Organizations (NGOs). The Central TB Division will directly report the Board.

Similar Board is also proposed at State level.

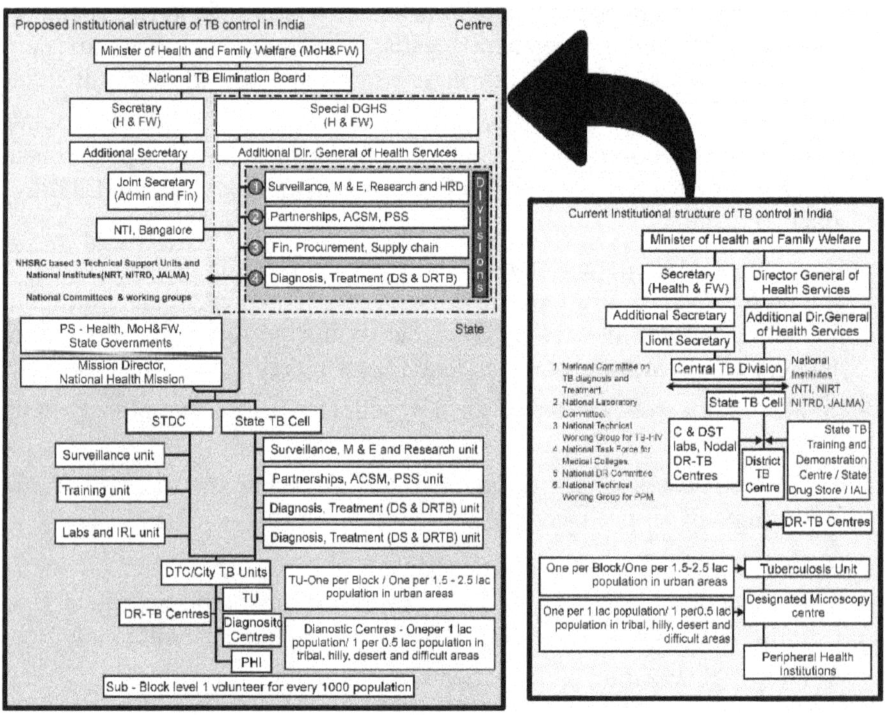


[Figure: Proposed Governing Structure of RNTCP Programme taken from National Strategic Plan for Tuberculosis Elimination 2017-2025, Government of India]

The significant changes proposed at different levels are:

1. **National Level:** creation of four divisions each in charge of key pragmatic area;
2. **State Level:** creation of four divisions similar to structure of National Level;

3. **District Level:** unified cadre for supervision to provide one TB supervisor for every block; and
4. **Block Level:** one community volunteer for communicable diseases for every 1000 population with task of active case finding and providing treatment support.
   - **Scaling up of Technical Assistance ant National and State level:** The World Health Organization Country Office for India has been providing Technical Assistance (TA) to RNTCP through its technical support network since 1999. The Technical Assistance needs to be scaled up in the priority areas: private sector engagement, drug resistant TB management and establishing TB surveillance system.
   - **Aligning & harmonizing partners' activities with programme needs to prevent duplication:** There is a need of synergistic efforts of all stake holders to achieve "universal access to TB care and treatment for all". The National Technical Working Group on Private – Public Mix is already in place to explore the participation of non-government partners. REACH and THALI, both supported by USAID, are working in several parts of the country. The programme proposes for harmonization of all partners to facilitate meaningful and sustainable collaboration.

## Bibliography

1. India TB Report 2018, Revised National TB Control Programme, Annual Status Report, Government of India.
2. Revised National Tuberculosis Programme, National Strategic Plan for Tuberculosis Elimination, 2017-2025, Government of India, March 2017.
3. FIP Challenge on TB round 1, Final Report, SEARPharm Forum, August 2012.
4. Pharmacists at the Frontlines – A Novel Approach at Combating TB, The DOTS TB Pharmacist Project, Indian Pharmaceutical Association, 2017.

# Worm Infestation

**After reading this chapter, you should be able to understand and appreciate:**

- Definition of Worm Infestation;
- Prevalence and Burden of Worm Infestation;
- India's effort tackling Worm Infestation; and
- Pharmacists' Role in Worm Infestation.

Worm infestations are the parasitic infection (also called Soil Transmitted Helminth Infections, STH in abbreviated form). The main species that infect people are the roundworm (*Ascaris lumbricoides*), the whipworm (*Trichuris trichiura*) and hookworms (*Necator americanus* and *Ancylostoma duodenale*).

Adult worms live in human intestines for food and survival where they produce thousands of eggs each day. Infected people who defecate outdoors spread worm eggs in their faeces. Subsequently, the eggs contaminate the soil which can spread infection in several ways:

- Attached to vegetables that are ingested when the vegetables are not carefully cooked, washed or peeled;
- Ingested from contaminated water sources;
- Ingested by children who play in soil and then put their hands in their mouths without washing them.

## Prevalence and Burden of Worm Infestation

**Global:** 4% of the world's population are affected. These infections affect the poorest and most deprived communities with poor access to clean water, sanitation and hygiene in tropical and subtropical areas, with the highest prevalence reported from sub-Saharan Africa, China, South America and Asia. They are transmitted by eggs present in human faeces, which in turn contaminate soil in areas where sanitation is poor.

**India:** STH is a significant public health concern for India, with 241 million children between the ages of 1 and 14 predicted to be at risk of STH infections. This represents approximately 68% of the world's children in this age group and approximately 28% of all children estimated to be at risk of STH infections globally. State-wide worm prevalence estimates are not available in all states, although plans are to conduct prevalence surveys in all states in the next five years.

**Symptoms of infection**

- Regular treatment of at-risk populations will reduce the intensity of infection and protect infected individuals from morbidity.
- The greater the amount of worms in an individual (intensity), the more symptoms the infected individual will have.
- People with light infections usually have no symptoms.
- Heavier infections can cause a range of symptoms including diarrhoea, abdominal pain, and weakness.
- Loss of appetite.

**Transmission of Infection**

1. An infected individual with faeces containing helminth eggs defecates outside. Eggs develop in soil.
2. Other individuals are infected by eggs ingested through food or dirty hands or by larvae penetrating the skin.
3. In an infected individual, eggs or larvae develop into adult worms which subsequently produces eggs.

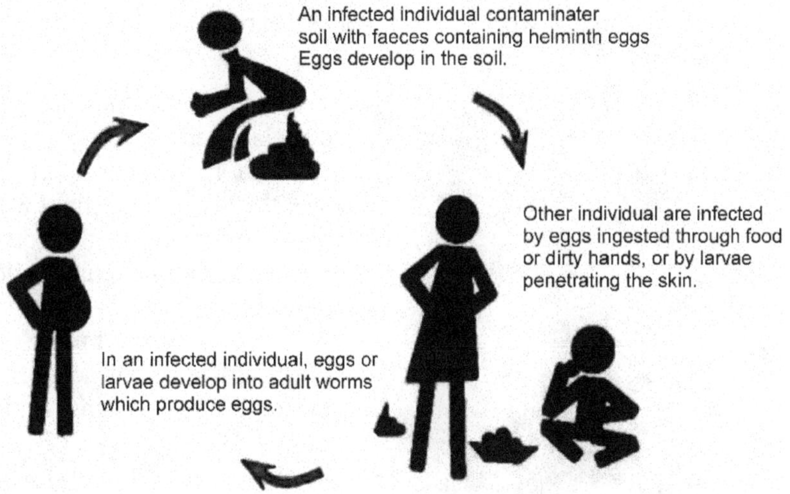


**Prevention of infection:**

- Infections can be prevented by taking precautions, including:
  - Using sanitary toilets, not defecating outside
  - Hand-washing, particularly before eating and after using toilets
  - Wearing slippers and shoes
  - Washing fruits and vegetables in safe and clean water
  - Properly cooking food
  - Keeping nails clean and short

**Nutritional and health consequences of infection**

STH impair the nutritional status of the people they infect in multiple ways:

- Worms feed on host tissues, including blood, which leads to anaemia.
- Worms increase malabsorption of nutrients. In addition, roundworm may compete for vitamin A in the intestine.
- The nutritional impairment caused by STH is recognized to have a significant impact on growth and physical development.

**Benefits of treatment**

- Rigorous studies have shown that deworming has a significant impact on the health, education and livelihoods of treated children. Outcomes of deworming can include:
    - o Decreases anaemia and improves nutrition
    - o Increases growth and weight gain
    - o Improves cognition and mental and physical development
    - o Increases resistance to other infections
    - o Supports more frequent school attendance
    - o Improves children's ability to learn better and be more active in school
    - o Increase hours worked and wages earned in the long-run in adulthood

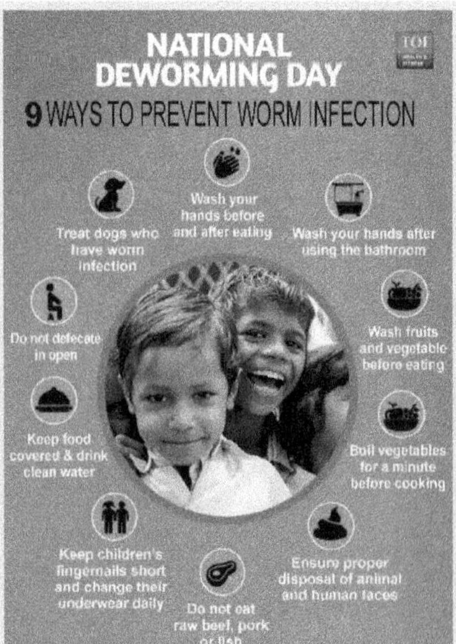


Two National Deworming Day used to be celebrated in a year: 10th February and 10th August. This aims to reduce the load of intestinal worms and related morbidity in the country. Under this programme, all children and adolescents from 1-19 years of age are given deworming tablet through the platform of schools and Anganwadi centres. During National Deworming Day (NDD) 2023, 88.3 percent children (1-19 years) against State target were covered in first round and 84.0 % children (119 years) against State target were covered during second round of NDD.

**Government Strategies**

- o Deworming treatment is delivered through mass campaigns in schools because teachers can safely and cost-effectively administer treatment to large numbers of children.

- Deworming treatment is delivered by teachers and Anganwadi Workers, with oversight from the health system including ASHAs. Children, the community and parents are comfortable with their teachers. Teachers can easily give deworming to children with basic treating and have been successfully deworming children in some states in India and over 30 countries.
- One tablet (400mg) of Albendazole is given to all children between the ages of 2 and 19 (both enrolled and non-enrolled) and half tablet (200mg) of Albendazole is given to all children between the ages of 1 and 2 (both enrolled and non-enrolled) at least once a year on National Deworming Day.
- Two National Deworming Day is celebrated.

**Treatment**

The WHO recommended medicines – albendazole (400 mg) and mebendazole (500 mg) – are effective, inexpensive and easy to administer by non-medical personnel (e.g. teachers). They have been through extensive safety testing and have been used in millions of people with few and minor side-effects.

**Worm Infestation and Sustainable Development Goals:** Worm infestation falls in the domain of neglected tropical diseases (NTDs). United Nations Sustainable Development Goal (SDG) 3.3. The goal is to end the epidemics of NTDs by 2030.

**Pharmacists' Role**

No specific role is defined, but the pharmacists can contribute through health education at school and community level. This can be considered as out reach activities.

**Bottom Line**

- Worm infestations are the parasitic infection (also called Soil Transmitted Helminth Infections, STH in abbreviated form).
- The main species that infect people are the roundworm, the whipworm and hookworms.
- Adult worms live in human intestines for food and survival where they produce thousands of eggs each day. Infected people who defecate outdoors spread worm eggs in their faeces. Subsequently, the eggs contaminate the soil which can spread infection in several ways.
- About 4% of the world's population are affected. These infections affect the poorest and most deprived communities with poor access to clean water, sanitation and hygiene.

- STH is a significant public health concern for India, with 241 million children between the ages of 1 and 14 predicted to be at risk of STH infections
- The greater the amount of worms in an individual (intensity), the more symptoms the infected individual will have.
- An infected individual with faeces containing helminth eggs defecates outside. Eggs develop in soil. This get transmitted to others if hygiene is not maintained.
- Infections can be prevented by Using sanitary toilets, not defecating outside; Hand-washing, particularly before eating and after using toilets; Wearing slippers and shoes; Washing fruits and vegetables in safe and clean water; Properly cooking food and Keeping nails clean and short.
- STH impair the nutritional status of the people they infect in multiple ways.
- Two National Deworming Day used to be celebrated in a year: 10$^{th}$ February and 10$^{th}$ August.
- Deworming treatment is delivered through mass campaigns in schools because teachers can safely and cost-effectively administer treatment to large numbers of children.
- One tablet (400mg) of Albendazole is given to all children between the ages of 2 and 19 (both enrolled and non-enrolled) and half tablet (200mg) of Albendazole is given to all children between the ages of 1 and 2 (both enrolled and non-enrolled) at least once a year on National Deworming Day.
- No specific role is defined, but the pharmacists can contribute through health education at school and community level.

**National Programme**

Though the mental health is managed as a part of general healthcare for quite long time, it was in 1982 for the first time, a National Programme, called National Mental Health.

## Bibliography

1. Annual Report 2023-24, Department of Health and Family Welfare, Ministry of Health and Family Welfare, Government of India.
2. https://www.who.int/news-room/fact-sheets/detail/soil-transmitted-helminth-infections accessed on 19th January 2025.
3. National Deworming Fact Sheet, Government of India.

# Pulse Polio Immunization

"Do Boond Zindagi ki"

**After reading this chapter, you should be able to understand and appreciate:**

- Definition of Pulse Polio Immunization (PPI);
- Prevalence and Burden of Polio;
- India's effort tackling Polio; and
- Pharmacists' Role in Polio Elimination.

The term "pulse" describes the simultaneous, mass administration of oral polio vaccine (OPV) on a single day to all children aged below 5 years. This is one of the most successful public health programmes where India could achieve the status of polio free country. India's polio eradication program is a shining example of total commitment and its success.

## Epidemiology and Programme

### Global

- In 1988, the World Health Assembly adopted a resolution for the worldwide eradication of polio, marking the launch of the Global Polio Eradication Initiative, spearheaded by national governments, WHO, Rotary International, the US Center for Disease Control and Prevention (CDC), UNICEF, and later joined by the Bill & Melinda Gates Foundation and Gavi, the Vaccine Alliance.
- Cases due to wild poliovirus have decreased by over 99% since 1988, from an estimated 350 000 cases in more than 125 endemic countries, to just two endemic countries: Pakistan and Afghanistan (as of 2022].
- In 1994, the WHO Region of the Americas was certified polio-free, followed by the WHO Western Pacific Region in 2000 and the WHO European Region in June 2002. On 27 March 2014, the WHO South-East Asia Region was certified polio-free, meaning that transmission of wild poliovirus has been interrupted in this bloc of 11 countries stretching from Indonesia to India. In 2020, Africa became the fifth region to be certified wild poliovirus-free.

### India:

- Prior to introduction of Polio vaccine in 1978, there were estimated 2,00,000 polio cases annually.

- Prior to introduction of Pulse Polio Programme in 1995 there were estimated 50,000 polio cases annually.
- Last case of wild virus type 2 in country was reported in 1999 from Aligarh, Northern India.
- In spite coverage of polio rounds being very high, polio virus type 1 & 3 continued to circulate.
- In 2005, India was the first country to use monovalent vaccine (type 1) globally, after country level research.
- In January 2010, based on country's research, India was the second country to introduce bivalent vaccine.
- At present in routine immunization, bivalent oral polio vaccine(bOPV) drops are being provided to all children less than five years of age and Inactivated Polio Vaccine (IPV) to children less than one year of age.

**Jonas Salk – Father of Polio Vaccine**

The American Scientist who refused to patent his invention of polio vaccine for sake of humanity. He is reported to have forfeited an estimated seven billion US Dollars.

**Pulse Polio Programme**

**Strategies (Polio Eradication}:**

(a) **Routine immunization:** Sustaining high levels of coverage with 3 doses of oral polio vaccine in the 0-1year age group.

(b) **Supplementary Immunization Activities (SIAs):** Simultaneous administration of oral polio vaccine to all children in the age group of 0-5 years, 4-6 weeks apart to interrupt wild poliovirus transmission and to increase immunity amongst children.

**SIAs include:**

- National Immunization Days (NIDs) when the entire country is covered.
- Sub National Immunization Days (SNIDs) when some states or parts of states are covered.
- Mop-ups are conducted, as soon as possible after identification of the virus as an end game strategy to interrupt transmission, when virus transmission is focalized and polio cases are found in specific areas.

The basic aim of conducting SIAs is to reach all under five children with potent vaccine in each round. The main strategy to achieve this is by offering:

(i) Immunization to all children at booths on the first day and

(ii) Follow up on missed children through house-to-house immune-zation teams and

(iii) Immunize children in transit through transit teams deployed throughout the duration of booth and house to house immunization activity.

(c) **Surveillance and investigation of cases of acute flaccid paralysis (AFP):** Surveillance data is used to identify areas of wild poliovirus transmission and to guide immunization activities

**Operational Guide Line**

The Union Government, the State Governments, and their international and national partners need to maintain and further enhance focus and momentum.

- Setting up of National / State / District / Block Committees.
- **Involvement of all government officials:** District Magistrate / District Collector / Chief Executive Officers; Chief Medical Officer/ District Health Officer/ Civil Surgeon / District Medical and Health Officer; District Immunisation Officer; Block / PHC Medical officer/Nodal Officer for planning in urban areas; and Key assistants at Block/PHC like Immunisation Official/Social Welfare Officer/ Health Supervisors/Public Health Nurse/ Computer.
- **Involvement other Government Departments and Organizations:** Education, NCC, NSS and NYK; Social Welfare; Panchayati Raj Institutions; Railways, Surface transport, Civil aviation, Shipping; Other Government departments like Home Affairs, Defence, MTNL, ESI etc.; Professional medical bodies; and NGOs/other voluntary organizations.

- **Meetings for NIDs/SNIDs:** State NID/SNID planning workshop; District Task Force Meetings; District Micro planning Meeting/Urban Area Planning Meeting; and State /District Review Meetings.
- **Monitoring by State and District Observers:** Preparatory phase; and Implementation phase;
- **Micro planning and Implementing NIDs/ SNIDs:** Booth activity; House-to-house activity; Transit site activity; Activity in high risk and underserved areas; and Activity at Brick kilns, construction sites, congregation sites, urban areas.
- **Other components of planning and implementation:** Supervision; Mapping of areas; Orientation training of vaccinators and supervisors; Vaccine, cold chain maintenance, other logistics and transportation; IEC/Social Mobilization Recording and reporting; Review of micro plans and data analysis for planning interventions and Use of data for planning actions; and
- Massive IEC Activities.

***National Immunization Day (NID) commonly known as Pulse Polio Immunization Day. This indicates country's commitment to eradicate polio which is a great success.***

| | **Time Line of Polio Immunization Initiatives in India** |
|---|---|
| 1978 | Vaccination against Polio introduced under Expanded Immunization Programme (EIP). |
| 1985 | Universal Immunization Programme Launched (Extended to whole country by 1989-90). |
| 1995 | Pulse Polio Immunization programme was launched in India. |
| 13th January, 2011 | India reported its last polio case from district Howrah, West Bengal. |
| 24th February 2012 | WHO removed India from the list of "endemic countries with active polio virus transmission". |
| March 2014 | Introduced mandatory requirement of polio vaccination to all international travellers for travel to India and other affected countries namely Afghanistan, Nigeria, Pakistan, Ethiopia, Kenya, Somalia Syria and Cameroon. |
| 27th March 2014 | India has been certified polio free by "The Regional Certification Commission (RCC)" of WHO. |
| | **Time Line of Polio Immunization Initiatives in India** |
| 2015 | Injectable Polio Vaccine (IPV) introduction as an additional dose along with 3rd dose of DPT in the entire country. |
| 25th April, 2016 | As part of Polio Endgame Strategy, India has switched from trivalent Oral Polio Vaccine (tOPV) to Bivalent Oral Polio Vaccine (bOPV) on both in polio campaigns and routine immunization. |

**Pharmacists in Pulse Polio Immunization Programme:** Though no specific responsibilities are assigned under the programme pharmacists can:

- Educate the public especially parents not to fall in to vaccine hesitancy trap and encourage them to take child for vaccination.
- Participate in vaccine logistics if opportunity comes.

**Bottom Line**

- Pulse Polio Immunization means the simultaneous, mass administration of oral polio vaccine (OPV) on a single day to all children aged below 5 years.
- In 1988, the World Health Assembly adopted a resolution for the worldwide eradication of polio, marking the launch of the Global Polio Eradication Initiative.
- Cases due to wild poliovirus have decreased by over 99% since 1988, from an estimated 350 000 cases in more than 125 endemic countries, to just two endemic countries: Pakistan and Afghanistan (as of 2022].
- In India, prior to introduction of Pulse Polio Programme in 1995 there were estimated 50,000 polio cases annually.
- At present in routine immunization, bivalent oral polio vaccine(bOPV) drops are being provided to all children less than five years of age and Inactivated Polio Vaccine (IPV) to children less than one year of age.
- ***Strategies for Polio Eradication:***
  - **(a) Routine immunization:** Sustaining high levels of coverage with 3 doses of oral polio vaccine in the 0-1 year age group.
  - **(b) Supplementary Immunization Activities (SIAs):** Simultaneous administration of oral polio vaccine to all children in the age group of 0-5 years, 4-6 weeks apart to interrupt wild poliovirus trans-mission and to increase immunity amongst children.
    - o The basic aim of conducting SIAs is to reach all under five children with potent vaccine in each round.
    - o Government machineries, NGOs, and all other groups are combinedly work for providing polio immunization to all children under 5 years.
- Though no specific responsibilities are assigned to pharmacists under the programme, they can educate the public especially parents not to fall in to vaccine hesitancy trap and encourage them to take child for vaccination.

### National Programme

Though the mental health is managed as a part of general healthcare for quite long time, it was in 1982 for the first time, a National Programme, called National Mental Health

## Bibliography


1. Annual Report 2023-24, Department of Health and Family Welfare, Ministry of Health and Family Welfare, Government of India.
2. Operational Guide for Pulse Polio Immunization in India, Government of India.
3. Roma Solomon, Involvement of Civil Society in India's Polio Eradication Program: Lessons Learned, Am. J. Trop. Med. Hyg., 2019.

# CHAPTER 8

# Community Service and Health Promotion

## Environment and Health (Climate and Health)

"At its core, the issue of a clean environment is a matter of public health."

- Gina McCarthy

Though the two terminologies environment and climate have been defined in different ways, in simplest sense, environment refers to anything surrounding us and climate is the overall weather pattern. Climate is part of environment. This chapter mainly uses climate. Environment and climate change adversely impact human health. Realizing this the worldwide action plan is initiated and so as in India too has plan in place to reduce their impact. The National Centre for Disease Control has developed the National Programme for Climate Change and Human Health (NPCCHH). Climate change is long term shift in temperature and weather pattern. Human activities immensely contribute towards climate change primarily due to burning of fossil fuels like coal, oil and gas. Burning fossil fuels generates greenhouse gas emissions that act like a blanket wrapped around the Earth, trapping the sun's heat and raising temperatures. The main greenhouse gases that are causing climate change include carbon dioxide and methane. Human activities are also equally responsible for global warming.

Clean environment is healthy environment. Clean air, stable climate, sanitation and hygiene are some of the prerequisites for good health. Globally, between 2030 and 2050, climate change is expected to cause approximately 250 000 additional deaths per year, from malnutrition, malaria, diarrhoea and heat stress alone. The direct damage costs to health is estimated to be between USD 2-4 billion per year by 2030.

The sustainable development Goal 13 (SDG 13) emphasises to "take urgent action to combat climate change and its impacts." This chapter deals with air pollution related and heat related illnesses.

**Air Pollution**

- **Air Pollution:** Air pollution is the contamination of indoor or outdoor environment by any chemical, physical or biological agent that modifies the natural characteristics of the atmosphere. Pollutants of major public health concern include particulate matter, carbon monoxide, ozone, nitrogen dioxide and sulphur dioxide. Outdoor and indoor air pollution cause respiratory and other diseases and are important sources of morbidity and mortality. Air quality is closely linked to climate. Air pollution is the second leading cause of NCDs after tobacco.
  - **Outdoor Air Pollution:** Air pollution may affect health by causing acid rain; eutrophication due to nitrogen oxides emission in air from power plants, cars, trucks, and other sources; haze; toxic effects on wildlife; ozone depletion; crop and forest damage etc.
  - **Indoor Air Pollution:** Worldwide, around 2.3 billion people cook using solid fuels (such as wood, crop waste, charcoal, coal and dung) and kerosene in open fires and inefficient stoves. Over 4 million people die prematurely from illness attributable to the household air pollution from cooking with solid fuels. 3.8 million premature deaths annually from non- communicable diseases including stroke, ischemic heart disease, chronic obstructive pulmonary disease (COPD) and lung cancer are attributed to exposure to household air pollution.
    - Strategies to reduce indoor air pollution:
      - Improving ventilation.
      - Improving quality of stoves.
      - Using cleaner fuels.
      - Using safer cleaning products.
      - Reducing outdoor air pollution.

Government policy along with education of general public would help in combating air pollution. The Pradhan Mantri Ujjwala Yojana (PMUY) is a scheme that provides free liquefied petroleum gas (LPG) connections to women from below-poverty-line households in India. This aims to reduce indoor air pollution.

**Heat related health issues:**

- Heat wave: A significant number of deaths occur every year in India due to heatwave. Heat stroke is a life-threatening situation.

  Heatwave is considered if the maximum temperature of a station reaches at least 40 °C or more for plains, 37 °C or more for coastal stations and at least 30 °C or more for hilly regions. Following criteria are used to declare a Heatwave:

  - **Based on Departure from Normal**
    - ***Heatwave:*** Departure from normal is 4.5 °C to 6.4 °C
    - ***Severe Heatwave:*** Departure from normal is >6.4 °C
  - **Based on Actual Maximum Temperature (for plains only)**
    - ***Heatwave:*** When actual maximum temperature ≥ 45 °C
    - ***Severe Heatwave:*** When actual maximum temperature ≥47 °C

  To declare a heatwave, the above criteria should be met for at least two stations in a Meteorological sub-division for at least two consecutive days. A heatwave will be declared on the second day.

  Acute Heat Waves are becoming increasingly frequent globally due to climate change.

  India Meteorological Department (IMD), Ministry of Earth Sciences, is the nodal agency for providing current and forecast weather information, including warnings for all weather- related hazards for optimum operation of weather-sensitive activities

The management work flow of suspected heatstroke cases at Primary Health Centre level:

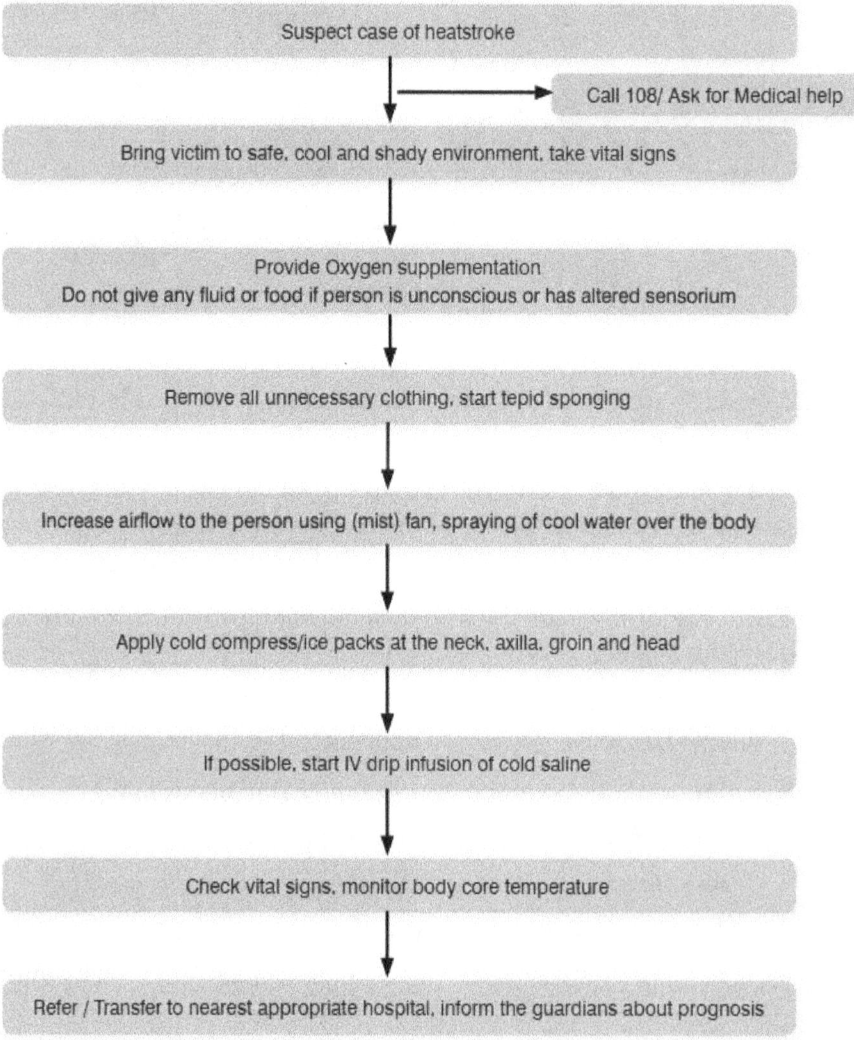

## Heat related illnesses are summarised below:

| Heat-Related Illness | Clinical Presentation | Treatment |
|---|---|---|
| **Heat oedema** | • Mild swelling of feet, ankle and hands<br>• It appears in a few days of exposure to the hot enviroment<br>• Does not progress to pretibial region | • Usually resolves spontaneously Within days to 6 weeks<br>• Elevate leg<br>• Compressive stocking<br>• Diuretics are not effective |
| **Prickly Heat** | • Pruritic, maculopapular, erythematous rash typically over covered areas of body<br>• Itchiness<br>• Prolonged pr repeated heat exposure may lead to chronic dermatitis | • Antihistamine<br>• Wear clean, light, loose-fitting clothing<br>• Avoid sweat generating situations<br>• Chlorhexidine is a light cream or lotion base<br>• Calamine lotion |
| **Heat Cramps** | • Painful, involuntary, spasmodic contraction of skeletal muscle (calves, thighs and shoulder)<br>• Occur in individuals sweating profusely and only drinking water or hypotonic solutions<br>• Limited duration<br>• Limited to specific muscle group | • Fluid and salt replacement (IV or oral)<br>• Rest in a relaxed environment |
| **Heat Tetany** | • Hyperventilation<br>• Extremity/s and circumoral paresthesia<br>• Carpopedal spasm | • Calm the patient to reduce respiratory rate<br>• Remove from hot environment |
| **Heat Syncope** | • Postural hypotension<br>• Commonly in non-acclimatized elderly | • Rule out other causes of syncope<br>• Rule out other causes of syncope<br>• Rest and IV drip |
| **Heat Exhaustion** | • Headache, nausea, vomiting<br>• Malaise, dizziness<br>• Muscle cramps<br>• Temperature less than 40°C or normal<br>• May progress to heatstroke if fails to improve with treatment<br>• No CNS involvment | • Remove the patient from the heat stress area<br>• Volume replacement<br>• If there is no response to treatment in 30 minutes, then aggressively cool the patient to a core temperature of 39°C |
| **Heatstroke** | • Core body temperature greater than 40°C<br>• Sign of CNS dysfunction: Confusion, delirium, ataxia, seizures, coma<br>• Other late findings: anhidrosis, coagulopathy, multiple organ failure | • Remove the patient from the heat stress area<br>• Volume replacement<br>• If there is no response to treatment in 30 minutes, then aggressively cool the patient to the core temperature of 39°C (further details later in document) |

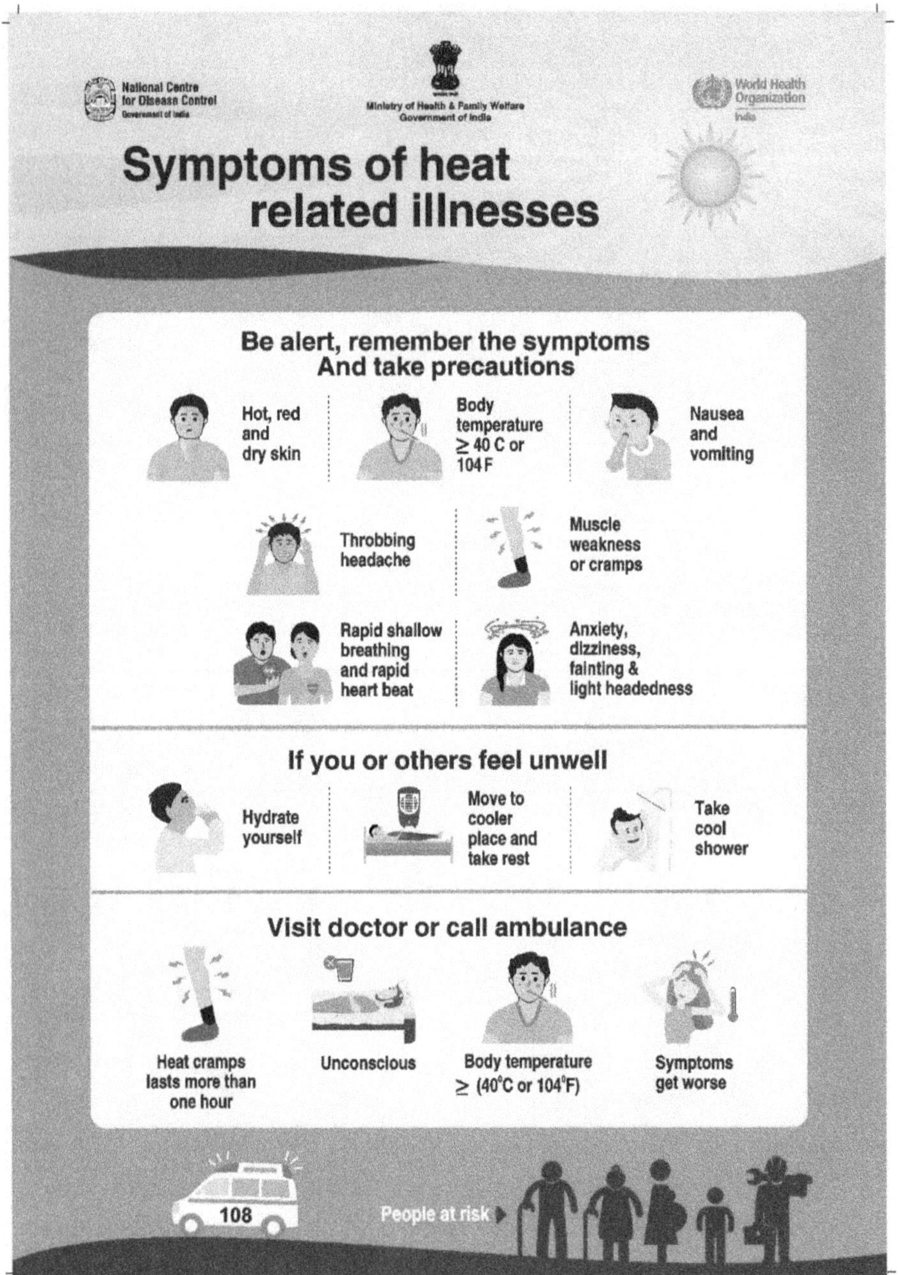
National Centre for Disease Control
Government of India
Ministry of Health & Family Welfare
Government of India
World Health Organization
India
Symptoms of heat related illnesses
Be alert, remember the symptoms And take precautions
Hot, red and dry skin
Body temperature ≥ 40 C or 104 F
Nausea and vomiting
Throbbing headache
Muscle weakness or cramps
Rapid shallow breathing and rapid heart beat
Anxiety, dizziness, fainting & light headedness
If you or others feel unwell
Hydrate yourself
Move to cooler place and take rest
Take cool shower
Visit doctor or call ambulance
Heat cramps lasts more than one hour
Unconscious
Body temperature ≥ (40°C or 104°F)
Symptoms get worse
108
People at risk

**Pharmacist's Role:**

- **Community Pharmacist:** The community pharmacists are usually first contact on health and related matters. The knowledge on health impact of environment and climate change would help them guiding the people / patients to take measures to protect. If they are trained, they can offer first aid to heat stroke patients.
- **Hospital Pharmacists:** The pharmacists must have knowledge of effective prevention and first -aid treatment of heat related illnesses. Odisha government has initiated Capacity building of Health Care Service Providers including pharmacists on diagnosis and management of heat related illness. They should ensure the availability of essential medicines. In many primary health centres, pharmacists are utilised to provide clinical services in absence of doctors.

  They can serve as data collection persons to collect the data of suspected heatstroke cases that were diagnosed previous day from emergency / casualty of medicine and paediatrics departments every day.

**Bottom Line**

- Environment refers to anything surrounding us and climate is the overall weather pattern. Climate is part of environment.
- The National Centre for Disease Control has developed the National Programme for Climate Change and Human Health (NPCCHH).
- Clean environment is healthy environment. Clean air, stable climate, sanitation and hygiene are some of the prerequisites for good health.
- The sustainable development Goal 13 (SDG 13) emphasises to "take urgent action to combat climate change and its impacts." This chapter deals with air pollution related and heat related illnesses.
- Air pollution is the contamination of indoor or outdoor environment by any chemical, physical or biological agent that modifies the natural characteristics of the atmosphere. Outdoor and indoor air pollution cause respiratory and other diseases and are important sources of morbidity and mortality. Air quality is closely linked to climate. Air pollution is the second leading cause of NCDs after tobacco.
- Strategies to reduce indoor air pollution: Improving ventilation; Improving quality of stoves; Using cleaner fuels; Using safer cleaning products; and Reducing outdoor air pollution.
- The Pradhan Mantri Ujjwala Yojana (PMUY) provides free liquefied petroleum gas (LPG) connections to women from below-poverty-line households to reduce indoor air pollution.
- Heat wave causes life threatening heat stroke.

Following criteria are used to declare a Heatwave:

- **Based on Departure from Normal**
  - ***Heatwave:*** Departure from normal is 4.5 °C to 6.4 °C
  - ***Severe Heatwave:*** Departure from normal is >6.4 °C
- **Based on Actual Maximum Temperature (for plains only)**
  - ***Heatwave:*** When actual maximum temperature ≥ 45 °C
  - ***Severe Heatwave:*** When actual maximum temperature ≥47 °C

- **Pharmacists' Role**: Thc pharmacists must have knowledge of effective prevention and first -aid treatment of heat related illnesses. They should ensure the availability of essential medicines.

## Bibliography

1. Compendium of WHO and other UN guidance on health and environment-2024 update, World Health Organization, 2024.
2. Heat Wave Action Plan, Year 2023, District Disaster Management Authority, Government of Odisha.
3. National Action Plan for Climate Change & Human Health, Ministry of Health and Family Welfare, Government of India, 2021.

## Antimicrobial Resistance (AMR)

"Some antibiotic stewardship is better than none"

-Jason Newland, MD,
Paediatric Infectious Diseases Physician

**After reading this chapter, you would be able to know / understand:**

- What is AMR;
- Impact of AMR in human health;
- Interventions suggested for combating AMR; and
- Pharmacist's role.

Antimicrobial Resistance (AMR) is a major public health challenge in the globe including India. AMR occurs when microorganisms such as bacteria, viruses, parasites or fungi become resistant to antimicrobial treatments to which they were previously susceptible. Development of resistance is a natural phenomenon that occurs over time through genetic changes in the microorganisms. Increased use and misuse of antimicrobials and other microbial stressors, such as pollution, create favourable conditions for microorganisms to develop resistance both in humans and the environment. Antimicrobial resistance threatens human and animal health and welfare, the environment, food and nutrition security and safety, economic development and equity within societies.

Microorganisms that develop antimicrobial resistance are sometimes referred to as "superbugs". World Health Organization (WHO) has identified AMR is one of the top ten threats of global health. AMR is threat to all countries independent of income levels. AMR has strong economic costs for health-care systems and national economies. In health-care systems, costs increase for example due to lengthier stays in hospitals, the requirement of more intensive care, and the need to use more expensive alternative treatments. AMR making common infections harder, increasing the risk of disease spread, severe illness and death. AMR is posing a significant threat as it undermines the effectiveness of antibiotics and antimicrobials, which are crucial for surgeries, chemotherapy and managing chronic infections.

AMR also has significant implications for the health of humans, animals and plants. Animal health, human health and environmental health are intrinsically intertwined and interdependent. Resistant bacteria can spread between and within animal, human and plant populations and travel through the waterways, soil and air, also infecting wild animals along the way. As more than 60% of emerging pathogens that cause human diseases originate from animals, protecting the health of animals and the environment protects human health. The concept of one health is significant.

There are many reasons for development of AMR, here are the main reasons related to human health:

- Indiscriminate and improper use.
- Misconception that antibiotics are prophylactics against many diseases leading to rampant overuse and misuse.
- Lack of money to buy proper antibiotic, thereby substituting it on one's own.
- Non-compliance of full regimen of the antibiotic
- Self medication with antibiotics as they are freely available (even without prescription)

In an attempt to optimize the use of antibiotics in human health, WHO has categorized the listed antibiotics (including other antibacterials) in Essential Medicine List into: Access Group, Watch Group and Reserve Group. The access group comprised of antibiotics which can be used as empiric therapy, with first or second choice, for common infectious conditions. The quality medicines of this type should be made available widely at an affordable costs. The first choice antibiotics are usually of narrow spectrum with low resistance potential. On the other hand, the second choice medicines are of broad spectrum either with higher resistance potential or less favourable benefit-risk ratio. In addition to Beta-lactum medicines, it contains: amikacin, azithromycin, chloramphenicol, ciprofloxacin, clarithromycin, clindamycin, doxycycline, gentamycin, metronidazole, nitrofurantoin, spectinomycin, sulfamethoxazole + trimethorprim, and vancomycin. The watch group antibiotics are considered to have higher resistance potential but still recommended as first or second line agents for a limited number of conditions. It contains the high priority medicines from the critically important antimicrobials for human medicines. The following seven classes of medicines are grouped under this category: Quinolones and fluoroquinolones, 3rd-generation cephalosporins (with or without beta-lactamase inhibitor), Macrolides, Glycopeptides, Anti-pseudomonal penicillins with beta-lactamase inhibitor, Carbapenems, and Penems. The reserve group of antibiotics are considered as last resort of treatment when all others are not feasible. They are tailored to highly specific patients and settings. They should be protected. Their use is restricted. The group has: Aztreonam, 4th and 5$^{th}$ generation cephalosporins, Polymyxins, Fosfomycin, Oxazolidinones, Tigecycline and Daptomycin.

**National Expert Consultations for Developing National Action Plan on Antimicrobial Resistance 2.0 has identified the following priorities for the country:**

1. Improving awareness and understanding of AMR through effective communication, education and training. In addition to healthcare professionals, community education is essential. Social media, religious leaders and other community leaders' help promotes awareness.
2. Strengthening knowledge and evidence through surveillance. ICMR has initiated the process of strengthening AMR surveillance. All medical colleges can be made part of it.
3. Reducing the incidence of infection through effective infection prevention and control practices. Expansion of HAI surveillance networks including public and private sectors; Promoting good animal welfare practices, Ethnoveterinary practices; Aligning with existing programs for hygiene and co-ordinate IPC indicators across programs e.g., Kayakalp, NABH etc are needed.
4. Optimizing the use of antimicrobial agents in health, animals and food. The prescribers and dispensers should be trained and sensitised on appropriate use of antimicrobials in human health. Antibiotic policy is needed at all levels including health facilities. Digital system may be introduced for effective monitoring and rational use.
5. Promoting investments for AMR activities, research and innovations. Initiatives by CSIR, DBT, ICMR, DST and start-up ecosystems are to be promoted to innovate new medicines and diagnostics. Sensitization towards integrative approach and traditional systems of medicine to tackle AMR is also necessary.
6. Strengthening India's commitment and collaborations on AMR at international, national, and sub-national levels. AMR activities are to be broadened. The best practices from states can be learnt and followed.

**Some of the strategies directly relevant to pharmacists include:**

- To train all the pharmacists, nurses and supporting staff, in antibiotic protocols, antibiotic abuse and antibiotic resistance.
- To reduce the sale of antibiotics like OTC medicines through regulatory provision, education and training of pharmacists.
- To conduct studies on KAP of pharmacists following education and training.

The training programme may be arranged as a part of continuing professional development programme by state pharmacy councils, pharmacy colleges, or any other agencies.

Utilization and Rational Use of Antimicrobials in India

- Production: They are locally produced.
- Regulation and Policy:
  - Regulation on Antimicrobial Sales is in place.
  - No updated medicine policy.
  - National Action Plan is available: STG is available.
- Selection:
  - AWaRe list not incorporated in NLEM.
  - Treatment Guideline is available.
- Consumption Monitoring Structure and Governance:
  - Budget - Data Not available.
  - Antimicrobials to be monitored by the national AMC surveillance are defined: AWaRe.
  - System for hospital antimicrobial consumption/use surveillance at the facility level: Limited.
  - Methodology for measuring AMC is defined: No data.
  - System for monitoring sales / use of antimicrobials in animals: Not available.
- Regulatory Agency: CDSCO.
- Data Sources:
  - AMC data from hospitals.
  - No IT system embedded.
- Use of Consumption Data:
  - Consumption Monitoring Data is publicly not available.
  - Enrollment to WHO GLASS – AMC: No data.

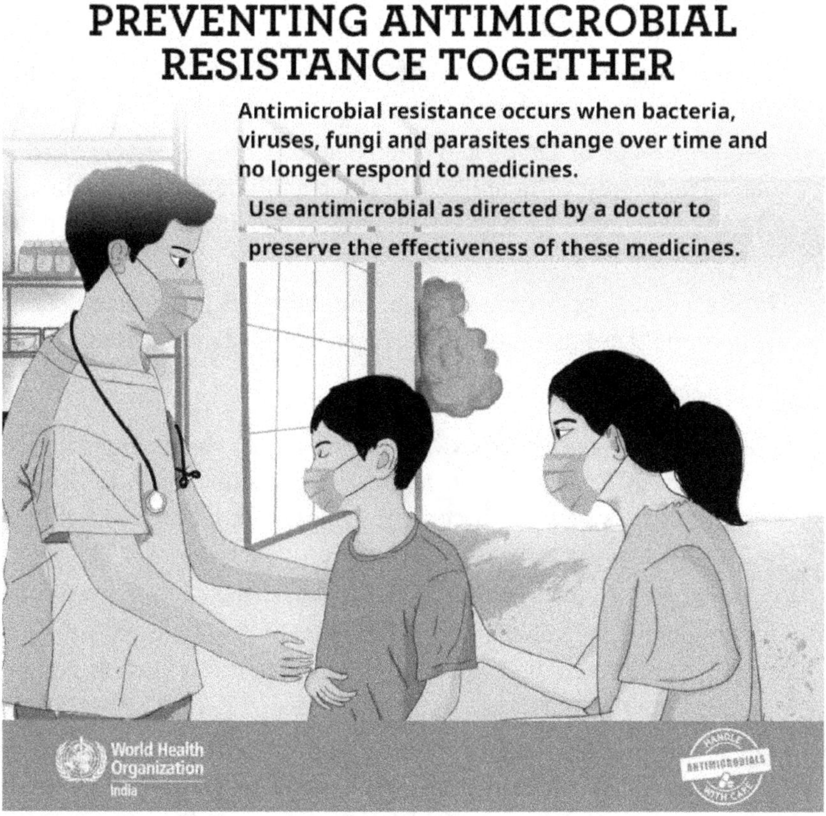


**Pharmacists' Role:** Pharmacists play a crucial role in promoting appropriate use of antimicrobial medicines in the health system and community.

- **Community pharmacists:**
  - Do not dispense these medicines without prescription.
  - Educate the patients / public to promote appropriate use of these medicines. Sensitize them on adverse impact of not using the antimicrobials appropriately – cure is difficult and development of AMR.
  - Counsel the patients on adherence for completing the course
  - Guide them on proper disposal of unused / expired antimicrobial medicines: not following the guideline would cause environmental pollution.
- **Hospital pharmacists:**
  - Ensure availability of essential antimicrobial medicines – this would prevent the use of high ended antibiotics. Non availability of desired antibiotics forces the health system to use whatever available.

- o Counsel the patients on appropriate use of antimicrobial medicines: adherence, completion of the course.
- o As a member of hospital infection control team, strengthen the infection control protocol.
- o As a member of Drugs and Therapeutics Committee (or, Pharmacy and Therapeutics Committee), develop antibiotics use guideline. The pharmacist takes part in developing and operation of stewardship programme.
- o As a clinical pharmacist (often antimicrobial pharmacist), ensures appropriate use of antimicrobials through prescription auditing.

**Bottom Line**

- Antimicrobial Resistance (AMR) is a major global public health challenge. AMR occurs when microorganisms such as bacteria, viruses, parasites or fungi become resistant to antimicrobial treatments to which they were previously susceptible.
- Development of resistance is a natural phenomenon that occurs over time through genetic changes in the microorganisms. Increased use and misuse of antimicrobials and other microbial stressors such as pollution create favourable conditions for microorganisms to develop resistance.
- AMR is threat to all countries independent of income levels. AMR has strong economic costs for health-care systems and national economies. In health-care systems, costs increase due to lengthier stays in hospitals, the requirement of more intensive care, and the need to use more expensive alternative treatments.
- In order to optimize the use of antibiotics in human health, WHO has categorized the listed antibiotics (including other antibacterials) in Essential Medicine List into: Access Group, Watch Group and Reserve Group.
- National Action Plan on Antimicrobial Resistance has identified six priority areas:
    1. Improving awareness and understanding of AMR through effective communication, education and training.
    2. Strengthening knowledge and evidence through surveillance.
    3. Reducing the incidence of infection through effective infection prevention and control practices.
    4. Optimizing the use of antimicrobial agents in health, animals and food.

5. Promoting investments for AMR activities, research and innovations.
6. Strengthening India's commitment and collaborations on AMR at international, national, and sub-national levels.

- Pharmacists play a crucial role in promoting appropriate use of antimicrobial medicines in the health system and community.

## Bibliography


1. Compiled Report of National Expert Consultations for Developing National Action Plan on Antimicrobial Resistance 2.0 (2023 – 2027), USAID, Ministry of Health and Family Welfare, and WHO-India.
2. Consumption and Rational Use of Antimicrobials in South East Asia Region, WHO Regional Office for South East Asia. 2023.
3. G. P. Mohanta, R. T. Saravana Kumar and P. K. Manna, *Promoting Rational Use of Antimicrobials,* ***Chronicle Pharmabiz,*** *December 15, 2010.*
4. G. P. Mohanta, S. Parimalakrishnan, P. K. Manna, *Antimicrobial Resistance,* ***Chronicle Pharmabiz,*** *January 27, 2011.*
5. Guru Prasad Mohanta, *Antibiotic Resistance Must be Checked,* ***Orissa Post,*** *19 March 2016.*
6. Guru Prasad Mohanta, Nisar Ahmed, and PK Manna, *WHO's New Mantra to Combat Antibiotic Resistance,* ***Chronicle Pharmabiz, October 27, 2017.***
7. Guru Prasad Mohanta, Zarine Khety and PK Manna, *Tackling Antibiotic Resistance: Need of Effective Strategies,* ***Pharmabiz,*** *April 22, 2015.*
8. Guru Prasad Mohanta, Zarine Khety, P. K. Manna, *Move from Schedule H to Hx to H1: Will it control antimicrobial resistance,* ***Chronicle Pharmabiz,*** *October 24, 2013.*
9. Vidya Sagar R.A, Anoop Paruchuri, Syed Zahed Pasha, Mohanta G P, and Manna P K, *Antimicrobial Resistance: Development and Prevention, The Pharma Review, July – August 2012.*

# School Education and Health Promotion

"I feel that we can't educate children who are not healthy, and we can't keep them healthy if they're not educated. There has to be a marriage between health and education. You can't learn if your mind is full of unhealthy images from daily life and confusion about right and wrong."

- Joycelyn Elders

**After reading this chapter, you would be able to know / understand:**

- Why children need to be educated about health;
- How most effectively this can be done; and
- Pharmacists' role.

Education and Health are fundamental to country's growth and prosperity. Schools create a unique opportunity to improve both the education and health status of learners, the futures of the nation. They constitute a sizeable proportion in our country. Besides, they have been recognized as means of bringing social changes in the society. They actively take part in bringing change in the family because the parents give importance to children's thought. A focus in children means informed children who can transfer their knowledge to their parents. Besides, the children are much more receptive than adults. If good concept is perceived at early age, it is much more sustainable. That is the reason why school children should be educated on good practices for health promotion.

The teachers, health workers, parents and communities should jointly engage educating the school children. The health workers including pharmacists should voluntarily take part in this cause of educating the children on health, hygiene and medicine use. Threat of antimicrobial resistance should also be a theme. The health days may be identified as the day for reaching the children, of course with permission of school authority, as a part of outreach activities or educational social responsibilities. The aspects: nutrition and health, Hand washing and antimicrobial resistance are discussed in separate chapter. This chapter concentrates on some areas of improving use of medicines.

- Do not believe "A pill for every ill".
- Do not follow self-medication. Consultation with healthcare professionals is necessary for even trivial conditions.
- Encourage them to read the label of medicines. Follow the instructions including storage conditions.

- Measure the liquid medicines with supplied spoon / sup.
- Medicines may cause adverse effects. These should be reported to the health professionals.

Lectures with LCD presentation, interactive sessions, use of cartoons are some useful strategies which may be employed to effectively deliver the message. At the end of the session, the impact of the programme should be assessed through feedback or conducting a test with multiple choice answers.

**Pharmacists' Role**

They can educate the school children as a part of outreach activities. They can voluntarily participate in providing health education in the following thematic areas:

- Practicing good hand hygiene;
- Taking nutritious food;
- Using medicines when necessary;
- Using medicines appropriately;
- Using antimicrobial agents prudently; and
- Disposing the unused / expired medicines properly.

Good nutrition and adopting healthy practices improve health condition: there may not have the need medicines.

**Bottom Line**

- Schools create a unique opportunity to improve both the education and health status of learners, the futures of the nation. If good concept is perceived at early age, it is much more sustainable.
- The health workers including pharmacists should voluntarily take part in the cause of educating the children on health, hygiene, medicine use and antimicrobial resistance.
- Some key messages:
    - Practicing good hand hygiene;
    - Taking nutritious food;
    - Using medicines when necessary;
    - Using medicines appropriately;
    - Using antimicrobial agents prudently; and
    - Disposing the unused / expired medicines properly.

## Bibliography

1. How to improve the use of medicines by consumers, World Health Organization, 2007.
2. Operational Guidelines on School Health Programme under Ayushman Bharat, A Joint initiative of Ministry of Health & Family Welfare and Ministry of Human Resource & Development, Government of India, April 2018.

# CHAPTER 9

# Miscellaneous

## Ayushman Bharat Pradhan Mantri Jan Arogya Yojana (PMJAY)

"Good health is the foundation of human progress and prosperity."

- Narendra Modi

**After reading this chapter, you should be able to understand and appreciate:**

- The theme of Ayushman Bharat Pradhan Mantri Jan Arogya Yojana;
- The eligibility criteria and benefits;
- Operational guidelines; and
- Pharmacists' Role.

Ayushman Bharat Pradhan Mantri Jan Arogya Yojana (PM-JAY) is the largest publicly funded health insurance scheme and launched by Government of India in September 2018.

It aims to reduce the financial burden on poor and vulnerable groups arising out of catastrophic hospital episodes and ensure their access to quality health services. PM-JAY is the world's largest healthcare scheme, and it seeks to accelerate India's progress towards achievement of Universal Health Coverage (UHC).

**Benefits:**

- Provides hospitalisation cover of up to Rs. 5,00,000 per entitled family per year.
- No cap on family size and age of members. All members of designated families get coverage;
- specifically, girl child and senior citizens.
- Covers secondary and tertiary care hospitalization.
- Free treatment available at all public and empanelled private hospitals.
- Cashless and paperless access to quality health care services.
- Benefits of national portability. Eligible beneficiaries can avail services across India.
- 1,350 medical packages covering surgery, medical and day care treatments, cost of medicines and diagnostics.
- All pre-existing diseases covered.

**Beneficiaries**: The categories in rural and urban that will be covered under PM-JAY are as follows:

**For Rural:**

- Total deprived Households targeted for PM-JAY who belong to one of the six deprivation criteria amongst D1, D2, D3, D4, D5 and D7:
  (a) Only one room with kuccha walls and kuccha roof (D1)
  (b) No adult member between age 16 to 59 (D2)
  (c) Female headed households with no adult male member between age 16 to 59 (D3)
  (d) Disabled member and no able-bodied adult member (D4)
  (e) Scheduled Caste/Scheduled Tribe households (D5)
  (f) Landless households deriving major part of their income from manual casual labour (D7)
- Automatically included:
  (a) Households without shelter
  (b) Destitute/ living on alms
  (c) Manual scavenger families
  (d) Primitive tribal groups
  (e) Legally released bonded labour

**For Urban:**

The following occupational categories of workers are included:

- Rag picker

- Beggar
- Domestic worker
- Street vendor/ Cobbler/hawker / Other service provider working on streets
- Construction worker/ Plumber/ Mason/ Labour/ Painter/ Welder/ Security guard/
- Coolie and another head-load worker
- Sweeper/ Sanitation worker / Mali
- Home-based worker/ Artisan/ Handicrafts worker / Tailor
- Transport worker/ Driver/ Conductor/ Helper to drivers and conductors/ Cart puller/ Rickshaw puller
- Shop worker/ Assistant/ Peon in small establishment/ Helper/Delivery assistant / Attendant/ Waiter
- Electrician/ Mechanic/ Assembler/ Repair worker
- Washer-man/ Chowkidar

In addition, all enrolled families under Rashtriya Swasthaya Bima Yojana (RSBY) that do not feature in the targeted groups as per SECC data will be included as well.

As per the SECC 2011, the following beneficiaries are automatically excluded:

- Households having motorized 2/3/4 wheeler/fishing boat
- Households having mechanized 3/4 wheeler agricultural equipment
- Households having Kisan Credit Card with credit limit above Rs. 50,000/-
- Household member is a government employee
- Households with non-agricultural enterprises registered with government
- Any member of household earning more than Rs. 10,000/- per month
- Households paying income tax
- Households paying professional tax
- House with three or more rooms with pucca walls and roof
- Owns a refrigerator
- Owns a landline phone
- Owns more than 2.5 acres of irrigated land with 1 irrigation equipment
- Owns 5 acres or more of irrigated land for two or more crop season
- Owning at least 7.5 acres of land or more with at least one irrigation equipment

There may still be some instances, where some of those who have to be automatically excluded in 2011, are figuring in the list of eligible beneficiaries. In such cases, States are advised to authorize the District Collectors/ District Magistrates or Deputy Commissioners to exclude such beneficiaries from the eligible list.

All citizens aged 70 and above, irrespective of income, are included in free health insurance under the scheme. Previously these groups were not covered but in 2024 they are included. This is big relief and boon to seniors.

**Pharmacists' Role**

For common man, the major source of information is accredited social health activists (ASHA)/anganwadi workers (AWW)/healthcare workers (HCW). The awareness among the general public is still an issue. Pharmacists are in better position to guide and sensitize people to avail the scheme for their health care.

**Operational Guideline**

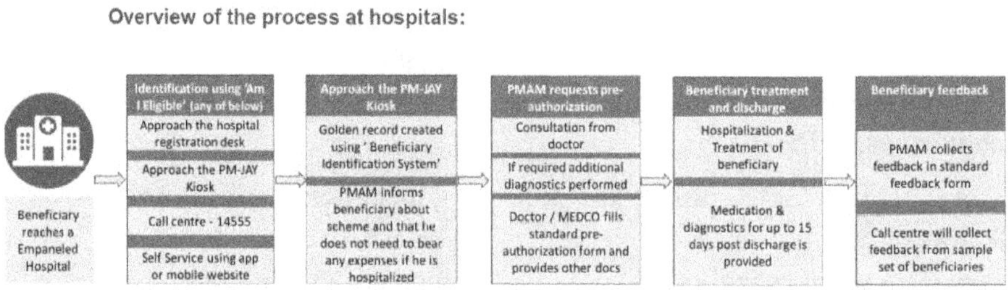


**Bottom Lines**

- Ayushman Bharat Pradhan Mantri Jan Arogya Yojana (PM-JAY) is the largest publicly funded health insurance scheme
- It aims to reduce the financial burden on poor and vulnerable groups arising out of catastrophic hospital episodes and ensure their access to quality health services.
- Provides hospitalisation cover of up to Rs. 5,00,000 per entitled family per year. No cap on family size and age of members. All members of designated families get coverage; specifically, girl child and senior citizens.
- It Covers secondary and tertiary care hospitalization.
- Households targeted for PM-JAY who belong to one of the six identified deprivation criteria.
- Pharmacists are in position to guide and sensitize people to avail the scheme for their health care.

## Bibliography

1. Information, Education and Communication (IEC) Guide Book for State Health Agencies (SHA), Ayushman Bharat – Pradhan Mantri Jan Arogya Yojana, National Health Agency, Government of India, 2018.
2. Swati Srivastava, Maria Paola Bertone, Sharmishtha Basu, Manuela De Allegri & Stephan Brenner, Implementation of PM-JAY in India: a qualitative study exploring the role of competency, organizational and leadership drivers shaping early roll-out of publicly funded health insurance in three Indian states, *Health Research Policy and Systems*, 2023.

# Responsible Use of Medicines

"The desire to take medicine is perhaps the greatest feature that distinguishes men from animals."

- William Osler

**After reading this chapter, you should be able to understand and appreciate:**

- The meaning of responsible use of medicines and rational use of medicines;
- Benefits of responsible use of medicines;
- Strategies available for promoting responsible use of medicines; and
- Pharmacists' role in promoting responsible use of medicines.

WHO estimates that more than half of all medicines worldwide are prescribed, dispensed or sold inappropriately, and that half of all patients fail to take medicines correctly. Overuse, underuse and misuse result in wastage of scarce resources, continued health problems or adverse reactions to drugs.

## Terminologies

In order to improve the use of medicines, WHO has coined the word 'Rational Use of Drugs' as "The rational use of drugs requires that patients receive medicines appropriate to their clinical needs, in doses that meet their own individual requirements, for an adequate period of time, and at the lowest cost to them and their community.". In short Right Medicine, Right Person [Right Indication], Right Dose, Right Route, Right Duration and Right Price.

Common types of irrational medicine use are:

- The use of too many medicines per patient (Polypharmacy)
- Inappropriate use of antibiotics, often in inadequate doses, for non-bacterial infections.
- Over use of injections where oral formulations would be more appropriate.
- Failure to prescribe in accordance with STG.
- Excessive use of irrational FIXED Dose Combinations.
- Under prescribing / under utilization of medicines.
- Prescribing medications with high risk of drug – drug / drug – disease interaction.
- Inappropriate self medication, often of prescription medicines only.

Irrational use of antimicrobial agents is one of the major drivers of developing antimicrobial resistance (AMR). AMR is a big threat to public health. If no effective action is taken, there will be a situation where simple bacterial infection can be life threatening.

WHO's definition of Rational Medicine Use is mainly concentrated in medical and financial terms. Irrationality defined from medical angle may be totally rational from consumer's point of view. Rational medicine use cannot be defined by the universal criteria of safety, efficacy, affordability and need. Some common terminologies similar to Rational Use of Medicines are in use: Responsible Use of Medicines; Quality Use of Medicines; Appropriate Use of Medicines. WHO defines "responsible use of medicines" that implies that the activities, capabilities, and existing resources of health system stakeholders are aligned to ensure patients receive the right medicines at the right time, use them appropriately, and benefit from them. The present text 'Rational Use of Medicine', 'Appropriate Use of Medicines' and 'Responsible Use of Medicine' are used interchangeably.

**Benefits of Responsible Use of Medicine**

Medicines are essential both at patient point and health system for patients' healthcare. They can save lives, decrease sufferings, and improve health. They differ from other commodities because the real consumers (who pays) have no choice. They should be appropriately used to maximise the benefits. Though the benefits of responsible use of medicines are many some are listed below:

- The patients are likely to get most appropriate treatment.
- Health system get strengthened: weeding out the irrational and harmful medicines from use within the health system, procurement is strengthened improving the availability of medicines even in challenging situation. It is easy to manage limited number of medicines.
- The use of antimicrobials would improve which is essential to combat development of AMR.
- The practice of polypharmacy may get reduced benefitting patients. In addition to cost reduction, limited number of medicines improves medication adherence especially in chronic condition.
- The medication cost at patient point and health system would be minimised substantially. Though the medicines' price is one of the lowest in our country, it pushed many to below the poverty line. The access to medicines can be improved.
- Improves satisfaction on health care professionals as provide the rational treatment.

- The adverse events are minimized as only safe and effective medicines are available for use.
- Improves patients' confidence on medicine and health facilities.

In short, responsible use of medicines is a solution to improve patient outcomes and support sustainable and cost effective health care.

**Strategies available for promoting responsible use of medicines**

The World Health Organization (WHO) suggested the following 12 interventions for promoting responsible use of medicines:

- establishment of a multidisciplinary national body to coordinate policies on medicine use
- use of clinical guidelines
- development and use of national essential medicines list
- establishment of drug and therapeutics committees in districts and hospitals
- inclusion of problem-based pharmacotherapy training in undergraduate curricula
- continuing in-service medical education as a licensure requirement
- supervision, audit and feedback
- use of independent information on medicines
- public education about medicines
- avoidance of perverse financial incentives
- use of appropriate and enforced regulation
- sufficient government expenditure to ensure availability of medicines and staff.

Some of these are implemented in our country too: use of clinical guidelines; development and use of national essential medicines list; establishment of drug and therapeutics committees in districts and hospitals; inclusion of problem-based pharmacotherapy training in undergraduate curricula; supervision, audit and feedback; use of independent information on medicines; public education about medicines; and sufficient government expenditure to ensure availability of medicines and staff.

**Pharmacists' Role**

- As pharmacist in Health Facilities / Health Management:
    - Member of Drug and Therapeutic Committee – Usually Member Secretary. Take part in developing Hospital Formulary.
    - Manager for procurement – Procurement based on essential medicine list.

- o Dispenser – Patient counselling to ensure the patient understands the instructions and adhere to it.
- o Educating the general public / patients on safe and rational use in reach out activities.

- As pharmacist in community pharmacy:
  - o Providing patient counselling for improving the use including promoting adherence.
  - o Educating the general public / patients on safe and rational use in reach out activities.

Responsible use of medicines requires, first and foremost, the commitment and competency of doctors, nurses, pharmacists and patients but also of politicians, policy-makers, patient groups and professional associations, which need to ensure availability of the needed resources, provide evidence for the best therapy choices, study the most effective prescribing regimens and get commitment from health professionals and patients to ensure the proper use of the medicines.

**Bottom Lines**

- Medicines save lives and promote health.
- More than half of all medicines worldwide are prescribed, dispensed or sold inappropriately, and that half of all patients fail to take medicines correctly. Overuse, underuse and misuse result in wastage of scarce resources, continued health problems or adverse reactions to drugs.
- Responsible use of medicines implies that the activities, capabilities, and existing resources of health system stakeholders are aligned to ensure patients receive the right medicines at the right time, use them appropriately, and benefit from them
- Responsible use of medicines requires, first and foremost, the commitment and competency of doctors, nurses, pharmacists and patients.
- 'Rational Use of Medicine', 'Appropriate Use of Medicines' and 'Responsible Use of Medicine' are similar terminologies.
- The benefits of responsible use of medicines are many. It ensures the best possible treatment. The responsible use of medicines is a solution to improve patient outcomes and support sustainable and cost effective health care.
- WHO has suggested 12 key interventions for promoting responsible use of medicines.
- Pharmacists in health facilities and community pharmacy have ample opportunities to promote responsible use of medicines among the patients and general publics.

## Bibliography


1. Akram Ahmad, Surya Chandra D, Krishna Kant T, Isha Patel, S. Parimalakrishnan, G. P. Mohanta, R. Balakrishnan, Changing Pharmaceutical Regulation in India to Promote Rational Use of Antimicrobials, Asian Journal of Biomedical and Pharmaceutical Sciences, 2012.
2. Arjun Poudel, Lisa M. Nissen, Rational and Responsible Medicine Use, in Social and Administrative Aspects of Pharmacy in Low and Middle Income Countries, 2018.
3. G. P. Mohanta and P. K. Manna, Rational Use of Medicines – Indian Perspective! International Journal of Risk and Safety in Medicine, 2015.
4. G. P. Mohanta, P.K. Manna, R. Manavalan, Drugs and Therapeutic Committee – a Need of Promoting Rational Drugs Use, Pharma Pulse, 19th February 2004.
5. Guru Prasad Mohanta, Good Pharmacy Practice – A Way to Promote Rational Use of Medicines, The Pharma Review, November – December 2013
6. Guru Prasad Mohanta, Medicine Utilization Studies: A Tool to Promote Rational Use of Medicines, Pharma Times, July 2011.
7. Guru Prasad Mohanta, Rational Use of Medicines: Opportunities and Challenges for Indian Pharmacists! Expressions, June 2014.
8. https://www.who.int/europe/activities/promoting-a-more-responsible-use-of-medicines accessed on 20.7.2024.
9. Responsible Use of Medicines, A Layman's Handbook, Indian Pharmaceutical Association and Pharmacy Council of India.
10. Sitanshu Kar, Himanshu Sekhar Pradhan, Guru Prasad Mohanta, Concept of Essential Medicines and Rational Use in Public Health, Indian Journal of Community Medicine, January 2010

# Infodemic

COVID-19-related infodemic is just as dangerous as the virus itself.

- World Health Organization

**After reading this chapter, you would be able to know / understand:**

- Meaning of infodemic;
- Contemporary situation and the impact of infodemic;
- Available strategies to overcome infodemic; and
- Pharmacists' contribution combating infodemic.

The WHO defines infodemic is an overflow of information of varying quality that surges across digital and physical environments during an acute public health event. Almost everyone has some experience of misinformation during COVID – 19. WHO has approved it as health topic in 2020. In a digital era, over flow of information is natural. But misinformation is harmful as it misguides the common man. There should be mechanism for infodemic management and reducing its impact.

**Harms caused by infodemic**: This can cause significant harm to the health of individual and communities; and response to epidemic. During health crisis, people may have lot of questions and concerns. They find information voids, misinformation, disinformation, and narratives.

- Individuals have challenges accessing or receiving credible, accurate health information;
- Individuals have challenges discerning between low-quality and higher quality health information;
- Individuals do not know always what health guidance applies to them;
- Individual and community information-seeking and health – seeking needs are constantly changing;
- Individuals try to make the best possible health decisions they can for themselves and families, even if only with limited or low quality information.

**The impacts of infodemic may be expressed as:**

- Direct harm to health may result from use of unapproved treatment that has been advertised as cure. During COVID – 19, people had used methanol as cure resulting several deaths.

- Fear and uncertainty associated with an epidemic can lead to behaviours that are not protective of health either for the individual or for the community. Effective communication can minimise the impact of fear and uncertainty by addressing people's questions, concerns, and information voids.
- It can adversely affect peoples trust in the health system. Health workers faced violent reactions from communities while promoting vaccination for COVID – 19.
- Stigma and discrimination are linked to infodemics during pandemics.

**Strategies to manage infodemics:**

The following strategies are suggested to manage infodemics:

- **Listening to concerns:** Listening to the community is the first step in formulating intervention, guidance, communication in a way that is more relevant, implementable, and acceptable to the community. Social media is a source for listening.
- **Communicate risk and translate science:** Often health authorities hide the outbreak of epidemic. This causes negative impact on trust. It is impossible to hide in the current information ecosystem. Regular, transparent, communication that acknowledges uncertainty is most certainly a more effective method of reassuring communities and keeping them informed. Risk communication must be timely and include efforts to translate scientific concepts into messaging that is understandable and relevant to target audiences.
- **Promote resilience to misinformation and disinformation:** During an epidemic, people tend to seek information actively, thereby increasing their exposure to all types of information. Fear and uncertainty impact a person's ability to analyse information objectively. Infodemic management includes dimensions of preparedness such as strengthening health and digital literacy.
- It is necessary to strengthen an individual's ability to distinguish between accurate and inaccurate information; recognise media manipulation; and successfully debunk misinformation with friends and family. On the other hand, a resilient community has both access and ability to disseminate credible, accurate information that is tailored and acceptable to the population.
- **Engage and empower communities:** During an epidemic, individual experience and responsibility as well as community/ collective experience and responsibility are important. In localised epidemics, geographical communities are an important focus. However, in the hyper-connected modern world, each individual belongs to multiple communities, including traditional communities (neighbours, friends,

family); virtual communities (social media platforms and networks); and communities defined by similar vocations or interests (faith, sport, workplace).

Upsala Monitoring Centre advises 6 tips to effectively fight misinformation online:

- **Target the fence sitters:** Spend your time and resources on those who have not fully made up their mind;
- **Avoid online arguments:** Fill the space with clear, accurate and true information;
- **Build trust to spread truth:** Be a regular source of reliable, truthful and transparent information;
- **Start with the truth before debunking the myth:** Explain the truth as simply and clearly as possible;
- **Understand the community:** Identify and work the trusted communities (patient groups, health centres and pharmacists); and
- **Use stories to make truth stick:** Sources of misinformation often uses personal narratives to make false facts stick, but stories of real patient experiences can be used ethically to help the truth stick.

**India's Situation**

A survey conducted just before the launch of India's vaccination programme showed that about 59% of Indians were sceptical about COVID – 19 vaccines. They expressed that they won't rush to take vaccines. Scepticism is common perhaps due to the speed at which the vaccines were developed and received emergency approval. People started perceiving the clinical study conducted in the development of vaccine as superficial one. This misunderstanding is further fuelled by some anti-vaccination and other generic disinformation. The minimum study required for assessing safety and efficacy is done and the vaccines were approved for emergency use just because sufficient period of follow up was not done because of the urgent need in pandemic. Choice is simple: we need vaccine or corona? In addition to the doubt on safety and efficacy of vaccines; wide spread rumours, false information and misinformed campaign further confuses the people.

Examples of some misinformation:

- Vaccines contain aluminium which is harmful. It can cause brain damage. The truth is: none of the COVID -19 vaccines approved has aluminium as component.

- Some people believe that the COVID vaccine contains cow blood, meat, or fat; aborted foetus, pigs, and chimpanzee; and could cause infertility and so on. List is endless. None of this information are true.
- Even the professionals too have their own reservation. In one leading hospital, when the vaccination was intended for only front-line health workers, the doctors and other hospital staff kept away from vaccination booth. In another incident, one medical officer instructed the nurse to hold a cotton ball to his arm to make it look like he took the injection. In another city, many of the hospital staff went on sudden leave just to skip vax dosing. All the incidents are reported in press. The irresponsible behaviours of these professionals cannot be justified but definitely influenced the attitude of general public towards corona vaccines.

In an attempt to safe guard public health and promote vaccination, the Prime Minister in his 76$^{th}$ edition of "Mann Ki Baat" called upon the country men to get information from the right sources and not to fall prey to rumours on vaccine. Proliferation of dangerous misinformation puts our lives and lively hood at risk. The unfounded and misleading rumours are social evils, Stay away from them!

**Pharmacists' Role**

Pharmacists being medicine information expert have lot of trust of individuals and the community. People come to pharmacy / pharmacist seeking reliable and trusted information. They can educate the common man providing the accurate and correct information. However, they should keep updated themselves on government guidelines during an epidemic. They can help the patients by refraining them from falling to the trap of misinformation spreading across including social media.

They can guide them on approved cure. The people should be advised to seek treatment from doctors / health facility.

**Bottom Lines**

- Infodemic is an overflow of information of varying quality that surges across digital and physical environments during an acute public health event. It is synonymous to misinformation.
- Infodemic may:
  - result in use of unapproved treatment that has been advertised as cure.
  - promote fear and uncertainty of epidemic.
  - adversely affect peoples' trust in the health system.
  - promote stigma and discrimination.

- Strategies to combat the impact:
    - o Listening to concerns;
    - o Communicating risk and translating science;
    - o Promoting resilience to misinformation; and
    - o Engaging and empowering communities.
- India has seen lot of misinformation concerning COVID – 19 especially vaccination.
- Pharmacists can provide accurate and reliable information on diseases and cure available. They must advise them to go doctor or health facilities for treatment.

## Bibliography


1. GP Mohanta, RT Saravanakumar and PK Manna, Vaccine hesitation – a threat to global health. *Chronicle Pharmabiz, Vol. 19 (32), page 10, July 10, 2019*
2. Guru Prasad Mohanta and PK Manna, *Fighting social stigma of corona virus, Chronicle Pharmabiz, 2nd September 2020*
3. Guru Prasad Mohanta, *Cure for misinformation, OrissaPost, Vol. 11, Issue 31, Page 6, 01 May 2021.*
4. Guru Prasad Mohanta, *Mandatory Vaccination against Covid – 19: Ethical Dilemma! Chronicle Pharmabiz, 29 September 2021.*
5. Tina D. Purnat, Tim Nguyen, Sylvie Briand (Editors), Managing Infodemics in the 21st Century, WHO, 2023.

# Glossary

1) **Access Group Antibiotics:** Essential antibiotics for common infections, recommended as first or second choice with low resistance potential.
2) **Access to Medicines:** Defined by WHO as having medicines continuously available and affordable at public or private health facilities within an accessible distance.
3) **Accredited Social Health Activist (ASHA):** A community health worker instituted by the Ministry of Health and Family Welfare under the National Rural Health Mission.
4) **ACE Inhibitors:** Medications that block the enzyme responsible for narrowing blood vessels, thus helping lower blood pressure.
5) **Acute Diarrhoeal Disease:** A sudden onset of diarrhoea, often caused by infections like cholera.
6) **Acute Flaccid Paralysis (AFP):** A clinical syndrome characterized by rapid onset of weakness or paralysis.
7) **Acute Suppurative Otitis Media:** A type of ear infection causing inflammation and pus in the middle ear.
8) **Addiction**: Substance dependence where the user cannot stop using the substance despite harmful consequences.
9) **Aedes aegypti:** A mosquito species primarily responsible for transmitting dengue and other viruses.
10) **Aedes albopictus:** Another species of mosquito responsible for transmitting chikungunya and other viral diseases.
11) **AEFI:** Adverse Event Following Immunization, which refers to any untoward medical occurrence after vaccination.
12) **Aetiology:** The study of the causes or origins of a disease.
13) **Affordability:** Economic access to medicines; relates to whether individuals can purchase the medicines they need.
14) **AIDS (Acquired Immunodeficiency Syndrome):** The most advanced stage of HIV infection, characterized by severe immune deficiency and susceptibility to opportunistic infections.
15) **AIDS:** A chronic, potentially life-threatening condition caused by the human immunodeficiency virus (HIV).
16) **Air Pollution:** The contamination of indoor or outdoor air by harmful substances, leading to health hazards and environmental damage.

17) **Albendazole:** A medication used to treat parasitic worm infestations.

18) **Anaemia:** A condition in which the number or size of red blood cells, or the haemoglobin concentration, is lower than normal, reducing the oxygen-carrying capacity of the blood.

19) **Anganwadi Worker (AWW):** Childcare providers under the Integrated Child Development Services (ICDS) program, offering nutrition and health advice.

20) **Antibacterial Soap:** Soap formulated to kill bacteria, though overuse may contribute to antimicrobial resistance.

21) **Antibiotic Resistance:** The ability of bacteria to resist the effects of drugs that once killed them.

22) **Antibiotic Stewardship:** Efforts to optimize the use of antibiotics to prevent overuse, misuse, and the development of resistance.

23) **Antimicrobial Resistance (AMR):** A phenomenon where micro-organisms such as bacteria, viruses, fungi, or parasites become resistant to antimicrobial treatments that were once effective.

24) **Anti-pyretic Drugs:** Medications used to reduce fever.

25) **ART (Antiretroviral Therapy):** A lifelong treatment combining three or more ARV drugs to suppress the virus.

26) **Artemisinin-based Combination Therapy (ACT):** A combination of drugs used to treat malaria, particularly effective against Plasmodium falciparum.

27) **Arthralgia:** Severe joint pain, often associated with viral infections like chikungunya.

28) **ASHA:** Accredited Social Health Activist, a community health worker in rural areas.

29) **Asthma:** A chronic inflammatory disease of the airways characterized by symptoms like wheezing, shortness of breath, chest tightness, and cough. It varies in intensity and is triggered by environmental factors.

30) **Availability:** Refers to medicines being in stock at health facilities or pharmacies.

31) **Ayushman Bharat Pradhan Mantri Jan Arogya Yojana (PM-JAY):** A government health insurance scheme providing financial protection to poor and vulnerable families for secondary and tertiary healthcare needs.

32) **Balanced Diet:** A diet that includes a variety of food groups to provide all essential nutrients for optimal health.

33) **Beedi:** A thin, Indian cigarette filled with tobacco and wrapped in a tendu or temburni leaf.

34) **Betel Quid (Pan):** A traditional preparation containing areca nut and other ingredients, sometimes combined with tobacco, widely used in India.

35) **Bilateral Organization:** Governmental agencies that provide aid to developing countries, such as USAID.

36) **Biopsy:** A medical test that involves removing a small sample of tissue from a suspected area to be examined under a microscope.

37) **Bipolar Disorder:** A mental health condition characterized by extreme mood swings that include emotional highs (mania or hypomania) and lows (depression).

38) **Bivalent Vaccine:** A vaccine that targets two strains of a virus.

39) **BMI (Body Mass Index):** A measure to classify weight status; calculated by dividing weight in kilograms by height in meters squared.

40) **Body Mass Index (BMI):** A measure of body fat based on height and weight.

41) **Bronchodilators:** Medications that relax and open the air passages in the lungs, often used in the management of asthma and COPD.

42) **Calcium Channel Blockers (CCBs):** A class of drugs that help relax and widen blood vessels, lowering blood pressure.

43) **Cancer:** A disease in which abnormal cells divide without control and can invade nearby tissues. Metastasis refers to the spread of cancer cells to other parts of the body.

44) **Cannabis:** A drug derived from the cannabis plant, commonly used for recreational and medicinal purposes.

45) **Carbohydrates:** Organic compounds, primarily sugars and starches, which are a main source of energy in the diet.

46) **Catastrophic Expenditure:** Health costs exceeding 20% of a household's annual income.

47) **Catastrophic Health Expenditure:** Health expenses that severely impact household finances, often leading to poverty.

48) **CD4 Cells:** White blood cells essential for immune defense, targeted and destroyed by HIV.

49) **Chemoprophylaxis:** Preventive treatment using medications to stop the development of a disease.

50) **Chikungunya:** A mosquito-borne viral disease characterized by fever and severe joint pain, caused by the Chikungunya virus (CHIKV).

51) **Chloroquine (CQ):** An antimalarial drug used to treat and prevent Plasmodium vivax infections.

52) **Cholera:** An acute diarrhoeal disease caused by Vibrio cholerae, transmitted through contaminated water or food.

53) **Cholera:** An acute diarrhoeal infection caused by ingesting food or water contaminated with *Vibrio cholerae.*

54) **Chronic Obstructive Pulmonary Disease (COPD):** A preventable and treatable lung disease marked by persistent airflow limitation, typically caused by long-term exposure to harmful particles like tobacco smoke or industrial pollutants.

55) **Chronic Suppurative Otitis Media:** A persistent ear infection that can result in a perforated eardrum and hearing loss.

56) **Cigarettes Act (1975):** Legislation requiring statutory warnings on cigarette packs.

57) **Climate Change:** A long-term alteration in temperature and weather patterns, largely influenced by human activities such as burning fossil fuels.

58) **Clinical Management Guidelines:** Protocols developed to standardize treatment and management of diseases.

59) **Clinical Pharmacy:** A branch of pharmacy focused on optimizing medication use for individual patient care.

60) **Commensal Flora:** Microorganisms that live on human skin without causing harm, though they may sometimes transmit infections.

61) **Community Health Centre (CHC):** A higher-level health facility, often providing specialist services, serving a population of 80,000–120,000.

62) **Community Pharmacist:** A healthcare professional working in a community setting to dispense medications, provide health advice, and ensure safe use of medicines.

63) **Compulsory Licensing:** Legal process allowing a government to permit the production of a patented product without the consent of the patent owner, usually in the interest of public health.

64) **Contraceptive Injectable (Antara):** A progestogen-only injectable contraceptive effective for three months.

65) **Country Cooperation Strategy (CCS):** A strategic plan outlining WHO's work with a country's government to achieve health goals.

66) **COVID-19:** An infectious disease caused by the SARS-CoV-2 virus, leading to a global pandemic starting in 2019.

67) **Co-WIN:** A cloud-based IT platform adopted in India for planning, implementing, monitoring, and evaluating COVID-19 vaccination.

68) **Culture:** A learned and socially acquired total way of life, encompassing customs, beliefs, values, and practices.

69) **Curative Care:** Medical care given to treat or cure disease or medical conditions.

70) **Deafness:** The inability to use hearing as a primary channel for receiving speech, even with amplification.

71) **Deficiency:** Lack of essential nutrients like vitamins and minerals, leading to disorders like anemia or scurvy.

72) **Dehydration:** A severe loss of body fluids, often a consequence of diseases like cholera.

73) **Demographic Indicators:** Statistical data about the population and particular groups within it, such as age, sex ratio, and life expectancy.

74) **Demography:** The statistical study of populations, including their size, growth, density, and distribution.

75) **Dengue Hemorrhagic Fever (DHF):** A severe form of dengue causing bleeding, plasma leakage, and low platelet counts.

76) **Depression:** A common and serious mood disorder causing persistent feelings of sadness and loss of interest.

77) **Designated Microscopy Centre (DMC):** A healthcare facility where microscopy services are provided for diagnosing TB by examining sputum samples under a microscope.

78) **Deworming:** The process of administering medication to eliminate parasitic worms that can contribute to anaemia.

79) **Diabetes:** A condition characterized by elevated blood glucose levels due to inadequate insulin production or action.

80) **Diagnosis:** Identification of a disease based on signs, symptoms, and laboratory tests.

81) **Diastolic BP:** The bottom number in a blood pressure reading, representing the pressure in the arteries when the heart is resting between beats.

82) **Diethylcarbamazine Citrate (DEC):** An anti-parasitic medication used specifically to target filarial infections.

83) **Diet-Related Non-Communicable Diseases:** Health conditions, such as CHD and type 2 diabetes, influenced by dietary habits.

84) **Digital Literacy:** The ability to find, evaluate, and use digital information effectively.

85) **Direct Benefit Transfer (DBT):** A government scheme that transfers subsidies or benefits directly to the bank accounts of beneficiaries, often used to provide financial support to patients undergoing TB treatment.

86) **Directly Observed Treatment (DOT):** A treatment method where a healthcare worker ensures the patient takes each dose of their TB

medication, promoting adherence to the treatment regimen and preventing the development of resistance.

87) **Disability Adjusted Life Years (DALY):** A measure of overall disease burden, representing the number of years lost due to ill-health, disability, or early death.

88) **Disabling Hearing Loss:** Hearing loss that impedes daily communication despite amplification.

89) **Disease:** A harmful deviation from normal health, involving symptoms and/or dysfunction in the body's structure or function.

90) **Disinformation:** Deliberately false information created and shared to deceive or harm others.

91) **District Hospital (DH):** A hospital that provides secondary-level healthcare to the population of a district, with specialized medical services and emergency care.

92) **Diuretics:** Medications that help remove excess salt and water from the body to lower blood pressure.

93) **Droplet Infection:** Infections transmitted through respiratory droplets expelled by sneezing, coughing, or talking, which can spread pathogens like viruses and bacteria.

94) **Drug (Substance) Abuse:** The harmful use of drugs in amounts or methods that cause harm to the user or others.

95) **Drug and Therapeutics Committee (DTC):** A multidisciplinary body responsible for promoting rational medicine use at institutional levels, such as hospitals or districts.

96) **Drug-Resistant TB (DRTB):** A form of TB that does not respond to the usual medications due to drug resistance. This includes Multi-Drug Resistant (MDR) TB and Rifampicin-Resistant (RR) TB, which require alternative and more complex treatment regimens.

97) **E. coli:** A bacterium commonly found in human intestines, often used in laboratory experiments to study bacterial transmission.

98) **Economic Growth:** An increase in the economic activity of a country, indicated by an increase in GDP and productivity.

99) **Education:** A fundamental determinant that enhances health literacy and equips individuals with knowledge to make informed health choices, often leading to improved job prospects and income.

100) **ELISA Test:** A diagnostic test used to detect antibodies against HIV in blood specimens.

101) **ELISA:** A laboratory technique used to detect antibodies or antigens in blood samples.

102) **Emergency Contraceptive Pill:** Pills taken within 72 hours of unprotected sex to prevent pregnancy.

103) **Employment Conditions:** The quality, security, and environment of one's job, which impact both mental and physical health.

104) **Epidemiological Transition:** Shift in disease patterns from infectious diseases to chronic non-infectious diseases.

105) **E-Prescription:** Electronic prescriptions, reducing the need for physical handling of paper prescriptions to limit infection spread.

106) **Essential Amino Acids:** Amino acids that the body cannot synthesize; they must be obtained from diet.

107) **Essential Medicines List (EML):** A list of medicines deemed necessary to meet the primary healthcare needs of a population, ensuring availability, affordability, and efficacy.

108) **Essential Medicines:** A set of drugs considered necessary to meet the healthcare needs of the population, ensuring availability and affordability at public health facilities.

109) **Ethnoveterinary Practices:** Traditional methods and treatments for managing animal health.

110) **Eutrophication:** Excessive nutrients in water bodies caused by nitrogen oxides, leading to dense plant growth and harm to aquatic life.

111) **Family Planning (FP):** The practice of controlling the number and spacing of children in a family through various contraceptive methods.

112) **Fats:** Nutrient providing energy, stored in the body and aiding in the absorption of fat-soluble vitamins.

113) **FEV1/FVC Ratio:** A diagnostic tool to distinguish between asthma and COPD, where a post-bronchodilator FEV1/FVC ratio of less than 70% suggests COPD.

114) **First Referral Unit (FRU):** A healthcare facility where patients are referred for specialized care beyond primary-level services, often including emergency obstetric care.

115) **Fist Bump:** A type of greeting involving lightly pressing knuckles, associated with lower germ transfer than handshakes.

116) **Florence Nightingale:** A pioneering nurse who promoted hygiene practices, including hand washing, in hospitals.

117) **Folic Acid:** A type of B-vitamin essential for the formation of red blood cells and prevention of neural tube defects during pregnancy.

118) **Foodborne Illness:** Diseases caused by consuming contaminated food, often due to poor hygiene during preparation.

119) **G6PD Deficiency:** A genetic condition causing a lack of an enzyme that protects red blood cells, making individuals susceptible to certain drugs and foods.

120) **Gastro-intestinal Tract:** Part of the digestive system where bacteria and viruses can be present and transmitted through hand contact.

121) **Gender:** Biological and social differences between men and women that influence health risks, disease prevalence, and healthcare needs.

122) **Genetics:** Biological factors inherited from parents that affect disease susceptibility and health outcomes.

123) **Gestational Diabetes:** Diabetes that develops during pregnancy and usually resolves after delivery.

124) **Global Hand Washing Day:** Observed on October 15 to promote hand washing as a key factor in preventing infections.

125) **Global Partnership:** Collaborative effort among nations to address global challenges, especially for sustainable development.

126) **Global Task Force on Cholera Control (GTFCC):** A partnership aimed at reducing the global burden of cholera.

127) **Glucometer:** A device used to measure blood glucose levels.

128) **Grade 2 Disability:** Visible deformity or damage caused by leprosy, such as severe impairments in hands, feet, or eyes.

129) **Greenhouse Gas Emissions:** Gases like carbon dioxide and methane that trap heat in the atmosphere, contributing to global warming.

130) **GTFCC:** Global Task Force on Cholera Control, a partnership to reduce global cholera burden.

131) **Gutkha:** A form of chewing tobacco mixed with areca nut and sweet or savory flavorings.

132) **Haemoglobin:** A protein in red blood cells responsible for transporting oxygen throughout the body.

133) **Hand Hygiene:** Practices such as washing hands with soap or using hand sanitizer to prevent the spread of germs.

134) **Hand Hygiene:** The practice of maintaining clean hands to reduce the spread of pathogens and prevent infection.

135) **Health Determinants:** Various factors influencing the health of individuals and populations, including the social and economic environment, physical environment, and individual characteristics and behaviours.

136) **Health Financing:** The management of funds to provide equitable healthcare access, covering public expenditure, insurance, and medical costs.

137) **Health Infrastructure:** Physical and organizational structures, facilities, and systems needed for the delivery of healthcare services.

138) **Health Literacy:** The ability of individuals to obtain, process, and understand basic health information and services needed to make appropriate health decisions.

139) **Health Promotion:** Activities or interventions aimed at enhancing the health and well-being of individuals or communities, often by encouraging healthy behaviours and environments.

140) **Health Services:** Medical care and preventive services that help to improve health outcomes and reduce health disparities.

141) **Health Status:** A measure of the health condition of individuals or populations, including disease prevalence and outcomes.

142) **Healthcare-Associated Infections (HAI):** Infections acquired in healthcare settings, often due to improper hygiene and infection control.

143) **Healthy Life Expectancy at Birth (HALE):** An estimate of the average number of years that a person can expect to live in "full health."

144) **Hearing Loss:** A range of hearing impairment from mild to profound affecting one or both ears.

145) **Heatwave:** Prolonged periods of excessively high temperatures, defined by specific thresholds based on regions and deviations from normal temperature.

146) **Hemagglutinin (H):** A glycoprotein found on the surface of influenza viruses, crucial for viral entry into host cells.

147) **Hereditary Disorder:** A disease or condition passed from parents to offspring through genes, such as hemophilia or thalassemia.

148) **High Dependency Unit (HDU):** A hospital unit that provides specialized care for patients who require more intensive observation and treatment than general wards.

149) **HIV (Human Immunodeficiency Virus):** A retrovirus that impairs the immune system by destroying CD4 cells.

150) **Hospital Pharmacists:** Pharmacists in hospitals who interact with patients, address health disparities, and guide on insurance and healthcare options.

151) **Hospital Pharmacy:** A pharmacy located within a hospital setting, where infection control is prioritized for patient and staff safety.

152) **Human Resources for Health (HRH):** Health sector workforce, including healthcare professionals essential for planning, development, and healthcare delivery.

153) **Hydrocele:** A swelling in the scrotum that occurs when fluid collects in the thin sheath surrounding a testicle, commonly associated with lymphatic filariasis.

154) **Hyperglycemia:** Excessively high blood sugar levels.

155) **Hypertension:** A condition where the blood pressure in the arteries is persistently elevated, commonly defined as a systolic BP of 140 mmHg or higher, or diastolic BP of 90 mmHg or higher.

156) **Hypoglycemia:** A condition where blood sugar levels drop below normal, potentially causing dizziness, confusion, or fainting.

157) **ICD (International Classification of Diseases):** A system by the WHO used globally for health statistics and tracking causes of illness and death.

158) **Ignaz Semmelweis:** Known as the "Father of Hand Hygiene," he introduced the practice of hand washing to reduce infection rates in hospitals in the 1840s.

159) **Immunization:** A process to make a person immune or resistant to an infectious disease, typically through vaccines.

160) **Immunoglobulin G (IgG):** A type of antibody that provides long-term immunity following infection.

161) **Immunoglobulin M (IgM):** An antibody produced by the immune system in response to infection.

162) **Immunoprophylaxis:** Prevention of disease using vaccines to boost immunity.

163) **Inactivated Vaccine:** A vaccine created from viruses or bacteria that have been killed or inactivated, making them incapable of causing disease.

164) **Income and Social Status:** Economic and social standing, which influences access to health resources such as nutritious food, safe housing, and healthcare.

165) **Indian Public Health Standards (IPHS):** A set of guidelines by the Government of India that define quality standards for public health facilities across various levels to ensure equitable healthcare delivery.

166) **Indoor Air Pollution:** Pollution within homes caused by cooking with solid fuels, leading to respiratory and cardiovascular diseases.

167) **Indoor Residual Spray (IRS):** Spraying insecticide on interior walls and ceilings to kill mosquitoes that transmit malaria.

168) **Infodemic:** An overflow of information, including both accurate and misleading content, that spreads rapidly during public health events, making it hard to find trustworthy information.

169) **Inhalants:** Substances whose volatile vapors are inhaled to produce mind-altering effects.

170) **Insecticide-Treated Nets:** Mosquito nets treated with insecticides to prevent mosquito bites and reduce disease transmission.

171) **Insulin:** A hormone produced by the pancreas that regulates blood sugar levels.

172) **Integrated Disease Surveillance Programme (IDSP):** An Indian government initiative for real-time monitoring of disease outbreaks.

173) **Integrated Health Information Platform (IHIP):** A real-time health information system for disease surveillance and emergency response.

174) **Intensive Care Unit (ICU):** A specialized department in hospitals that provides intensive treatment medicine.

175) **Intrauterine Contraceptive Device (IUCD):** A small, T-shaped device inserted into the uterus to prevent pregnancy for an extended period.

176) **IPR (Intellectual Property Rights):** Legal rights that protect creations of the mind, such as inventions, literary works, and symbols.

177) **Iron Deficiency Anaemia:** A common type of anaemia caused by inadequate iron intake, leading to reduced red blood cell production.

178) **Kuppuswamy's Scale:** A tool for assessing socio-economic status using education, occupation, and income as parameters.

179) **Latent Tuberculosis Infection (LTBI):** A condition where an individual is infected with *Mycobacterium tuberculosis* but does not have active TB disease. People with LTBI are not contagious but may develop active TB later if their immune system weakens.

180) **Leprosy:** A chronic infectious disease caused by *Mycobacterium leprae*, primarily affecting the skin, peripheral nerves, and mucosa.

181) **Life Expectancy:** The average period a person may expect to live, often used as a key indicator of public health.

182) **Live Attenuated Vaccine:** A vaccine created from live bacteria or viruses that have been weakened so they do not cause disease in healthy individuals.

183) **Long-Lasting Insecticidal Nets (LLINs):** Mosquito nets treated with insecticide, effective for several years without re-treatment.

184) **Lymphatic System:** A network of vessels through which lymph drains from tissues into the blood.

185) **Macronutrients:** Nutrients required in large quantities, including proteins, fats, and carbohydrates.

186) **Malignant Tumor:** A cancerous tumor that can invade surrounding tissues and spread to other parts of the body.

187) **Maternal and Child Health (MCH):** Care provided to mothers and children to improve their health outcomes, reduce mortality, and enhance well-being.

188) **Maternal Mortality Rate (MMR):** The number of maternal deaths per 100,000 live births, used as an indicator of maternal health and healthcare quality.

189) **Medicine Use Evaluation:** A systematic assessment of medicine use in health facilities or the community to ensure optimal patient outcomes.

190) **Medroxyprogesterone Acetate (MPA):** A hormonal contraceptive injection.

191) **Mental Health:** A state of mental well-being involving a balance between oneself and surroundings, contributing to harmony with others and society.

192) **Mental Health:** A state of well-being in which an individual can cope with stress, work productively, and contribute to their community.

193) **Metastasis:** The process by which cancer cells spread from the primary site to other parts of the body.

194) **Micro Planning:** Detailed planning at the local level for effective immunization campaigns.

195) **Microfilariae:** The immature larval stage of filarial worms found in the bloodstream.

196) **Micronutrients:** Essential vitamins and minerals required by the body in small amounts for proper functioning.

197) **Micronutrients:** Nutrients needed in small amounts, such as vitamins and minerals.

198) **Millennium Development Goals (MDGs):** Eight international development goals that were established following the Millennium Summit of the UN in 2000, aimed at reducing extreme poverty and improving health outcomes by 2015.

199) **Minerals:** Inorganic elements necessary for body functions, such as calcium and iron.

200) **Mishri:** A smokeless tobacco product used for dental application, prevalent in India.

201) **Misinformation:** False or inaccurate information spread without harmful intent.

202) **Mission Indradhanush (MI):** A targeted immunization program launched by India in 2014 to immunize children who have missed vaccines or received partial immunization.

203) **Mission Parivar Vikas:** A government initiative to improve access to contraceptives and family planning services in high fertility districts.

204) **Monovalent Vaccine:** A vaccine that targets one strain of a virus.

205) **Multibacillary (MB):** A form of leprosy with more than five lesions, often with visible nodules and skin infiltration.

206) **Multidimensional Health:** Health comprising multiple aspects such as physical, mental, and social well-being.

207) **Multidrug Therapy (MDT):** A combination of medications (Rifampicin, Clofazimine, Dapsone) used to treat leprosy effectively.

208) **Multidrug-Resistant TB:** TB that does not respond to at least two first-line anti-TB drugs.

209) **Multi-Drug-Resistant Tuberculosis (MDR-TB):** A type of DRTB resistant to at least two of the most effective first-line anti-TB drugs: Isoniazid and Rifampicin.

210) **Namaskar/Namaste:** A non-contact form of greeting in India, involving pressing palms together as a sign of respect and greeting.

211) **Namaste:** A traditional Indian greeting that involves a slight bow with palms pressed together, considered a safe, contactless way to greet others.

212) **National Accreditation Board for Testing and Calibration Labora-tories (NABL):** An autonomous body that provides accreditation to laboratories based on quality standards and ensures the credibility of diagnostic tests performed in TB management.

213) **National Family Health Survey (NFHS):** A large-scale survey conducted periodically to collect information on health and family welfare indicators.

214) **National Health Mission (NHM):** A national initiative in India aimed at improving access to affordable and quality healthcare through the National Rural Health Mission (NRHM) and National Urban Health Mission (NUHM).

215) **National Reference Laboratory System (NRLS):** A network of laboratories that provide diagnostic support, quality assurance, and technical expertise in TB diagnosis and surveillance.

216) **National Strategic Plan (NSP)**: A comprehensive plan designed to eliminate TB in a country, outlining key strategies, objectives, and timelines for achieving TB control and elimination.

217) **National Vector Borne Disease Control Programme (NVBDCP):** A government initiative to manage and prevent vector-borne diseases in India.

218) **National Vector Borne Diseases Control Programme:** A government initiative in India aimed at controlling vector-borne diseases like malaria, dengue, and chikungunya.

219) **Neoplasm:** An abnormal growth of tissue, commonly known as a tumor. It can be benign or malignant.

220) **Neuraminidase (N):** An enzyme found on the surface of influenza viruses, important for viral release from host cells.

221) **Neuropathy:** Nerve damage often caused by high blood sugar, leading to numbness or pain, especially in the extremities.

222) **Nicotine Replacement Therapy (NRT):** Medical products that provide nicotine in forms such as gums, patches, or lozenges to help quit tobacco.

223) **Nocturnal Periodicity:** A characteristic of certain parasites where they appear in the host's blood during the night.

224) **Non-Communicable Disease (NCD):** Chronic diseases such as diabetes and cancer, not transmissible between people.

225) **Non-Governmental Organization (NGO):** Independent organizations providing voluntary assistance, like MSF.

226) **One Health:** An approach recognizing that human, animal, and environmental health are interconnected, emphasizing coordinated efforts to address public health issues.

227) **Open Defecation Free (ODF):** A status indicating that a community or area has eliminated open defecation by ensuring access to toilets.

228) **Open Defecation:** The practice of defecating outdoors in open spaces such as fields, forests, or bodies of water, often due to lack of sanitation facilities.

229) **Opioids:** A class of drugs used to reduce pain but often associated with addiction and misuse.

230) **Opportunistic Infections (OIs):** Infections that occur more frequently in individuals with weakened immune systems, such as TB and oral candidiasis.

231) **Oral Rehydration Solution (ORS):** A type of fluid replacement used to prevent and treat dehydration, especially due to diarrhoea.

232) **ORS:** Oral Rehydration Solution, a fluid replacement therapy to treat dehydration caused by diarrhoeal diseases.

233) **Orthopoxvirus:** A genus of viruses that includes Mpox and smallpox.

234) **Otitis Media with Effusion:** A condition characterized by the presence of fluid in the middle ear without signs of infection.

235) **Ototoxic Drugs:** Medications that can cause damage to the ear, leading to hearing loss.

236) **Out of Pocket (OOP) Expenditure:** Direct costs borne by patients for healthcare services or medicines due to lack of coverage in public or insurance systems.

237) **Overcrowding:** A condition where too many people live in a small space, often leading to poor sanitation.

238) **Parasitic Infection:** Illnesses caused by parasites, such as malaria or filariasis.

239) **Patent Protection:** A legal right granted to the innovator of a new drug, which can impact the availability and cost of new medicines.

240) **Pathogen:** A microorganism that causes disease, such as bacteria, viruses, or fungi.

241) **Paucibacillary (PB):** A milder form of leprosy with up to five lesions, without extensive nerve involvement.

242) **Peripheral Capillary Oxygen Saturation ($SpO_2$):** A measure of the oxygen saturation level in the blood.

243) **Peripheral Nerves:** Nerves outside the brain and spinal cord responsible for transmitting signals to and from the limbs and organs.

244) **Personal Behaviours:** Individual lifestyle choices, such as diet, exercise, and coping mechanisms, that contribute to health and can prevent or contribute to chronic diseases.

245) **Pharmaceutical Public Health:** Application of pharmaceutical knowledge to prevent disease and promote health on a population level.

246) **Pharmacoeconomics:** The study of the costs and benefits of pharmaceutical products and services.

247) **Pharmacovigilance:** The science and activities related to the detection, assessment, and prevention of adverse effects of medicines, aiming to enhance drug safety.

248) **Pharmacovigilance:** The science of monitoring and assessing adverse effects of medicines, vaccines, and other health products.

249) **Physical Distancing:** Another term for social distancing, focusing on maintaining a physical gap between individuals.

250) **Physical Environment:** The external surroundings that affect health, including access to clean water, air quality, safe housing, and transportation infrastructure.

251) **Physical Health:** Body's optimal functioning with indicators like clear skin, sound sleep, and regular bodily movements.

252) **Physiological Disorder:** A dysfunction in the normal physical function of the body, like diabetes or asthma.

253) **Polio-Free:** A status declared by the WHO when there is no transmission of the polio virus within a country or region.

254) **Polymerase Chain Reaction (PCR):** A method used to amplify specific DNA or RNA sequences for diagnostic purposes.

255) **Polypharmacy:** The simultaneous use of multiple medicines by a patient, often leading to increased risks of adverse drug interactions and non-adherence.

256) **POSHAN Abhiyaan:** A government initiative to improve nutritional outcomes in India, focusing on maternal and child health.

257) **Pradhan Mantri Ujjwala Yojana (PMUY):** A government initiative providing free LPG connections to reduce indoor air pollution.

258) **Prediabetes:** A condition where blood sugar levels are higher than normal but not yet in the diabetes range.

259) **Prescription Auditing:** A process to review and analyze prescriptions to ensure the appropriate use of medicines.

260) **Prevention and Control:** Strategies that aim to reduce risk factors, such as smoking cessation, reducing exposure to air pollutants, and ensuring proper diagnosis and treatment.

261) **Prevention of Mother-to-Child Transmission (PMTCT):** Measures taken to prevent HIV transmission from mother to child during pregnancy, childbirth, or breastfeeding.

262) **Preventive Healthcare:** Medical practices that focus on disease prevention and health maintenance, aiming to reduce the risk of chronic diseases and other conditions.

263) **Primaquine (PQ):** An antimalarial drug used to prevent relapse in Plasmodium vivax infections.

264) **Primary Health Care:** Basic or first-contact care that includes preventive, promotive, curative, and rehabilitative services.

265) **Primary Health Centre (PHC):** A healthcare facility that serves as the first level of healthcare above the SC, catering to a population of 20,000–30,000.

266) **Primary/Essential Hypertension:** Hypertension with no identifiable cause, typically associated with lifestyle factors such as diet, stress, and inactivity.

267) **Prime Minister (PM):** The head of government in India.

268) **Problem-Based Pharmacotherapy Training:** An educational approach in medical and pharmacy curricula focusing on solving real-world patient scenarios to improve pharmacotherapy skills.

269) **Project Implementation Plan (PIP):** A detailed plan for executing TB control initiatives, outlining the steps, responsibilities, and resources required to achieve the objectives set out in the NSP.

270) **Prophylactic Supplementation:** Preventive intake of vitamins or minerals to maintain health and prevent deficiencies.

271) **Proteins:** Nutrients necessary for body structure, growth, and repair, composed of amino acids.

272) **Psychoactive Substance:** A chemical substance that alters mental processes, such as mood, perception, or consciousness.

273) **Psychotropic Medicines:** Drugs that affect a person's mental state and are used to treat mental health conditions.

274) **Public Health Emergency of International Concern (PHEIC):** A formal declaration by WHO for an extraordinary event posing a public health risk.

275) **Public Health Facility Utilization:** The rate at which public healthcare services are used by the population, often reflecting accessibility and trust in public health systems.

276) **Pulmonary TB:** TB that primarily affects the lungs.

277) **Pulse Polio:** A public health initiative involving the mass administration of OPV to children under five on a single day.

278) **Rashtriya Swasthya Bima Yojana (RSBY):** A health insurance scheme for workers in the unorganized sector and their families.

279) **Rational Selection of Medicines:** The process of selecting medicines that are most needed, based on criteria such as health impact and cost-effectiveness.

280) **Rational Use of Medicines:** The practice of prescribing, dispensing, and using medicines that meet clinical needs, in appropriate doses, for an adequate duration, and at the lowest cost to patients and the community.

281) **Reproductive Age Group:** Women aged 15–49 years, considered in public health programmes for maternal and child health interventions.

282) **Reserve Group Antibiotics:** Antibiotics reserved as a last resort for specific conditions when other treatments fail.

283) **Responsible Use of Medicines:** Ensuring the alignment of health system resources and stakeholders to provide the right medicines at the right time for appropriate use and maximum benefit.

284) **Retinopathy:** Eye disease resulting from damage to the blood vessels of the retina, commonly associated with diabetes.

285) **Reverse-Transcriptase Polymerase Chain Reaction (RT-PCR):** A laboratory technique used to detect the presence of specific genetic material from pathogens like viruses.

286) **Ribonucleic Acid (RNA):** A nucleic acid involved in coding, decoding, regulation, and expression of genes, including in viruses.

287) **Rifampicin-Resistant Tuberculosis (RR-TB):** A type of DRTB where the tuberculosis strain is resistant specifically to Rifampicin, a crucial anti-TB drug.

288) **Right to Health:** A fundamental human right to access the highest standard of health, including medical care, as advocated by WHO.

289) **Right to Health:** The concept of health as a fundamental human right, upheld by the Supreme Court as part of the Right to Life in India.

290) **Risk Communication:** The exchange of real-time information and advice between experts and the public during a health crisis to enable informed decision-making.

291) **Secondary Hypertension:** High blood pressure caused by another underlying medical condition, such as kidney disease or endocrine disorders.

292) **Secondhand Smoke:** Smoke inhaled involuntarily by non-smokers due to tobacco smoking nearby.

293) **Social Determinants:** Conditions and factors like income, education, employment, and social support that significantly impact overall health.

294) **Social Distancing:** A public health practice of maintaining a safe physical distance from others to reduce the spread of infectious diseases, especially respiratory infections like COVID-19.

295) **Social Environment:** The societal conditions and factors that influence the well-being and behavior of individuals and communities.

296) **Social Health:** Quality and quantity of relationships with others and the community, reflecting social skills and participation in society.

297) **Social Support Networks:** Connections with family, friends, and community that offer emotional and practical support, helping to reduce stress and enhance well-being.

298) **Socio-Economic Caste Census (SECC):** A survey to identify households eligible for government schemes based on socio-economic conditions.

299) **Socioeconomics:** Relating to or concerned with the interaction of social and economic factors.

300) **Sparsh Leprosy Elimination Campaign (SLEP):** An initiative to increase leprosy awareness, early detection, and treatment in India.

301) **Spirometry**: A common test used to assess lung function by measuring the volume and speed of air exhaled from the lungs.

302) **Standard Operating Procedures (SOPs):** Detailed, written instructions to ensure consistency and quality in performing specific tasks such as procurement, storage, and dispensing of medicines.

303) **Staphylococcus:** A type of bacteria commonly found on the skin, which can cause foodborne illness if transferred to food.

304) **Stigma:** Negative stereotypes or discrimination against individuals with mental health issues.

305) **Sub-Centre (SC):** The first point of contact in rural healthcare infrastructure, designed to serve a population of 3,000–5,000.

306) **Sulfadoxine-Pyrimethamine (SP):** A combination drug used in malaria treatment and prophylaxis, particularly effective against Plasmodium falciparum.

307) **Superbugs:** Microorganisms that have developed resistance to multiple antibiotics and are difficult to treat.

308) **Surfactant:** A substance that reduces surface tension, making it easier to remove dirt and microbes; soaps are common surfactants.

309) **Sustainable Development Goal 13 (SDG 13):** A global goal emphasi-zing urgent action to combat climate change and mitigate its impacts.

310) **Sustainable Development Goals (SDGs):** A collection of 17 global goals set by the United Nations, aiming to address global challenges, including those related to health, poverty, and inequality, to be achieved by 2030.

311) **Swachh Bharat Mission (SBM):** A nationwide campaign by the Indian government to eliminate open defecation and improve waste manage-ment. Launched on October 2, 2014, it operates under the Ministry of Jal Shakti with two subdivisions, SBM (Gramin) for rural areas and SBM (Urban) for urban areas.

312) **Swachh Bharat Scheme:** An initiative by the Indian government to improve sanitation and eliminate open defecation.

313) **Swachh Swasth Sarvatra:** A joint initiative by the Ministry of Health & Family Welfare and the Ministry of Drinking Water & Sanitation to ensure high sanitation standards at healthcare facilities, including separate toilets for males and females.

314) **Systolic BP:** The top number in a blood pressure reading, representing the pressure in the arteries when the heart contracts and pumps blood.

315) **Tetravalent Vaccine:** A vaccine designed to protect against four different strains of the dengue virus.

316) **Tobacco Cessation Centres:** Facilities providing services to help individuals quit using tobacco through counseling and treatment.

317) **Total Fertility Rate (TFR):** The average number of children born to a woman over her lifetime, an important measure for population studies.

318) **Tuberculosis (TB):** A contagious bacterial infection caused by *Mycobacterium tuberculosis*, primarily affecting the lungs but can also impact other organs. TB is transmitted through the air when an infected person coughs, sneezes, or talks.

319) **Tumor Markers:** Substances, often proteins, found in the blood, urine, or tissues that can indicate the presence of cancer.

320) **Union Territories (UTs):** Administrative divisions in India governed directly by the Central Government.

321) **Universal Health Coverage:** Ensuring that all people have access to necessary health services without suffering financial hardship.

322) **Universal Immunization Programme (UIP):** A national vaccination program initiated by the Government of India in 1985 aimed at providing vaccines to all children across the country to reduce vaccine-preventable diseases.

323) **Urbanization:** The demographic shift from rural to urban living, often associated with economic growth and societal changes.

324) **Vaccination:** The act of administering a vaccine to an individual to induce immunity.

325) **Vaccine-Preventable Diseases:** Illnesses that can be prevented through immunization, including measles and polio.

326) **Vector Control:** Strategies to prevent the spread of diseases by targeting the vectors (e.g., mosquitoes) responsible for their transmission.

327) **Vector-Borne Diseases:** Illnesses caused by pathogens transmitted to humans through vectors like mosquitoes.

328) **Vertical Transmission:** The transfer of a pathogen from a mother to her fetus during pregnancy or delivery.

329) **Vibrio cholerae:** A bacterium responsible for causing cholera.

330) **Vitamins:** Organic compounds required for bodily functions, often classified as fat- or water-soluble.

331) **WASH:** Acronym for Water, Sanitation, and Hygiene, a key intervention to prevent waterborne diseases.

332) **Watch Group Antibiotics:** Antibiotics with higher resistance potential, recommended for limited use in specific conditions.

333) **Water, Sanitation, and Hygiene (WASH):** Interventions aimed at improving access to clean water, proper sanitation, and hygiene practices to prevent diseases.

334) **WHO:** World Health Organization, a United Nations agency focused on international public health.

335) **Wild Poliovirus:** The naturally occurring virus that causes poliomyelitis.

336) **Window Period:** The time between initial infection with HIV and the appearance of detectable antibodies.

337) **World Hand Hygiene Day:** Observed on May 5, focusing on the importance of hand hygiene in healthcare settings.

338) **World Health Organization (WHO):** A specialized agency of the United Nations responsible for international public health, which sets global TB control guidelines and provides technical assistance to countries.

339) **Worm Infestation:** The presence of parasitic worms in the intestine, which can cause nutrient deficiencies, including iron deficiency.

340) **Zoonotic:** A disease that can be transmitted between animals and humans.

# Index

2030 Agenda for Sustainable Development 51, 57

A

Access Group Antibiotics 369
Access to Essential Medicines 34-37
Access to Medicines 34, 37, 56, 287, 359
Accreditation (NABL) 381
Accredited Social Health Activist (ASHA) 262, 369
ACE Inhibitors 204, 369
Achievements of NMBA 229
Achievements of NPPCD 224, 225
Active Case Finding 307, 309, 323
Acute Diarrhoeal Disease 369, 372
Adherence to Medication 200
Adverse Drug Reaction (ADR) Monitoring 25
Adverse Event Following Immunization (AEFI) 369
Aedes aegypti: Transmission Cycle, Mosquito Characteristics, and Control Measures 90, 107, 369
Aedes Albopictus 90, 108, 369
Aedes Albopictus: Role in Dengue Transmission and Characteristics 90, 108, 369
Affordability 369
Age at Marriage 233, 237
Ahimsa – Religious Influence on Hand Hygiene 66
AIDS Control Programme 119, 122, 124, 235, 245-247
Air Pollution – Causes, Effects, and Strategies for Reduction 336, 341
Albendazole 143-145, 213, 327, 370
Alcohol-Based Sanitiser – Use and Limitations 63, 156, 179, 181
Amino Acids: Essential and Non-Essential Amino Acids 78
Anaemia 149, 209, 370
Anaemia in India 209, 210, 211
Anaemia Mukt Bharat Strategy 209, 211-213
Annual Mass Drug Administration 143-145
Antara (MPA) 234
Antenatal Care 9, 15, 54, 241, 294
Antibacterial Soap – Environmental Impact and Usage 62, 370
Antibiotic Stewardship 343, 370
Anti-leprosy MDT – Side Effects 137
Antimicrobial Pharmacist 348
Antimicrobial Resistance (AMR) 139, 343, 345
Antimicrobial Use Committee 25
Antiretroviral Therapy (ART) 370
Anti-TB Drugs 167, 316, 381
Anti-TB Drugs (Regulation) 321
Appropriate Use of Antimicrobials 345, 348

ART Centres 239, 245, 320
Arthralgia 90, 257, 370
Asthma 2, 19, 109, 170, 182, 189, 190, 370
Atharva Veda – Reference to Leprosy 132
Availability 8, 10, 255, 257
Awareness Programmes 263
Ayushman Bharat 13, 24, 45, 270, 353
Ayushman Bharat Initiatives 13
Ayushman Bharat Pradhan Mantri Jan Arogya Yojana (PM-JAY) 14, 87, 353, 356, 370

## B

Bacterial Transmission – Studies on Handshake and Germ Spread 374
Bacteriological Positive DS/DR TB 320
Balanced Diet: Importance and Components 83, 370
Barriers to Medicine Access 34, 35, 287
BCG Vaccine 254
Beedi Smoking 298
Below Poverty Line (BPL) Classification 36, 87, 336, 341
Beneficiaries, Direct Benefit Transfer (DBT) 318, 373
Beneficiaries: Rural and Urban Criteria 354
Benefits of Quitting Tobacco 298, 302
Benefits of Responsible Use of Medicines 358, 361
Biological Determinants 21, 285
Blood Glucose, BMI 192, 199
BMI (Body Mass Index): Definition and Classifications 371
Body Mass Index (BMI) 371
Bronchodilators 187, 371

## C

Calcium Channel Blockers 204, 371
Cancer 173, 180, 371
Cancer Risk 174
Cancer Treatment Options 180
Capacity Building – Role of Pharmacists in Heat-Related Illness Management 341
Carbohydrates: Types, Sources, and Role in the Body 78, 371
Case Detection – Strategies 136, 272
Causes of Anaemia 210, 294
Causes of Hearing Loss 222-225
Center for Disease Control and Prevention (CDC) 60, 329
Central Bureau of Health Intelligence 39, 42
Chemoprophylaxis 138, 267, 278, 309, 371
Chemoprophylaxis – Definition 278, 279
Chikungunya Virus (CHIKV) 90, 94, 371
Child Health 14, 28, 291-293, 295, 296, 380
Child Health Improvement 45, 70
Cholera 95-99, 372
Cholera Burden (Global) 96, 376
Chronic Disease Prevention 20, 383
Chronic Obstructive Pulmonary Disease (COPD) 28, 170, 182, 336, 372

Cigarettes Act (1975) 299, 372
Climate Action 52
Climate Change – Definition, Impacts on Health, and Mitigation Strategies 335, 336, 372
Clinical Management Guidelines 372
Clofazimine – Use in MDT 135, 381
Common Types of Irrational Medicine Use 358
Community Engagement – Strategies to Involve and Empower Individuals 29
Community Health 41,86,161, 285
Community Health Centre (CHC) 22, 24, 41, 285, 372
Community Pharmacists 20, 31, 37, 41, 71, 168, 199, 205, 309, 347
Community Pharmacy 38, 304, 312, 361
Community Volunteer 323
Comorbid Conditions 319
Compensations 321
Confidentiality 320
Contact Tracing 270, 272, 320
Contraceptive Methods 375
COPD Diagnosis 184, 188
Copper IUCD: Page 14 234
COTPA Act 299
Cough Corners 320
Cough Etiquette 319
Counselling and Testing 239
COVID-19 73, 89, 100-103, 267, 372
COVID-19 Symptoms 100
Co-WIN 101, 102, 372
CSF (Cerebrospinal Fluid) 93
CSIR (Council of Scientific and Industrial Research) 345
Cultural Aspects – Impact on Hand Hygiene Practices 66
Cultural Factors in Health 84
Cultural Influences on Health 84
Curative Care 34, 373
Customs, Beliefs, Values, and Religious Taboos 84

## D

Dapsone – Side Effects 137
Deafness and Sustainable Development Goals 223
Definition and Scope 232
Demographic Indicators 39, 42, 373
Demography 232, 373
Dengue Hemorrhagic Fever (DHF): Definition and Severity 373
Density of Population 233
Determinants of Health 45, 49, 84, 86
Deworming Strategy 213, 215, 326-328, 373
Diabetes (Type 1, Type 2, Gestational), Diagnosis 77, 81
Diagnosis 93, 373
Diagnosis and Testing 196, 239
Diagnosis and Treatment 93, 97, 275
Diagnosis of Anaemia 209, 210
Diagnosis of Malaria 274, 275
Diarrhoea 69,70,294
Diastolic Blood Pressure 201, 205
Diethylcarbamazine Citrate 145, 373

Diet-Related Diseases: Includes CHD, Hypertension, Type 2 Diabetes 81, 373

Digital Literacy – Importance in Combating Infodemics 373

Direct Benefit Transfer (DBT) 318, 373

Disability Prevention and Morbidity Management 143

Disease 374

Disease Burden 127, 258

Disease Classification 2, 3

Disease Surveillance 46

Disinformation – Definition and Impacts 363, 374

Disposal Sputum 320

District Hospitals (DH) 22, 374

District Mental Health Programme 285

District Tobacco Control Cell 300

Diuretics 374

DMC (Designated Microscopy Centre) 373

Doctors Without Borders 48

DOT (Directly Observed Treatment) 373

DPT Vaccine 255

Droplet Infection 374

Drug Abuse and Sustainable Development Goals 227, 387, 51

Drug-Resistant TB (DRTB) 307, 374

Drug-Sensitive TB (DSTB) 308, 315

# E

Ebola 115-118

Economic Burden 140, 145, 217, 223

Economic Burden of Tobacco Use 302

Economic Growth 7, 52, 374, 388

Economic Status and Health 84, 87

Economic Survey Report 70

Education 11, 18, 20, 85, 197

Eligibility for PM-JAY: Criteria, Exclusions 353, 354, 356

Elimination Program 146, 263, 281, 306

Emergency Contraceptive Pill 234, 237, 375,

Employment Conditions 375

Environmental Health 45, 343, 382

Environmental Pollution 319, 347

Epidemiology 209, 217, 282

Essential Medicines 23, 35, 55, 56, 375

Essential Medicines List 30, 35, 360, 375

Ethnoveterinary Practices 345, 375

# F

Facility Risk Assessment 320

Family Planning Programme 232, 233

Fast-Tracking Mask 319, 320

Fats: Role, Sources, and Health Implications 375

Fertility Rate 235, 388

Filarial Worms 380

Filariasis Control Programme 144

First Referral Units (FRU) 15

Florence Nightingale 375

Follow-Up 311

Food Safety 80
Foodborne Illness 375

## G

Gastro-Intestinal Tract 376
Genetics and Disease Risk 19, 376
Global and National Burden of HIV 121
Global Burden – Statistics 194, 202
Global Burden 376
Global Burden of Cancer 174
Global Economic Burden 289
Global Epidemiology 217, 282
Global Hand Washing Day 376
Global Impact 102
Global Impact and Death Rates 102
Global Maternal Mortality 52, 54
Global Polio Eradication Initiative 329
Global Prevalence 132
Global Programme to Eliminate Lymphatic Filariasis 142
Global Task Force on Cholera Control (GTFCC) 376
Glucose, Glucometer, Gestational Diabetes 193, 376
Good Health and Well-being 51, 83
Government Initiatives 208
Grade 2 Disability – Definition and Concern 376
Greenhouse Gases – Role in Climate Change 335
Greetings – Health Implications of Different Forms 63, 75
GTFCC 376
Gutkha 299

## H

H1N1 217, 130
H3N2 127, 128
HALE 102, 377
Hand Hygiene – Importance and Techniques 376
Hand Hygiene 351, 376
Handshake – Infection Risks and Cultural Significance 61
Hansen's Disease – Alternative Name for Leprosy 132, 133
HbA1c, Hypoglycemia, Hyperglycemia 378
HDU 377
Health and Wellness Centres 13
Health Care Workers – Role in Preventing Disease Transmission 66, 74
Health Disparities 377
Health Expenditure 10, 11, 87, 302, 371
Health Facilities 14, 31, 36
Health Financing 40, 42
Health Impact of SBM 70
Health Information Systems 363, 371
Health Infrastructure 41, 42
Health Literacy – Role in infodemic resilience 377
Health Literacy 18, 374, 377
Health Promotion 45, 345
Health Services and Access 20, 377
Health Status 40, 42
Health Systems Strengthening 174, 180
Health Warning Labels 300

Healthcare Workers (HCW): Role in Public Awareness 356
Healthcare-Associated Infections (HAI) 377
Healthy Diet 171
Heatwave – Definition, Criteria, and Health Impacts 337
Hepatitis B Vaccine 262
High-Risk Groups 224, 225
HIV/AIDS 89
HIV/AIDS Programs 208
Hospital Pharmacists 180, 189
Hospital Pharmacy 265
Human Resources in Healthcare 377
Human Resources 281
Hygiene Practices 60, 376
Hypertension 28

# I

ICD 3,378
ICMR (Indian Council of Medical Research) 80, 82
ICU 104, 105
IDA (Triple Drug Therapy) 144
IEC Campaigns 236
Ignaz Semmelweis 378
Immunization 249, 250
Immunization Programs 250
Impact of COVID-19 363, 372
Impact of Drug Abuse 228
Income and Health Outcomes 380
India 7, 10, 11, 23
India's Burden and Initiatives 202
India's Burden 194
India's Efforts in Tackling Drug Abuse 227, 229
India's Polio Eradication Timeline 329
India's TB Elimination Goals 167
Indian Public Health Standards (IPHS) 25, 378
Indoor Air Pollution – Causes and Reduction Strategies 336
Indoor Residual Spray (IRS) 378
Infant and Maternal Mortality 291, 380
Infection Control 25
Infection Prevention and Control (IPC) 73
Infectious Patients 319
Infodemic – Definition and Effects on Public Health 363
Injectable Contraceptive 372
Injection Drug Users (IDUs) 239
Inpatient Facility 319
Insecticides 379
Insecticide-Treated Nets 379
Institutional Structure 321
Insulin 192,379
Integrated Disease Surveillance Programme (IDSP) 379
Integrated Vector Management (IVM) 275
Intellectual Property Rights 379
Introduction to Anaemia 2
Introduction to HIV/AIDS 52
Isolation of Patients 117, 130
IUCD 234, 235

## J

JAMA – Recommendations on Handshake-Free Zones 61

Jonas Salk 330

## L

Latent Tuberculosis Infection (LTBI) 379

Life Below Water 52

Life Expectancy Goals 57

Lifestyle and Health 195

Lifestyle Changes 197, 200

Lifestyle Modifications for NCDs 170, 171

Linkage with Health Insurance Schemes 321

Long-Lasting Insecticidal Nets (LLINs) 150, 379

Lymphatic Parasites 140

Lymphoedema 142, 143

## M

Management of TB 381

Mask Provision 41

Maternal and Child Health 292, 384

Maternal Mortality Ratio 52, 292

MDR-TB (Multi-Drug Resistant TB) 381

MDT – Regimen and Importance 137

Medicine Availability in India 143, 145

Medicines and Accessibility 37

Mental Health 285, 287

Mental Health Overview 285, 287

Microfilariae 144, 380

Micronutrient Deficiency: Types and Impacts 28, 81

Microorganism Infections 63, 370

Millennium Development Goals (MDGs) 380

Minerals: Types and Functions in the Body 71, 380

Ministry of Jal Shakti 69, 71, 387

Misinformation – Impacts on Individual and Community Health 260, 364, 365

Mission Indradhanush 380

Mission Parivar Vikas 236, 381

Mixed Infections 278

Mode of Taking Drugs 228, 230

Modes of Transmission 239

Monitoring (Ongoing) 242

Monkeypox 153, 157

Mpox 153

## N

NABH (National Accreditation Board for Hospitals and Healthcare Providers) 345

Namaskar/Namaste – Cultural and Health Benefits 385

Namaste 381

Nasha Mukt Bharat Abhiyaan (NMBA) 229

National Action Plan on Drug Demand Reduction (NAPDDR) 229

National AIDS Control Organization (NACO) 122, 238

National Family Health Survey (NFHS) 381

National Health Mission (NHM) 381

National Health Policy 7, 8

National Health Profile 39, 42
National Iron Plus Initiative (NIPI) 7, 211
National Leprosy Eradication Programme (NLEP) – Strategies 135, 269
National Level Implementation 280, 300
National Malaria Programmes 274
National Mental Health Policy 284, 286
National Programme for Prevention and Control of Deafness (NPPCD) 224, 225
National Programme on Mental Health 285
National Strategic Plan (NSP) 240, 381
National TB Elimination Board 322
National Tobacco Control Programme 298, 304
National Urban Health Mission (NUHM) initiatives 13, 88, 381
National Vector Borne Disease Control Programme 110, 114
Neuropathy, Nutrition 193, 382
Nicotine Replacement Therapies 298, 304
No Poverty 51
Non-Communicable Diseases (NCDs) 45, 170
Non-Communicable Diseases 53, 81
Non-Stigmatization of TB Patients 246, 307
Notification of TB Patients 321
NPCDCS and NP-NCD Programs 171
NTQLS (Quit Line Service) 302
Nutrition: Definition and role in health 351
NVBDCP: Role in India's dengue prevention program 381

# O

One Health 382
Operational Guidelines 248, 353
Opioid Substitution Therapy (OST) 239
Oral Polio Vaccine (OPV) 252, 255
Oral Rehydration Solution (ORS) 97, 99, 382
Oral Rehydration Solution (ORS) 382
ORS (Treatment) 97, 382
OTC (Over the Counter) Medications 345
Out of Pocket (OOP) Expenditure 36, 23, 383
Out-of-Pocket Expenditure 36, 87

# P

Partnership for the Goals 52
Patent Protection and Medicines 35, 383
Pathogens – Definition and Transmission through Hand Contact 60
PaucibacillE ary (PB) – Definition and Characteristics 132, 383
PCR 156
Personal Protective Equipment (PPE) 75, 117
Pharmaceutical Management Practices 36
Pharmaceutical Public Health 27, 33, 383

Pharmacist's Role 68, 74, 341
Pharmacological Treatment 205, 207, 301
Pharmacovigilance 25, 29, 280, 383
Physical Activity 20, 83, 172, 188
Physical Distancing 73, 75, 383
Physical Environment and Health 19, 363, 383
Physical Health 1, 19, 51
PIP (Project Implementation Plan) 306, 385
Polio Vaccine 255, 260, 329, 333
Population Growth Factors 233, 237
Portability in PM-JAY 87, 353, 356
POSHAN Abhiyaan 211, 384
PPE (Personal Protective Equipment) for Staff 75, 117
Pradhan Mantri Jan Arogya Yojana (PM-JAY) 353, 356
Pradhan Mantri Ujjwala Yojana (PMUY) – Description and Benefits 336, 341,384
Pharmacist's Role 348, 384
Prevalence of Drug Abuse 277
Prevalence of Hearing Loss 222, 224
Prevention and Control of Cancer 40, 171, 301
Prevention Strategies 99, 153, 224
Preventive Healthcare 384
Preventive Measures 19, 157,
Primary and Secondary Care 10
Primary Health Centres (PHCs) 41, 42
Primary Hypertension 384
Prime Minister (PM) 384
Prophylactic Iron and Folic Acid (IFA) Supplementation 212
Proteins: Functions, Sources, and Essential Amino Acids 77, 78
Public Health Emergencies 46
Public Health Goals 8
Pulse Polio Programme 330, 333

## Q

Quality Education 51, 223

## R

Rashtriya Swasthya Bima Yojana (RSBY) 385
Rational Medicine Use 358, 359
Reduction in Out-of-Pocket Expenditure (OOPE) 87
Reproductive-Maternal-Neonatal-Child Health (RMNCH+A) 13, 22, 241
Reserve Group Antibiotics 385 358, 361, 362
Retinopathy 385
Reverse-Transcriptase Polymerase Chain Reaction (RT-PCR) 103, 105, 386
Rifampicin-Resistant Tuberculosis (RR-TB) 386
Right to Health 11, 37, 386
Risk Assessment 320
Risk Communication 386
RNA (Ribonucleic Acid) 90, 386
Road Traffic Accidents 53, 55
Role of family and child-rearing practices 19, 21

## S

Safe Housing and Communities 19, 21
Sanitation and Hygiene 66, 69, 324
Screening 175
SDGs 34, 51, 387
Secondary Hypertension 83, 386
Severe Malaria 277, 278
Sexual and Reproductive Health 53, 55
Sexually Transmitted Infection (STI) 89, 124, 156, 238
Smokeless Tobacco 178, 299, 380
Smoking in Public Places 301
Soap – Efficacy in Removing Microbes 62
Social Determinants of TB 320
Social Distancing 73, 386
Social Health 262, 369, 370, 386
Social Support Networks 19, 21, 386
Sociocultural Determinants of Health 84
Socio-Economic Caste Census (SECC) 386
Socioeconomics Data 40, 42, 386
Sociology 84, 88
Sparsh Leprosy Elimination Campaign – Objective and Results 136, 386
Spirometry 184, 190
Standard Operating Procedures (SOPs) for Pharmacy 387
Staphylococcus 59, 387
State AIDS Control Societies (SACS) 239, 247
State Level Implementation 280
State Tobacco Control Cell 300
Stigma – Effects during pandemics 364
Stigma – Impact on Affected Individuals 387
Stigma 387
Strategies for Promoting Responsible Use 358, 360
Sub-Centres (SCs) 41, 42, 234
Superbugs – Definition and Threat 387
Supplementary Immunization Activities (SIAs) 330, 333
Surveillance and Investigation 331
Sustainable Development Goal 13 (SDG 13) – Overview and Relevance 336, 341, 387
Swachh Bharat Mission Launch Date 69, 387
Swachh Bharat Scheme 96, 387
Symptoms of Cancer 173
Systolic Blood Pressure 201, 205

## T

Tamil Nadu Medical Service Corporation 35
Target Goals of Anaemia Mukt Bharat 212, 294
Targeted Interventions (TI) 238
TB Bill 321
Technical Assistance 275, 323
Testing Services 239, 246
Tetanus Toxoid (TT) 255, 256,
Time Line of Anaemia Control Programme in India 211
Tobacco Cessation Centres 299, 388
Tobacco Control 46, 56, 175, 298

Total Fertility Rate (TFR) 235, 388
Treatment Initiation 318
Treatment of Plasmodium falciparum Malaria 277
Treatment Options 29, 175, 181, 182
Tuberculosis (TB) 164, 302, 388
Tuberculosis (TB) and HIV/AIDS 89, 289, 306
Types of HIV 199, 239

## U

UN Sustainable Development Summit 51, 57
UNICEF – WASH Programme in Schools 46, 47, 66
Union Territories (UTs) 96, 388
United Nations International Children's Emergency Fund 46
Universal Health Coverage (UHC) 34, 166
Universal Immunization Programme (UIP) 250, 293, 388
Urbanization and Health 86, 88

## V

Vaccination in India 101
Vector Control: Environmental, biological, and chemical methods 111, 112
Vector-Borne Diseases 388
Vertical Transmission 388
Vitamins: Types, sources, and functions 79, 210

## W

WASH Interventions 96, 98
Watch Group Antibiotics 344, 389
Water, Sanitation, and Hygiene (WASH) 389
Weekly Iron and Folic Acid Supplementation (WIFS) 211, 212
WHO (World Health Organization) 45, 49
WHO End TB Strategy 167, 306
WHO Estimate on SBM 69, 387
WHO Guidelines: Food Safety Practices 81
WHO NCD Profile – India, 2018 170, 171
World Hearing Day and World Deafness Week 223, 224

## Z

Zoonotic Diseases 89

www.ingramcontent.com/pod-product-compliance
Lightning Source LLC
Chambersburg PA
CBHW071222230926
51849CB00001B/11